Dive Into

ARTIFICIAL INTELLIGENCE

KUMAR ANIKET

KAITRA

First Edition:2025

*Dive Into ARTIFICIAL INTELLIGENCE : Kumar Aniket

Auther:

Kumar Aniket

Email:kaitra79@gmail.com

KAITRA

Price:199/-(In India)
Price: $10

ISBN: 978-93-5812-812-3

9 789358 128123

Published in India

Content

7. Natural Language Processing (NLP)

- NLTK & SpaCy (Text Processing, Tokenization)
- Transformers & BERT
- Text Classification & Sentiment Analysis
- Speech Recognition

8. Computer Vision

- OpenCV (Image Processing)
- CNNs (Convolutional Neural Networks)
- Object Detection (YOLO, SSD, Faster R-CNN)

9. AI Applications

- Chatbots (Using NLP & Deep Learning)
- AI-powered Recommendation Systems
- AI-based Image Recognition

10. AI Deployment

- Flask / FastAPI (Deploy AI Models as APIs)
- Docker & Kubernetes (Containerization)
- Cloud AI (AWS, Google Cloud, Azure)

Preface

Artificial Intelligence (AI) has emerged as one of the most transformative technologies of the 21st century, revolutionizing industries, reshaping human interactions, and redefining the way we approach problem-solving. From self-driving cars to intelligent chatbots, AI is no longer a concept of the distant future—it is here, and it is evolving at an unprecedented pace.

This book, *Dive Into ARTIFICIAL INTELLIGENCE*, is designed to provide a comprehensive and accessible journey into the fascinating world of AI, catering to both beginners and experienced practitioners. It explores the fundamental and advanced concepts that drive modern AI systems, including Machine Learning, Deep Learning, Computer Vision, Natural Language Processing (NLP), and Large Language Models (LLMs).

We begin by laying the groundwork with an introduction to AI and its historical evolution, followed by a deep dive into the core principles of machine learning—the backbone of AI applications. As we progress, we explore deep learning techniques that power complex neural networks, uncover the magic behind computer vision, and delve into NLP, which enables machines to understand and generate human language. The book also sheds light on LLMs, the cutting-edge AI models driving advancements in conversational AI and content generation.

Each chapter is designed to balance theory with practical applications, offering real-world case studies, code implementations, and insights into industry trends. Whether you are a student, a researcher, or a professional looking to integrate AI into your work, this book serves as a valuable resource to enhance your understanding and expertise in AI technologies.

The world of AI is vast, dynamic, and full of possibilities. I invite you to embark on this exciting journey with me as we dive into artificial intelligence and unlock its limitless potential.

Let's get started!

Kumar Aniket

Acknowledgments

Writing *Dive Into ARTIFICIAL INTELLIGENCE* has been an incredible journey, and I am deeply grateful to everyone who has contributed to its completion. This book would not have been possible without the support, guidance, and inspiration of many individuals.

First and foremost, I would like to express my sincere gratitude to my mentors and teachers, whose knowledge and encouragement have played a vital role in shaping my understanding of Artificial Intelligence. Their insights and guidance have been invaluable in structuring the concepts presented in this book.

I am also thankful to my father Prof. Dr. Mahesh Mohan Jha,HOD(Geography) and mother Anjana Jha for their unwavering support, patience, and belief in my work. Their encouragement kept me motivated throughout this writing journey.

A special thanks to the AI research community, whose groundbreaking work continues to push the boundaries of innovation. The contributions of researchers, developers, and engineers in the fields of Machine Learning, Deep Learning, Computer Vision, Natural Language Processing, and Large Language Models have been the foundation of this book.

I would also like to acknowledge my readers—students, professionals, and AI enthusiasts—who inspire me to share knowledge and make AI more accessible. Your curiosity and passion for learning fuel my dedication to writing and teaching.

Lastly, I extend my appreciation to everyone who provided feedback, reviewed drafts, or contributed in any way to improving the content of this book. Your valuable input has helped shape it into what it is today.

Thank you all for being part of this journey. I hope this book serves as a stepping stone for your exploration into the world of Artificial Intelligence.

About The Auther

Kumar Aniket is a passionate researcher and AI enthusiast with a strong background in Artificial Intelligence, Machine Learning, Deep Learning, and Computer Vision. He has made significant contributions as a researcher at OrbitX India Aerospace, where he worked in the Reusable Launch Vehicle (RLV) department. His research focused on applying AI techniques to enhance aerospace technology, pushing the boundaries of intelligent systems in space exploration.

Beyond aerospace applications, Kumar Aniket has worked extensively on various AI-driven projects in Machine Learning, Deep Learning, Computer Vision, and Natural Language Processing (NLP). His expertise spans from building intelligent models for automation to developing innovative solutions for real-world challenges.

With a deep curiosity for cutting-edge technology, he is dedicated to making AI more accessible and impactful. Through *Dive Into ARTIFICIAL INTELLIGENCE*, he aims to share his knowledge and experience, helping readers understand the fundamentals and advancements of AI in a practical and engaging way.

Section-1

Python Basics for AI

- Introduction to Python
- Variables & Data Types
- Lists, Tuples, Dictionaries, Sets
- Control Flow (if-else, loops)
- Functions & Lambda Functions
- List Comprehensions
- File Handling
- Exception Handling

Python Basics for AI

0.Introduction to Python

Python is a versatile, high-level programming language known for its simplicity and readability. Created by Guido van Rossum and first released in 1991, it's one of the most popular languages today, used in web development, data science, automation, artificial intelligence, scientific computing, and more.

Key features that make Python great for beginners and experts alike:

- Easy to learn: Clean syntax that resembles English, with minimal boilerplate code.
- Interpreted: Code runs line-by-line, making debugging straightforward.
- Dynamically typed: No need to declare variable types explicitly.
- Extensive standard library: Comes with batteries included for common tasks.
- Large ecosystem: Millions of third-party packages available via PyPI.
- Cross-platform: Runs on Windows, macOS, Linux, and more.

Your first Python program is traditionally "Hello, World!":

```
print("Hello, World!")
```


Installing Python & Setting Up the Environment

The best way to get started is to download and install the official Python distribution from the Python website.

Step 1: Download Python

Visit the official downloads page: https://www.python.org/downloads/

The site automatically suggests the latest version (3.14.2 as of now) for your operating system.

Step 2: Installation Instructions by Operating System

Windows:

1. Download the executable installer (.exe).
2. Run it.
3. **Important**: Check the box "Add python.exe to PATH" at the bottom of the installer.
4. Select "Install Now" or customize if needed.
5. Python will include pip (package manager) and IDLE (simple editor).

macOS:

1. Download the .pkg installer.
2. Open the file and follow the prompts.
3. It installs Python in /Applications and adds it to your PATH automatically in most cases.

Linux:

- Many distributions come with Python pre-installed (check with python3 --version).
- For the latest version, use your package manager (e.g., sudo apt update && sudo apt install python3 on Ubuntu/Debian) or download and compile from source.
- Alternatively, use tools like pyenv for managing multiple versions.

After installation, open a terminal/command prompt and type:

python –version

or

python3 –version

It should show something like Python 3.14.2

Step 3: Verify and Run Your First Program

1. Open the Python shell (type python or python3 in terminal).
2. Type print("Hello, World!") and press Enter.

Or create a file hello.py with the code above, then run python hello.py.

Recommended Setup for Development

For serious projects:

- Use **virtual environments** to isolate dependencies: python -m venv myenv then activate it.

- Install packages with pip install package_name.
- Choose an editor/IDE: Visual Studio Code (free, with Python extension) is highly recommended for beginners.

You're now ready to start coding in Python!

1.Variables & Data Types

Variables

Variables are used to store data values.

```
x = 10          # Integer
pi = 3.14       # Float
name = "AI"   # String
is_ai = True   # Boolean
```

Data Types

- **Integers**: Whole numbers (e.g., 10, -5)
- **Floats**: Decimal numbers (e.g., 3.14, -0.01)
- **Strings**: Sequence of characters ("Hello")
- **Booleans**: True or False

```
print(type(x))          # <class 'int'>
print(type(pi))         # <class 'float'>
print(type(name))    # <class 'str'>
print(type(is_ai))     # <class 'bool'>
```

2.Lists, Tuples, Dictionaries, Sets

Lists (Mutable, Ordered)

A list is an ordered collection of items.

```
numbers = [1, 2, 3, 4, 5]
numbers.append(6)          # Add element
print(numbers[0])          # Access first element
```

Tuples (Immutable, Ordered)

Tuples are similar to lists but immutable.

```
tuple_example = (10, 20, 30)
print(tuple_example[1])       # Access second element
```

Dictionaries (Key-Value Pairs, Mutable)

Dictionaries store key-value pairs.

```
person = {"name": "Alice", "age": 25}
print(person["name"])                    # Alice
person["age"] = 26                       # Modify value
```

Sets (Unique Elements, Unordered)

A set contains unique elements.

```
unique_numbers = {1, 2, 3, 4, 5, 5}   # Duplicates are removed
print(unique_numbers)                  # {1, 2, 3, 4, 5}
```

3. Control Flow (if-else, loops)

if-else Statements

```
age = 18
if age >= 18:
   print("You are an adult.")
else:
   print("You are a minor.")
```

Loops

for loop

```
for i in range(5):
   print(i)          # Prints 0 to 4
```

while loop

```
x = 0
while x < 5:
   print(x)
   x += 1
```

4. Functions & Lambda Functions

Using the def statement is the most common way to define a function in python. This statement is a so called *single clause compound statement* with the following syntax:

```
def function_name(parameters):
    statement(s)
```

function_name is known as the *identifier* of the function. Since a function definition is an

executable statement its execution *binds* the function name to the function object which can be called later on using the identifier.
parameters is an optional list of identifiers that get bound to the values supplied as arguments when the function is called. A function may have an arbitrary number of arguments which are separated by commas.
statement(s) – also known as the *function body* – are a nonempty sequence of statements executed each time the function is called. This means a function body cannot be empty, just like any *indented block*.
Here is an example of a simple function definition which purpose is to print Hello each time it is called:

```
def greet():
    print("Hello")
```

Now let`s call the defined greet() function:

```
greet()
# Out: Hello
```

That`s another example of a function definition which takes one single argument and displays the passed in value each time the function is called:

```
def greet_two(greeting):
    print(greeting)
```

After that the greet_two() function must be called with an argument:

```
greet_two("Howdy")
# Out: Howdy
```

Regular Function

```
def greet(name):
   return f"Hello, {name}!"

print(greet("AI"))
```


Lambda Function

A lambda function is an anonymous function.

```
square = lambda x: x * x
print(square(5))              # Output: 25
```

You'll notice that unlike many other languages, you do not need to explicitly declare a return type of the function. Python functions can return values of any type via the **return** keyword. One function can return any number of different types!

```
def many_types(x):
```

```
    if x < 0:
        return "Hello!"
    else:
            return 0
print(many_types(1))
print(many_types(-1))
# Output:
0
Hello!
```

As long as this is handled correctly by the caller, this is perfectly valid Python code.
A function that reaches the end of execution without a return statement will always return None:

```
def do_nothing():
    pass
print(do_nothing())
# Out: None
```

As mentioned previously a function definition must have a function body, a nonempty sequence of statements. Therefore the **pass** statement is used as function body, which is a null operation – when it is executed, nothing happens. It does what it means, it skips. It is useful as a placeholder when a statement is required syntactically, but no code needs to be executed.

5. List Comprehensions

List comprehensions provide a concise way to create lists.

```
squares = [x**2 for x in range(5)]
print(squares)                              # Output: [0, 1, 4, 9, 16]
```

6. File Handling

Writing to a File

```
with open("data.txt", "w") as file:
   file.write("Hello, AI!")
```

Reading from a File

```
with open("data.txt", "r") as file:
   content = file.read()
   print(content)  # Output: Hello, AI!
```

7. Exception Handling

try-except Block

```
try:
    result = 10 / 0          # Division by zero error
except ZeroDivisionError:
    print("Cannot divide by zero!")
```

Handling Multiple Exceptions

```
try:
    num = int("AI")          # ValueError
except ValueError:
    print("Invalid number format!")
```

Section-2

Mathematics for AI

- Linear Algebra (Vectors, Matrices)
- Probability & Statistics (Mean, Variance, Standard Deviation)
- Calculus (Derivatives, Integrals)
- Optimization Techniques (Gradient Descent)

Mathematics for AI

1.Linear Algebra (Vectors, Matrices)

Linear algebra is the foundation of modern artificial intelligence and machine learning. Almost everything in AI — from data representation to neural networks, optimizations, and dimensionality reduction — relies heavily on vectors and matrices. Understanding these concepts intuitively will make topics like neural networks, transformers, and embeddings much clearer.

We'll focus on the key ideas relevant to AI, with visual aids for formulas and operations.

Vectors

A vector represents a quantity with magnitude and direction, but in AI, we treat vectors as ordered lists of numbers (features or coordinates).

In $\mathbb{R}^n$(n-dimensional space), a vector vis:

$$\mathrm{v} = \begin{pmatrix} v_1 \\ v_2 \\ \vdots \\ v_n \end{pmatrix}$$

or as a row: $[v_1, v_2, \ldots, v_n]$.

In AI:

- An image pixel might be a vector in $\mathbb{R}^{784}$(28x28 flattened).
- Word embeddings (e.g., in NLP) are vectors in $\mathbb{R}^{300}$.
- A data point in a dataset is a feature vector.

Key Operations:

1. Vector Addition (parallelogram rule — combines displacements or features):

Never underestimate a child`s ability to do maths _Esther White

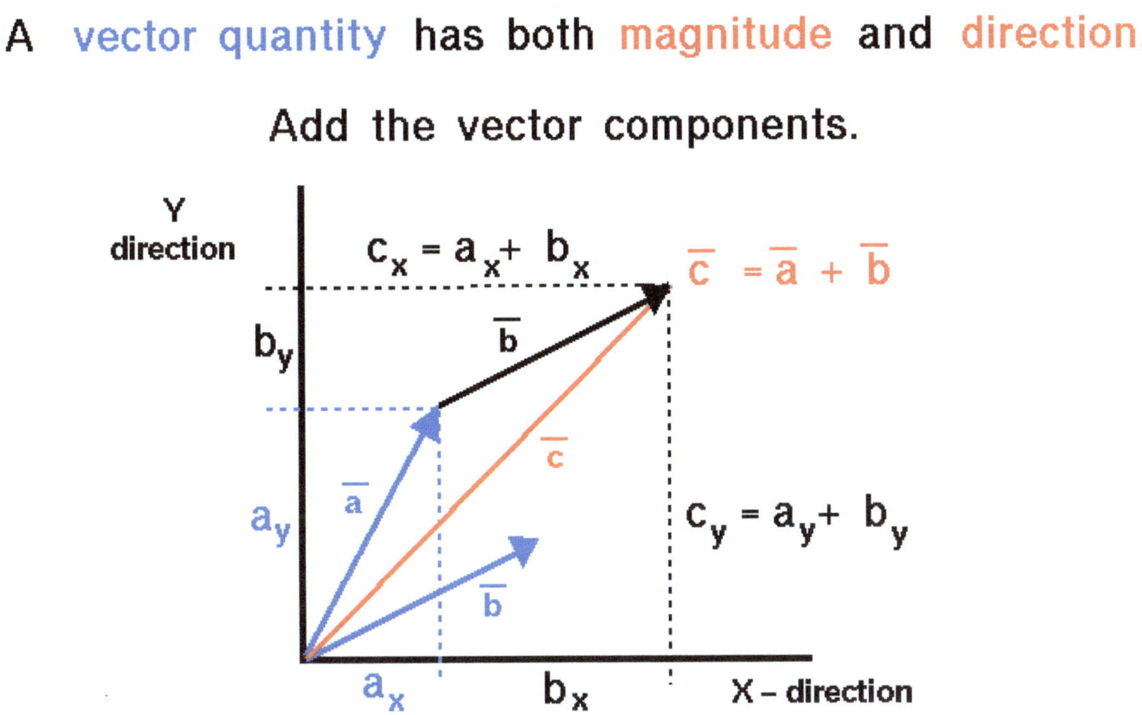

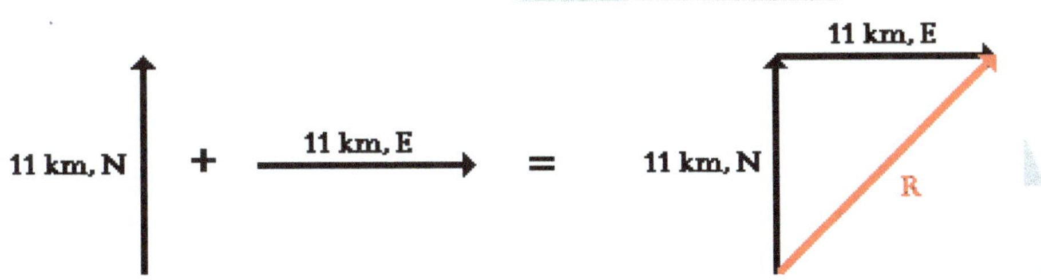

$$11^2 + 11^2 = R^2$$

$$242 = R^2$$

$$15.6 = R$$

Formula: $u + v = \begin{pmatrix} u_1 + v_1 \\ u_2 + v_2 \\ \vdots \end{pmatrix}$

2. Scalar Multiplication (stretches or shrinks the vector):

Scalar multiplication - Wikipedia

Formula: $c\mathrm{v} = \begin{pmatrix} cv_1 \\ cv_2 \\ \vdots \end{pmatrix}$

3. Dot Product (measures similarity or projection):

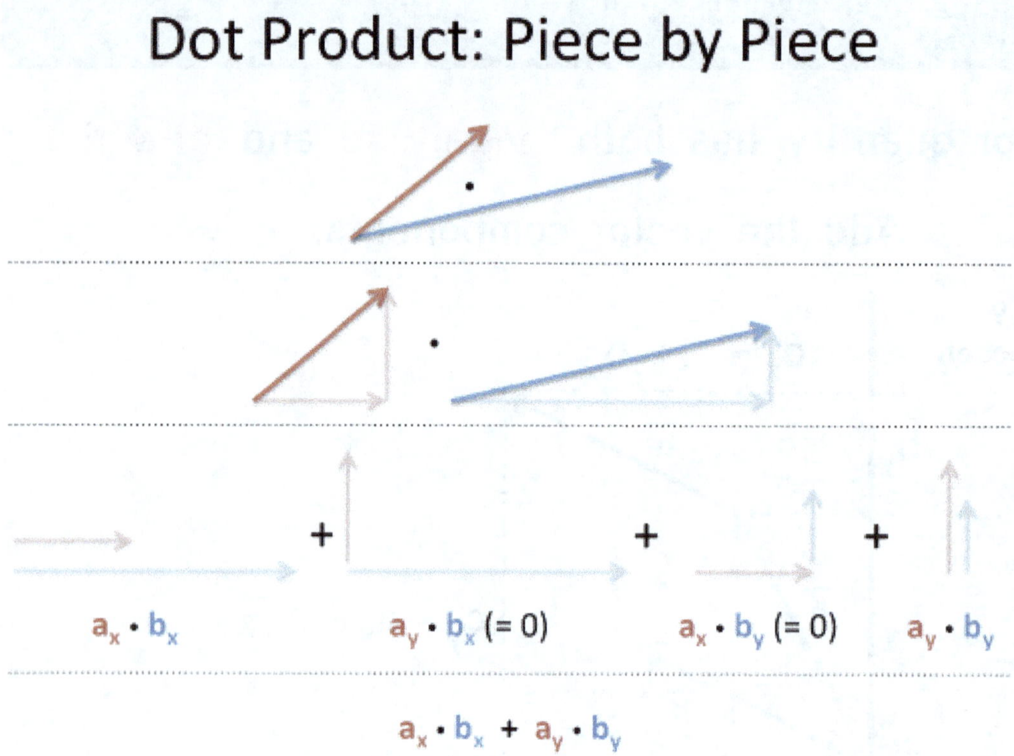

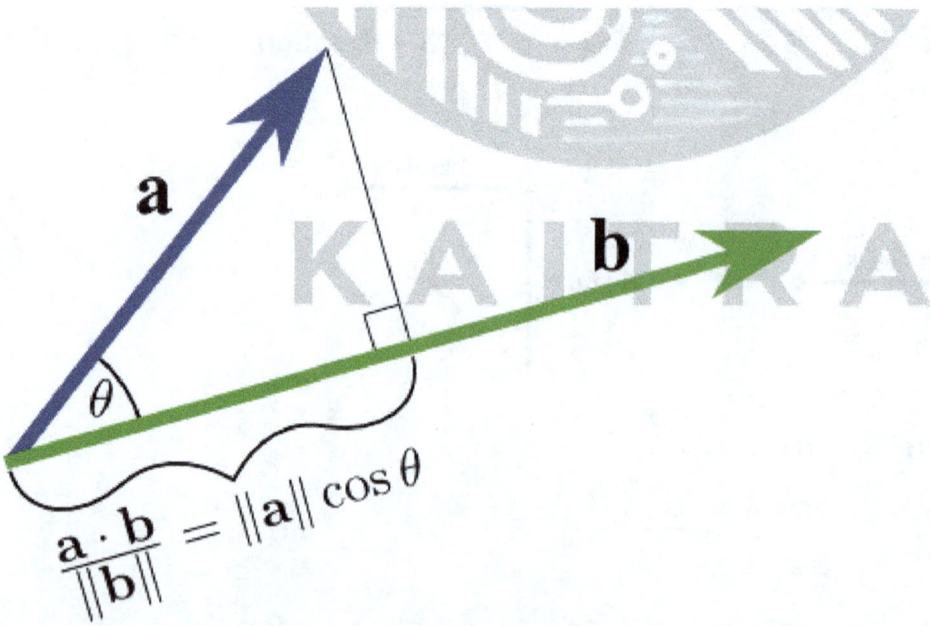

Formula: $\mathrm{u} \cdot \mathrm{v} = u_1 v_1 + u_2 v_2 + \cdots + u_n v_n = \| \mathrm{u} \| \| \mathrm{v} \| \cos\theta$

In AI: Crucial for attention mechanisms (e.g., query-key dot products in transformers measure similarity), cosine similarity for recommendations, and projections.

Other useful concepts: Vector norm ($\| \mathrm{v} \| = \sqrt{\mathrm{v} \cdot \mathrm{v}}$) for normalization, common in embeddings.

Matrices

A matrix is a rectangular array of numbers, used to represent linear transformations or datasets.

An $m \times n$matrix A:

$$A = \begin{pmatrix} a_{11} & a_{12} & \cdots & a_{1n} \\ a_{21} & a_{22} & \cdots & a_{2n} \\ \vdots & \vdots & \ddots & \vdots \\ a_{m1} & a_{m2} & \cdots & a_{mn} \end{pmatrix}$$

In AI:

- A dataset with $m$samples and $n$features is an $m \times n$matrix.
- Weights in a neural network layer are matrices.

Key Operation: Matrix Multiplication

To multiply $A(p \times q)$ and $B(q \times r)$, result is $p \times r$: Each entry $(AB)_{ij} = \sum_k a_{ik} b_{kj}$(row i of A dot column j of B).

$$\begin{bmatrix} 1 & 2 & 3 \\ 4 & 5 & 6 \end{bmatrix} \times \begin{bmatrix} 10 & 11 \\ 20 & 21 \\ 30 & 31 \end{bmatrix}$$

$$= \begin{bmatrix} 1\text{x}10 + 2\text{x}20 + 3\text{x}30 & 1\text{x}11 + 2\text{x}21 + 3\text{x}31 \\ 4\text{x}10 + 5\text{x}20 + 6\text{x}30 & 4\text{x}11 + 5\text{x}21 + 6\text{x}31 \end{bmatrix}$$

$$= \begin{bmatrix} 10+40+90 & 11+42+93 \\ 40+100+180 & 44+105+186 \end{bmatrix} = \begin{bmatrix} 140 & 146 \\ 320 & 335 \end{bmatrix}$$

Multiplication of Matrices

Dive into AI

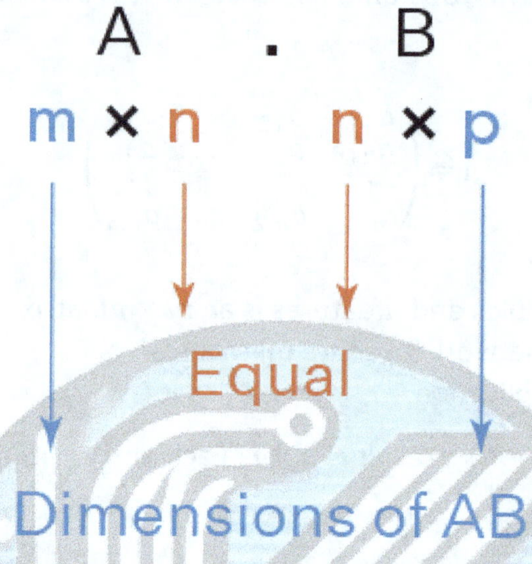

Why critical in AI? A fully connected neural network layer is exactly matrix multiplication: Input vector x(batch as matrix X) transformed to output $y = Wx + b$, where $W$is the weight matrix.

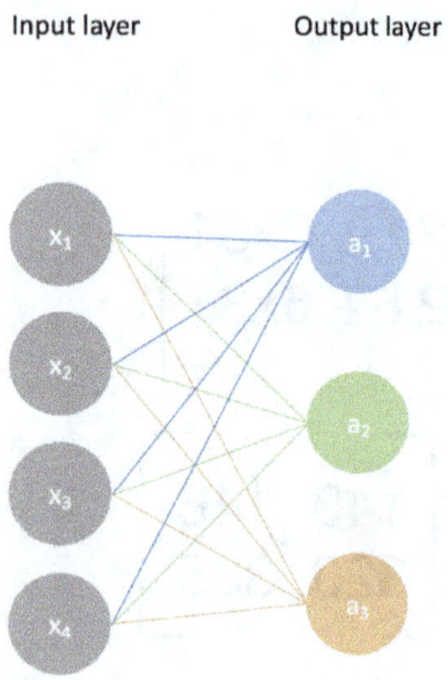

Using multiple observations

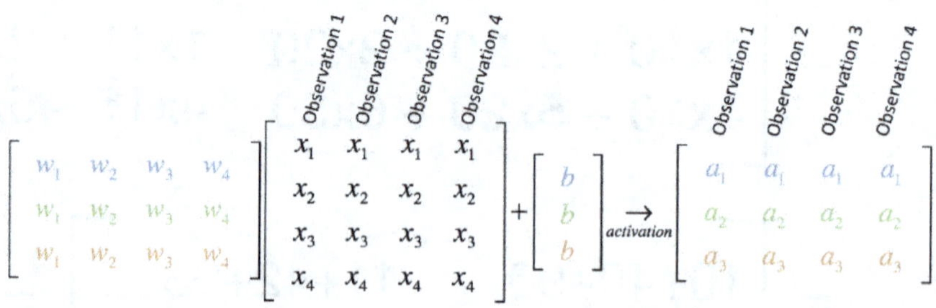

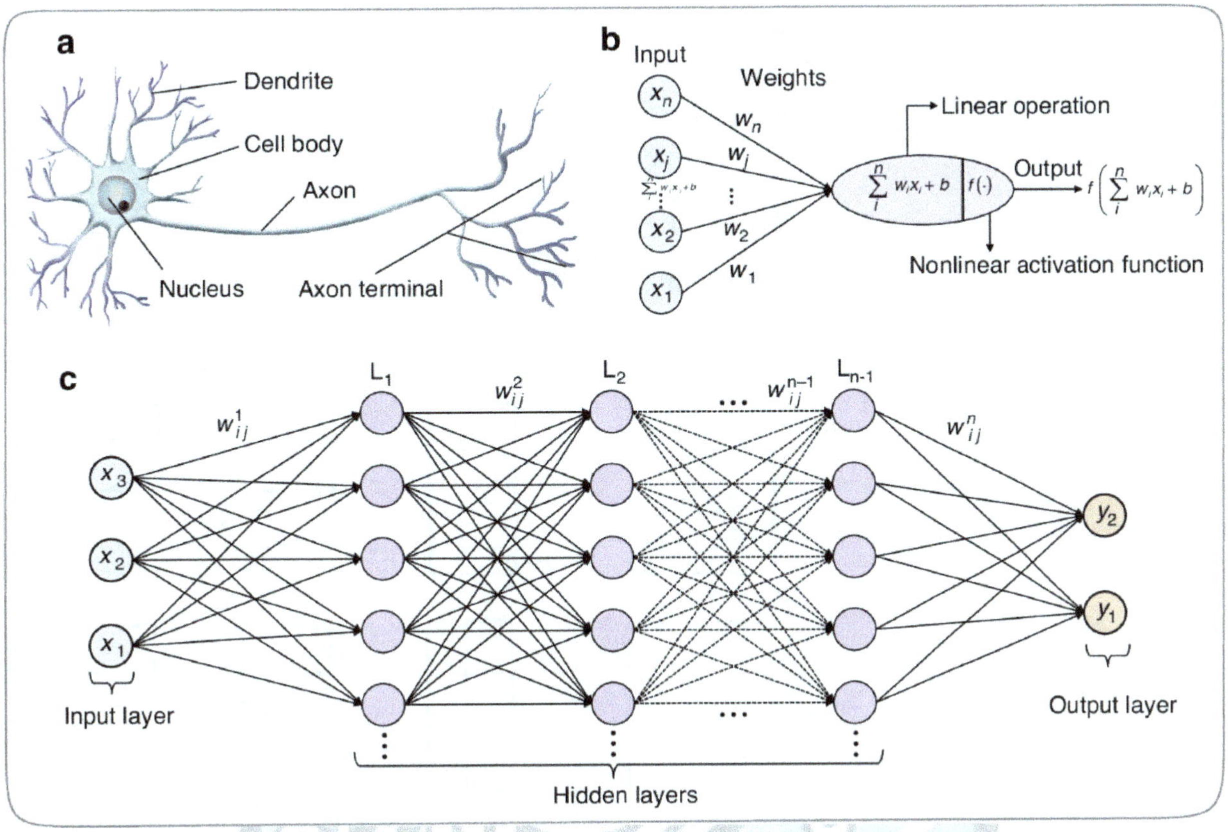

Entire deep networks are stacked matrix multiplications — that's why GPUs (great at matmul) accelerate AI.

Other operations: Transpose A^T, inverse A^{-1}(for solving systems), determinants (less common in deep learning).

Advanced Concepts in AI

1. Eigenvalues and Eigenvectors For square matrix A: $A\mathrm{v} = \lambda\mathrm{v}$(vector vscaled by λ, direction unchanged).

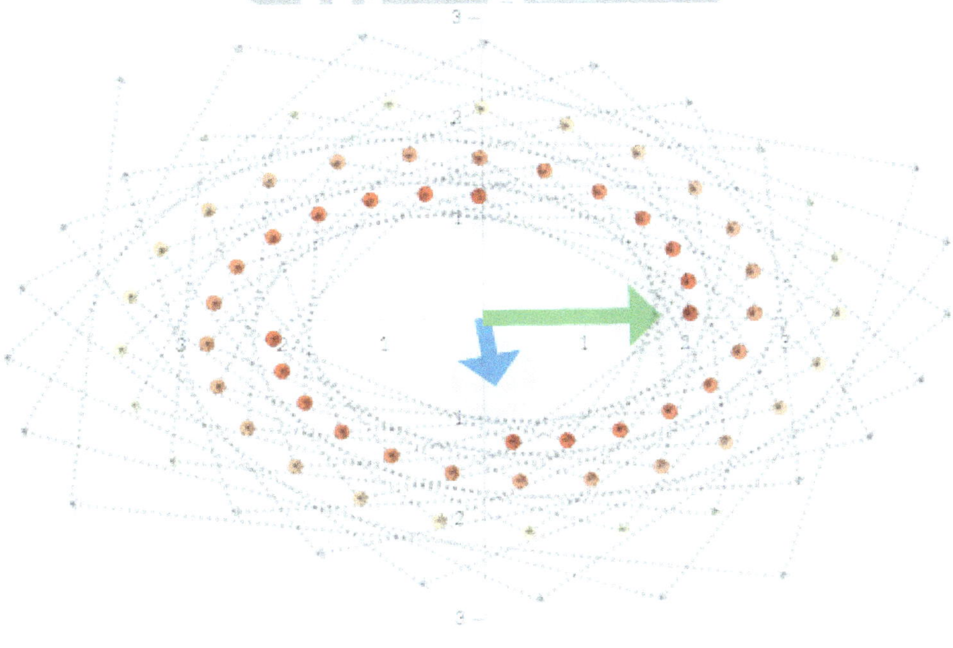

Used in: Spectral analysis, stability in recurrent networks, and foundational for PCA/SVD.

2. Singular Value Decomposition (SVD) Any matrix $A = U\Sigma V^T$, where U,$V$are orthogonal, Σdiagonal (singular values).

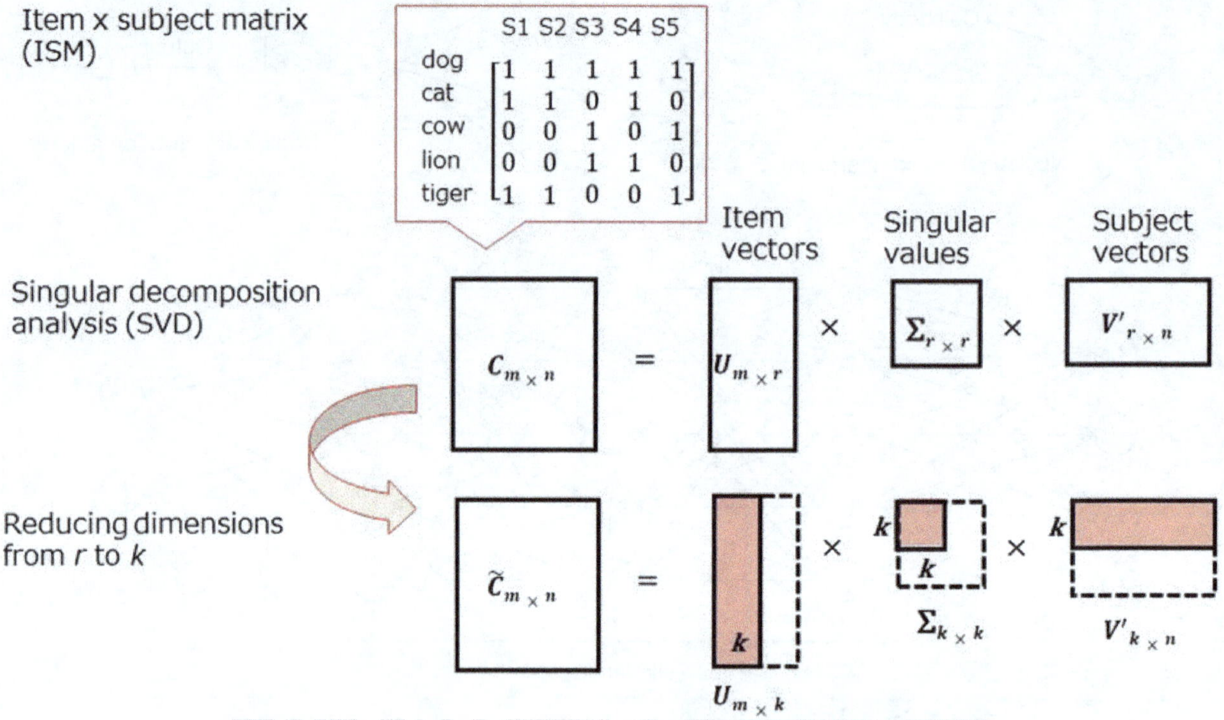

Powers: Compression, latent semantics (in old-school NLP), and recommendation systems.

3. Principal Component Analysis (PCA) Uses eigenvectors of covariance matrix to project data onto directions of maximum variance (dimensionality reduction).

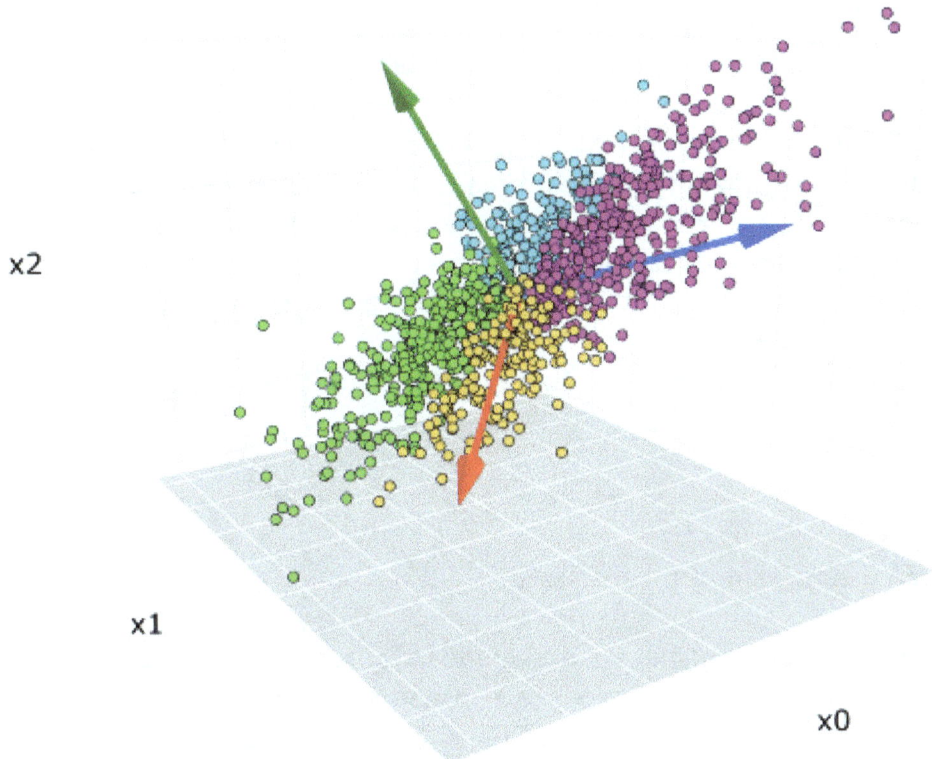

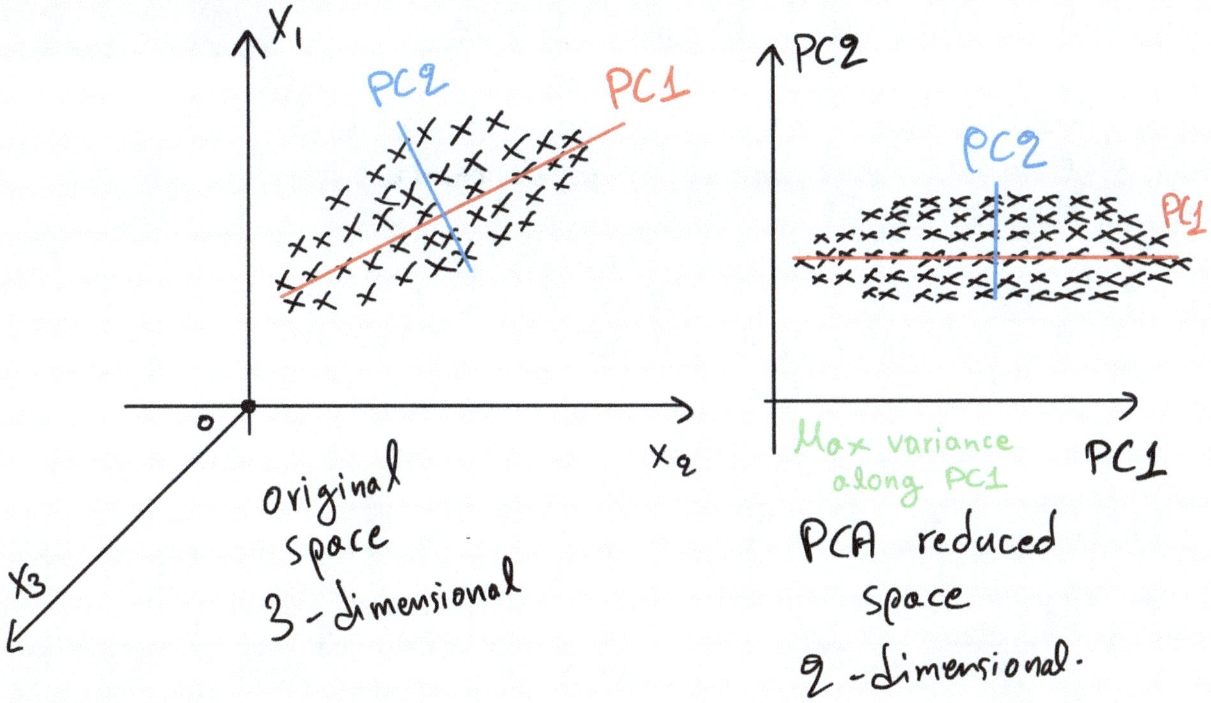

Common for preprocessing high-dimensional data before feeding to models.

Mastering vectors and matrices will unlock deeper understanding of how AI models work under the hood. In libraries like NumPy, PyTorch, or TensorFlow, these operations are highly optimized.

2. Probability & Statistics (Mean, Variance, Standard Deviation)

Probability and statistics form the core of artificial intelligence and machine learning. They help us model uncertainty, quantify data patterns, evaluate models, and make decisions under noise. Concepts like **mean**, **variance**, and **standard deviation** are everywhere—from data preprocessing to loss functions, regularization, and understanding model errors. We'll dive deep into these, with formulas, intuitions, AI relevance, and visuals.

Basic Measures of Central Tendency and Spread

1. **Mean (Average)** The mean is the "center of mass" of the data. For a dataset x_1,x_2,..., x_n:

$$\mu = \grave{x} = \frac{1}{n}\sum_{i=1}^{n} x_i$$

(Population mean uses μ, sample mean uses $\grave{x}$.)

In AI:

- Used for centering data (subtract mean for zero-centered features).
- Basis for many loss functions (e.g., Mean Squared Error).
- Expected value in probability: $E[X] = \sum x \cdot P(x)$for discrete, or $\int x \cdot f(x)\, dx$ for continuous.

Mean is sensitive to outliers, unlike median or mode.

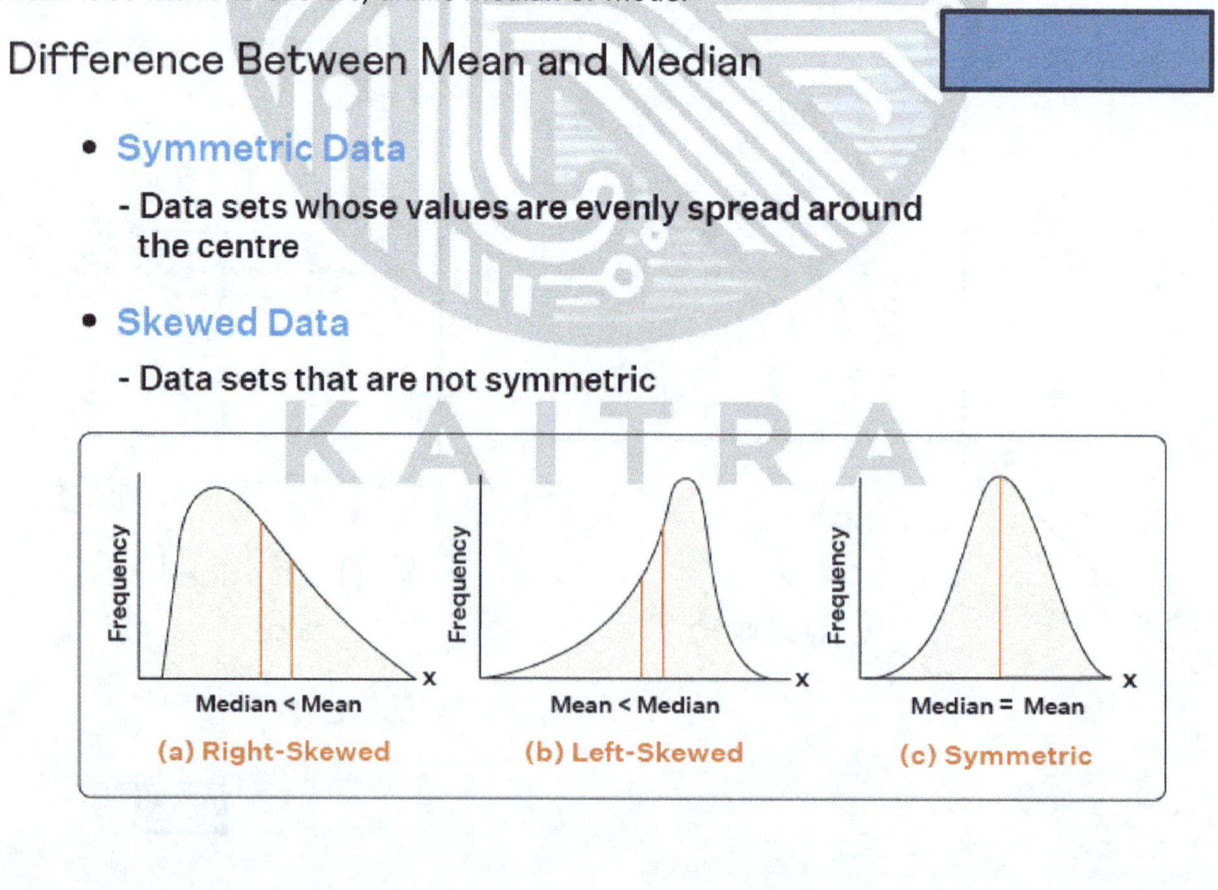

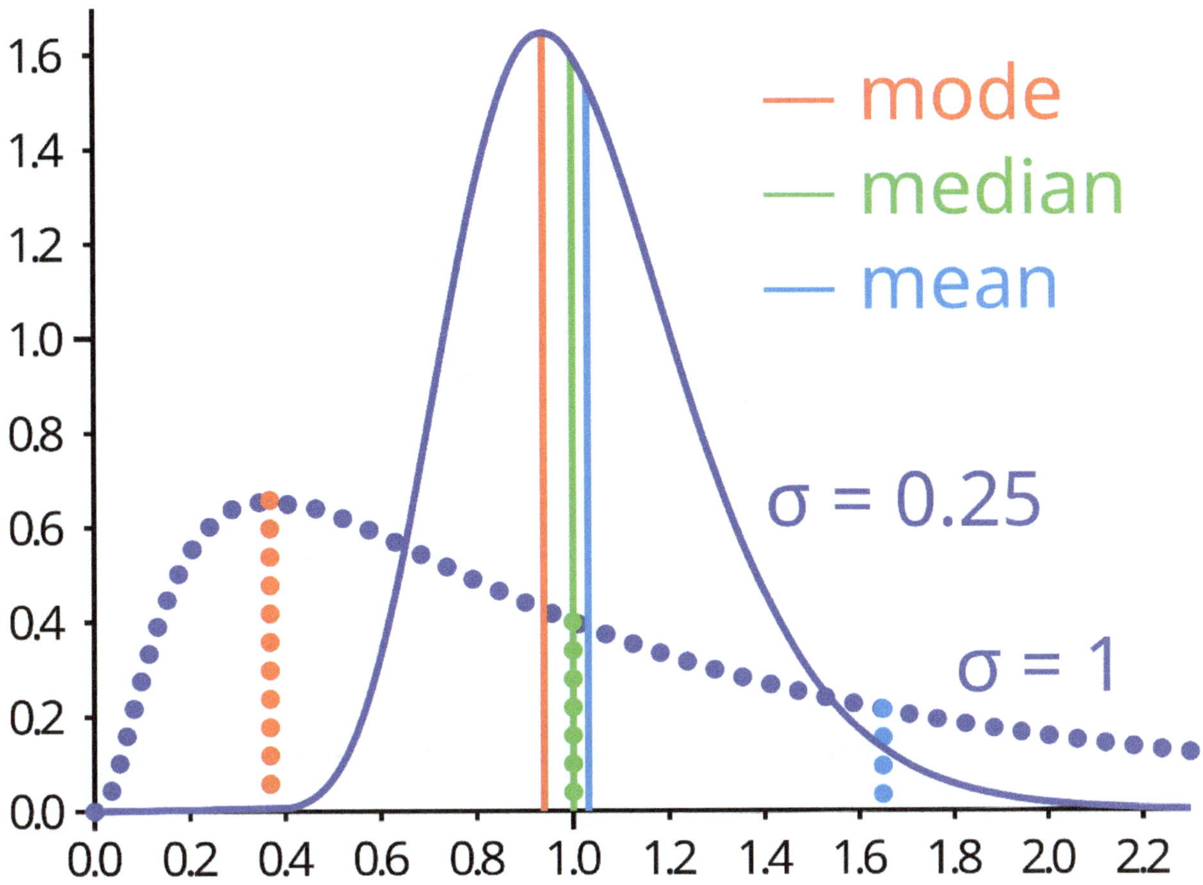

2. **Variance** Variance measures how spread out the data is from the mean—average squared deviation. Population variance:

$$\sigma^2 = \frac{1}{n}\sum_{i=1}^{n}(x_i - \mu)^2$$

Sample variance (unbiased, uses $n - 1$):

$$s^2 = \frac{1}{n-1}\sum_{i=1}^{n}(x_i - \grave{x})^2$$

In AI:

- Key in understanding model error decomposition (bias-variance tradeoff).
- Used in regularization (e.g., weight decay penalizes large variances in parameters).
- Covariance matrices in multivariate Gaussians for generative models.

Visualizing how points far from the mean contribute more (squared term):

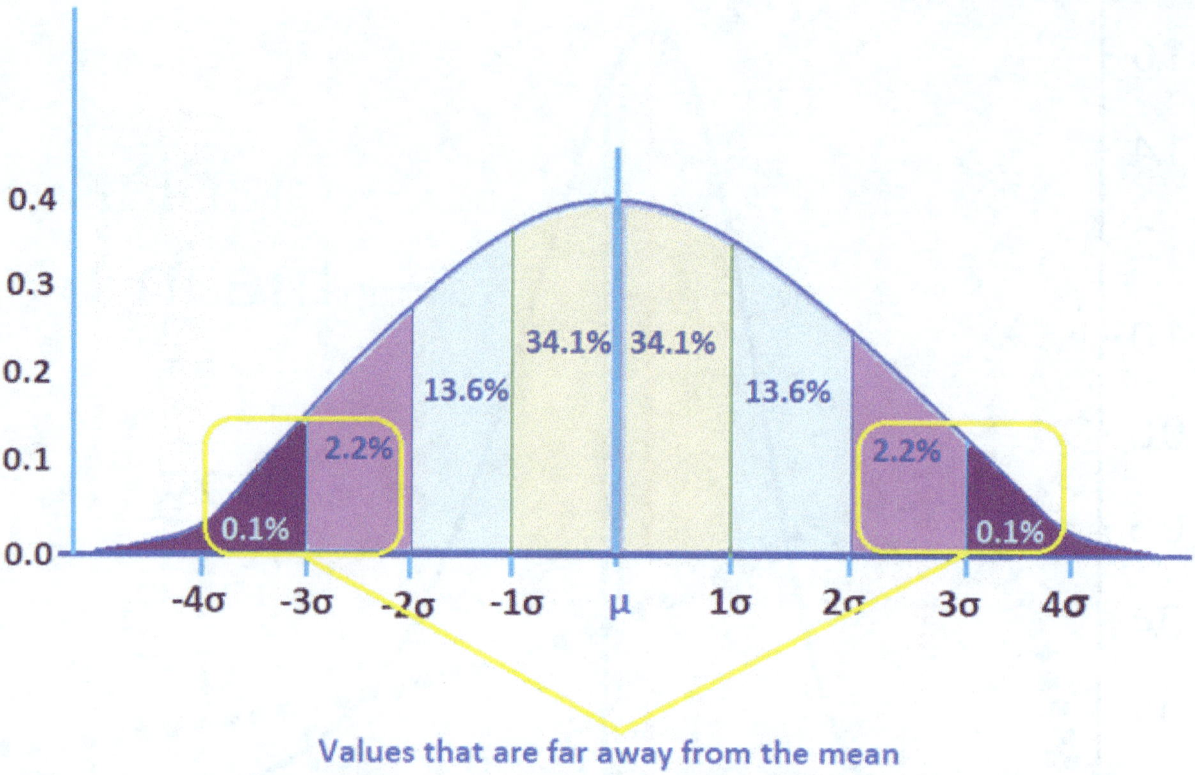

Population Variance	Sample Variance
$\sigma^2 = \dfrac{\sum_{i=1}^{N}(x_i-\mu)^2}{N}$	$s^2 = \dfrac{\sum_{i=1}^{n}(x_i-\bar{x})^2}{n-1}$
σ^2 = population variance x_i = value of ith element μ = population mean N = population size	s^2 = sample variance x_i = value of ith element $\bar{x}$ = sample mean n = sample size

3. **Standard Deviation** Square root of variance—brings it back to original units.

$$\sigma = \sqrt{\sigma^2} = \sqrt{\frac{1}{n}\sum_{i=1}^{n}(x_i-\mu)^2}$$

(Sample: $s = \sqrt{s^2}$.)

In AI:

- Data normalization: Subtract mean and divide by std dev (z-score) for stable training.
- In normal distributions: ~68% of data within 1σ, 95% within 2σ, 99.7% within 3σ (empirical rule).
- Uncertainty estimation in models (e.g., Gaussian processes).

The iconic bell curve showing mean as center and std dev as spread:

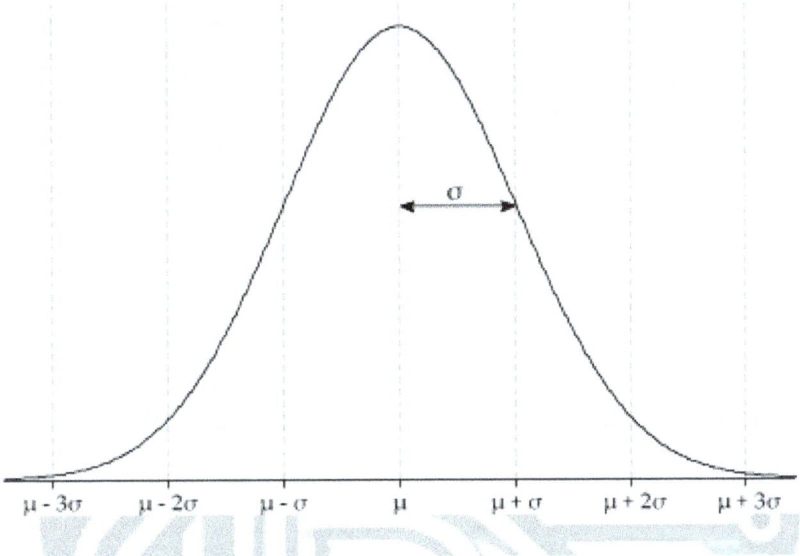

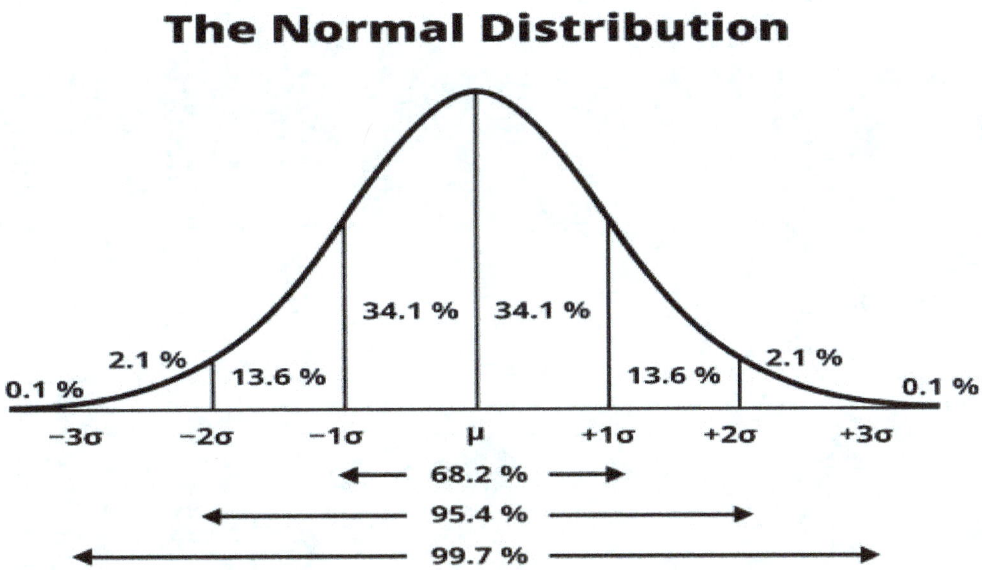

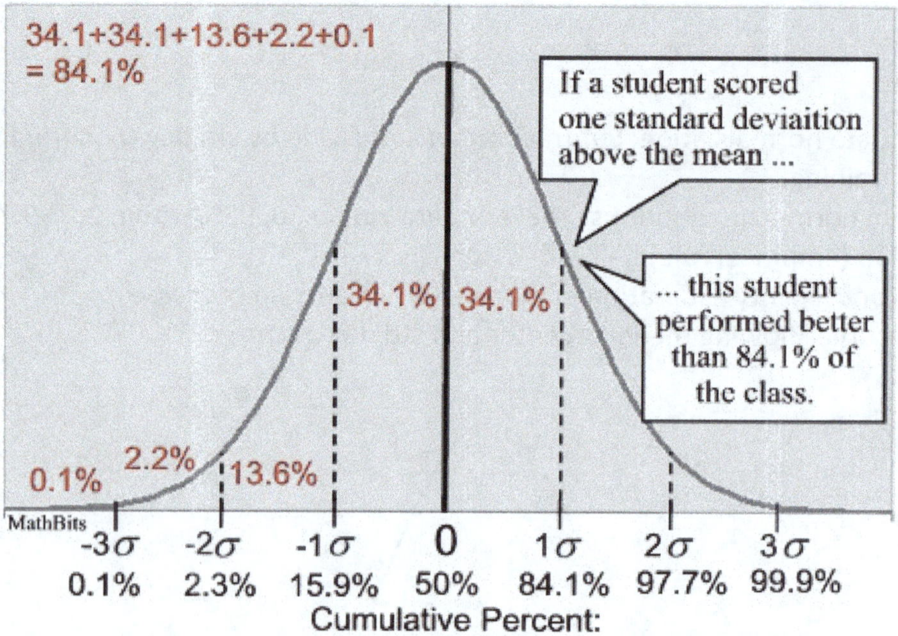

Probability Foundations

- **Probability Mass Function (PMF)**: For discrete variables, $P(X = x)$.
- **Probability Density Function (PDF)**: For continuous, $f(x)$where area under curve gives probability.

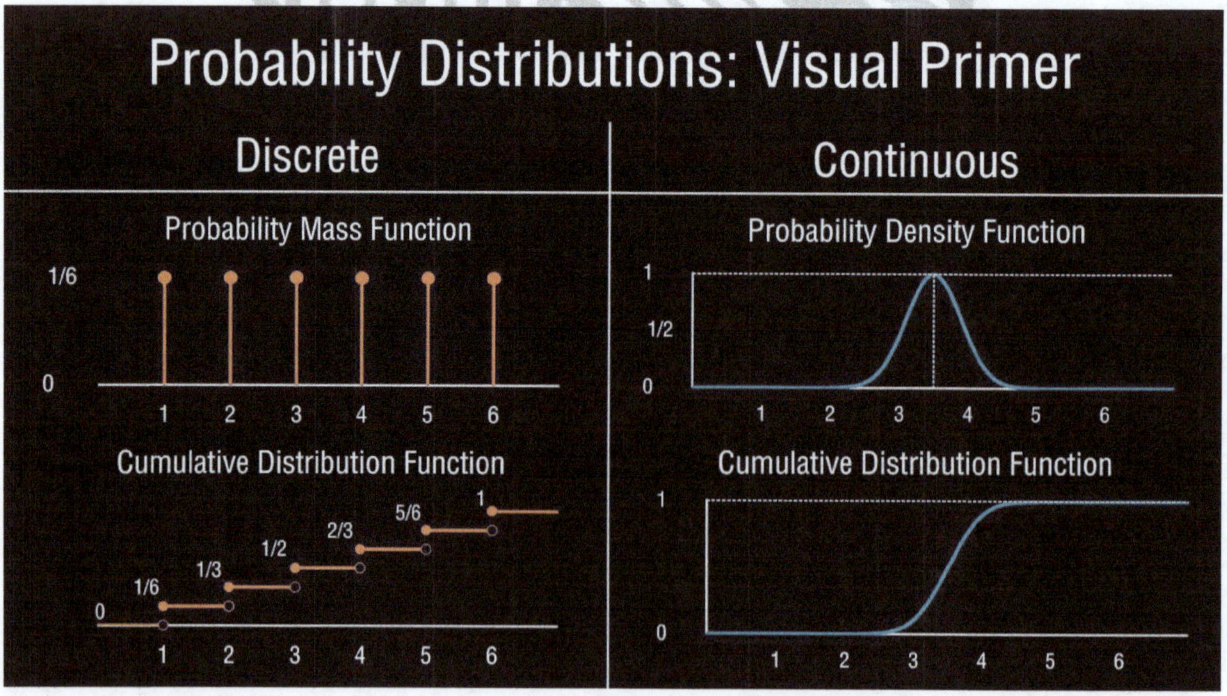

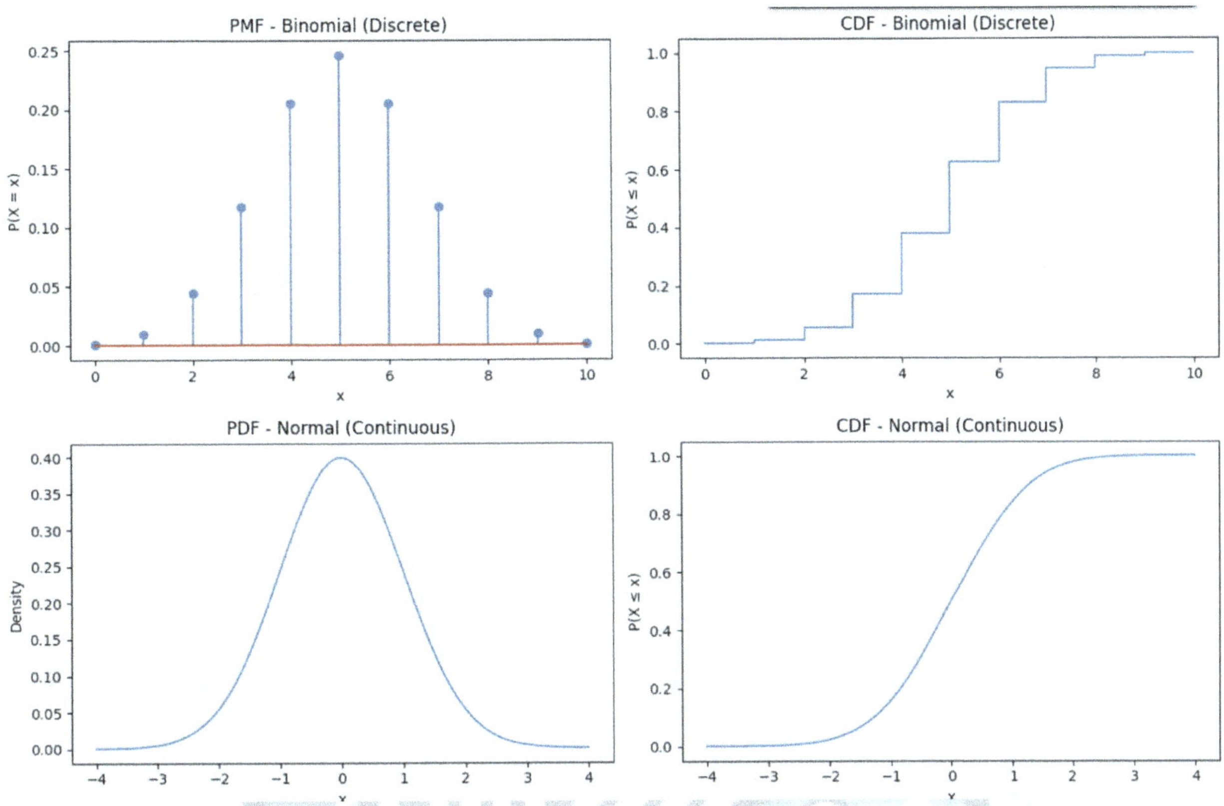

Many AI models assume Gaussian (normal) distributions because of nice properties (mean/variance fully describe it).

Key Theorems in AI

1. **Law of Large Numbers (LLN)** As sample size $n \to \infty$, sample mean $\grave{x} \to$ true mean μ. Why it matters in AI: Training on large data ensures empirical averages (e.g., gradients) approximate true expectations.

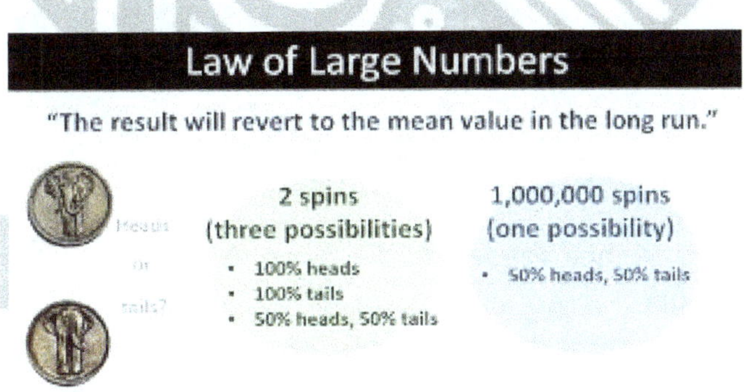

2. **Central Limit Theorem (CLT)** Sum/mean of many independent random variables (regardless of original distribution) approaches a normal distribution as $n$grows. In AI: Explains why errors, gradients, and many real-world features are approximately normal—enables Gaussian assumptions in models.

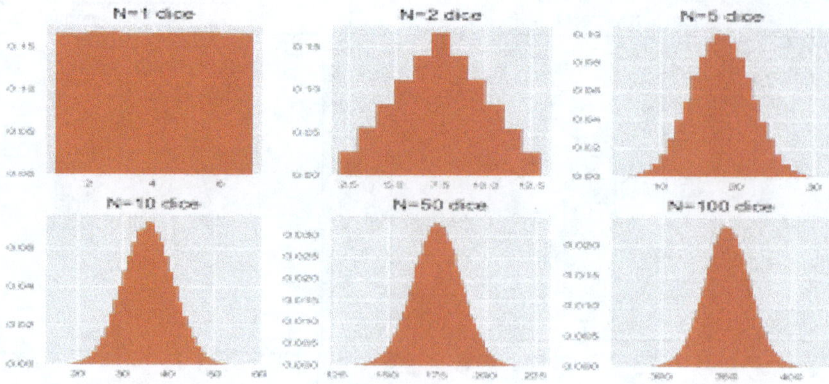

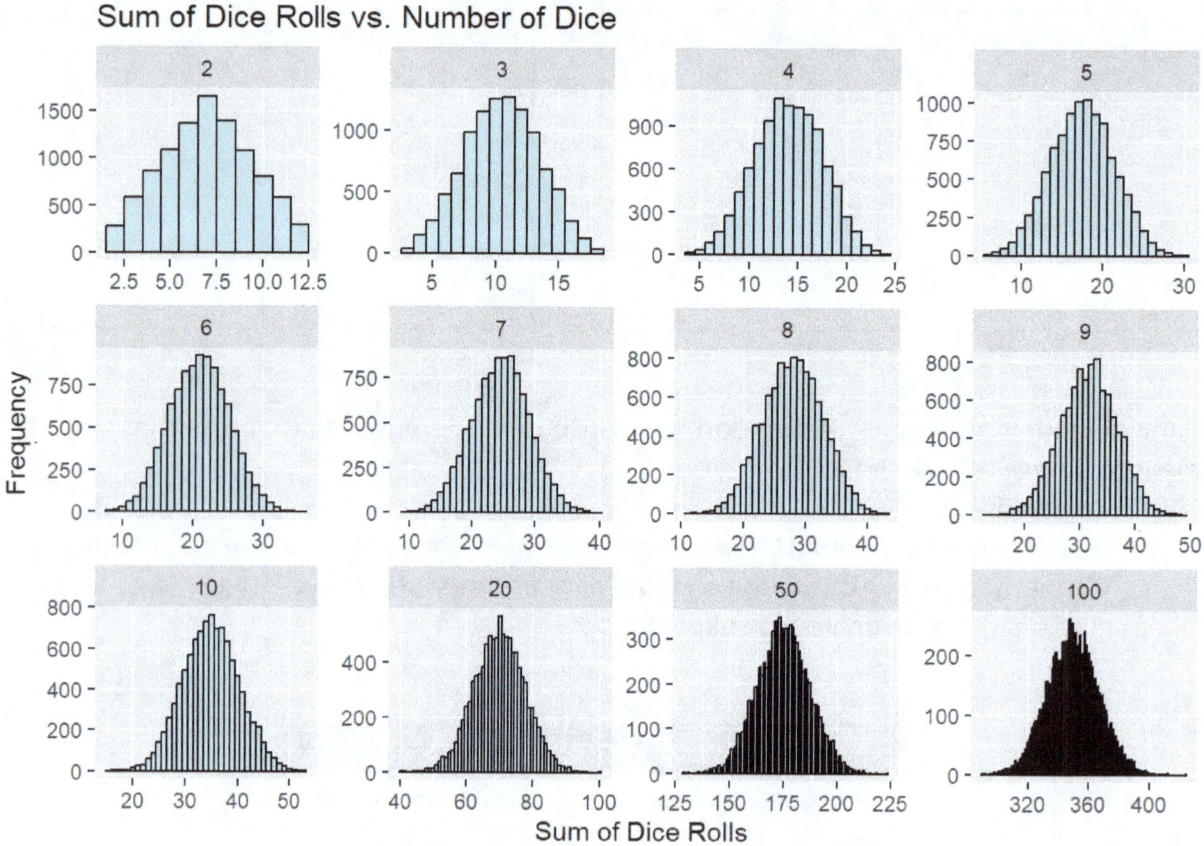

Critical AI Concept: Bias-Variance Tradeoff

Total error = $Bias^2$ + Variance + Irreducible error.

- **High bias**: Underfitting (model too simple, high error on train/test).
- **High variance**: Overfitting (model too complex, low train error but high test error).

Goal: Balance for optimal generalization.

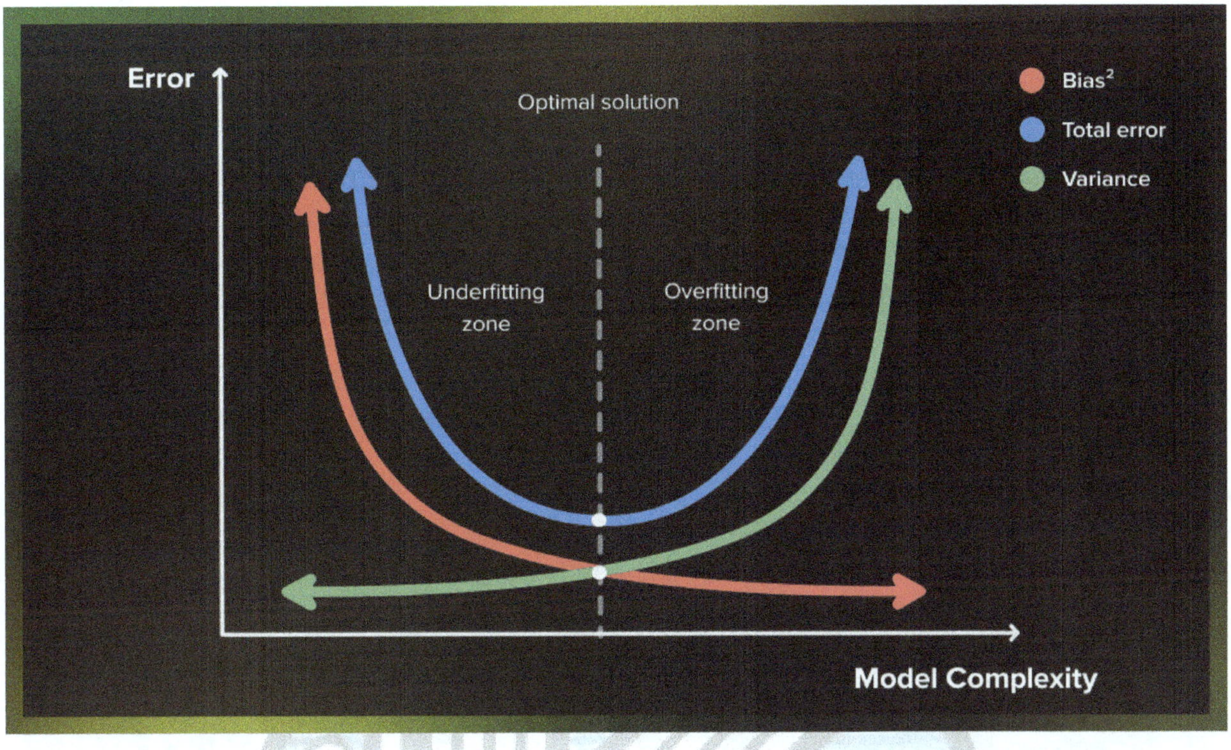

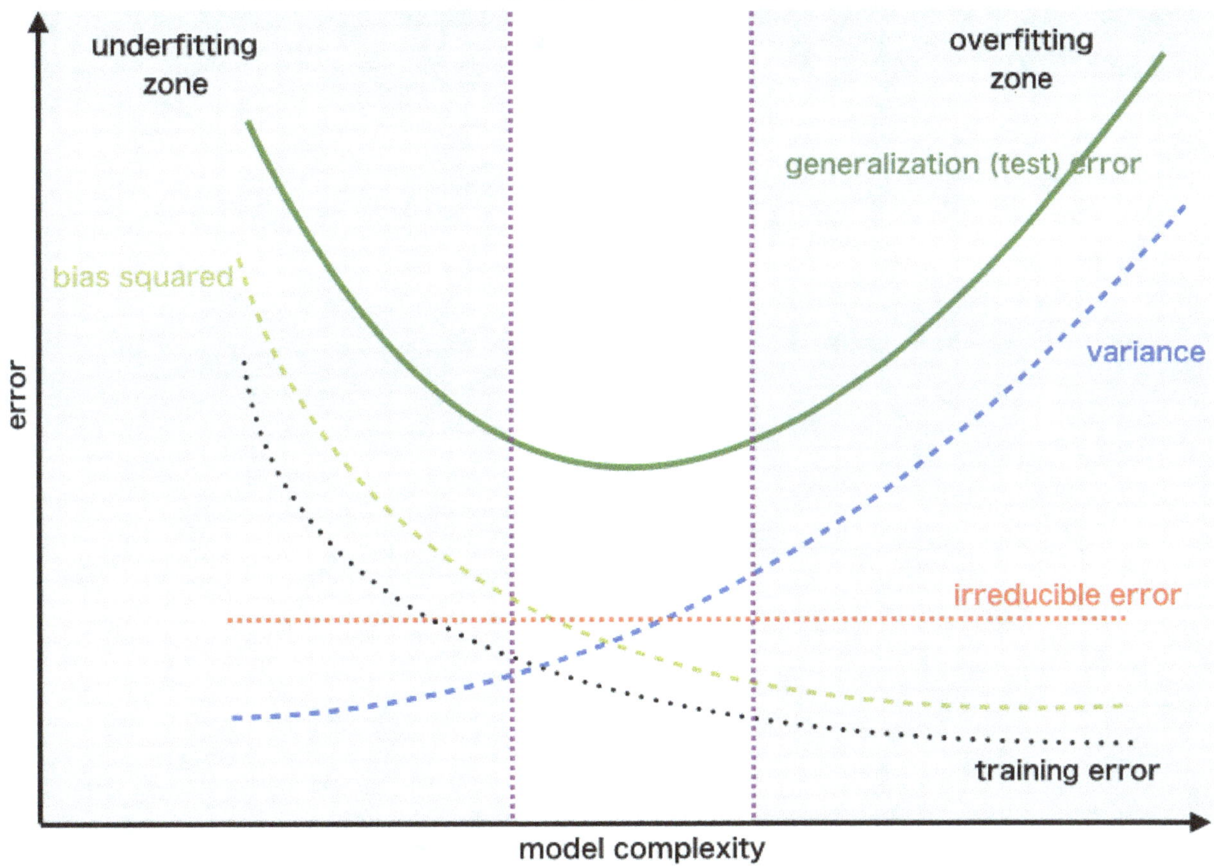

These fundamentals drive preprocessing (normalization), model selection, and error analysis in AI.

3.Calculus (Derivatives, Integrals)

Calculus is essential in artificial intelligence, particularly for **optimization** (training models via gradient descent) and understanding how changes propagate in neural networks. Derivatives tell us how functions change (rates of change), while integrals accumulate quantities (areas, expectations). In AI, derivatives drive learning, and integrals appear in probability densities, expectations, and some advanced models.

Derivatives

The **derivative** of a function $f(x)$at a point is the instantaneous rate of change—the slope of the tangent line.

Formal definition (limit):

$$f'(x) = \lim_{h \to 0} \frac{f(x+h) - f(x)}{h}$$

Intuition: How small changes in input affect output.

The tangent line to the graph of function f at the point $(2, 3)$ passes through the point $(7, 6)$.

Find $f'(2)$.

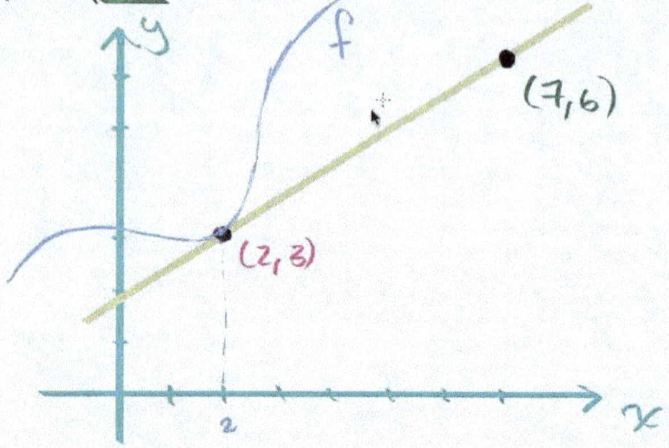

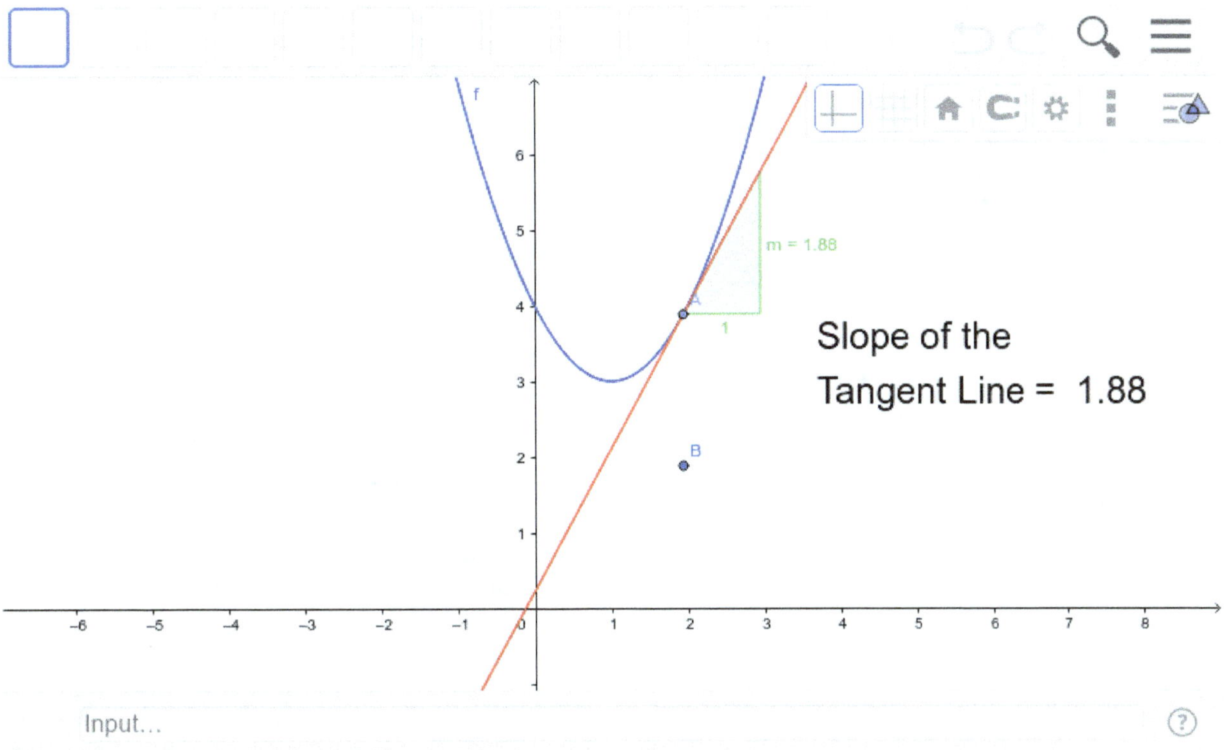

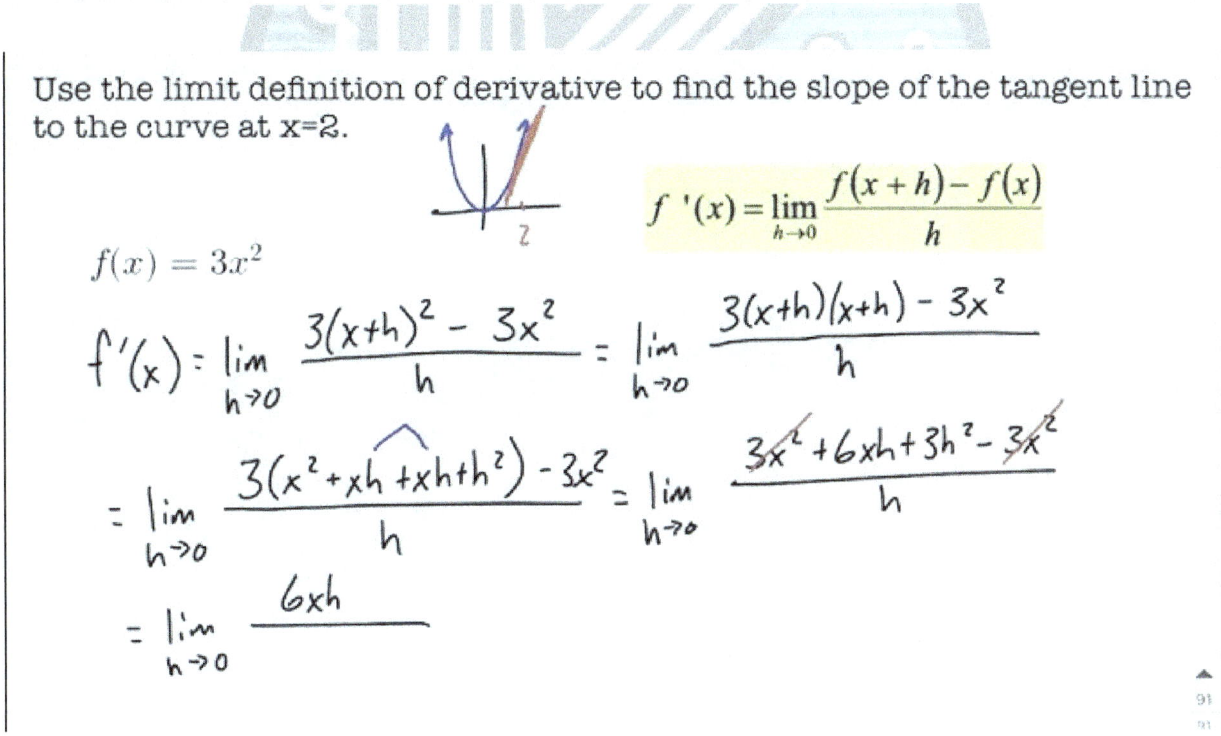

Why crucial in AI?

- **Gradients**: For a loss function $L(\mathbf{w})$(where $\mathbf{w}$are model weights), the gradient $\nabla L$is a vector of partial derivatives $\frac{\partial L}{\partial w_i}$, pointing toward the steepest increase in loss.
- **Gradient Descent**: Update weights by moving opposite the gradient: $\mathbf{w} \leftarrow \mathbf{w} - \eta \nabla L$(η= learning rate).

Linear regression models converge because the loss surface is convex and contains a point where the weight and bias have a slope that's almost zero.

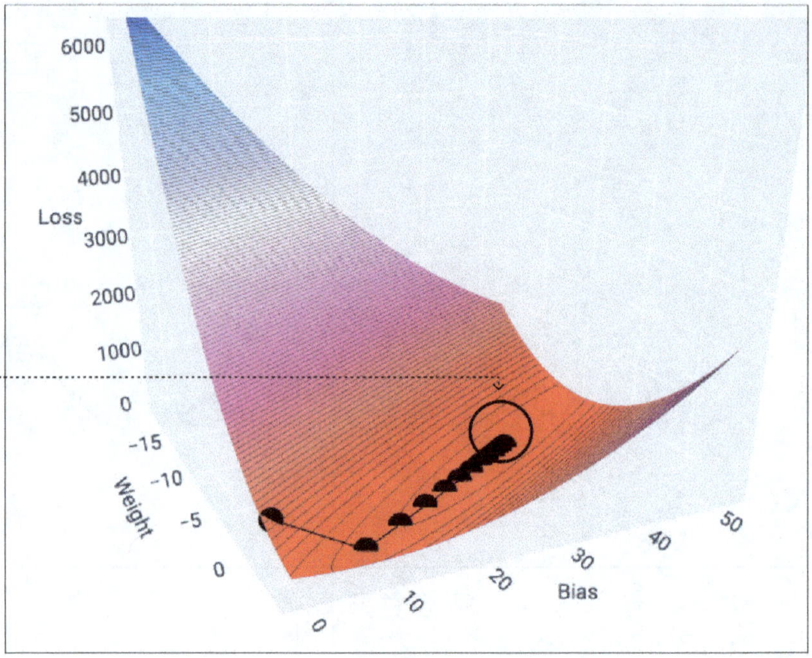

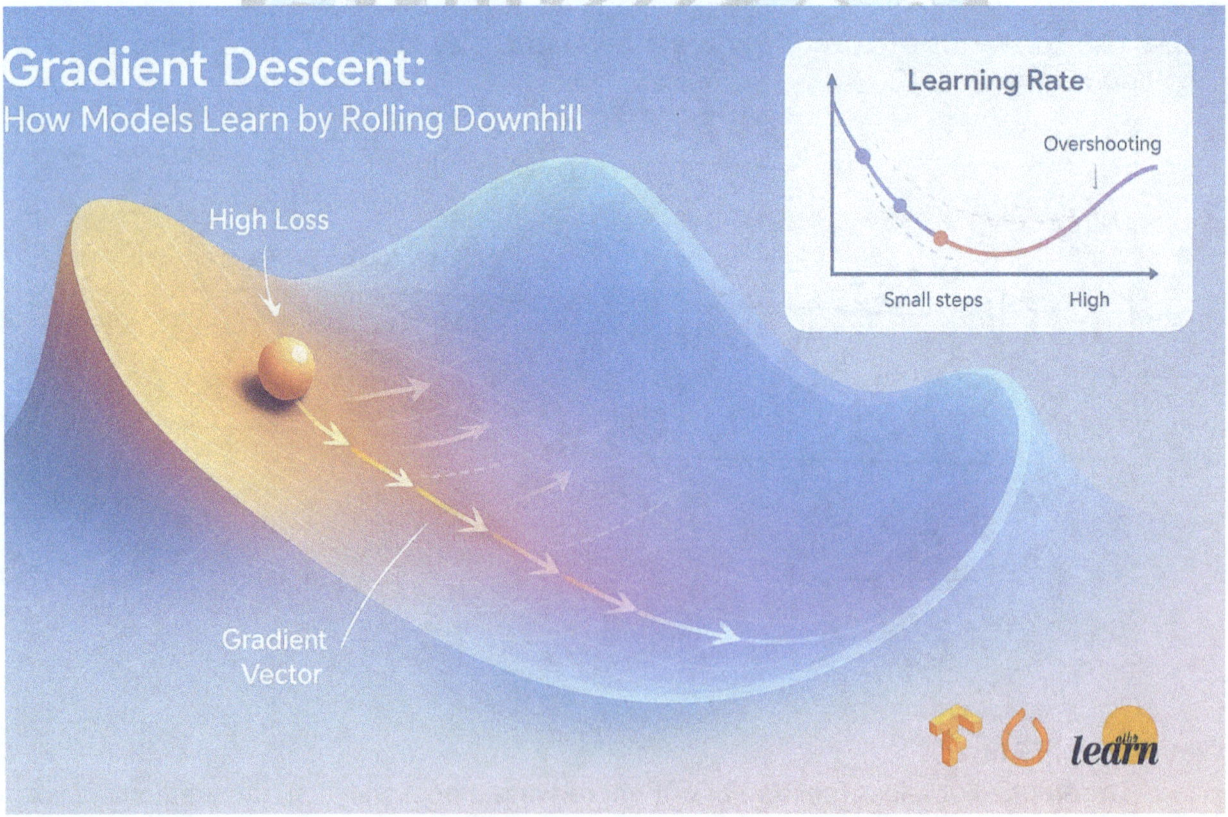

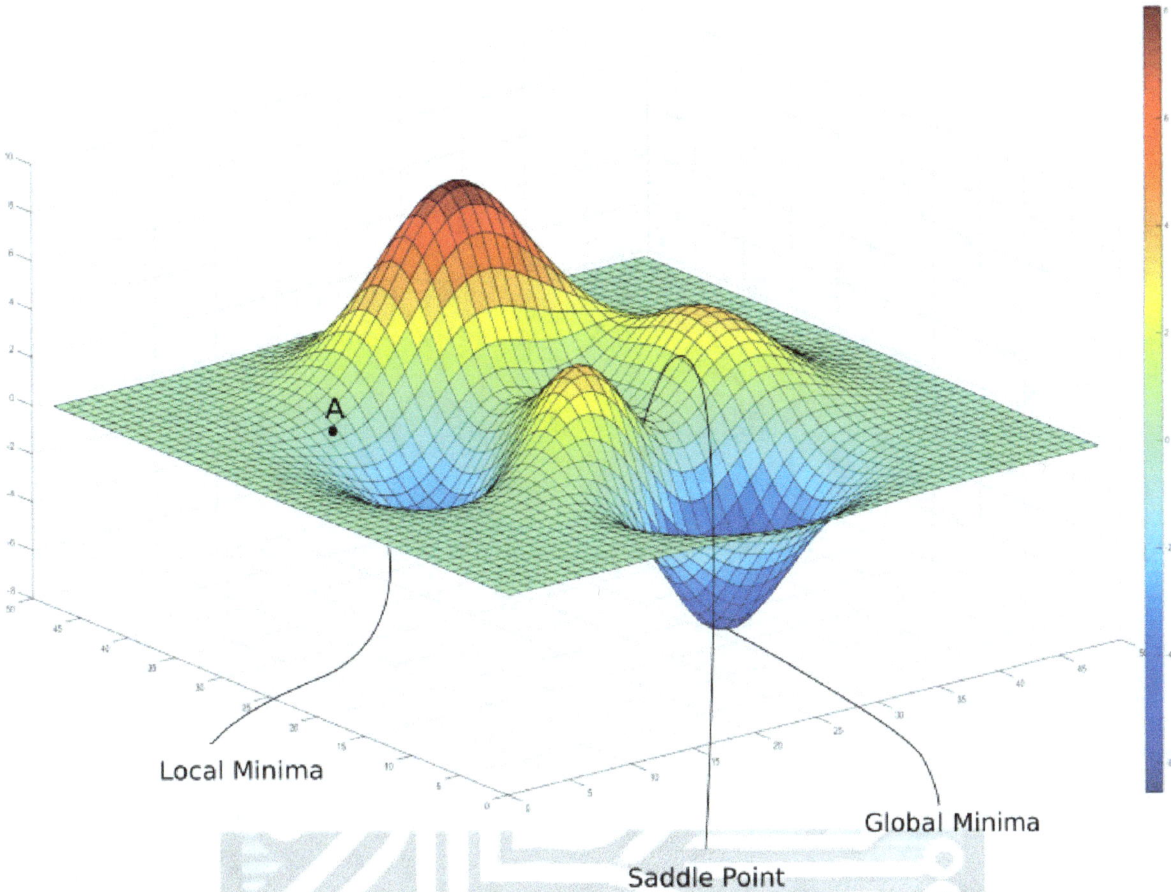

This minimizes loss, "descending" the loss surface to find good parameters.
Chain Rule (key for deep networks): If $y = g(u)$and $u = h(x)$, then

$$\frac{dy}{dx} = \frac{dy}{du} \cdot \frac{du}{dx}$$

In multilayer networks, extends to partials for backpropagation—computing gradients efficiently layer by layer.

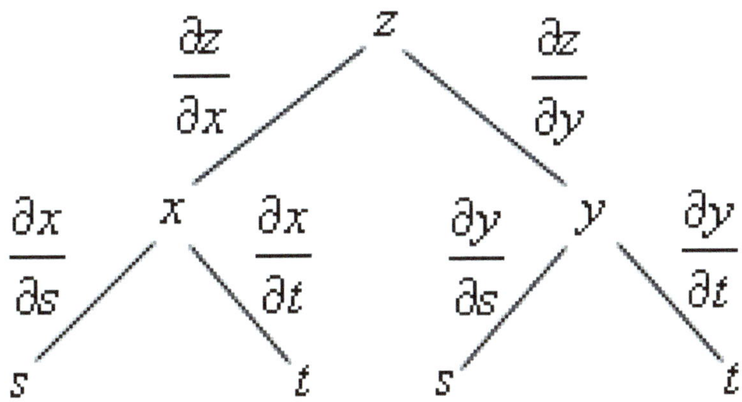

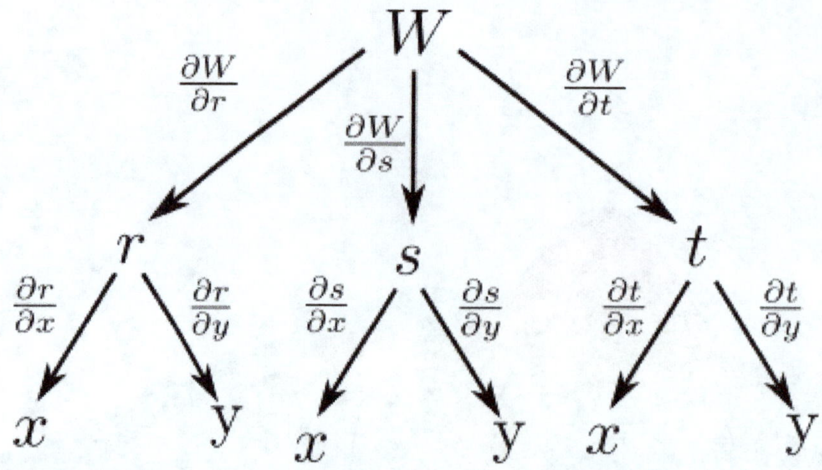

Backpropagation visualizes this chain in reverse, propagating error gradients backward.

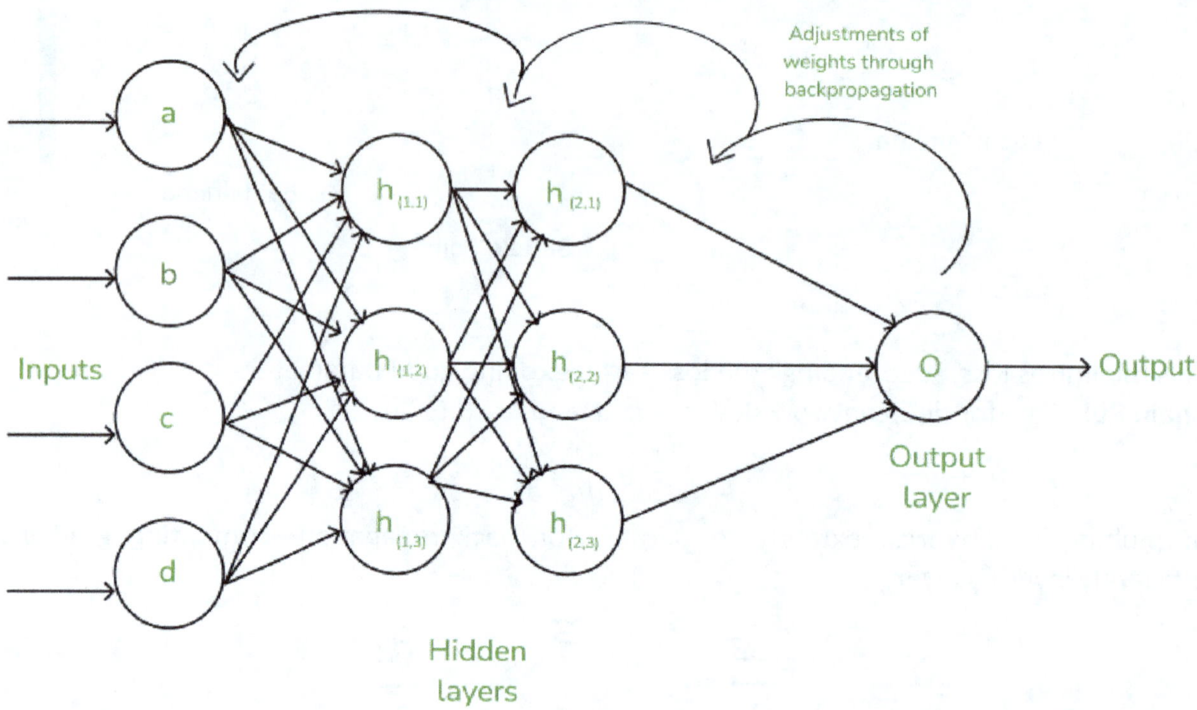

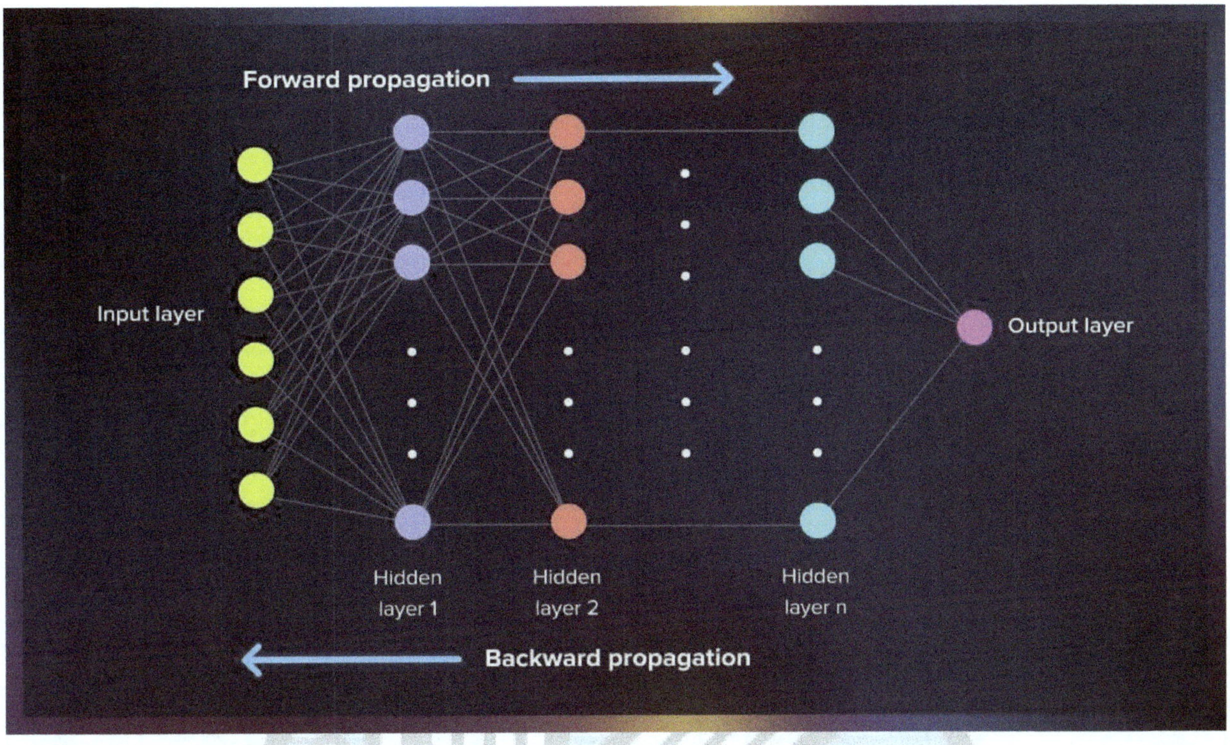

Integrals

The **definite integral** $\int_a^b f(x)\,dx$ represents the signed area under the curve of $f(x)$ from a to b.

Riemann sum approximation:

$$\int_a^b f(x)\,dx = \lim_{n\to\infty} \sum_{i=1}^{n} f(x_i^*)\Delta x$$

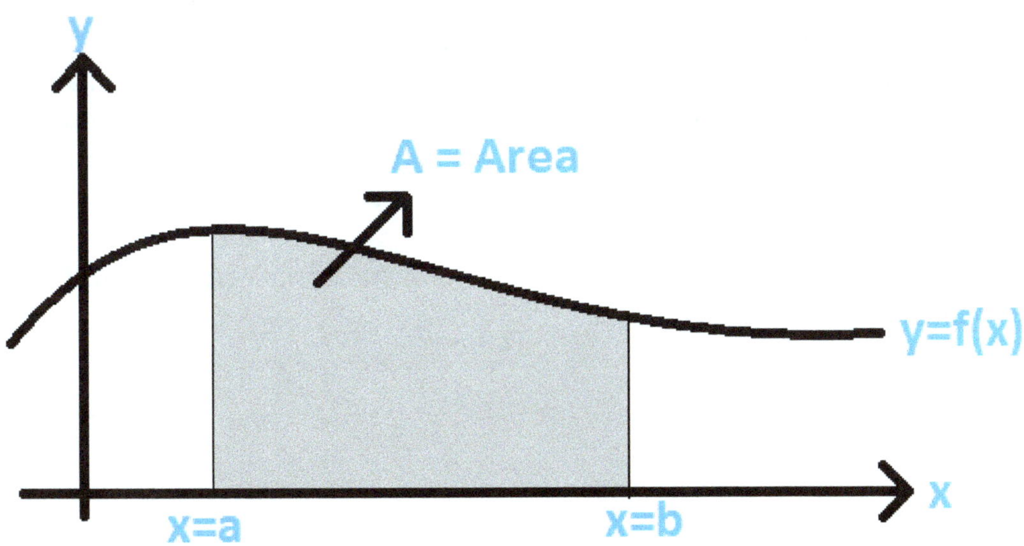

Fundamental Theorem of Calculus (links derivatives and integrals):

1. If $F(x) = \int_a^x f(t)\, dt$, then $F'(x) = f(x)$.
2. $\int_a^b f(x)\, dx = F(b) - F(a)$where $F' = f$.

This shows integration as the inverse of differentiation.

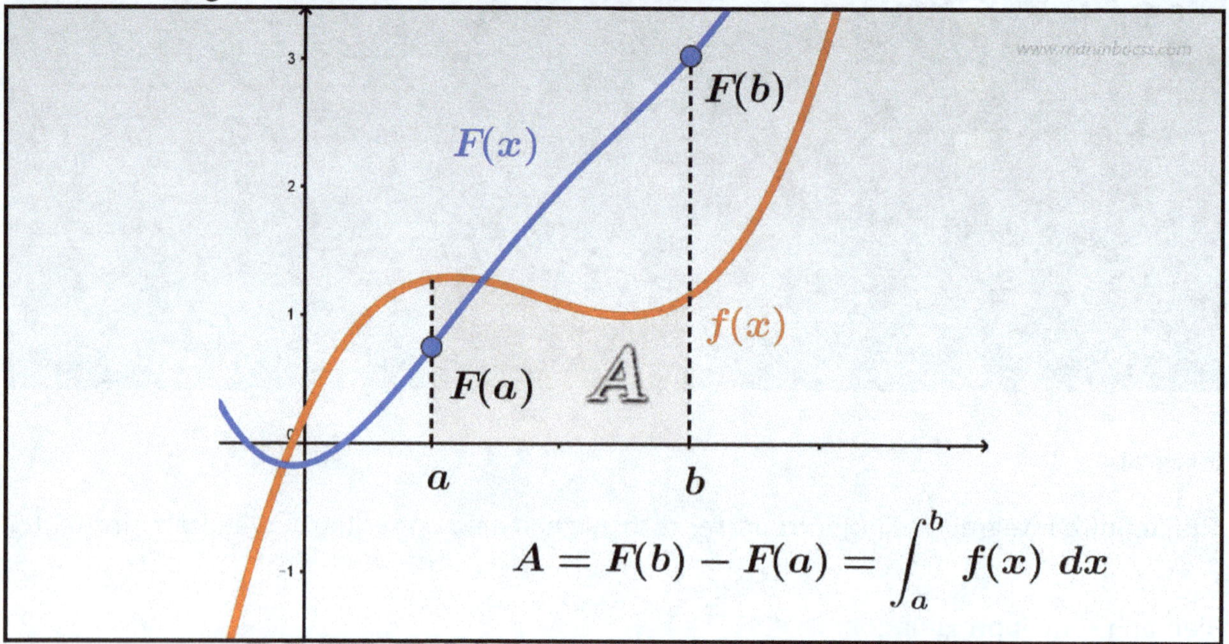

Relevance to AI:

- **Probability**: Continuous distributions (e.g., Gaussian) use integrals for expectations $E[X] = \int x f(x)\, dx$and normalization (PDF integrates to 1).
- **Loss functions**: Cross-entropy often involves integrals in continuous formulations.
- **Variational inference** and **reinforcement learning**: Integrals over state/action spaces.
- Less direct in basic deep learning (discrete sums dominate), but vital in probabilistic models, Bayesian ML, and physics-informed networks.

These concepts power how models learn (derivatives/gradients) and handle uncertainty (integrals/probability). Mastering them unlocks intuition for optimizers (Adam, RMSprop), vanishing gradients, and generative models.

4.Optimization Techniques (Gradient Descent)

Optimization is the heart of training AI models, especially in machine learning and deep learning. The goal is to minimize a **loss function** $L(\mathbf{w})$, where $\mathbf{w}$represents model parameters (e.g., weights and biases). This loss quantifies how poorly the model performs on data, and optimization finds the $\mathbf{w}$that makes Las small as possible.

In AI, loss landscapes are high-dimensional and non-convex, full of valleys, plateaus, and ridges. Gradient-based methods, rooted in calculus, dominate because they use derivatives (gradients) to guide updates. We'll focus on **Gradient Descent (GD)** and its variants, with detailed explanations, formulas, AI applications, and visuals.

Gradient Descent Basics

Vanilla (Batch) Gradient Descent computes the gradient over the entire dataset and updates parameters in the direction of steepest descent.

Update rule:

$$\mathbf{w}_{t+1} = \mathbf{w}_t - \eta \nabla L(\mathbf{w}_t)$$

- η: Learning rate (step size).
- ∇L: Gradient of the loss (vector of partial derivatives).

Intuition: Imagine descending a mountain by always taking a step downhill based on the slope at your feet. In AI, this minimizes errors in neural networks during training.

Pros: Smooth, converges to local minima in convex cases. Cons: Computationally expensive for large datasets; can get stuck in local minima or saddle points.

Visualizations of GD on a loss surface:

Linear regression models converge because the loss surface is convex and contains a point where the weight and bias have a slope that's almost zero.

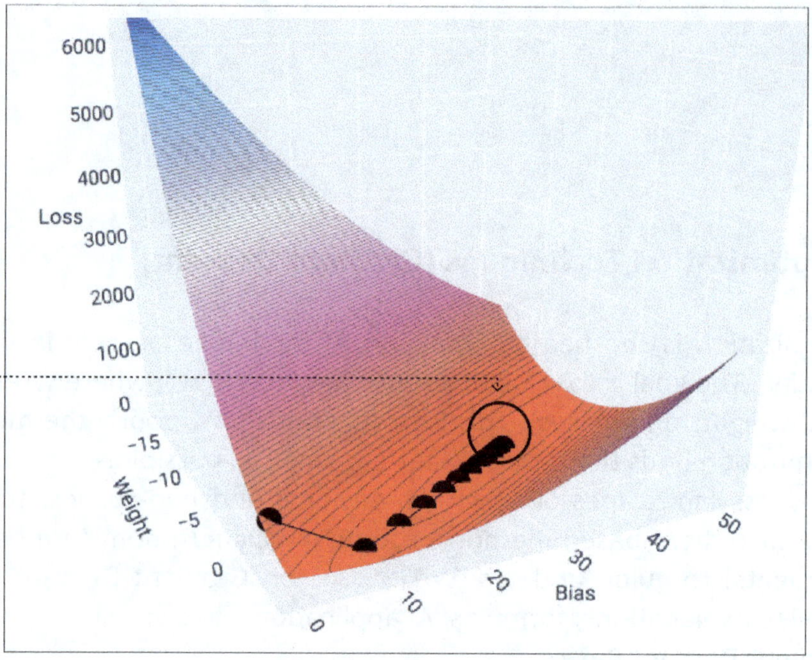

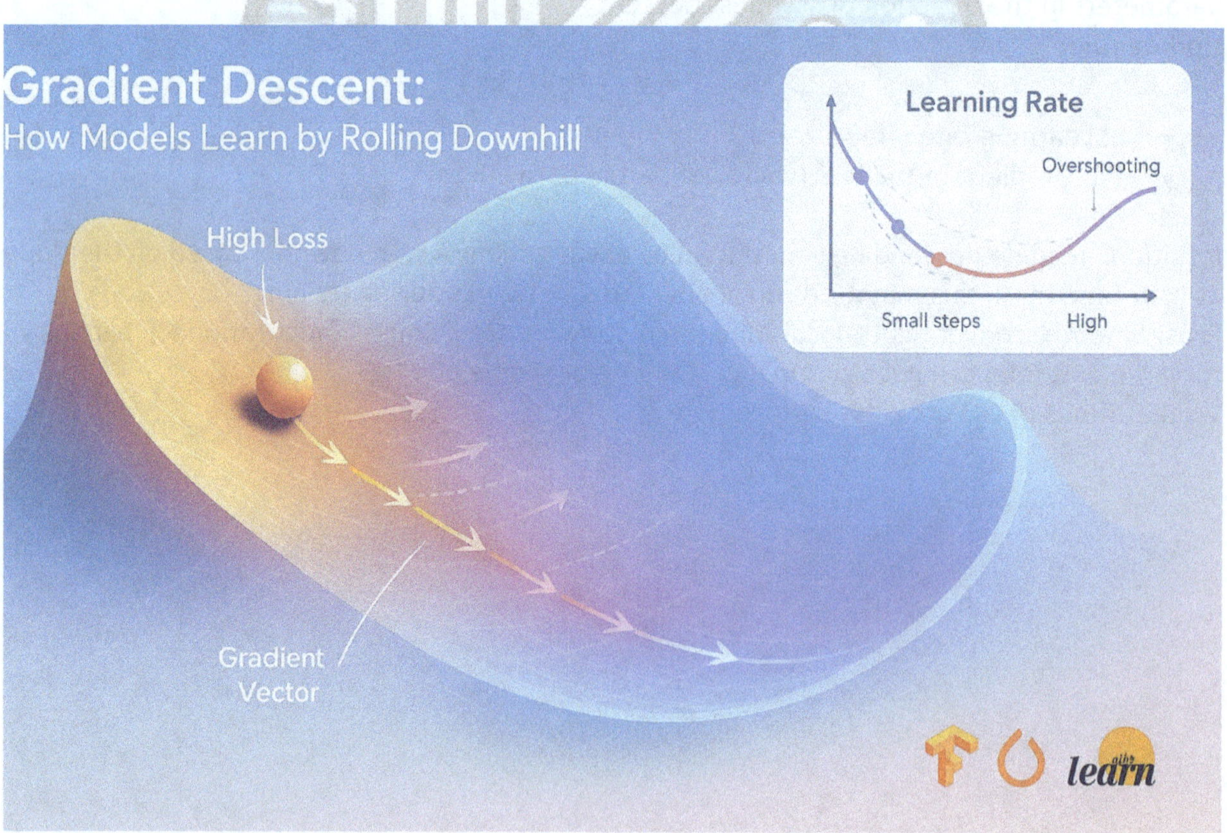

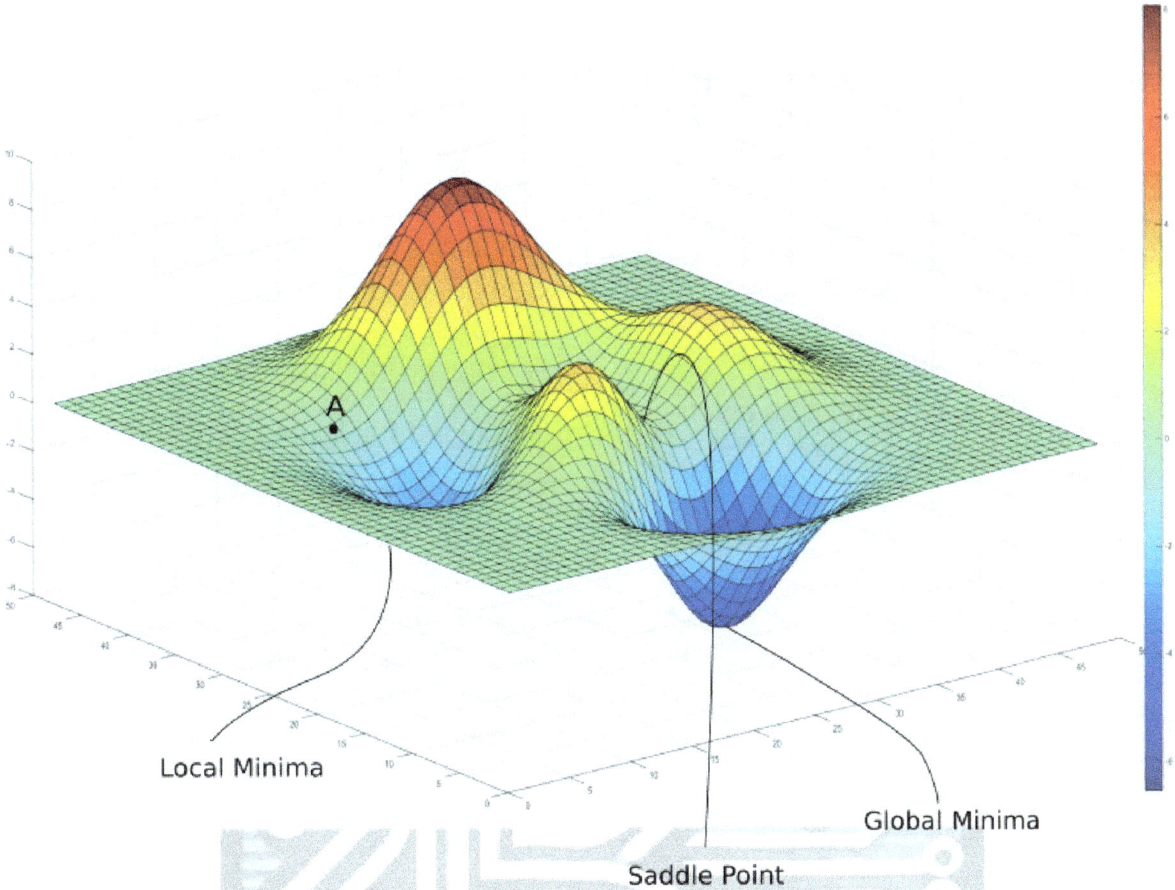

In AI: Used in simple linear regression or small-scale models, but rarely alone in deep learning due to scale.

Stochastic and Mini-Batch Gradient Descent

To handle big data, we approximate the gradient.

- **Stochastic Gradient Descent (SGD)**: Updates using a single random sample per step. Noisy but fast.

$$\mathbf{w}_{t+1} = \mathbf{w}_t - \eta \nabla L_i(\mathbf{w}_t)$$

(Where $L_i$is loss on one example.)

- **Mini-Batch GD**: Compromise—uses a small batch (e.g., 32-256 samples). Balances noise and computation.

$$\mathbf{w}_{t+1} = \mathbf{w}_t - \eta \frac{1}{b} \sum_{i=1}^{b} \nabla L_i(\mathbf{w}_t)$$

(b= batch size.)

In AI: Mini-batch is standard in frameworks like PyTorch/TensorFlow. SGD's noise helps escape local minima; mini-batch enables GPU parallelism.

Comparison visuals:

A	B	C
S.NO.	**BATCH GRADIENT DESCENT**	**STOCHASTIC GRADIENT DESCENT**
1	Computes gradient using the whole Training sample	Computes gradient using a single Training sample
2	Slow and computationally expensive algorithm	Faster and less computationally expensive than Batch GD
3	Not suggested for huge training samples.	Can be used for large training samples.
4	Deterministic in nature.	Stochastic in nature.
5	Gives optimal solution given sufficient time to converge.	Gives good solution but not optimal.
6	No random shuffling of points are required.	The data sample should be in a random order, and this is why we want to shuffle the training set for every epoch.
7	Can't escape shallow local minima easily.	SGD can escape shallow local minima more easily.
8	Convergence is slow.	Reaches rthe convergence much faster.

Momentum and Nesterov Accelerated Gradient

Vanilla GD can oscillate or slow down. **Momentum** adds inertia, like a ball rolling downhill, accumulating velocity from past gradients.

Update with momentum:

$$\mathbf{v}_{t+1} = \beta \mathbf{v}_t - \eta \nabla L(\mathbf{w}_t)$$

$$\mathbf{w}_{t+1} = \mathbf{w}_t + \mathbf{v}_{t+1}$$

- β: Momentum coefficient (e.g., 0.9), damps oscillations.

Nesterov Accelerated Gradient (NAG): "Looks ahead" by computing gradient at $\mathbf{w}_t + \beta \mathbf{v}_t$:

$$\mathbf{v}_{t+1} = \beta \mathbf{v}_t - \eta \nabla L(\mathbf{w}_t + \beta \mathbf{v}_t)$$

In AI: Speeds convergence in RNNs or CNNs; reduces zigzagging in ravines.

Momentum illustrations:

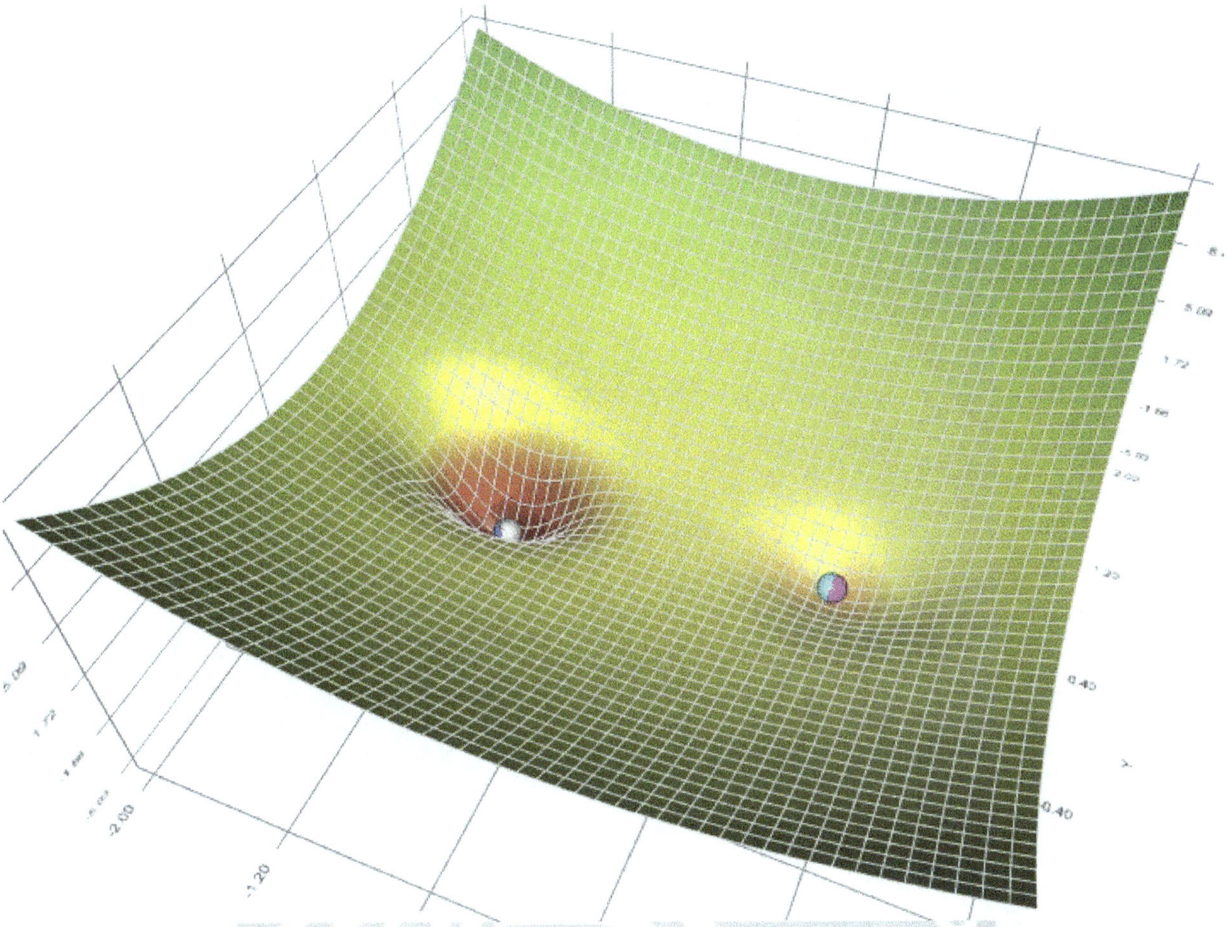

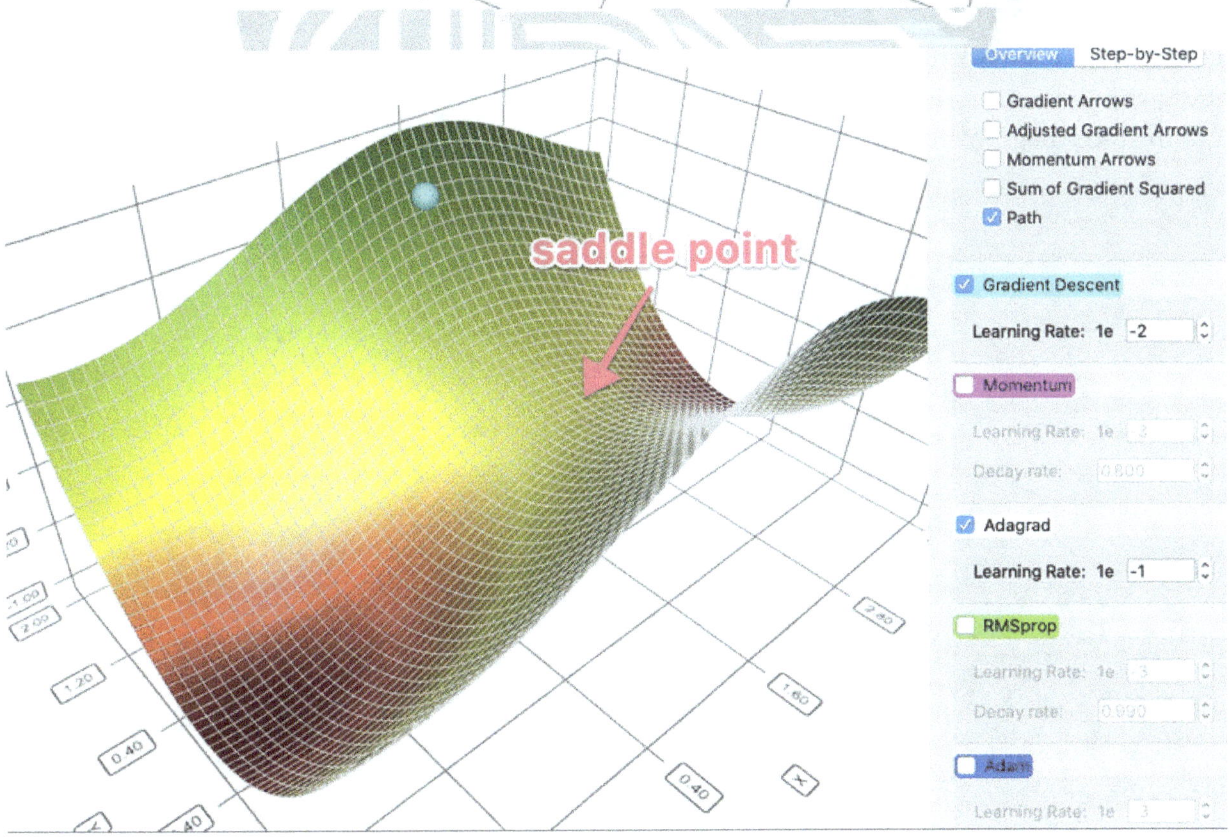
saddle point
Overview
Step-by-Step
Gradient Arrows
Adjusted Gradient Arrows
Momentum Arrows
Sum of Gradient Squared
Path
Gradient Descent
Learning Rate: 1e -2
Momentum
Adagrad
Learning Rate: 1e -1
RMSprop
Adam

Adaptive Optimizers: RMSprop, Adam

These adapt ηper parameter, handling sparse gradients or varying scales.

- **RMSprop** (Root Mean Square Propagation): Divides learning rate by sqrt of exponentially weighted moving average of squared gradients.

$$\mathbf{s}_{t+1} = \beta \mathbf{s}_t + (1-\beta)(\nabla L)^2$$

$$\mathbf{w}_{t+1} = \mathbf{w}_t - \frac{\eta}{\sqrt{\mathbf{s}_{t+1}} + \epsilon} \nabla L$$

(ϵ: Small constant for stability.)

- **Adam** (Adaptive Moment Estimation): Combines momentum (first moment) and RMSprop (second moment), with bias correction.

$$\mathbf{m}_{t+1} = \beta_1 \mathbf{m}_t + (1-\beta_1)\nabla L \text{(1st moment)}$$

$$\mathbf{v}_{t+1} = \beta_2 \mathbf{v}_t + (1-\beta_2)(\nabla L)^2 \text{(2nd moment)}$$

$$\hat{\mathbf{m}} = \frac{\mathbf{m}_{t+1}}{1-\beta_1^{t+1}}, \hat{\mathbf{v}} = \frac{\mathbf{v}_{t+1}}{1-\beta_2^{t+1}}$$

$$\mathbf{w}_{t+1} = \mathbf{w}_t - \frac{\eta \hat{\mathbf{m}}}{\sqrt{\hat{\mathbf{v}}} + \epsilon}$$

Defaults: $\beta_1 = 0.9, \beta_2 = 0.999, \eta = 0.001$.

In AI: Adam is default for transformers (e.g., BERT, GPT); handles noisy gradients in NLP/CV. RMSprop good for non-stationary problems.

Adam steps diagram:

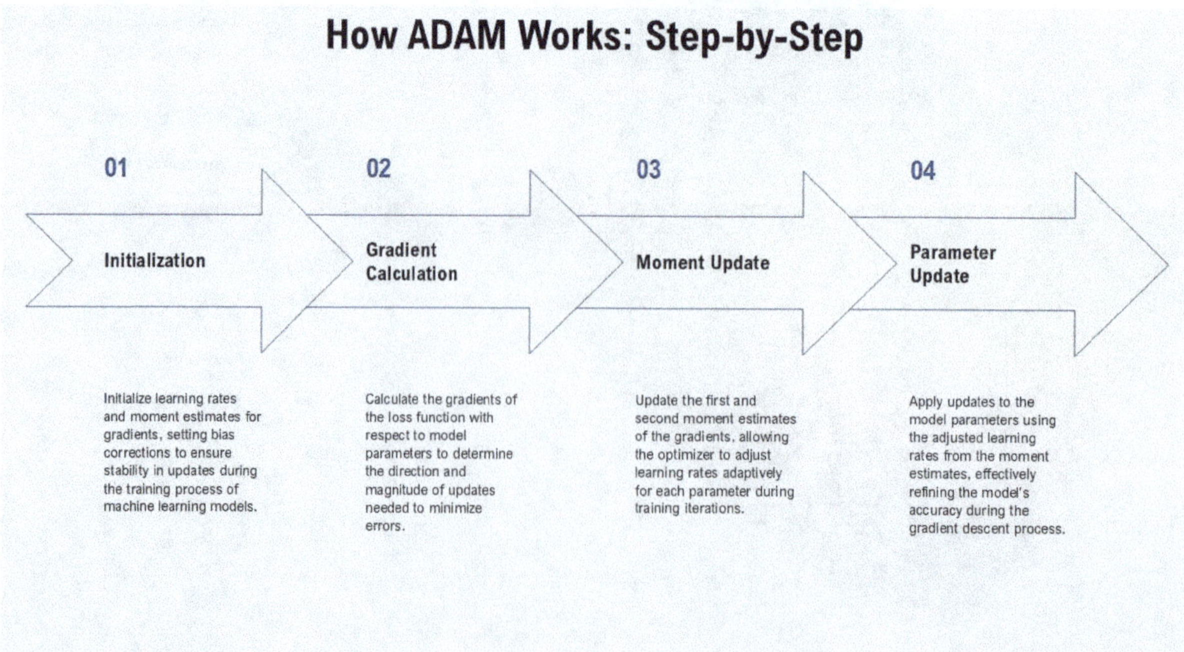

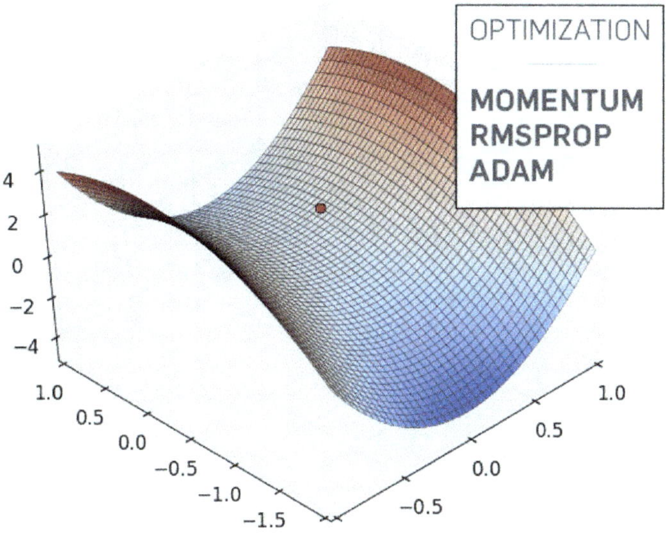

Learning Rate Schedules

Fixed ηcan be suboptimal—too high causes divergence, too low slows training. Schedules adjust ηover time/epochs.

- **Step Decay**: Halve ηevery few epochs.
- **Exponential Decay**: $\eta_t = \eta_0 \cdot \alpha^t (\alpha < 1)$.
- **Cosine Annealing**: $\eta_t = \eta_{\min} + \frac{1}{2}(\eta_{\max} - \eta_{\min})(1 + \cos(\frac{t\pi}{T}))$(cycles for better exploration).
- **Warmup**: Start low, ramp up (helps large batches/minima escape).

In AI: Crucial for large models; e.g., linear warmup + cosine decay in transformers.

Schedule graphs:

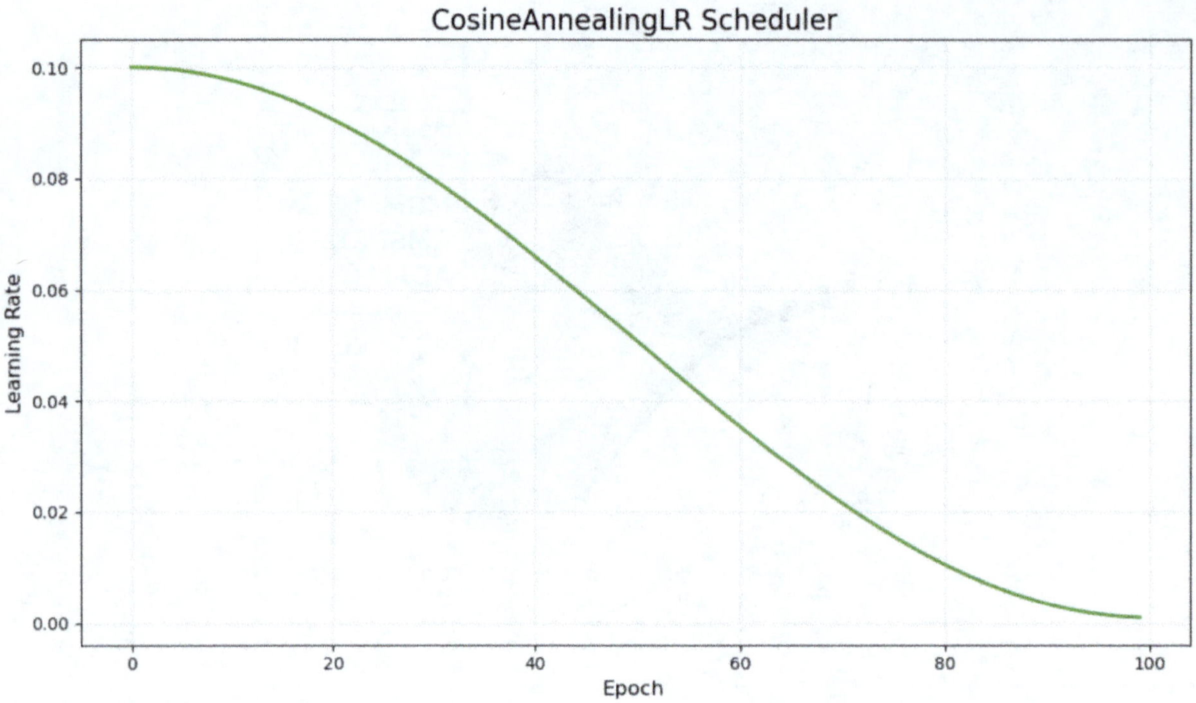

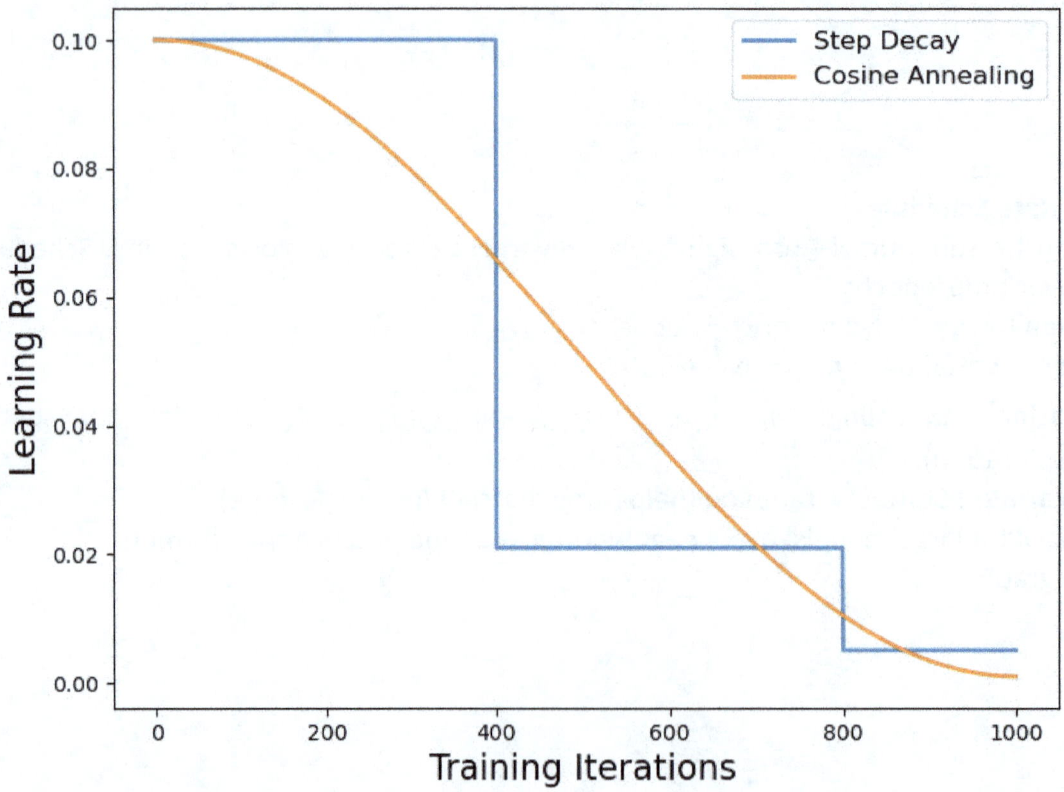

Challenges in Optimization

- **Local Minima**: Suboptimal valleys; noise in SGD helps escape.
- **Saddle Points**: Flat regions with positive/negative curvature; common in high

dimensions—momentum/Adam navigate better.

- **Vanishing/Exploding Gradients**: In deep nets; mitigated by initialization (e.g., Xavier), normalization (BatchNorm), or architectures (ResNets).
- **Plateaus**: Gradients near zero; adaptive methods or learning rate warm restarts help.

Visuals of local minima and saddles:

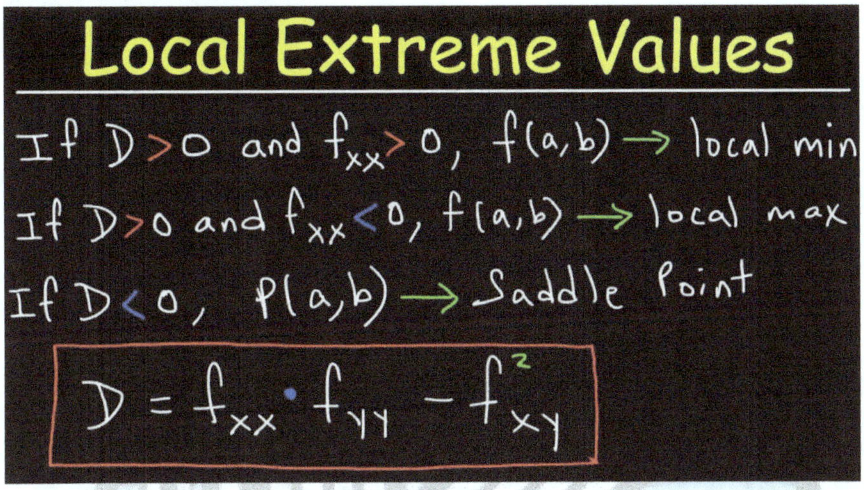

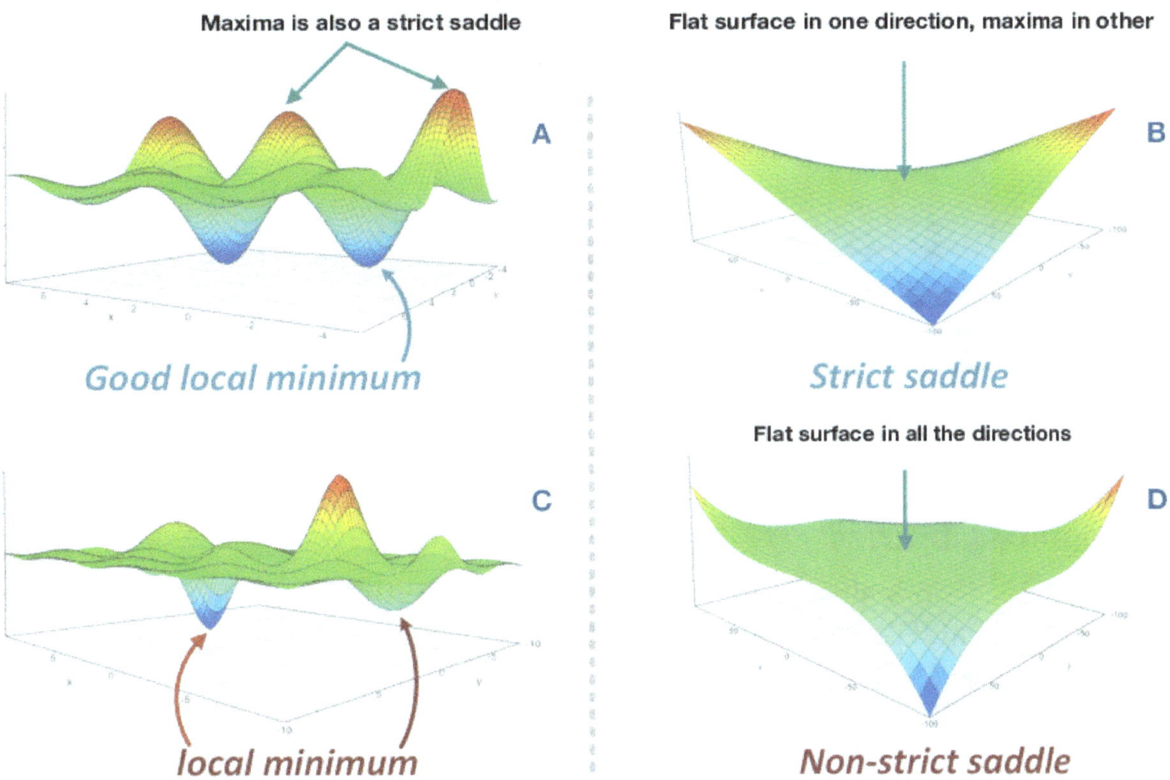

Section-3

Data Science Libraries

- NumPy (Arrays, Linear Algebra, Statistical Operations)
- Pandas (DataFrames, Data Manipulation)
- Matplotlib & Seaborn (Data Visualization)

Data Science Libraries

1.NumPy (Arrays, Linear Algebra, Statistical Operations)

NumPy: As the foundational library for numerical computing, NumPy provides support for large, multi-dimensional arrays (ndarrays) and matrices, along with a vast collection of high-level mathematical functions (e.g., linear algebra, statistics). Many other libraries, including Pandas, are built on top of NumPy.
Use Cases: Mathematical operations, linear algebra, and random number generation on large arrays. Many other libraries, like Pandas and Scikit-learn, are built on top of NumPy.
Key Functions: np.array(), np.dot(), np.mean(), np.linspace()

Why NumPy is essential for AI/ML:

- Vectors, matrices, and tensors in neural networks are NumPy arrays (or built on them in PyTorch/TensorFlow).
- Operations are vectorized (no explicit loops) → much faster than pure Python lists.
- Underpins libraries like Pandas, SciPy, scikit-learn, TensorFlow, and PyTorch.

NumPy arrays (ndarray) are homogeneous, fixed-size, and stored contiguously in memory.

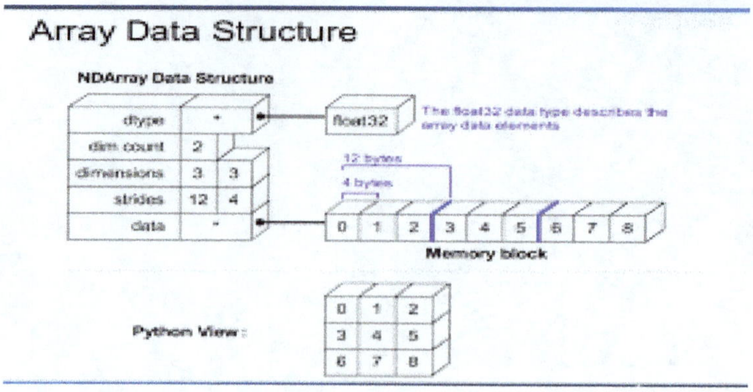

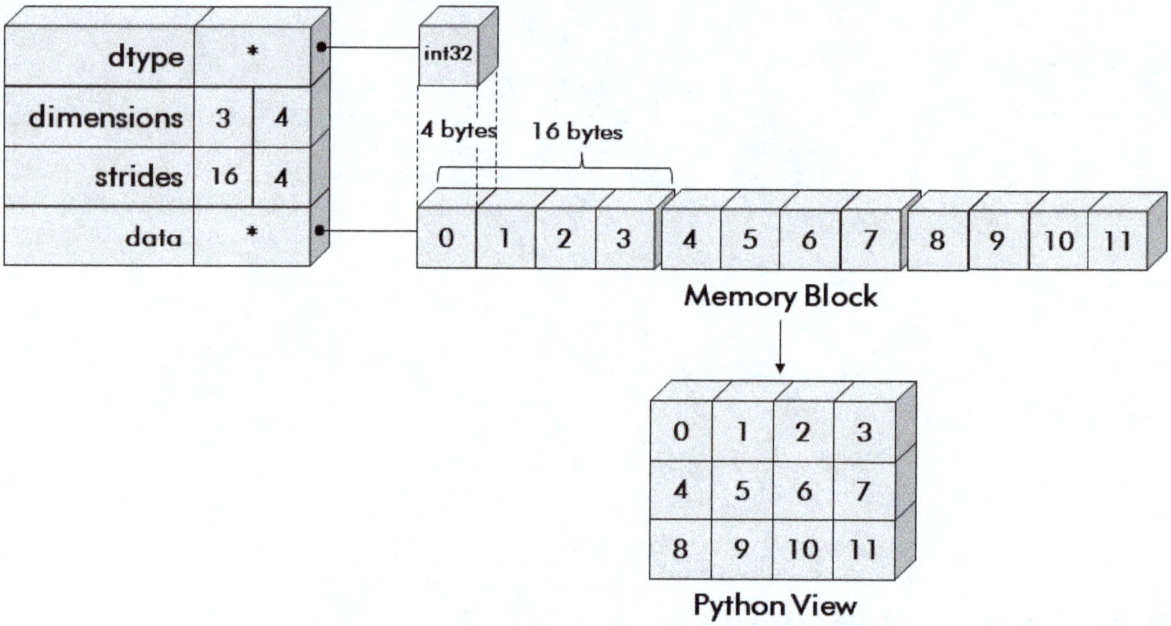

Performance comparison: NumPy is often 10–100x faster than Python lists for numerical operations.

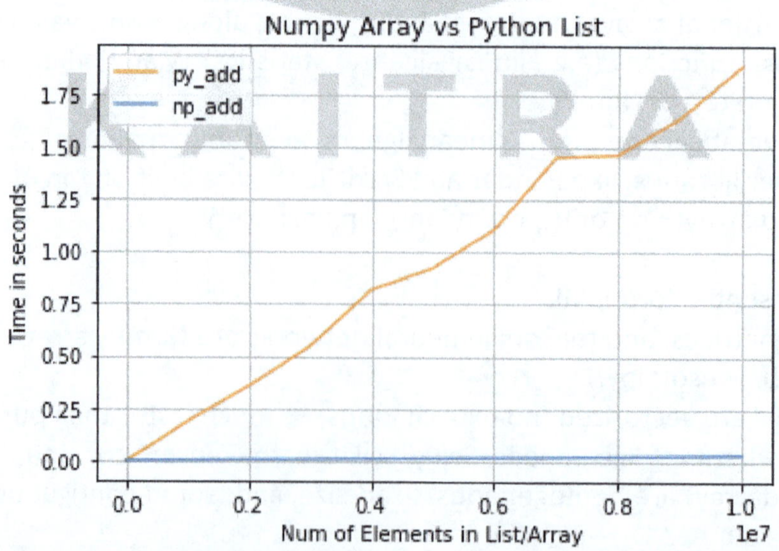

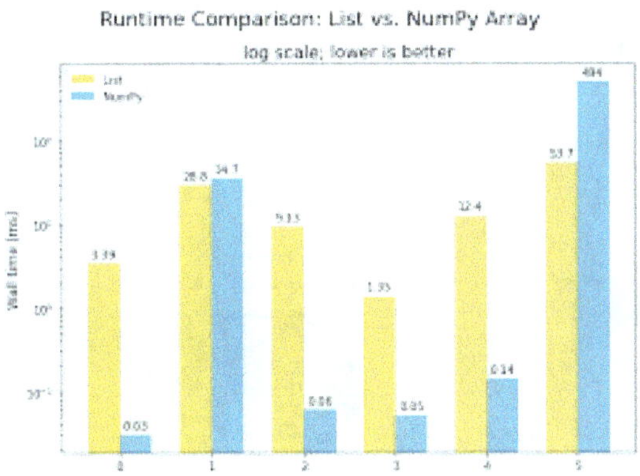

1. Creating Arrays

Python

```
import numpy as np

# From Python list
arr1 = np.array([1, 2, 3, 4])
print(arr1)          # [1 2 3 4]
print(arr1.shape)    # (4,)
print(arr1.dtype)    # int64

# 2D array (matrix)
arr2 = np.array([[1, 2, 3], [4, 5, 6]])
print(arr2)
# [[1 2 3]
#  [4 5 6]]
print(arr2.shape)    # (2, 3)

# Special arrays
zeros = np.zeros((3, 4))      # 3x4 array of zeros
ones = np.ones((2, 2))        # 2x2 array of ones
full = np.full((3, 3), 7)     # 3x3 array filled with 7
eye = np.eye(4)               # 4x4 identity matrix
random = np.random.random((5, 5))  # 5x5 random floats [0,1)

# Sequences
lin = np.linspace(0, 10, 11)  # 11 points from 0 to 10 inclusive
arange = np.arange(0, 10, 2)  # 0,2,4,6,8
```

Visual examples of array creation and reshaping:

Python numpy reshape and stack cheatsheet

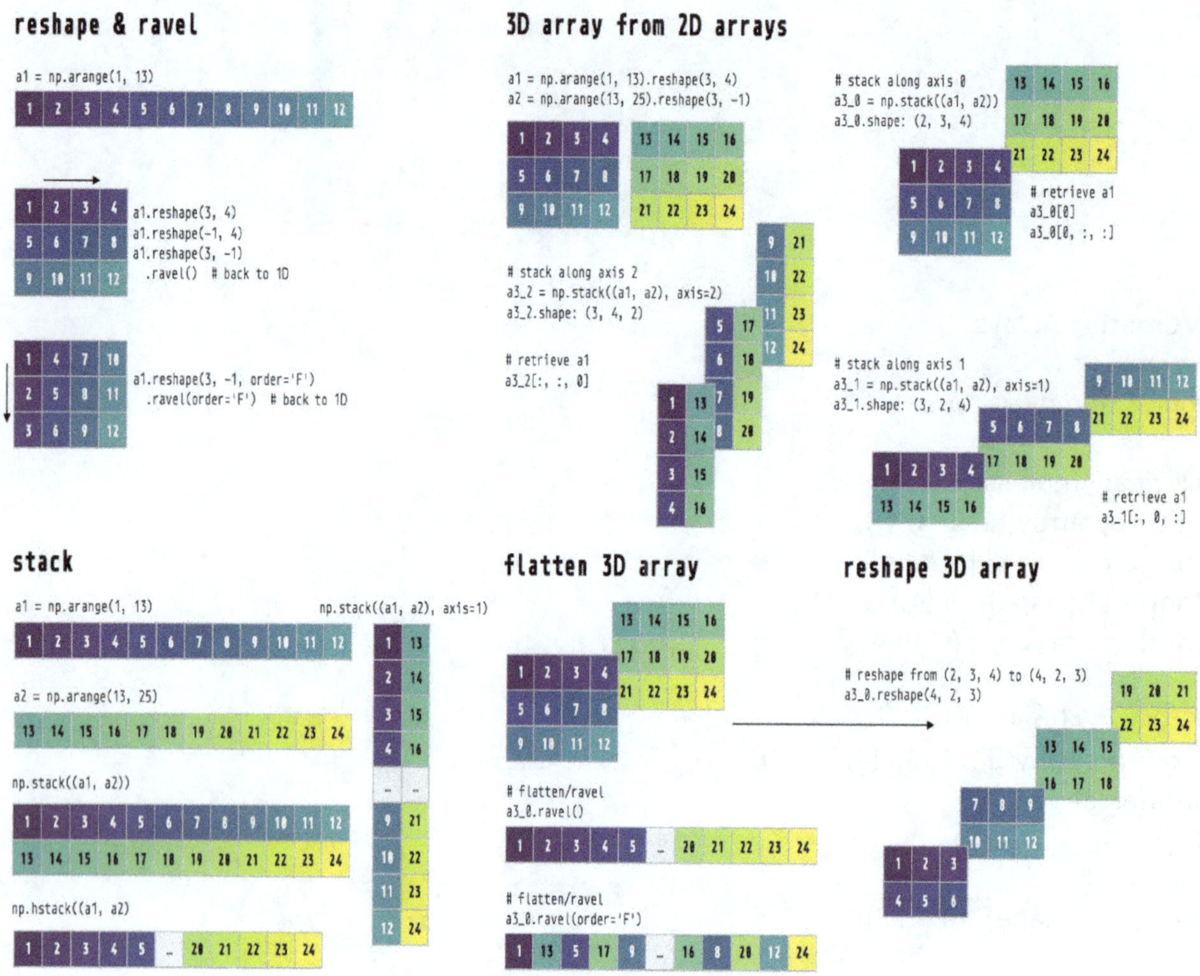

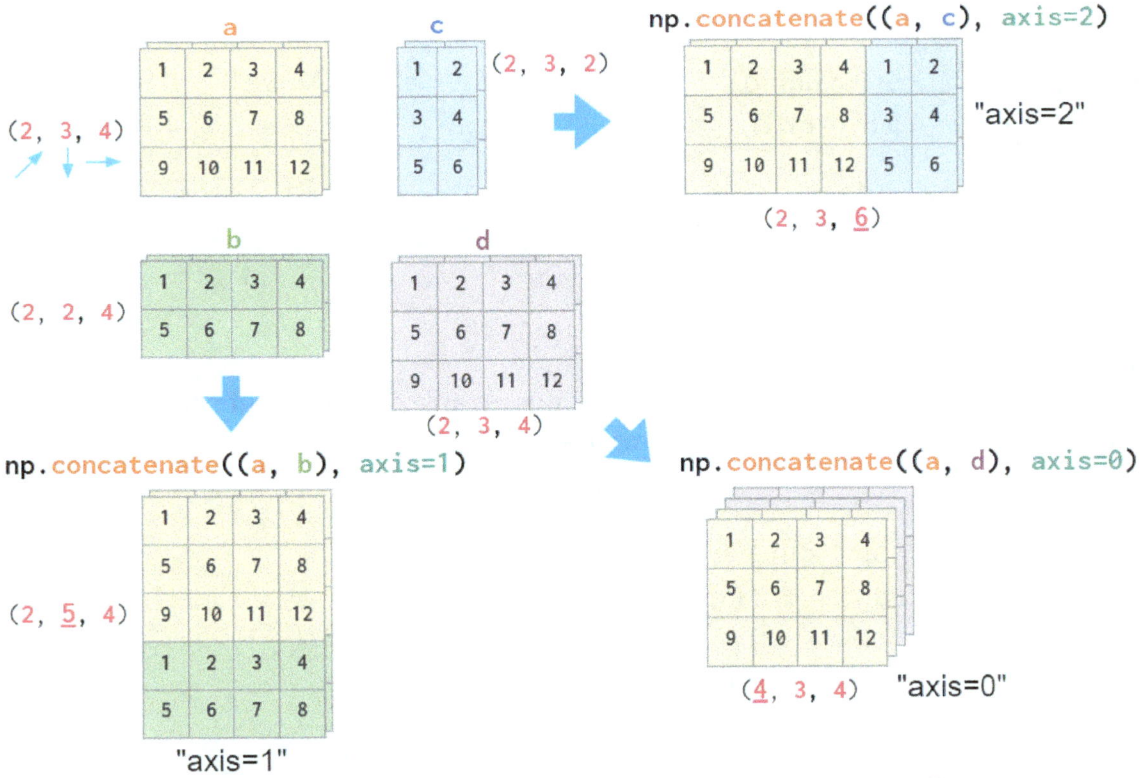

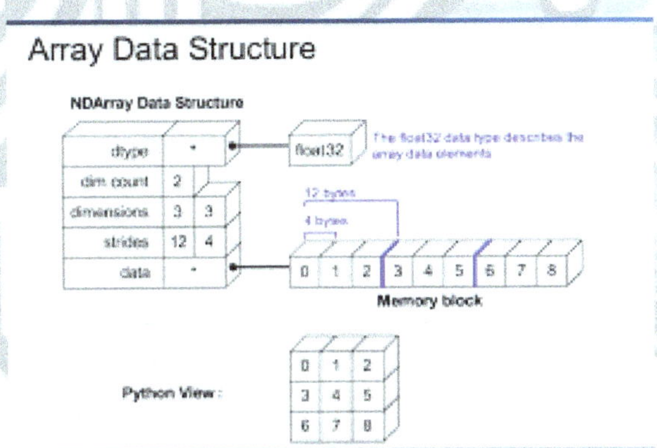

2. Array Attributes & Operations

Python

```
arr = np.array([[1, 2, 3], [4, 5, 6]])

print(arr.ndim)   # 2 (dimensions)
print(arr.size)   # 6 (total elements)
print(arr.shape)  # (2, 3)

# Reshaping (doesn't change data)
reshaped = arr.reshape(3, 2)
print(reshaped)
# [[1 2]
#  [3 4]
#  [5 6]]
```

```
# Indexing & Slicing
print(arr[0, 1])     # 2
print(arr[:, 1])     # [2 5] (column 1)
print(arr[1, :])     # [4 5 6] (row 1)

# Boolean indexing
mask = arr > 3
print(arr[mask])     # [4 5 6]
```

3. Broadcasting

Broadcasting allows NumPy to perform operations on arrays of different shapes without copying data — crucial for efficient AI computations.

Python
```
a = np.array([[1, 2, 3], [4, 5, 6]])  # (2, 3)
b = np.array([10, 20, 30])            # (3,)

result = a + b  # b is "stretched" across rows
print(result)
# [[11 22 33]
#  [14 25 36]]
```

Broadcasting rules visualized:

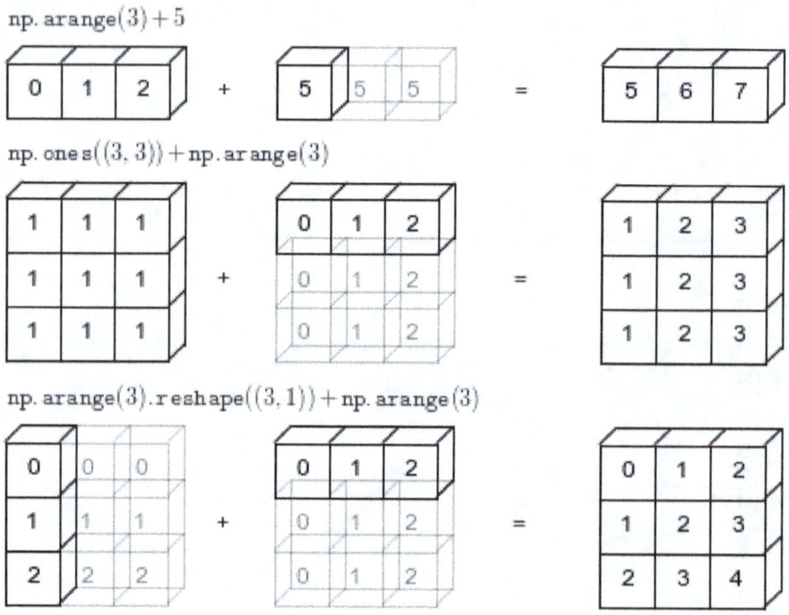

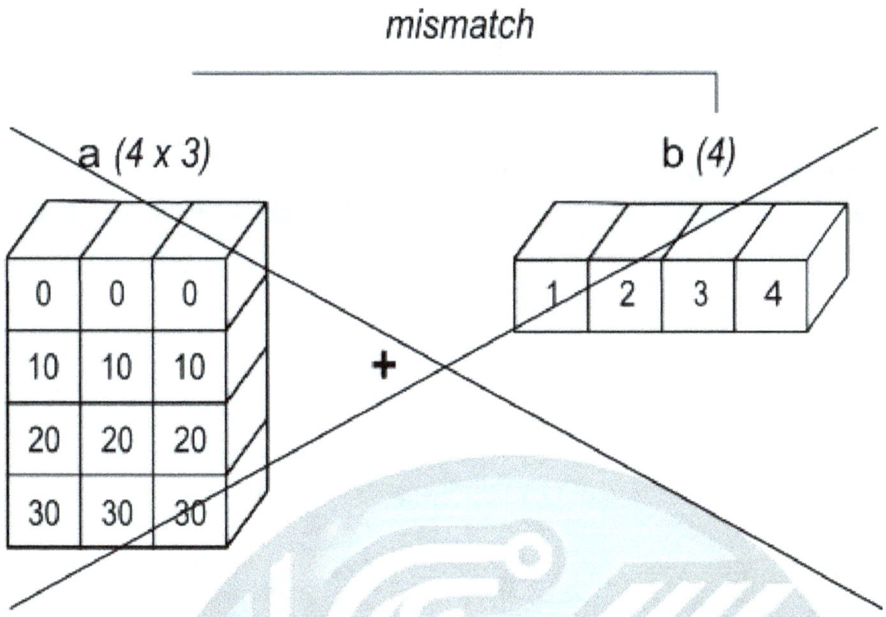
mismatch
a (4 x 3)
b (4)
0 0 0
10 10 10
20 20 20
30 30 30
+
1 2 3 4

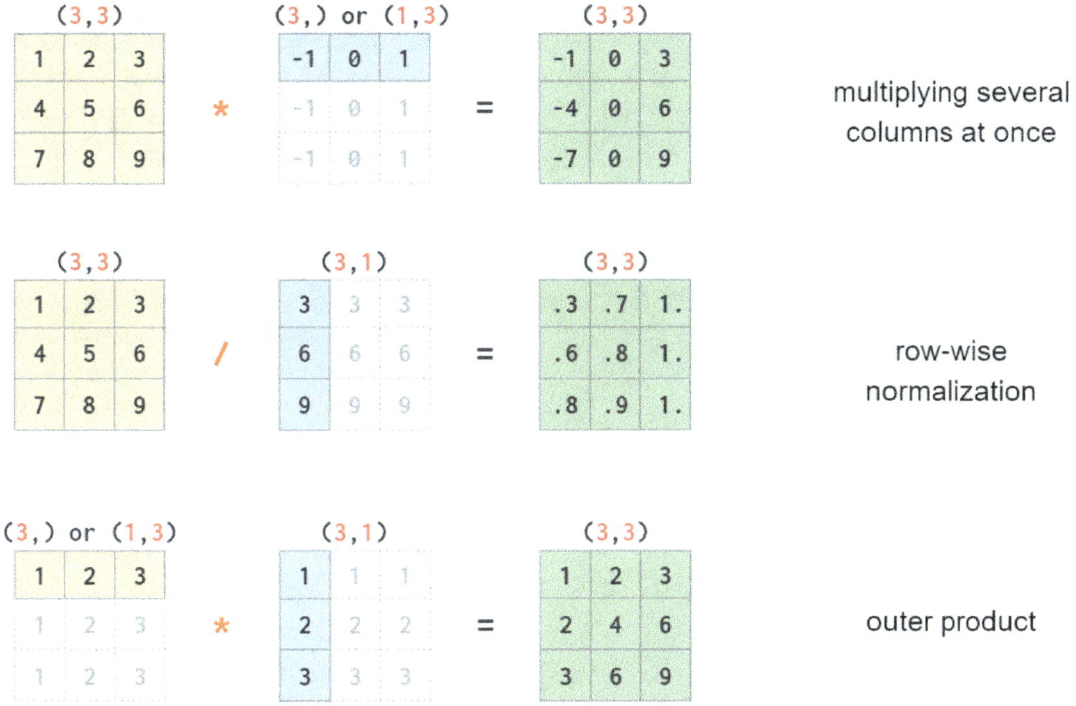
(3,3)
(3,) or (1,3)
(3,3)
multiplying several columns at once
(3,3)
(3,1)
(3,3)
row-wise normalization
(3,) or (1,3)
(3,1)
(3,3)
outer product

4. Linear Algebra Operations (via numpy.linalg)

NumPy provides efficient implementations of core linear algebra — heavily used in ML for projections, decompositions, etc.

Python

```
A = np.array([[3, 1], [1, 2]])
B = np.array([[1, 4], [2, 3]])

# Matrix multiplication
matmul = np.matmul(A, B)  # or A @ B
print(matmul)
# [[5 15]
#  [5 10]]

# Dot product (for vectors)
v1 = np.array([1, 2])
v2 = np.array([3, 4])
dot = np.dot(v1, v2)  # 1*3 + 2*4 = 11

# Transpose, inverse, eigenvalues
print(A.T)                # Transpose
inv = np.linalg.inv(A)
print(np.round(A @ inv))      # Should be identity

eigvals, eigvecs = np.linalg.eig(A)

# Solve linear system Ax = b
b = np.array([5, 6])
x = np.linalg.solve(A, b)
print(x)  # Solution to [3 1; 1 2] * x = [5; 6]
```

Matrix multiplication and operations visualized:

```
a@b
np.dot(a,b)
np.matmul(a,b)
```

Equivalent Semantics:
Matrix Multiplication

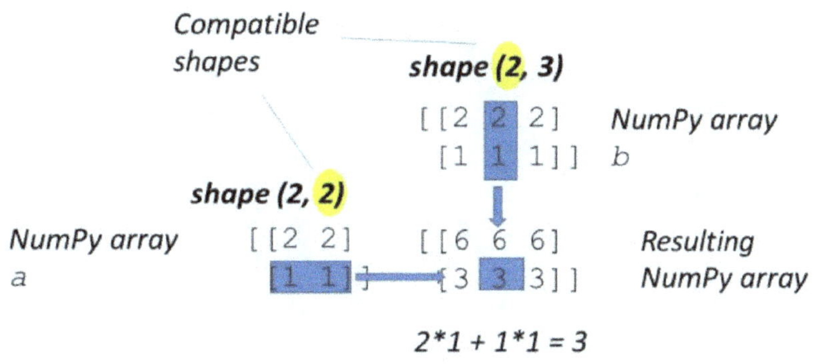

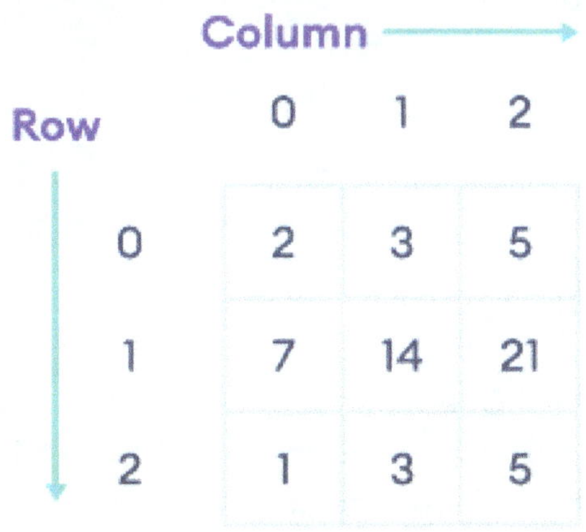

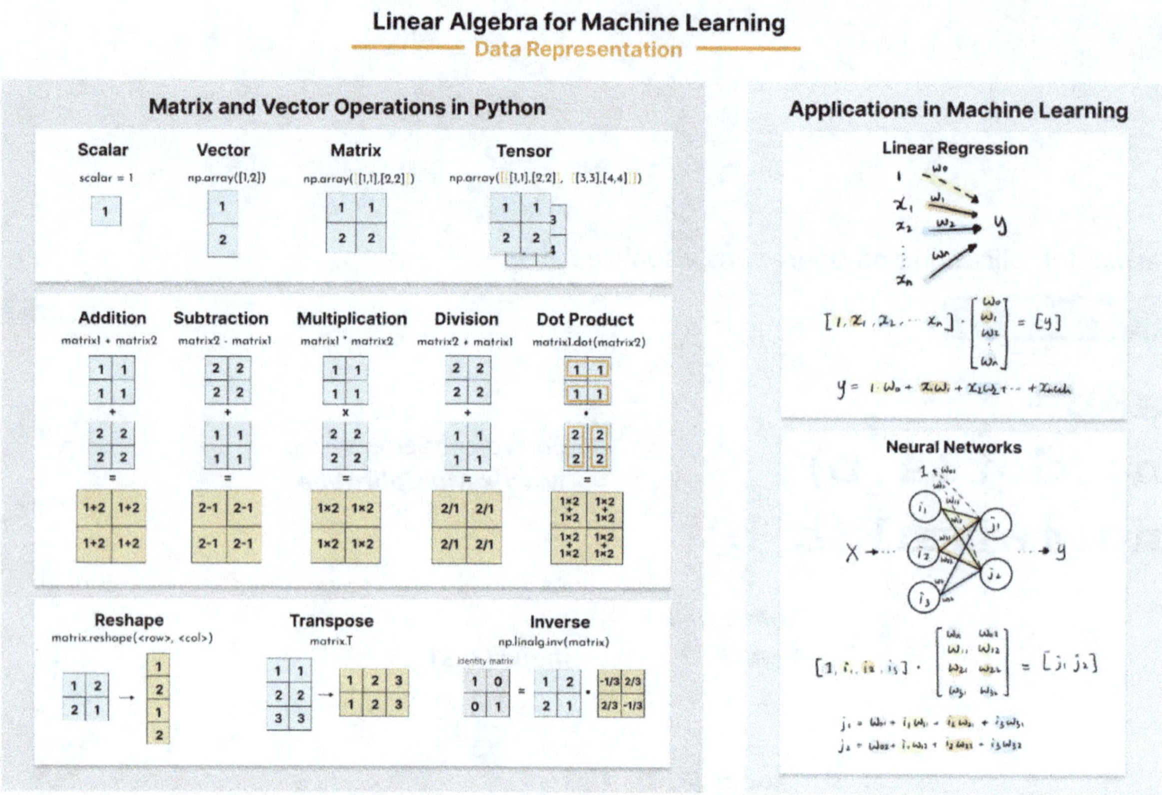

5. Statistical Operations

NumPy makes computing statistics across axes trivial — essential for data normalization in AI.

Python

```
data = np.random.randn(1000)  # 1000 samples from standard normal

print(np.mean(data))    # ~0
print(np.median(data))
print(np.std(data))     # ~1
print(np.var(data))     # ~1

# 2D example
matrix = np.array([[1, 2, 3], [4, 5, 100]])

print(np.mean(matrix))          # Overall mean
print(np.mean(matrix, axis=0))  # Column means: [2.5 3.5 51.5]
print(np.mean(matrix, axis=1))  # Row means: [2. 36.333...]

# Percentiles
print(np.percentile(data, 95))  # 95th percentile

# Correlation
x = np.random.rand(100)
```

```
y = 2 * x + np.random.randn(100) * 0.1
print(np.corrcoef(x, y)[0,1])     # Close to 1
```

Visualizing mean, variance, and standard deviation:

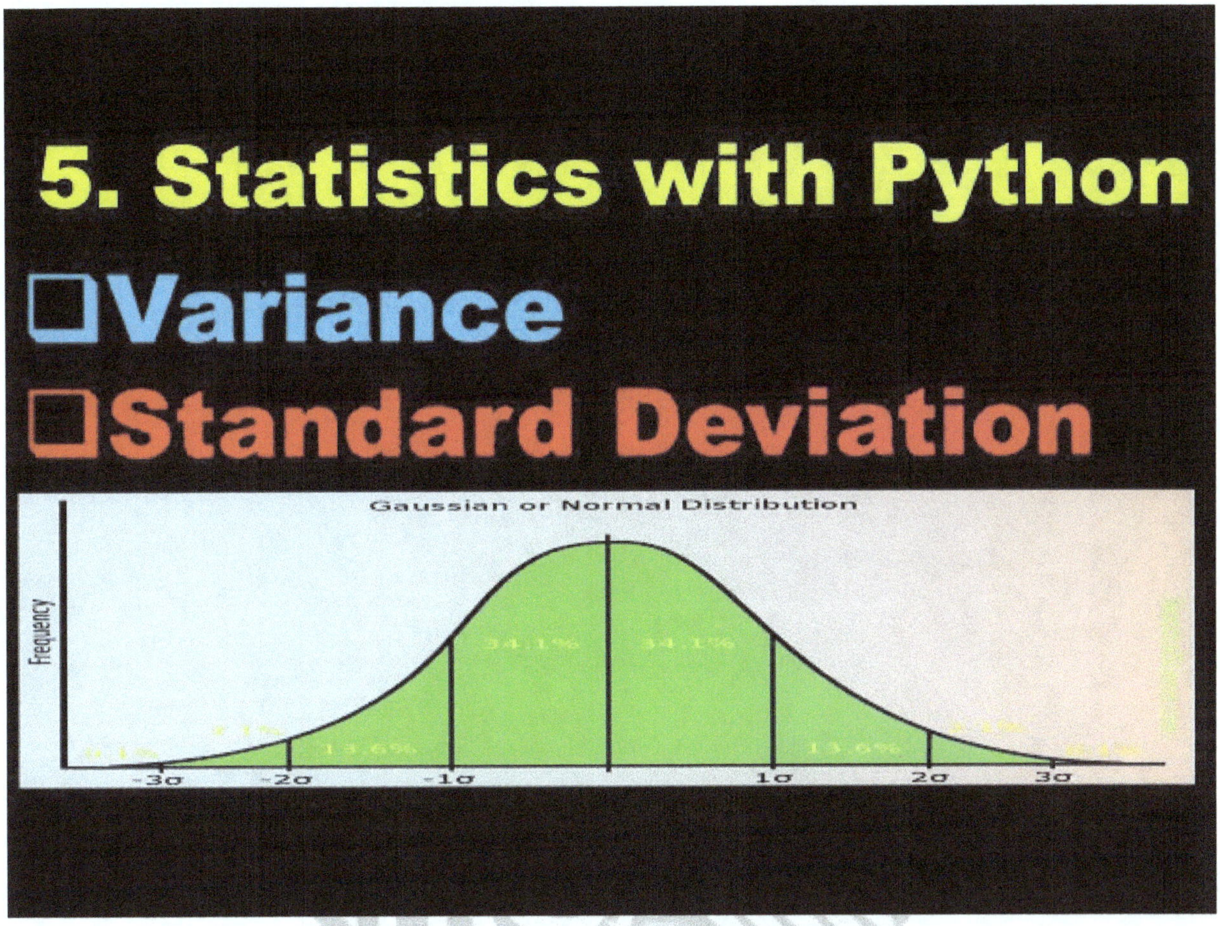

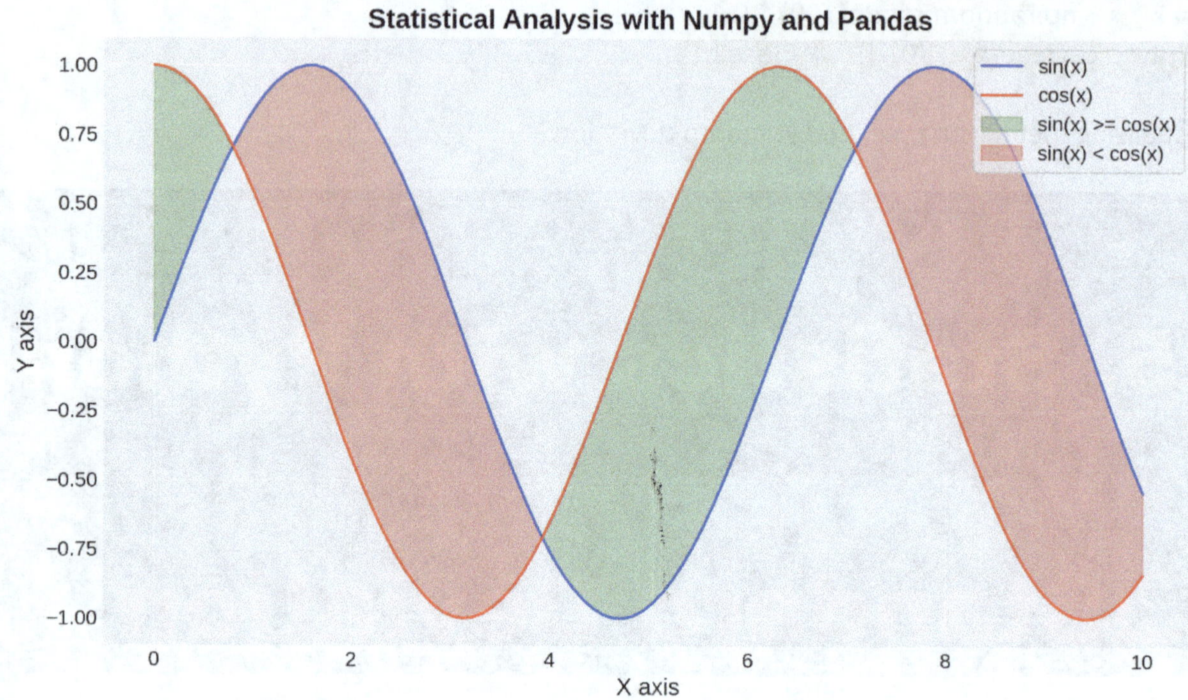

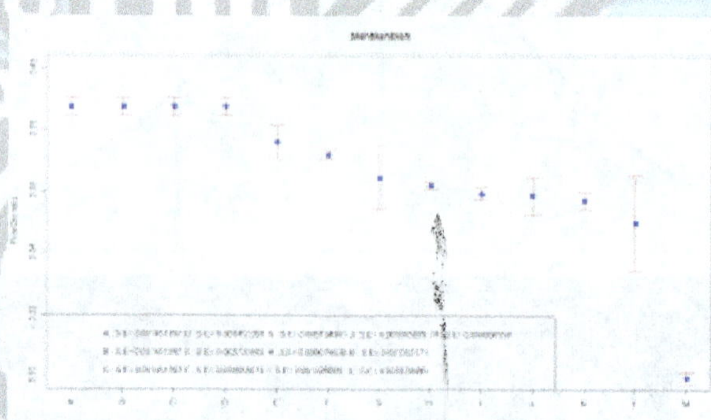

NumPy is the bedrock of data manipulation and numerical operations in AI.

2.Pandas (DataFrames, Data Manipulation)

Pandas: This is the most widely used library for data analysis and manipulation. It provides powerful and flexible data structures, most notably the DataFrame (similar to a spreadsheet or SQL table), which makes it easy to handle and analyze structured data, including cleaning, filtering, joining, and aggregating datasets.

Use Cases: Reading/writing various file formats (CSV, Excel, SQL), handling missing data (.dropna(), .fillna()), grouping, joining, and filtering datasets.

Key Functions: .head(), .describe(), .groupby(), .merge(), pd.read_csv().

Why Pandas for AI?

- Data cleaning, exploration, and feature engineering (80% of ML work!).
- Seamless integration with NumPy, scikit-learn, TensorFlow, and PyTorch.
- Fast operations on large datasets via vectorization.

Examples of Pandas DataFrames in action:

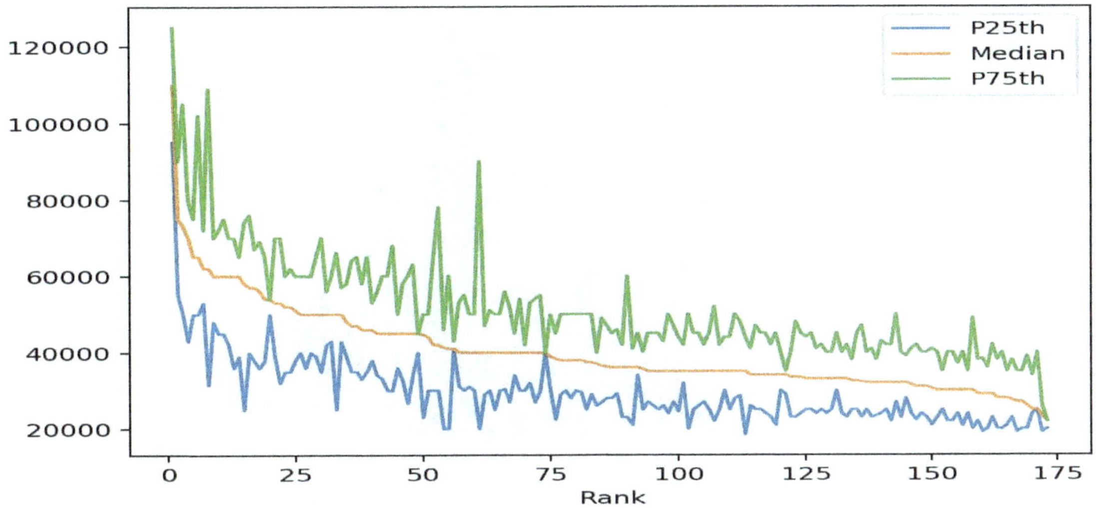


```
import pandas as pd
df = pd.read_csv("https://raw.githubusercontent.com/datasets/covid-19/master/data/countries-aggrega

display(df)
```

Plot Builder

Search...

Date	Country	Confirmed	Recovered	Deaths
2020-01-22	Afghanistan	0	0	0
2020-01-22	Albania	0	0	0
2020-01-22	Algeria	0	0	0
2020-01-22	Andorra	0	0	0
2020-01-22	Angola	0	0	0
2020-01-22	Antigua and Barbuda	0	0	0
2020-01-22	Argentina	0	0	0
2020-01-22	Armenia	0	0	0
2020-01-22	Australia	0	0	0
2020-01-22	Austria	0	0	0

« 1 2 3 ... 100 »

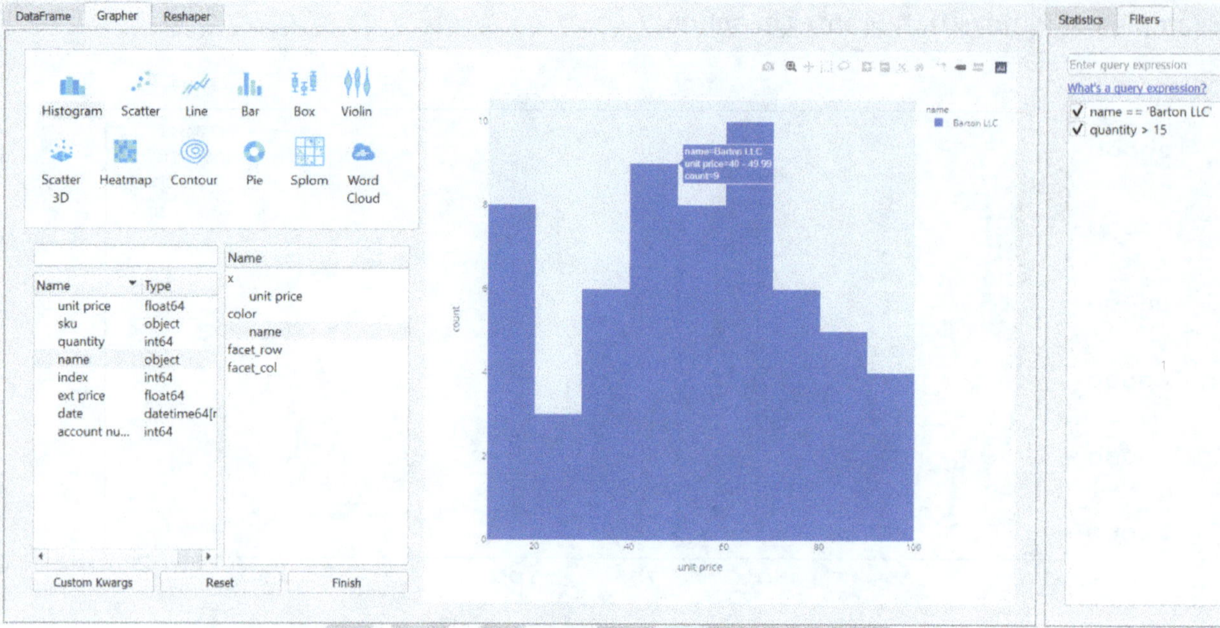

1. Creating DataFrames

Python

```
import pandas as pd
import numpy as np

# From dictionary
data = {
    'Name': ['Alice', 'Bob', 'Charlie', 'Diana'],
    'Age': [25, 30, 35, 28],
    'Salary': [50000, 60000, 75000, 55000],
    'Department': ['HR', 'IT', 'IT', 'Marketing']
}
df = pd.DataFrame(data)
print(df)
#      Name  Age  Salary Department
# 0   Alice   25   50000         HR
# 1     Bob   30   60000         IT
```

```
# 2  Charlie   35   75000        IT
# 3    Diana   28   55000  Marketing

# From NumPy array
arr = np.random.randn(5, 3)
df2 = pd.DataFrame(arr, columns=['A', 'B', 'C'])

# Reading from files (common in ML)
# df = pd.read_csv('data.csv')
# df = pd.read_excel('data.xlsx')
# df = pd.read_sql(query, connection)
```

2. Basic Inspection and Attributes

Python

```
print(df.head(2))     # First 2 rows
print(df.tail(2))     # Last 2 rows
print(df.info())      # Summary: dtypes, non-null counts
print(df.describe())  # Stats: mean, std, min/max for numeric
print(df.shape)       # (4, 4)
print(df.columns)     # Index(['Name', 'Age', 'Salary', 'Department'], dtype='object')
print(df.dtypes)      # Data types per column
```

3.Indexing, Selection, and Slicing

Pandas has flexible ways: label-based (.loc), integer-based (.iloc), and boolean.

Python

```
# Column selection
print(df['Name'])                 # Series
print(df[['Name', 'Salary']])     # DataFrame

# Row selection
print(df.loc[0])                # Row 0 by label
print(df.iloc[1:3])             # Rows 1-2 by position

# Label-based slicing
print(df.loc[1:3, ['Name', 'Age']])

# Boolean filtering (crucial for data prep in ML)
high_salary = df[df['Salary'] > 55000]
```

```
it_dept = df[df['Department'] == 'IT']

# Multiple conditions
print(df[(df['Department'] == 'IT') & (df['Age'] > 30)])
```

Visual guides to indexing and selection:

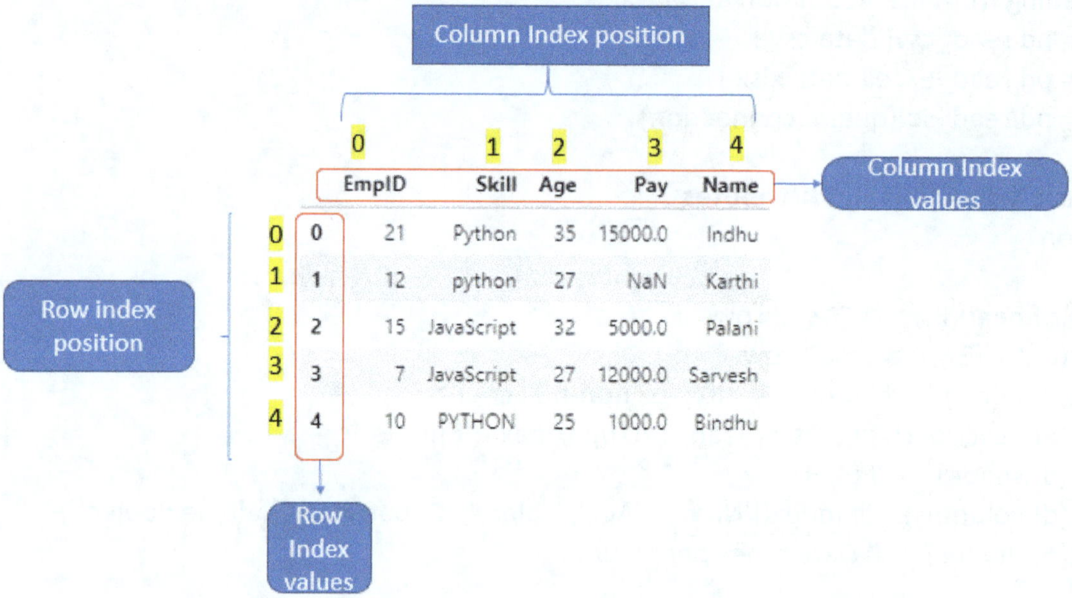

Dataset

Name	Team	Number	Position	Age	Height	Weight	College	Salary
Avery Bradley	Boston Celtics	0.0	PG	25.0	6-2	180.0	Texas	7730337.0
Jae Crowder	Boston Celtics	99.0	SF	25.0	6-6	235.0	Marquette	6796117.0
John Holland	Boston Celtics	30.0	SG	27.0	6-5	205.0	Boston University	NaN
R.J. Hunter	Boston Celtics	28.0	SG	22.0	6-5	185.0	Georgia State	1148640.0
Jonas Jerebko	Boston Celtics	8.0	PF	29.0	6-10	231.0	NaN	5000000.0

Single Column selected from Dataset

Name	Age
Avery Bradley	25.0
Jae Crowder	25.0
John Holland	27.0
R.J. Hunter	22.0
Jonas Jerebko	29.0

dtype: float64

4. Adding/Modifying Data

Python

```
# New column
df['Experience'] = [2, 5, 10, 4]

# Apply functions
df['Salary_K'] = df['Salary'] / 1000

# Conditional column
df['Senior'] = df['Age'] > 30

# Drop columns/rows
df.drop('Senior', axis=1, inplace=True)  # axis=1 for columns
df.drop(0, inplace=True)                 # Drop row 0
```

5. Handling Missing Data

Real-world datasets are messy — Pandas makes cleaning easy.

Python

```
# Introduce NaN
df.loc[1, 'Age'] = np.nan
```

```
print(df.isnull().sum())  # Count NaNs per column
```

```
# Drop rows with any NaN
df_clean = df.dropna()

# Fill NaN
df['Age'].fillna(df['Age'].mean(), inplace=True)  # Mean imputation
df.fillna({'Age': 0, 'Department': 'Unknown'}, inplace=True)

# Forward/backward fill
df.fillna(method='ffill')
```

Handling missing values visuals:

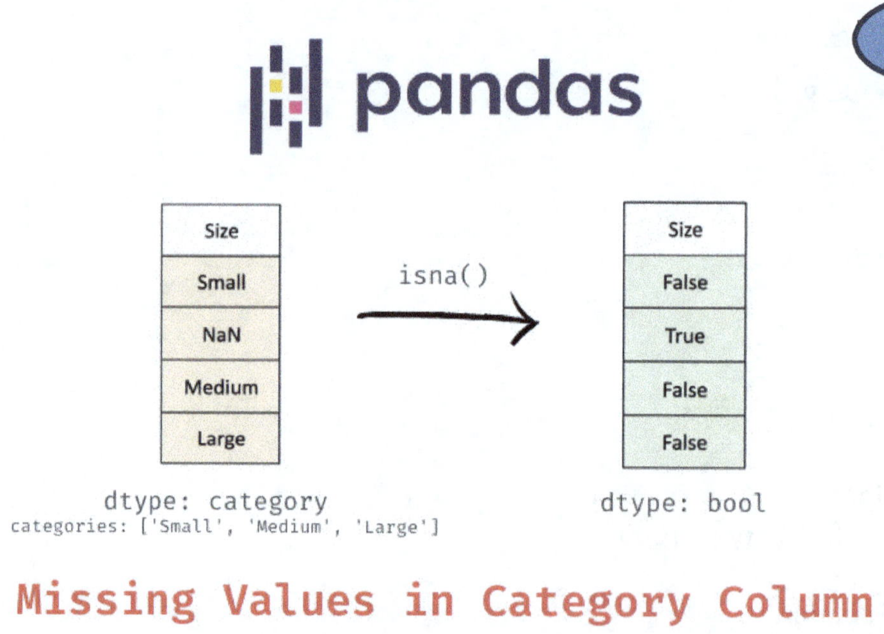

6. GroupBy: Split-Apply-Combine

Powerful for aggregation — e.g., average salary per department.

Python

```
# Group and aggregate
dept_stats = df.groupby('Department')['Salary'].agg(['mean', 'count', 'max'])

# Multiple aggregations
print(df.groupby('Department').agg({'Salary': 'mean', 'Age': 'median'}))
```

```
# Custom functions
df.groupby('Department')['Salary'].apply(lambda x: x.max() - x.min())
```

The classic split-apply-combine paradigm:

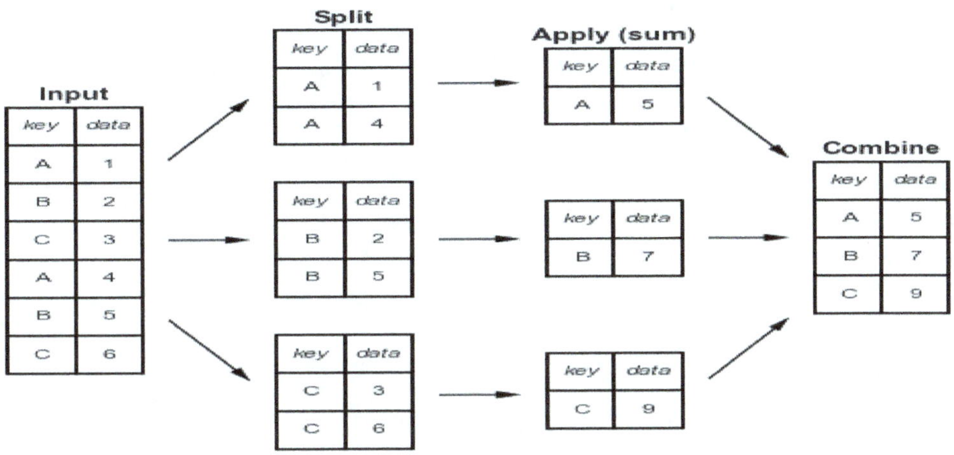

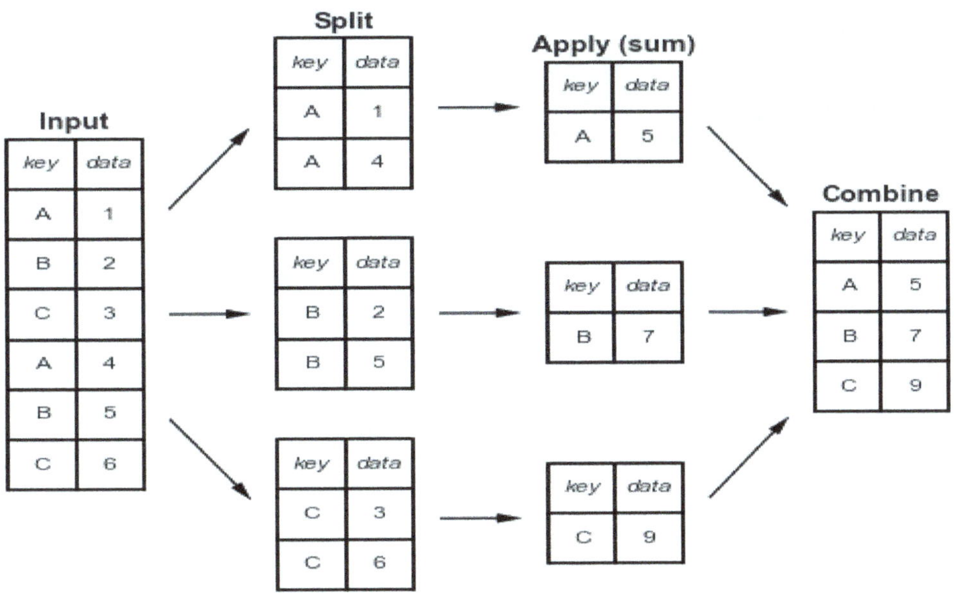

7.Merging and Joining DataFrames

Like SQL joins — essential for combining features from multiple sources.
Python

```
df2 = pd.DataFrame({
    'Department': ['HR', 'IT', 'Marketing'],
    'Manager': ['Eve', 'Frank', 'Grace']
})

# Inner merge (default)
merged = pd.merge(df, df2, on='Department', how='inner')

# Left, right, outer
pd.merge(df, df2, on='Department', how='left')   # Keep all from left
pd.merge(df, df2, on='Department', how='outer') # All rows

# Concatenate vertically/horizontally
pd.concat([df, new_rows], axis=0)  # Stack rows
pd.concat([df, new_cols], axis=1)  # Add columns
```

Merge/join types visualized:

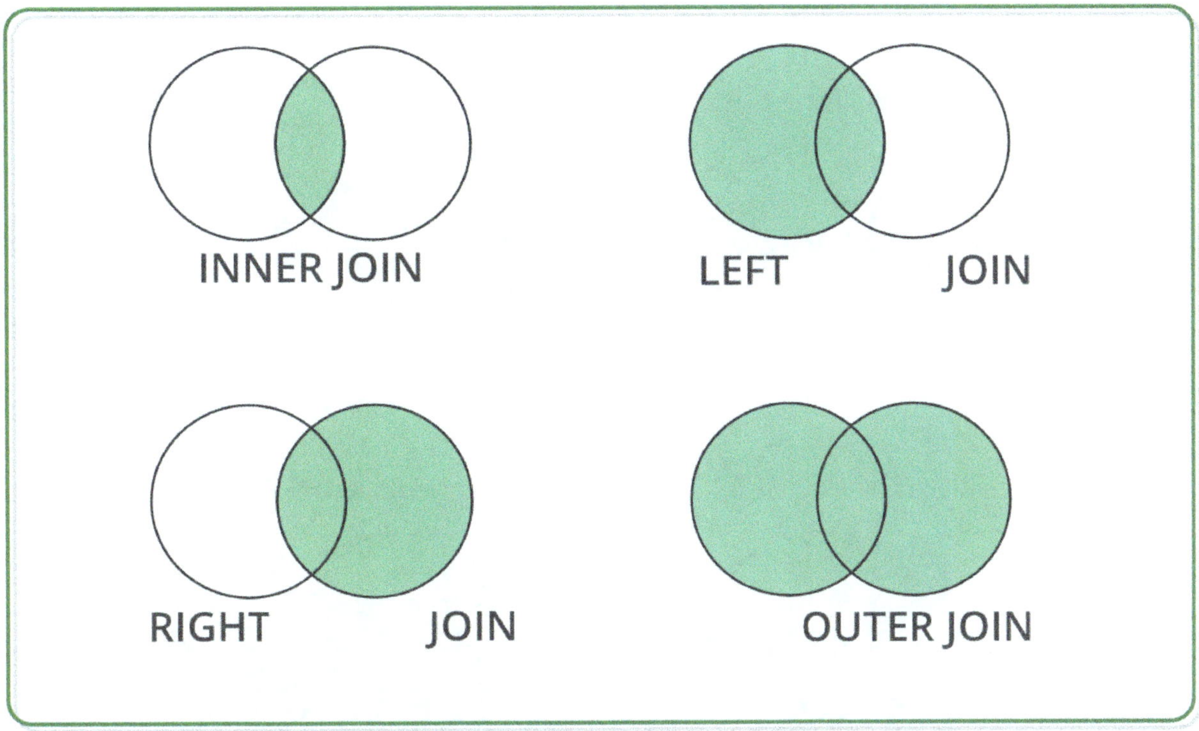
INNER JOIN
LEFT JOIN
RIGHT JOIN
OUTER JOIN

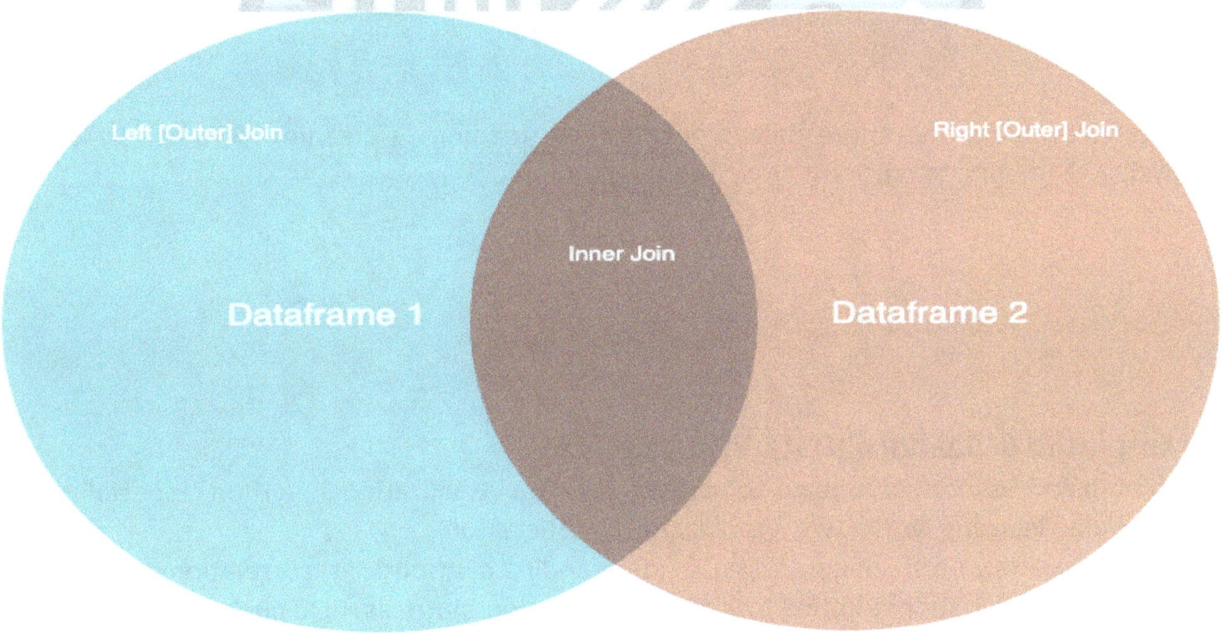
Left [Outer] Join
Right [Outer] Join
Inner Join
Dataframe 1
Dataframe 2

Outer Join

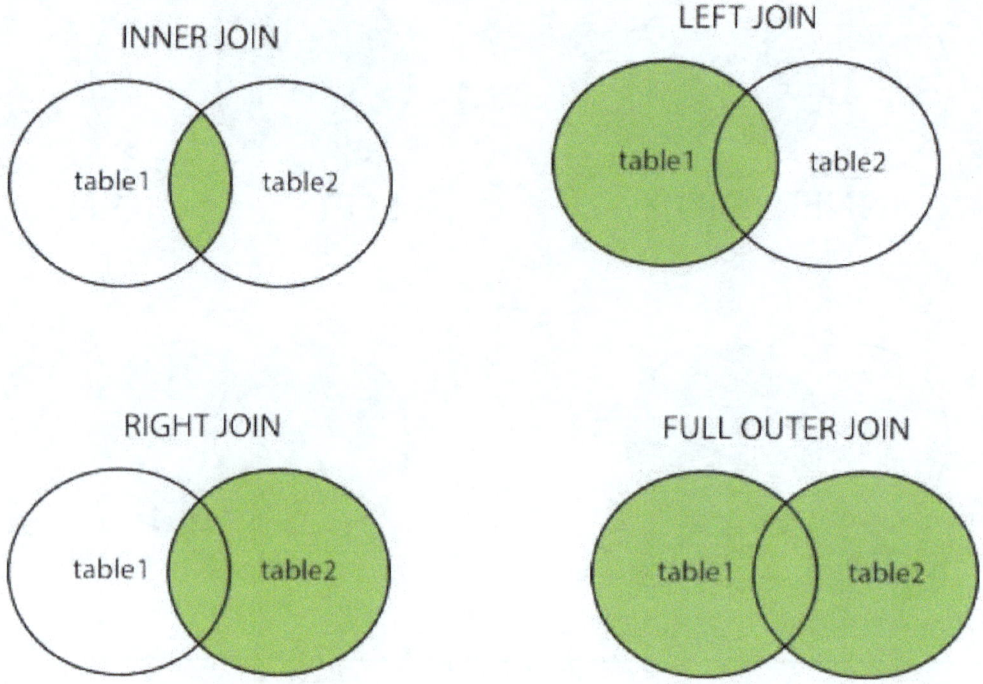

Pandas streamlines the entire data pipeline in AI: loading → cleaning → transforming → analyzing → feeding to models.

3.Matplotlib & Seaborn (Data Visualization)

Matplotlib and Seaborn are the go-to libraries for data visualization in Python, especially in AI and machine learning workflows. Visualization is crucial for:

- Exploratory Data Analysis (EDA): Understanding distributions, correlations, outliers.
- Model evaluation: Plotting loss curves, confusion matrices, ROC curves.
- Communicating insights: Presenting results clearly.

Matplotlib is a low-level, highly customizable plotting library (the foundation). Seaborn is built on Matplotlib, providing high-level, statistical plots with beautiful defaults and easier syntax. Both integrate seamlessly with NumPy and Pandas.

Matplotlib Basics

Matplotlib's core concepts: Figure (the canvas) and Axes (the actual plot area). A figure can have multiple axes (subplots).

Diagram explaining Figure and Axes structure:

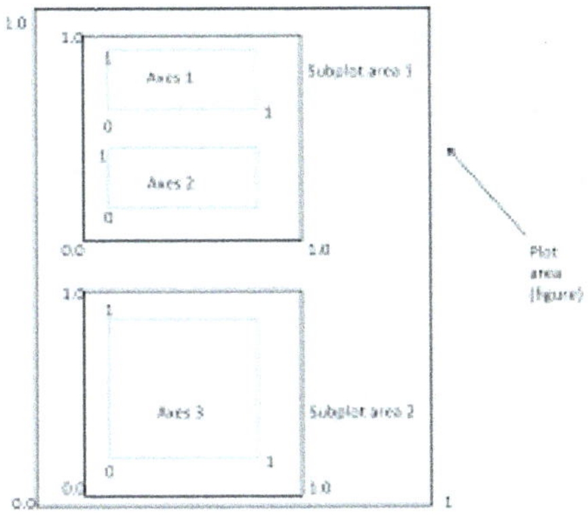
Axes 1
Axes 2
Subplot area 1
Plot area (figure)
Axes 3
Subplot area 2

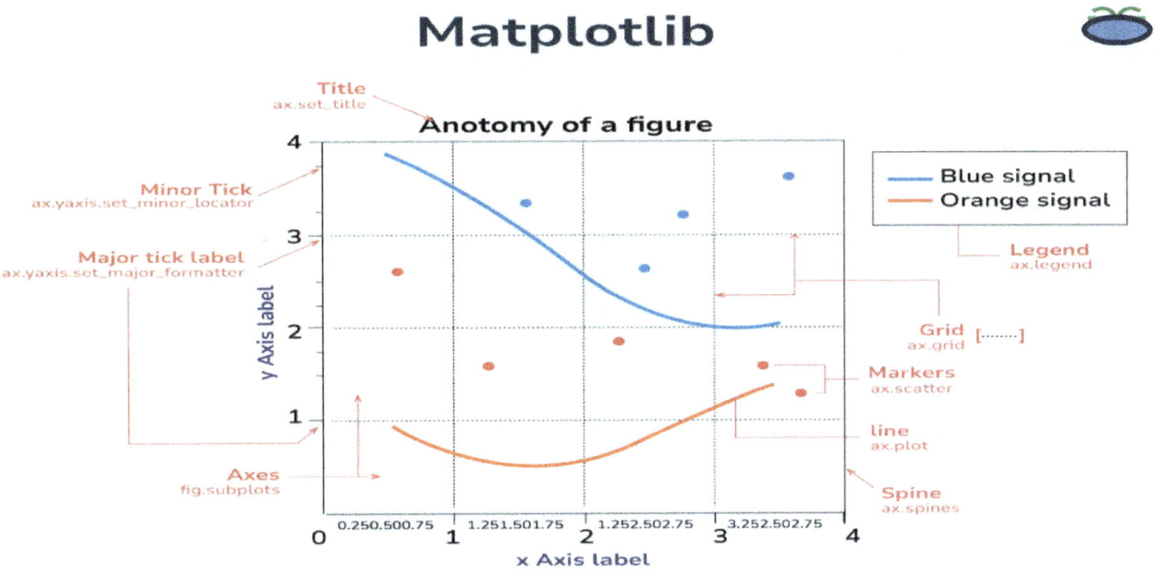
Matplotlib
Anotomy of a figure
Title
ax.set_title
Minor Tick
ax.yaxis.set_minor_locator
Major tick label
ax.yaxis.set_major_formatter
Blue signal
Orange signal
Legend
ax.legend
Grid
ax.grid
[........]
Markers
ax.scatter
line
ax.plot
Axes
fig.subplots
Spine
ax.spines
y Axis label
x Axis label

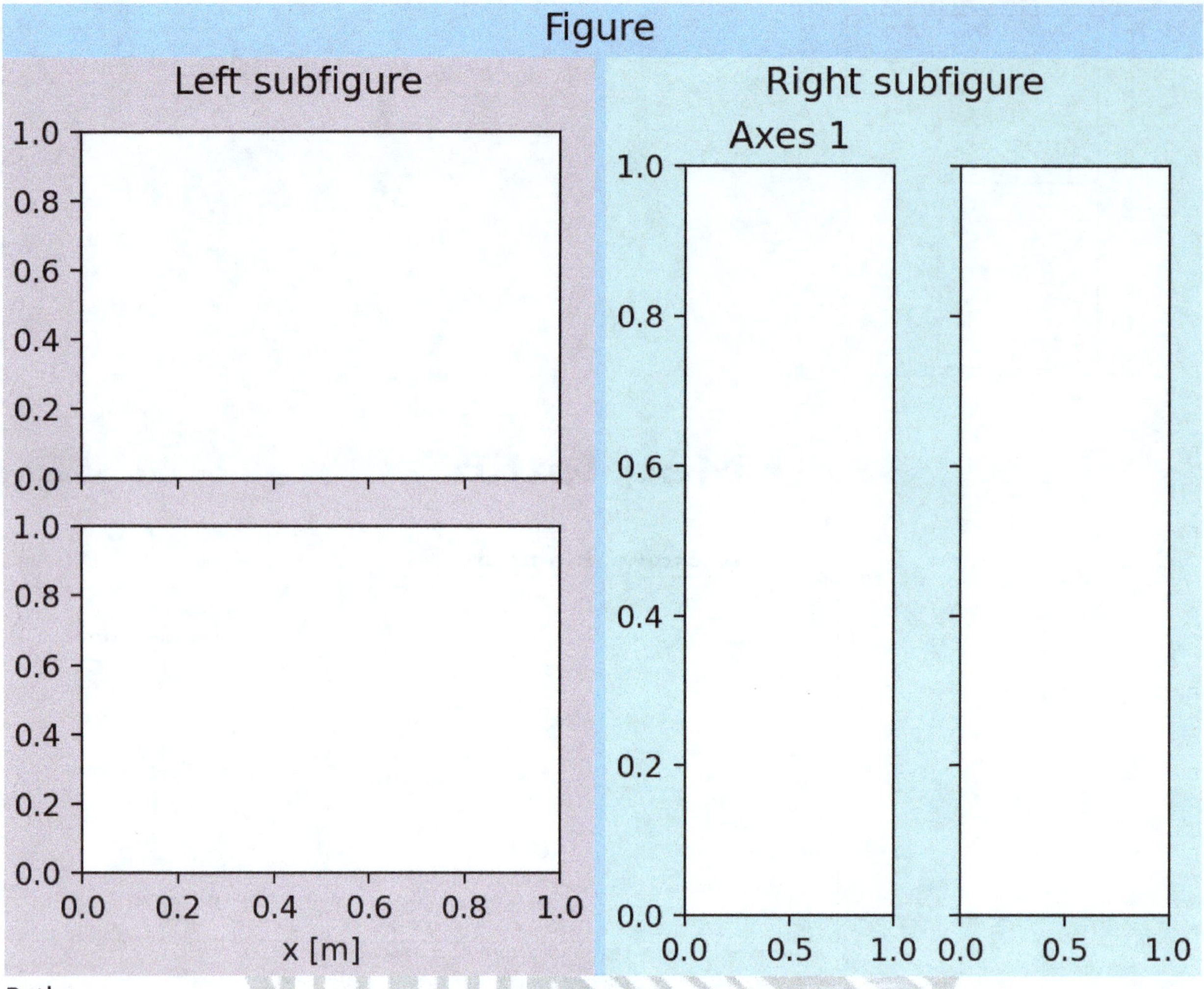

Python

```
import matplotlib.pyplot as plt
import numpy as np

# Simple line plot
x = np.linspace(0, 10, 100)
y = np.sin(x)

plt.figure(figsize=(8, 6))  # Create figure
plt.plot(x, y, label='sin(x)', color='blue', linewidth=2)
plt.title('Simple Sine Wave')
plt.xlabel('X axis')
plt.ylabel('Y axis')
plt.grid(True)
plt.legend()
plt.show()  # Required in scripts; not in Jupyter
```

Examples of basic line plots:

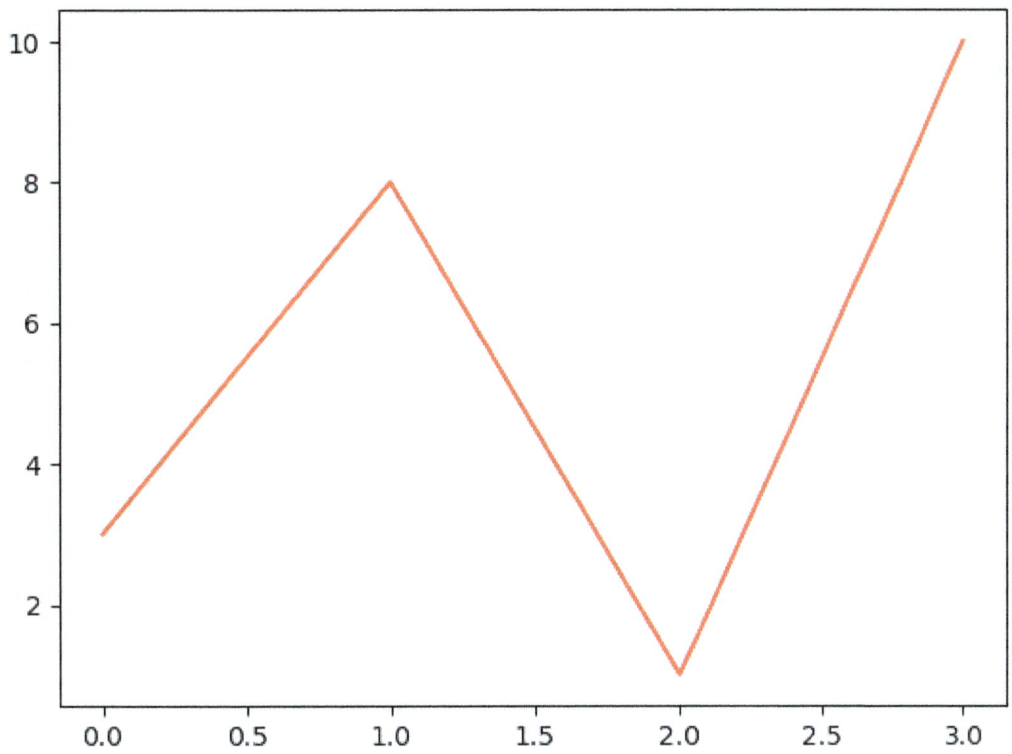

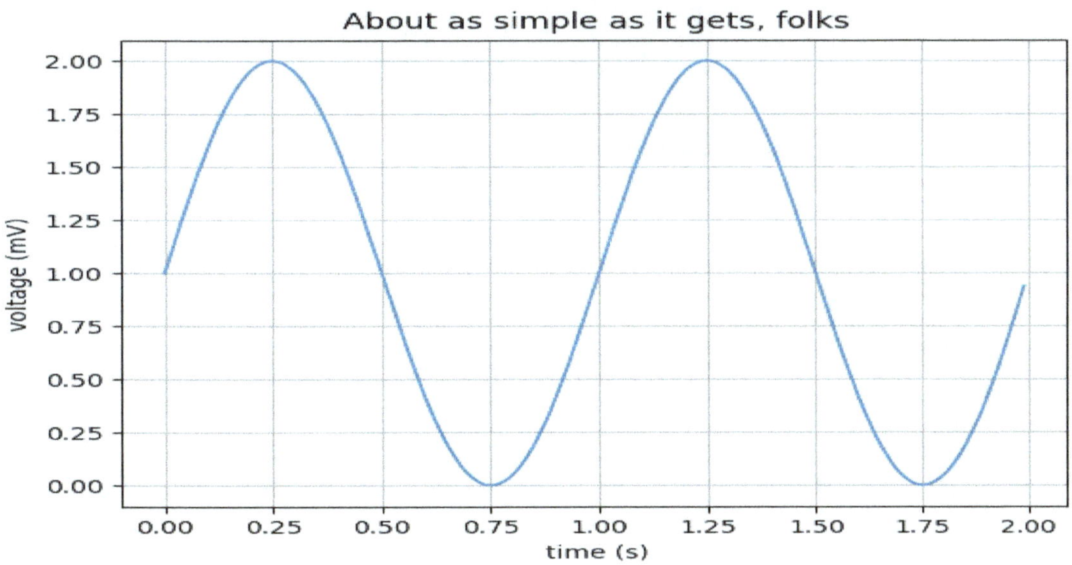

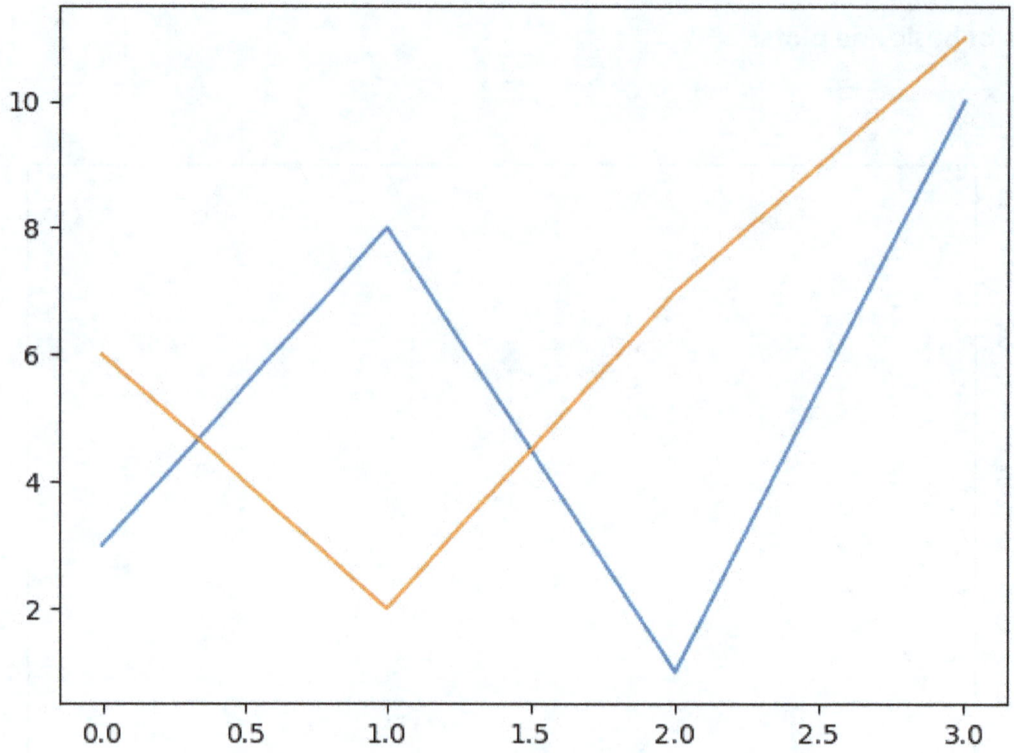

Common Matplotlib Plots
1.Scatter Plot
Python

```
plt.scatter(x, np.cos(x), c='red', marker='o', alpha=0.7)
plt.title('Scatter: Cosine')
plt.show()
```

2.Histogram (great for feature distributions in ML)
Python

```
data = np.random.randn(1000)
plt.hist(data, bins=30, alpha=0.7, color='green', edgecolor='black')
plt.title('Histogram of Normal Distribution')
plt.xlabel('Value')
plt.ylabel('Frequency')
plt.show()
```

Customized histograms:

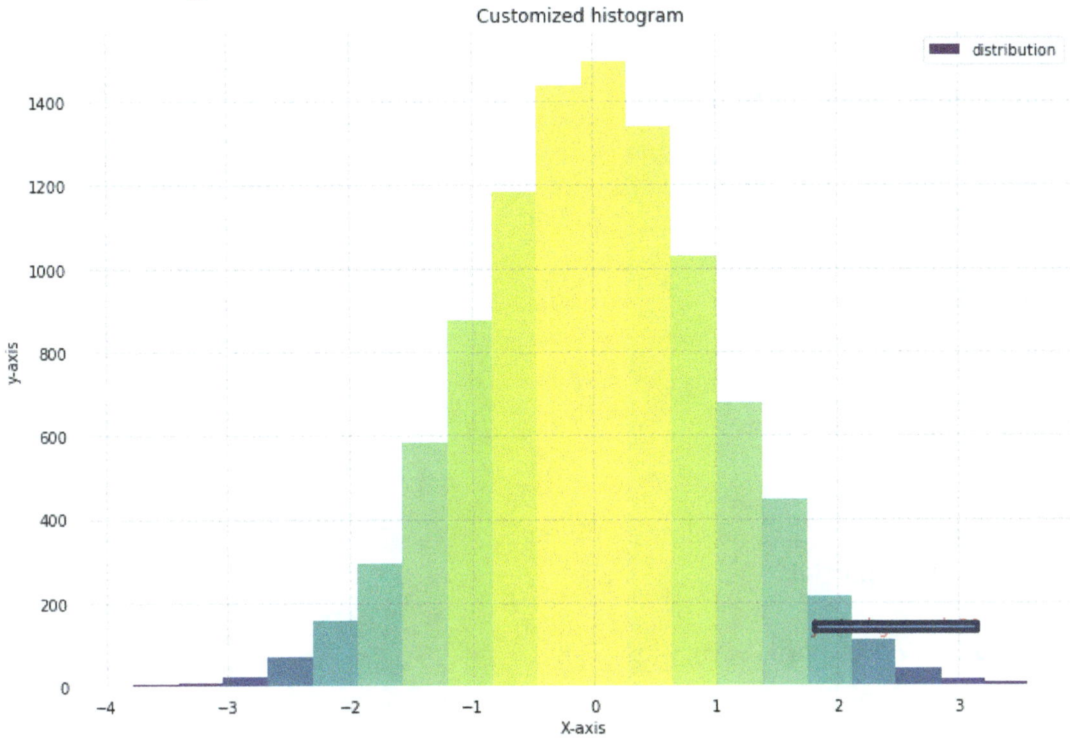

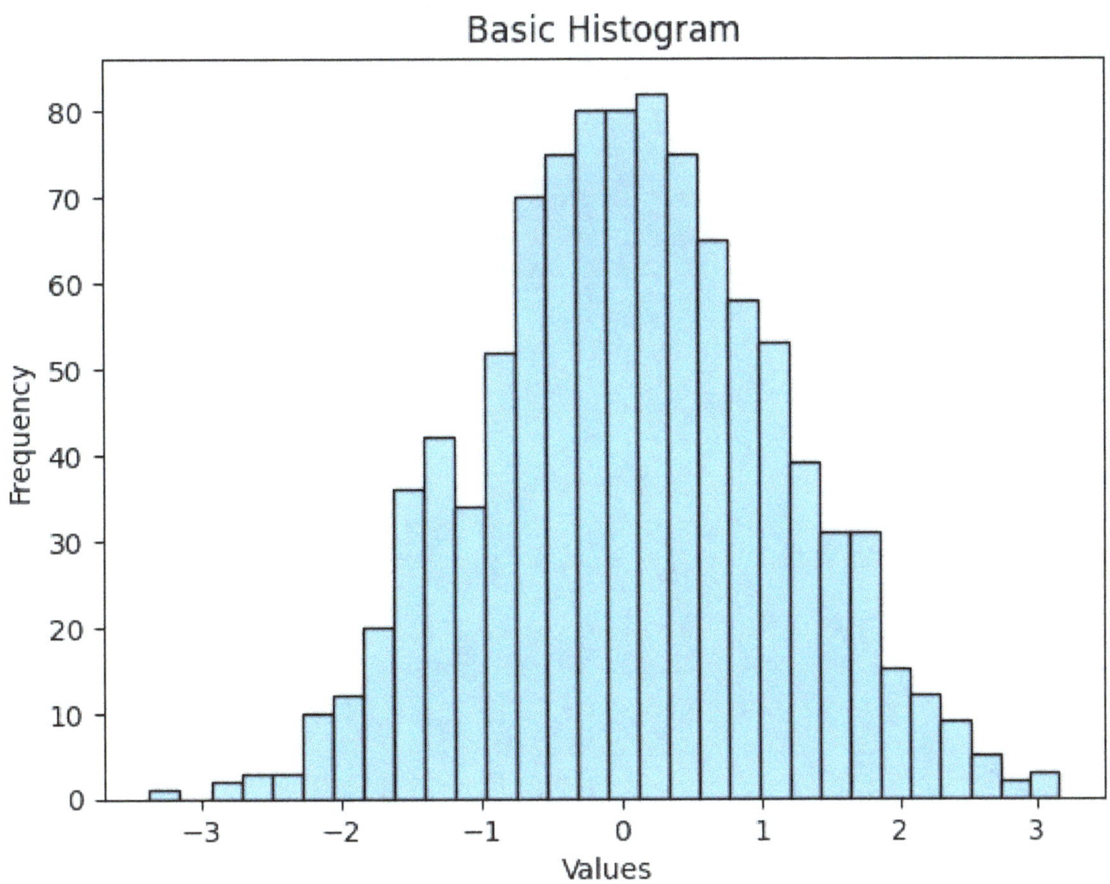

3.Subplots (multiple plots in one figure)
Python

```
fig, axs = plt.subplots(2, 2, figsize=(10, 8))  # 2x2 grid

axs[0, 0].plot(x, np.sin(x))
axs[0, 0].set_title('Sin')

axs[0, 1].plot(x, np.cos(x))
axs[0, 1].set_title('Cos')

axs[1, 0].scatter(x, np.tan(x[:50]))  # Limited points
axs[1, 0].set_title('Tan (partial)')

axs[1, 1].hist(np.random.randn(1000), bins=20)
axs[1, 1].set_title('Histogram')

plt.tight_layout()  # Prevents overlap
plt.show()
```

Subplot examples:

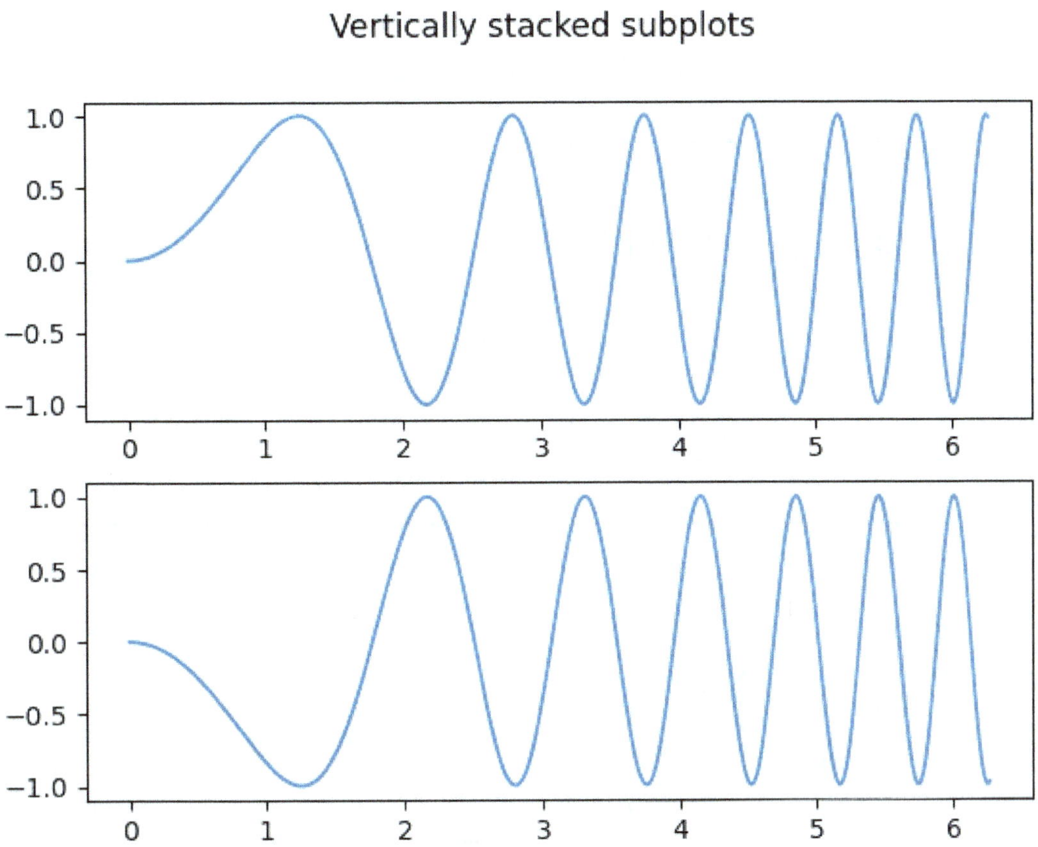
Vertically stacked subplots
1.0
0.5
0.0
−0.5
−1.0
0 1 2 3 4 5 6

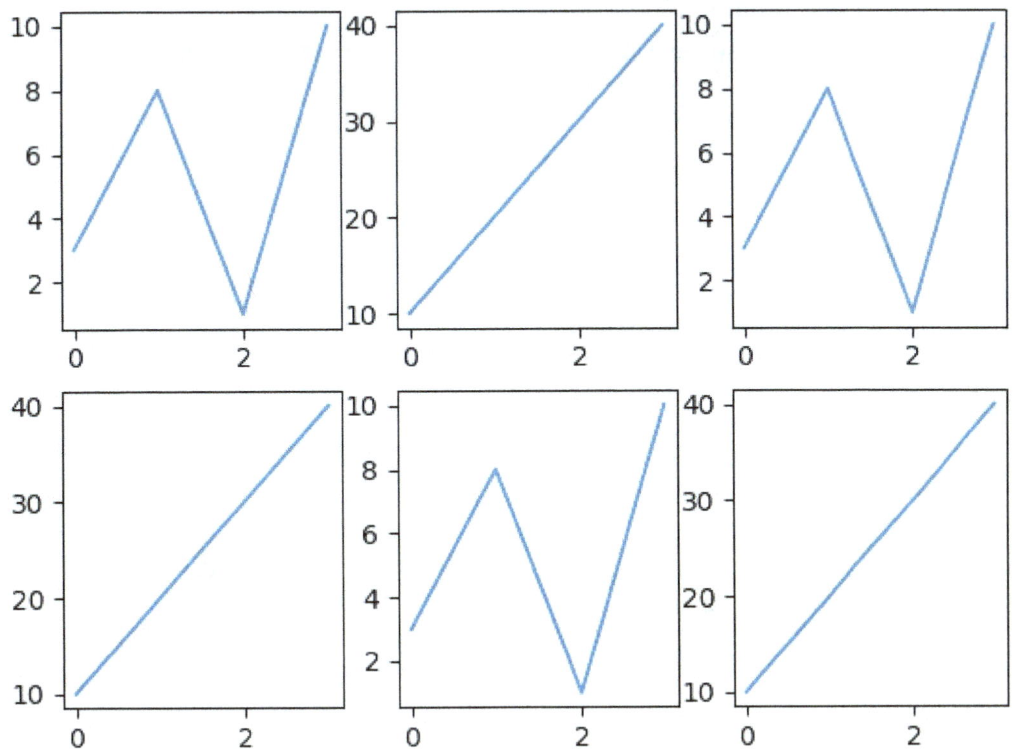
10 8 6 4 2
40 30 20 10
0 2

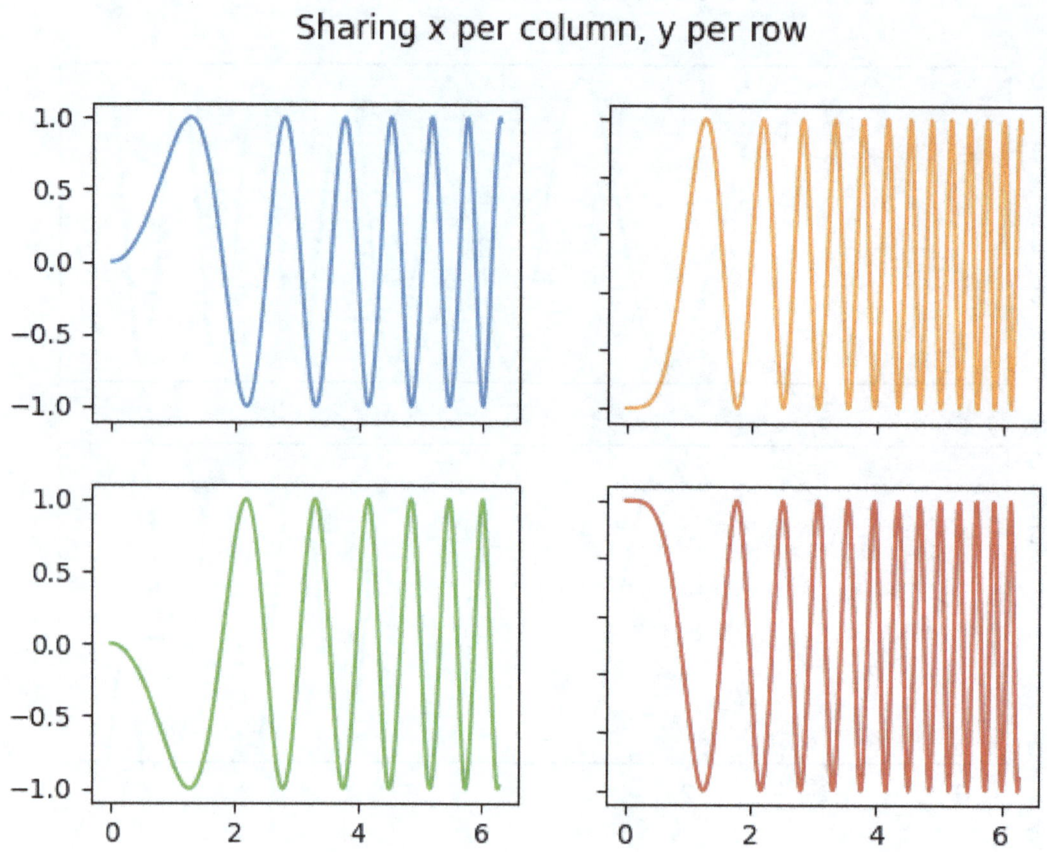

Seaborn: Statistical Visualization Made Easy

Seaborn works directly with Pandas DataFrames and adds themes/colors.

Python

```
import seaborn as sns
import pandas as pd

# Load sample dataset (Seaborn has built-ins)
df = sns.load_dataset('iris')  # Classic ML dataset
print(df.head())
```

1.Distribution Plots

Python

```
sns.histplot(data=df, x='sepal_length', kde=True)  # Histogram + density
plt.title('Sepal Length Distribution')
plt.show()

sns.violinplot(data=df, x='species', y='petal_length')
plt.title('Violin Plot: Petal Length by Species')
```

```
plt.show()
```

Violin plots showing distributions:

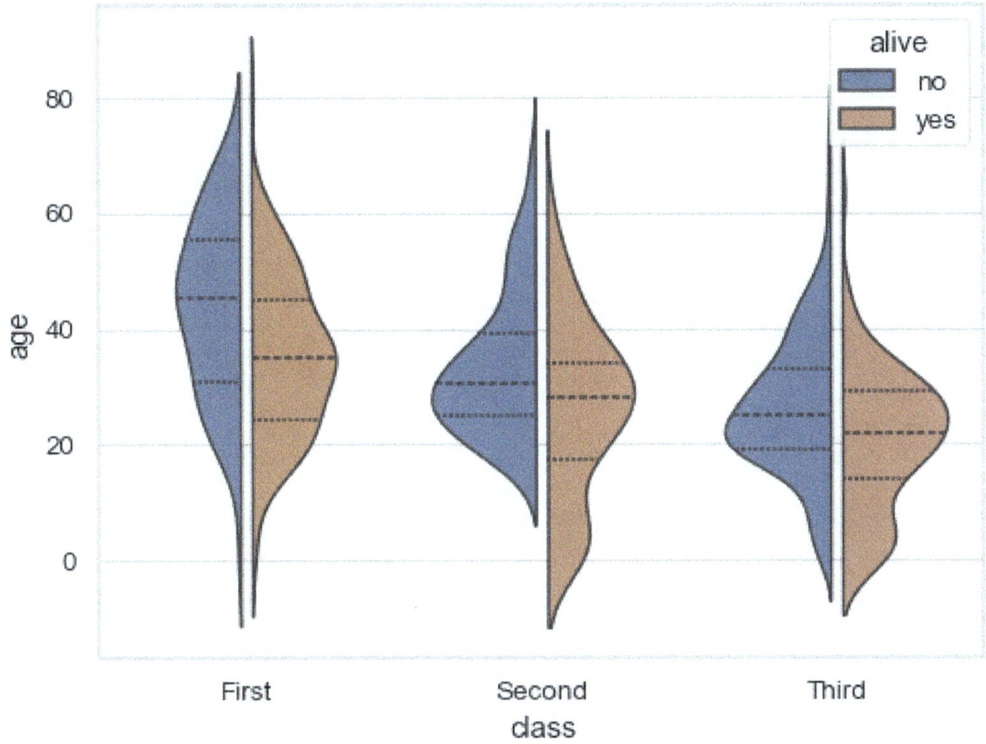

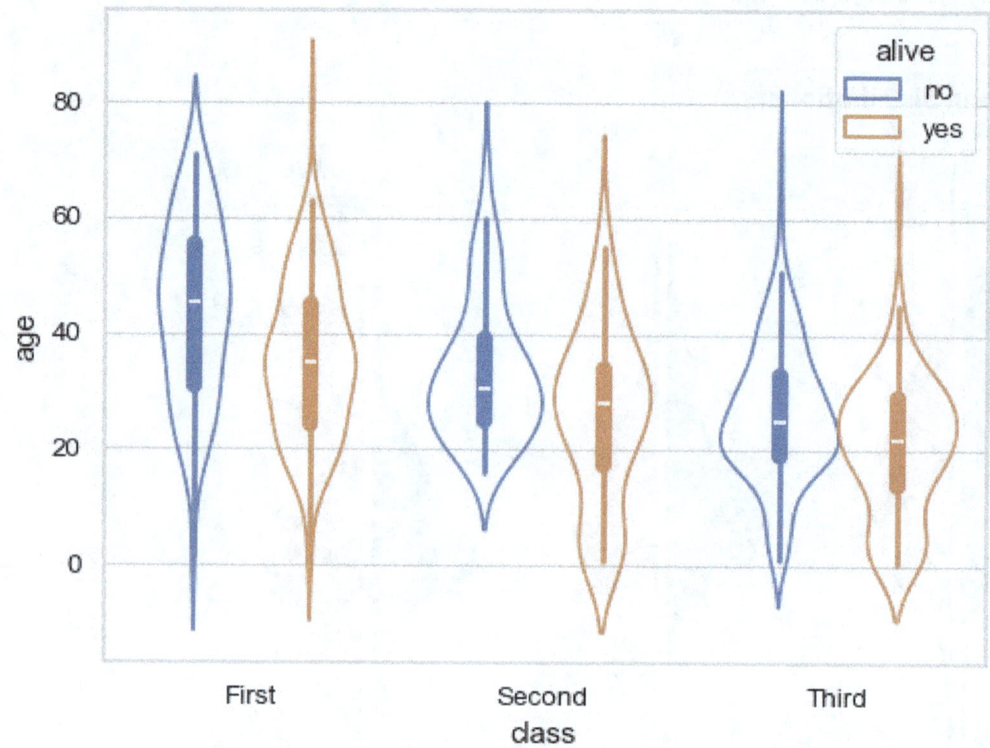

2.Categorical Plots
Python

```
sns.boxplot(data=df, x='species', y='sepal_width')
plt.title('Boxplot: Sepal Width by Species')
plt.show()

sns.swarmplot(data=df, x='species', y='petal_length', size=5)
plt.show()
```

Boxplots for categorical data:

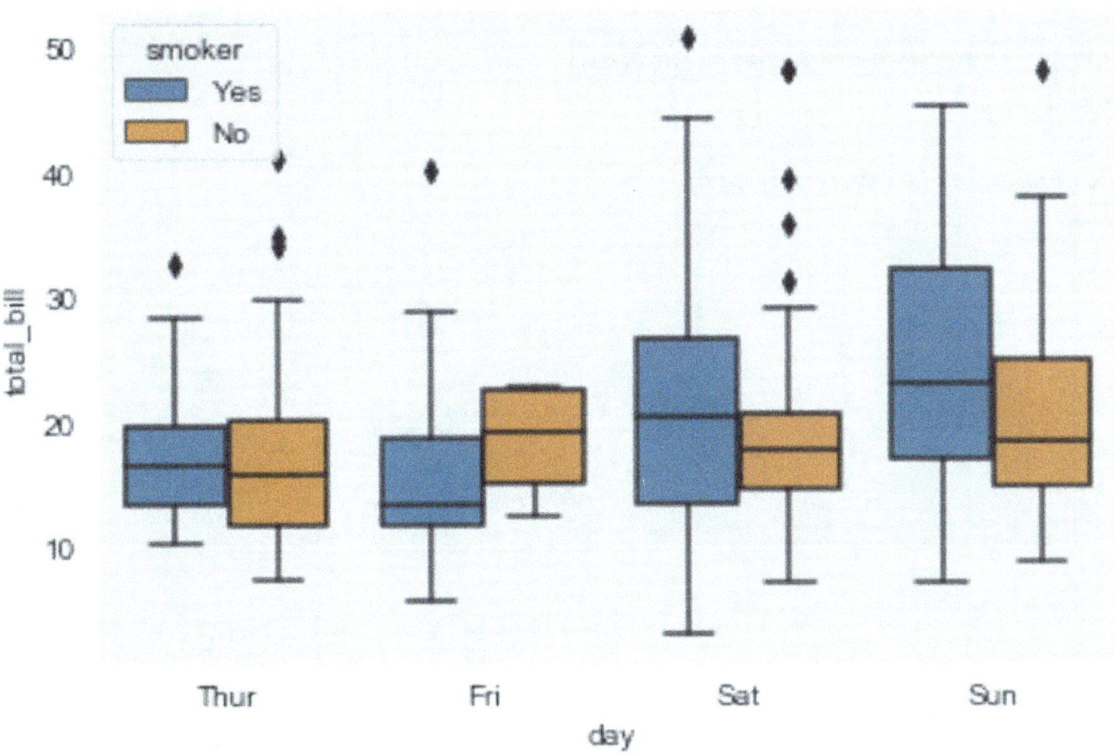

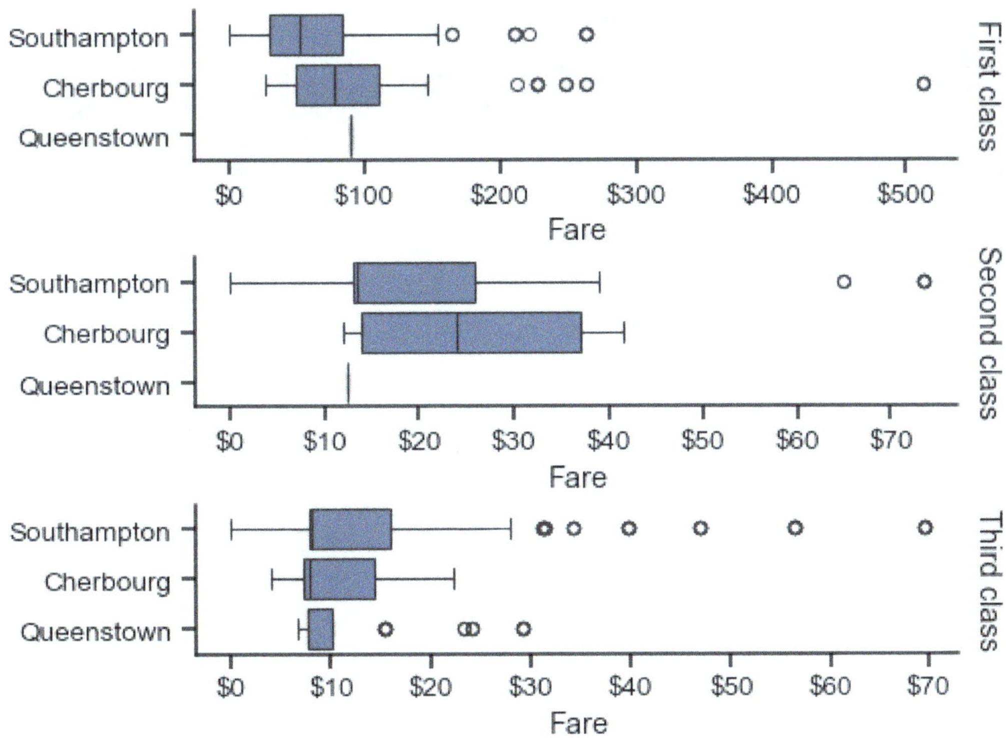

3.Pairplot (scatter matrix — essential for EDA)
Python

```
sns.pairplot(df, hue='species', diag_kind='kde')
plt.show()
```

Pairplot examples (scatter matrices):

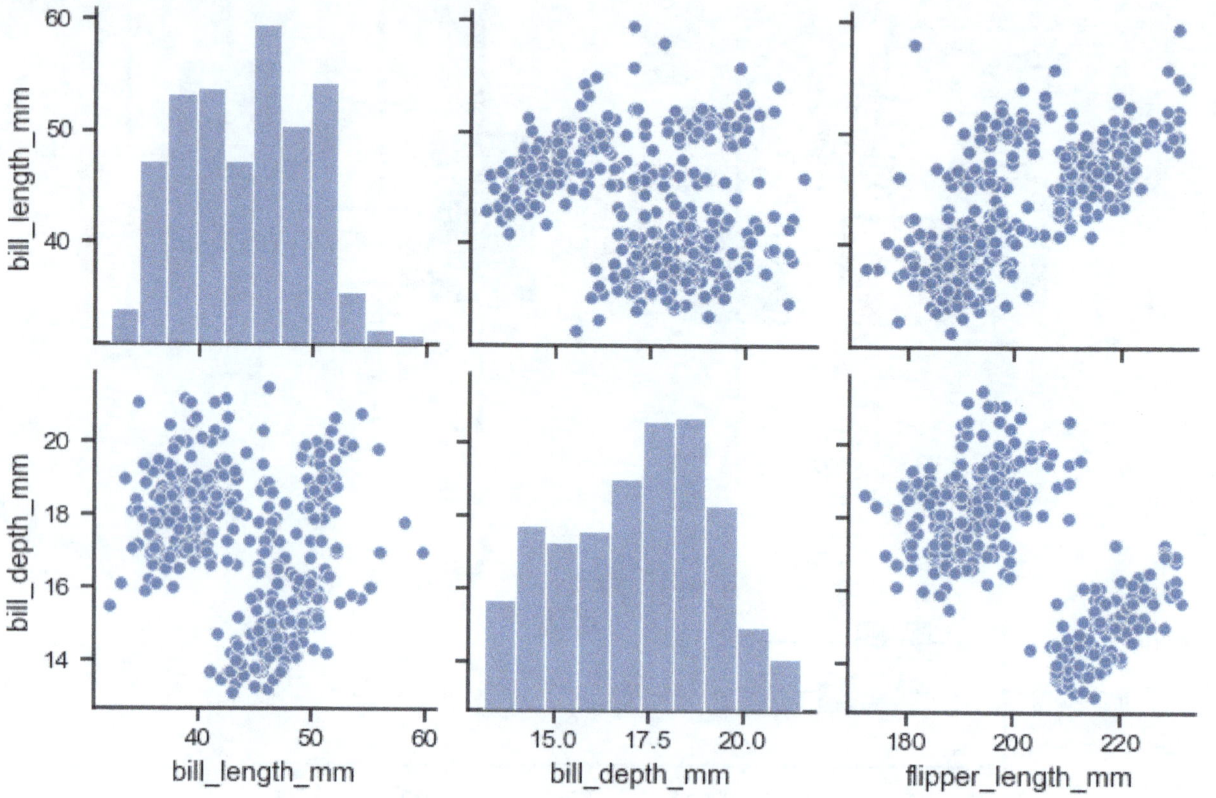

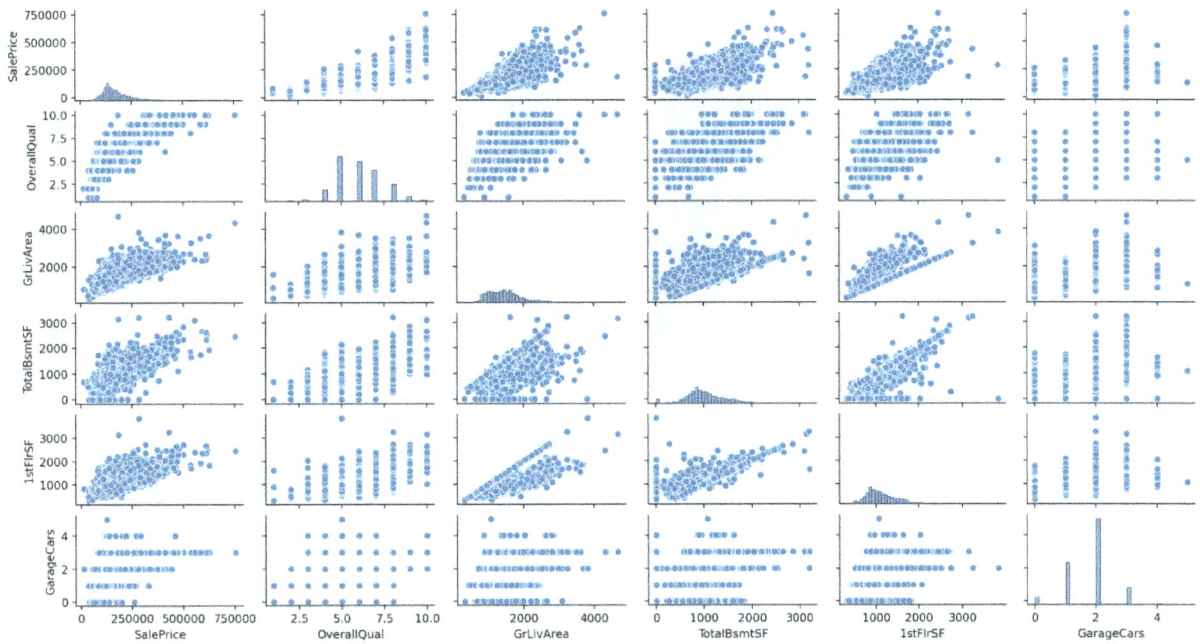

4.Heatmap (correlation matrix — key for feature selection)
Python

```
corr = df.select_dtypes(include=np.number).corr()
sns.heatmap(corr, annot=True, cmap='coolwarm', center=0)
plt.title('Correlation Heatmap')
plt.show()
```

Correlation heatmaps:

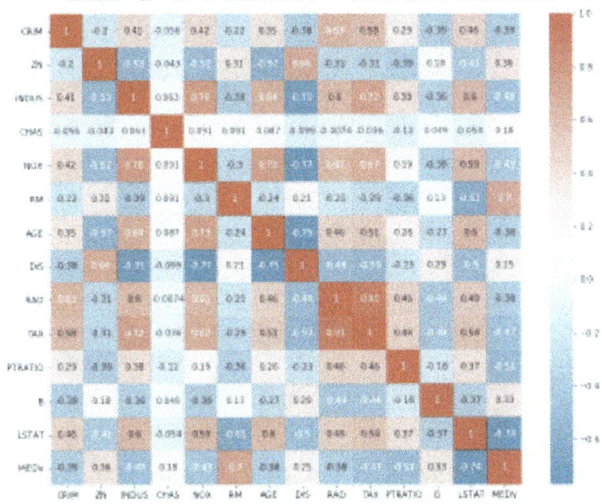

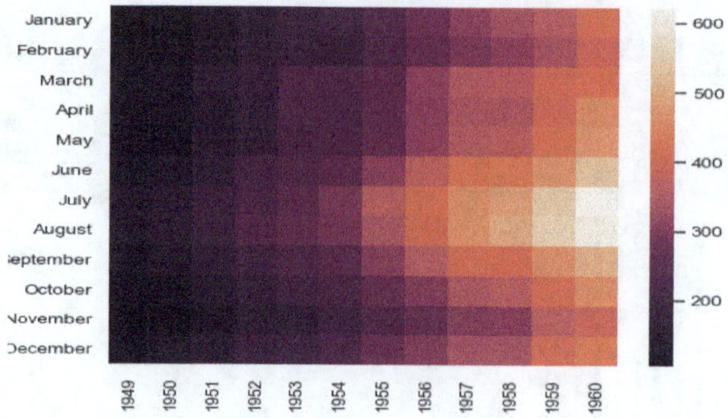

Python

```
# Set style
sns.set_style('whitegrid')
sns.set_palette('husl')
```

These libraries help you spot patterns, validate assumptions, and debug models visually. In Jupyter notebooks, plots display inline automatically (%matplotlib inline).

Section-4

Machine Learning Basics

- Supervised Learning (Regression, Classification)
- Unsupervised Learning (Clustering, Dimensionality Reduction)
- Reinforcement Learning (Markov Decision Process)
- Model Evaluation (Confusion Matrix, Precision, Recall, F1-score)

Machine Learning Basics

1.Supervised Learning (Regression, Classification)

In supervised learning, algorithms learn from labeled data to predict outcomes. **Regression** algorithms predict continuous values (e.g., prices, temperatures), while **classification** algorithms predict discrete categories (e.g., spam/not spam, disease/no disease). We'll cover key algorithms for each, with detailed explanations, workings, pros/cons, and Python code examples using scikit-learn. Examples use synthetic or built-in datasets for simplicity.
I'll include visuals to illustrate concepts.

Regression Algorithms

Regression minimizes the difference between predicted and actual continuous values, often using metrics like Mean Squared Error (MSE).

1. **Linear Regression** Assumes a linear relationship between features (X) and target (y): $y = w_0 + w_1x_1 + \cdots + w_nx_n + \epsilon$(where $w$are weights, $\epsilon$is error). It fits a straight line by minimizing the sum of squared residuals via ordinary least squares (OLS) or gradient descent. Pros: Simple, interpretable, fast. Cons: Assumes linearity; sensitive to outliers; no regularization (can overfit). In AI: Baseline for predictive modeling, e.g., sales

forecasting.

Visual example of line fitting:

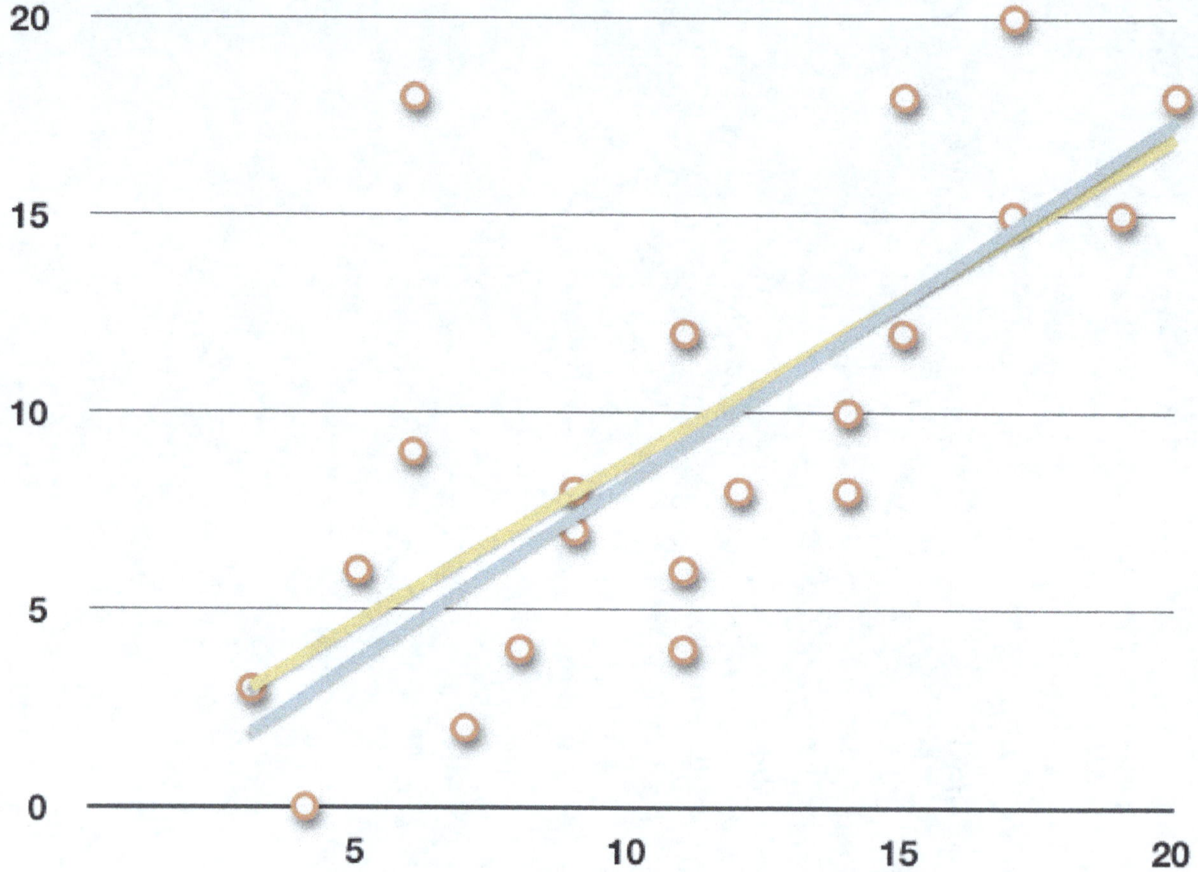

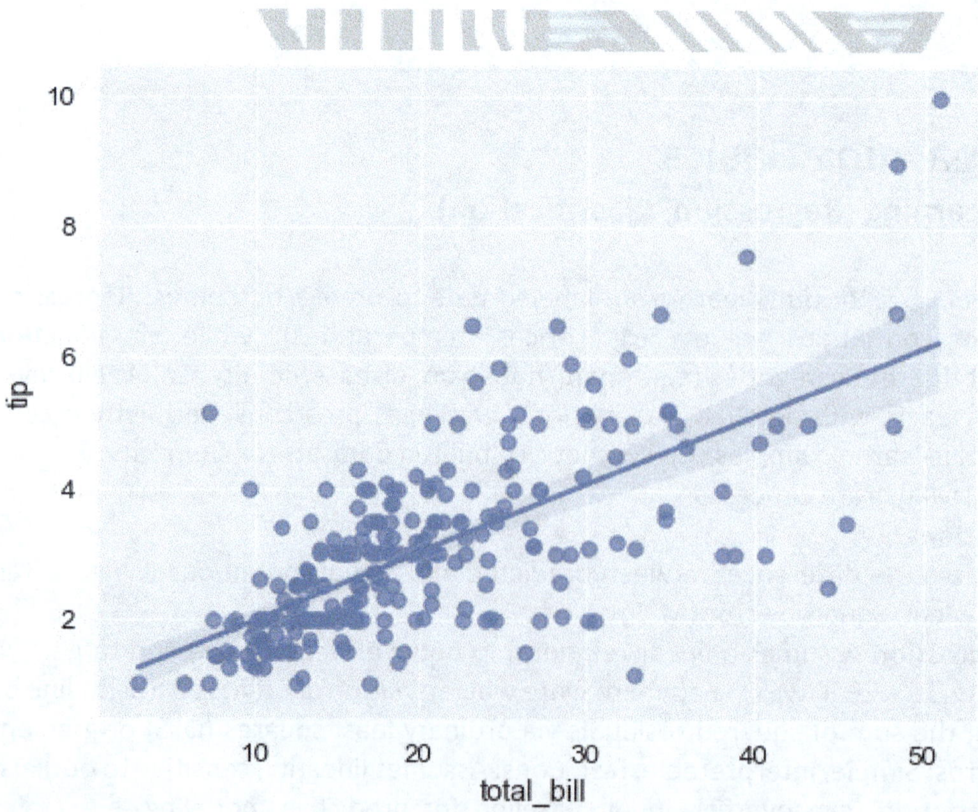

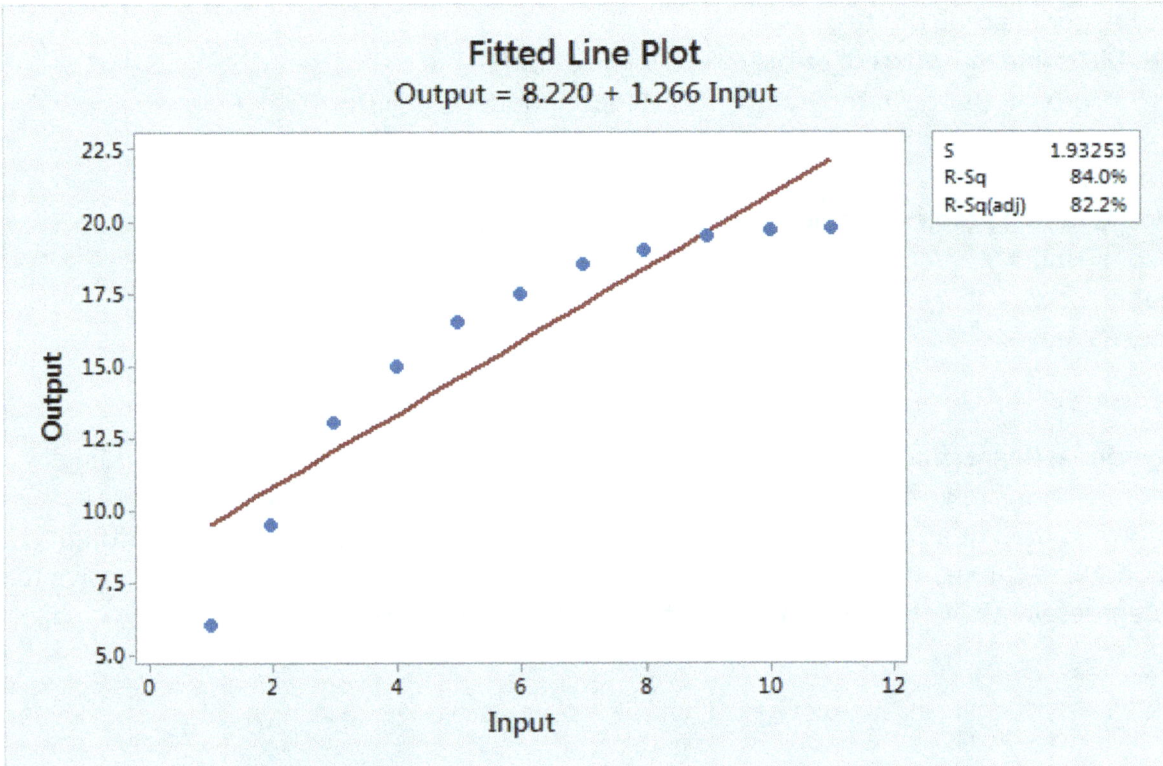

Python

```
import numpy as np
import matplotlib.pyplot as plt
from sklearn.linear_model import LinearRegression
from sklearn.model_selection import train_test_split
from sklearn.metrics import mean_squared_error

# Synthetic data: X (hours studied) vs. y (exam score)
np.random.seed(42)
X = np.random.rand(100, 1) * 10
y = 2 * X + np.random.randn(100, 1) * 2 + 5

X_train, X_test, y_train, y_test = train_test_split(X, y, test_size=0.2)

model = LinearRegression()
model.fit(X_train, y_train)
```

```
y_pred = model.predict(X_test)
print(f"MSE: {mean_squared_error(y_test, y_pred):.2f}")
print(f"Intercept: {model.intercept_[0]:.2f}, Slope: {model.coef_[0][0]:.2f}")

plt.scatter(X, y)
plt.plot(X, model.predict(X), color='red')
plt.xlabel('Hours Studied')
plt.ylabel('Score')
plt.show()
```

2.Polynomial Regression Extends linear regression for non-linear relationships by adding polynomial terms (e.g., x^2,x^3): $y = w_0 + w_1x + w_2x^2 + ...$ Use PolynomialFeatures to transform X, then fit a linear model. Degree is a hyperparameter (higher risks overfitting). Pros: Captures curves; still interpretable. Cons: Overfits easily; computationally expensive for high degrees. In AI: Modeling complex patterns like growth curves.

Curve fitting visual:

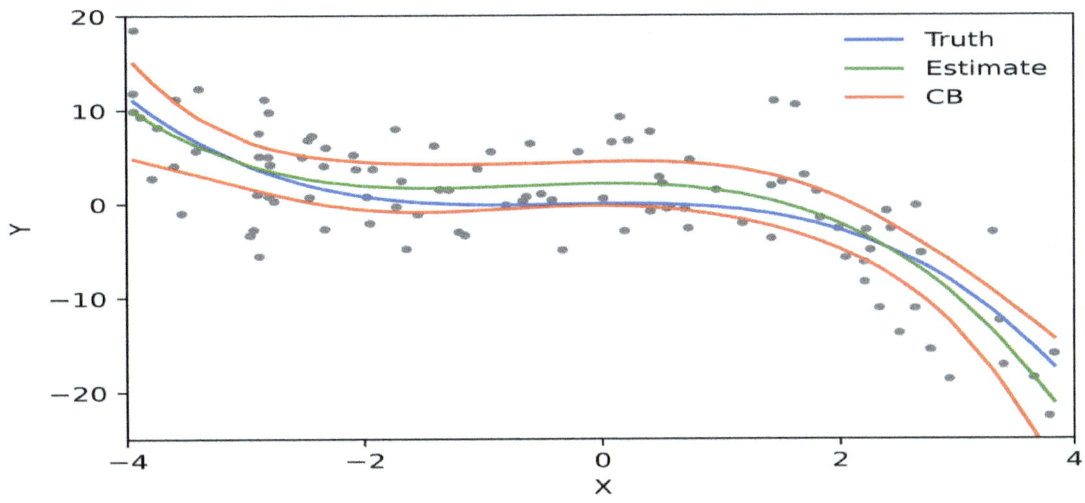

Truth
Estimate
CB
Y
X
20
10
0
−10
−20
−4
−2
0
2
4

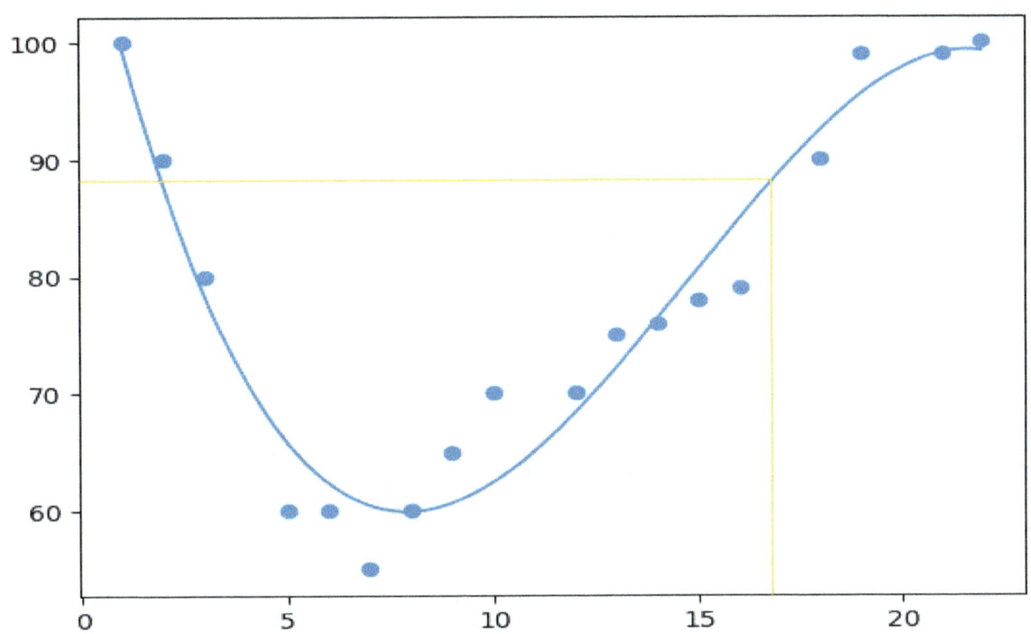

100
90
80
70
60
0
5
10
15
20

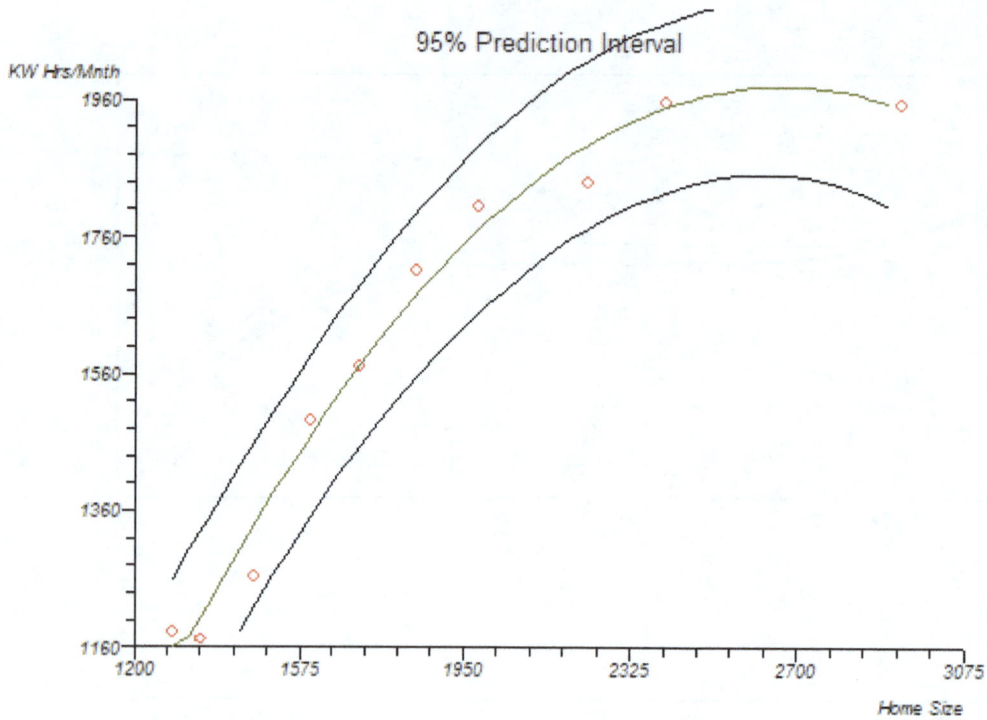

Python

```
from sklearn.preprocessing import PolynomialFeatures
from sklearn.pipeline import make_pipeline

# Synthetic quadratic data
X = np.random.rand(100, 1) * 6 - 3
y = X**2 + np.random.randn(100, 1) * 0.5

X_train, X_test, y_train, y_test = train_test_split(X, y, test_size=0.2)

degree = 2
model = make_pipeline(PolynomialFeatures(degree), LinearRegression())
model.fit(X_train, y_train)

y_pred = model.predict(X_test)
print(f"MSE: {mean_squared_error(y_test, y_pred):.2f}")

X_plot = np.linspace(-3, 3, 100).reshape(-1, 1)
plt.scatter(X, y)
plt.plot(X_plot, model.predict(X_plot), color='red')
plt.show()
```

3.Ridge Regression Linear regression with L2 regularization to prevent overfitting: Adds penalty $\alpha\sum w_i^2$to loss. Shrinks coefficients. Pros: Handles multicollinearity; stable with noisy data. Cons: All features retained (use Lasso for selection). In AI: When features are correlated, e.g., in genomics.

Python

```
from sklearn.linear_model import Ridge

# Use same data as linear
model = Ridge(alpha=1.0)  # Alpha controls regularization
model.fit(X_train, y_train)
y_pred = model.predict(X_test)
print(f"MSE: {mean_squared_error(y_test, y_pred):.2f}")
```

Classification Algorithms

Classification assigns inputs to categories, minimizing errors like cross-entropy. Metrics: Accuracy, Precision, Recall, F1.

1.Logistic Regression For binary/multi-class: Uses sigmoid (binary) or softmax (multi) for probabilities. Decision boundary from $P(y = 1|X) = \frac{1}{1+e^{-(wX+b)}}$. Pros: Probabilistic; handles linear separability. Cons: Assumes linearity; poor with complex boundaries. In AI: Sentiment analysis, churn prediction.

Sigmoid and boundary visuals:

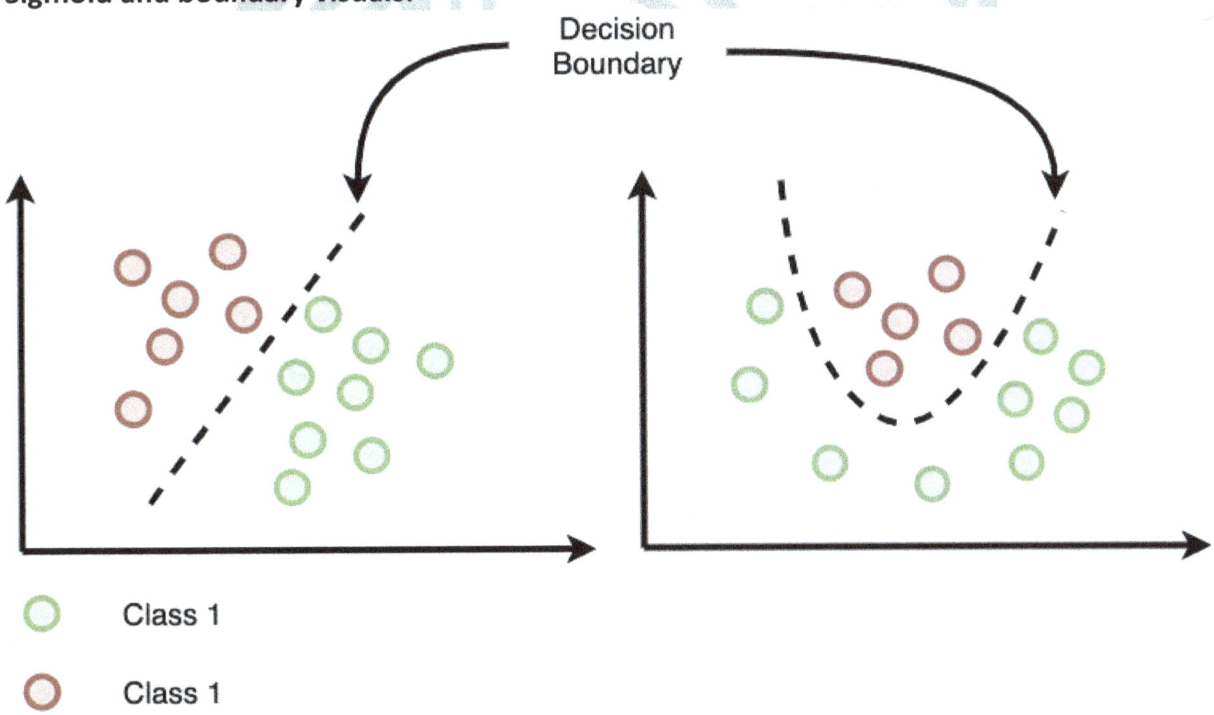

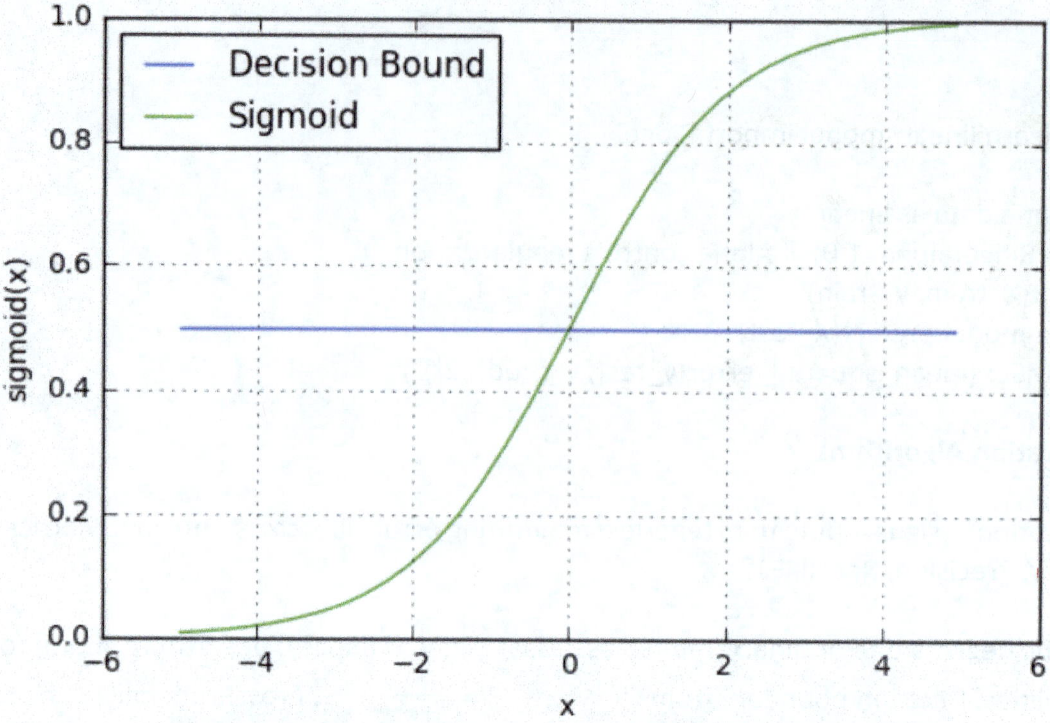
Decision Bound
Sigmoid
sigmoid(x)
x

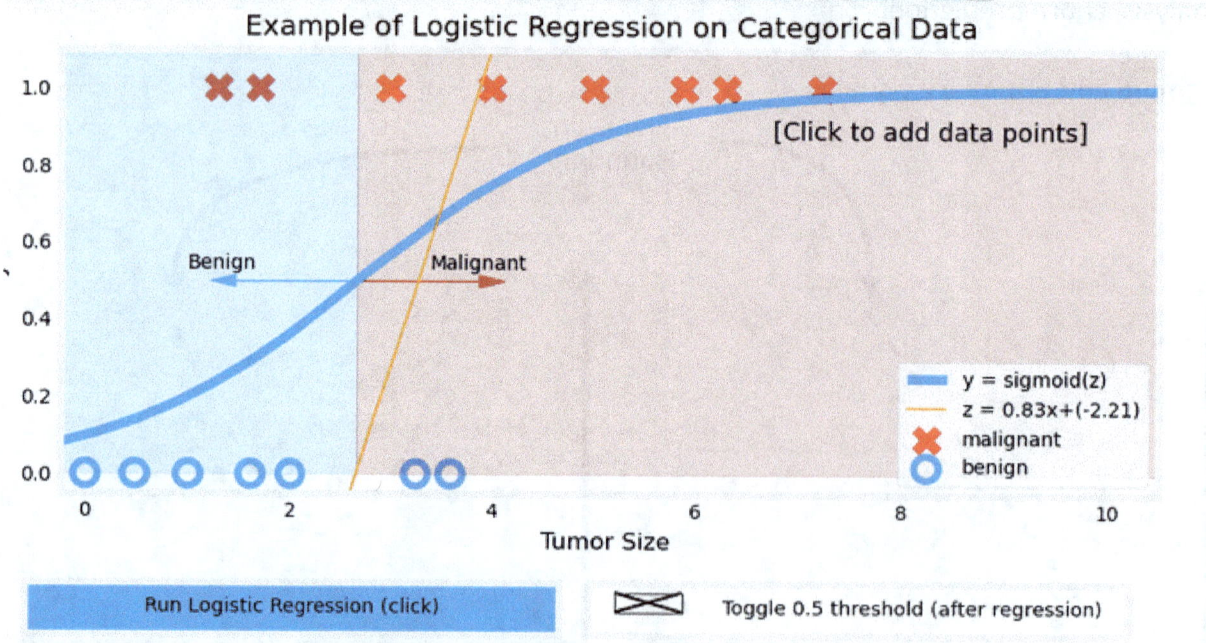
Example of Logistic Regression on Categorical Data
[Click to add data points]
Benign
Malignant
y = sigmoid(z)
z = 0.83x+(-2.21)
malignant
benign
Tumor Size
Run Logistic Regression (click)
Toggle 0.5 threshold (after regression)

Python

```
from sklearn.datasets import load_iris
from sklearn.linear_model import LogisticRegression
from sklearn.metrics import accuracy_score

iris = load_iris()
X = iris.data
y = iris.target

X_train, X_test, y_train, y_test = train_test_split(X, y, test_size=0.2)

model = LogisticRegression(max_iter=200)
model.fit(X_train, y_train)

y_pred = model.predict(X_test)

print(f"Accuracy: {accuracy_score(y_test, y_pred):.2f}")
```

2.K-Nearest Neighbors (KNN) Non-parametric: Predicts class by majority vote of K nearest training points (distance: Euclidean). Lazy learner (no training phase). Pros: Simple; no assumptions. Cons: Slow on large data; sensitive to K and noise. In AI: Recommendation systems, image recognition.

KNN visualization:

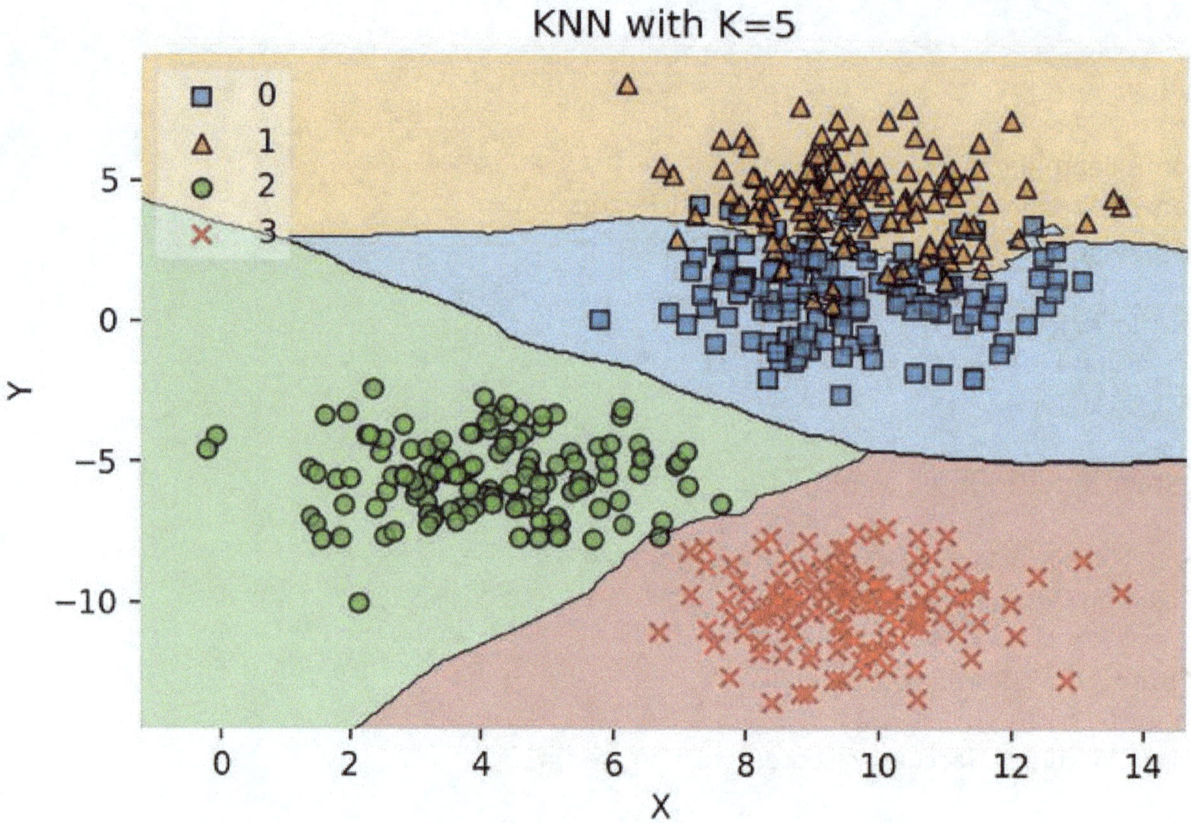

KNN with K=5
0
1
2
3
5
0
−5
−10
Y
0
2
4
6
8
10
12
14
X

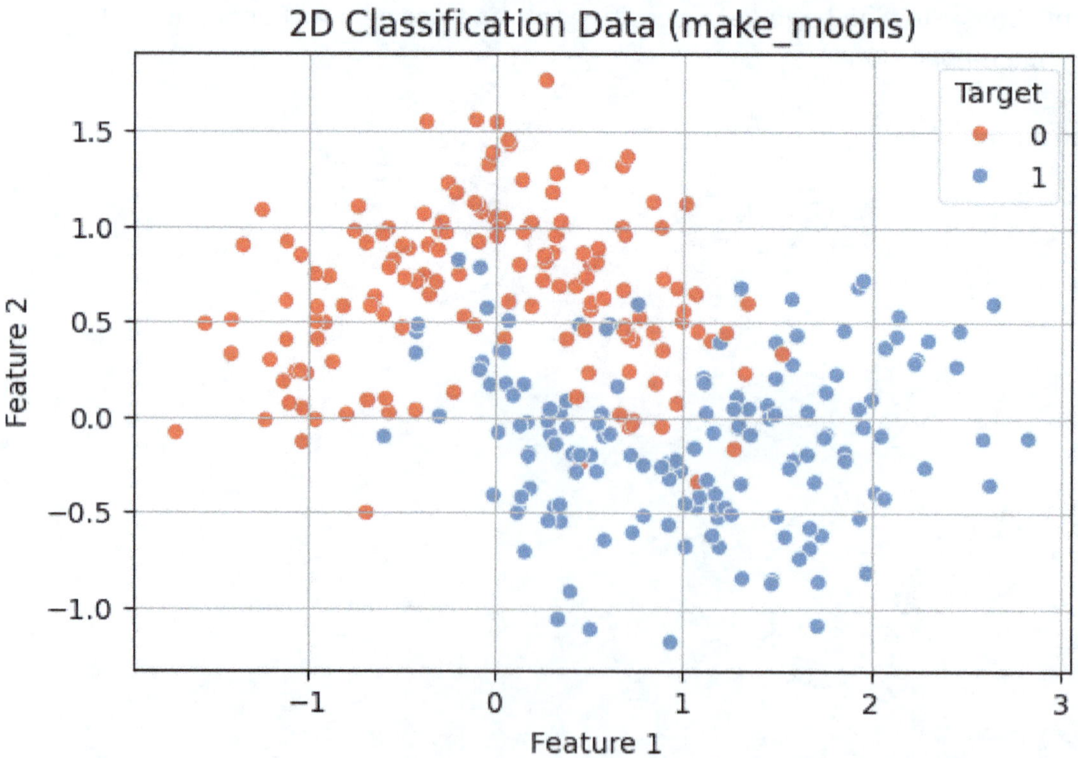

2D Classification Data (make_moons)
Target
0
1
1.5
1.0
0.5
0.0
−0.5
−1.0
Feature 2
−1
0
1
2
3
Feature 1

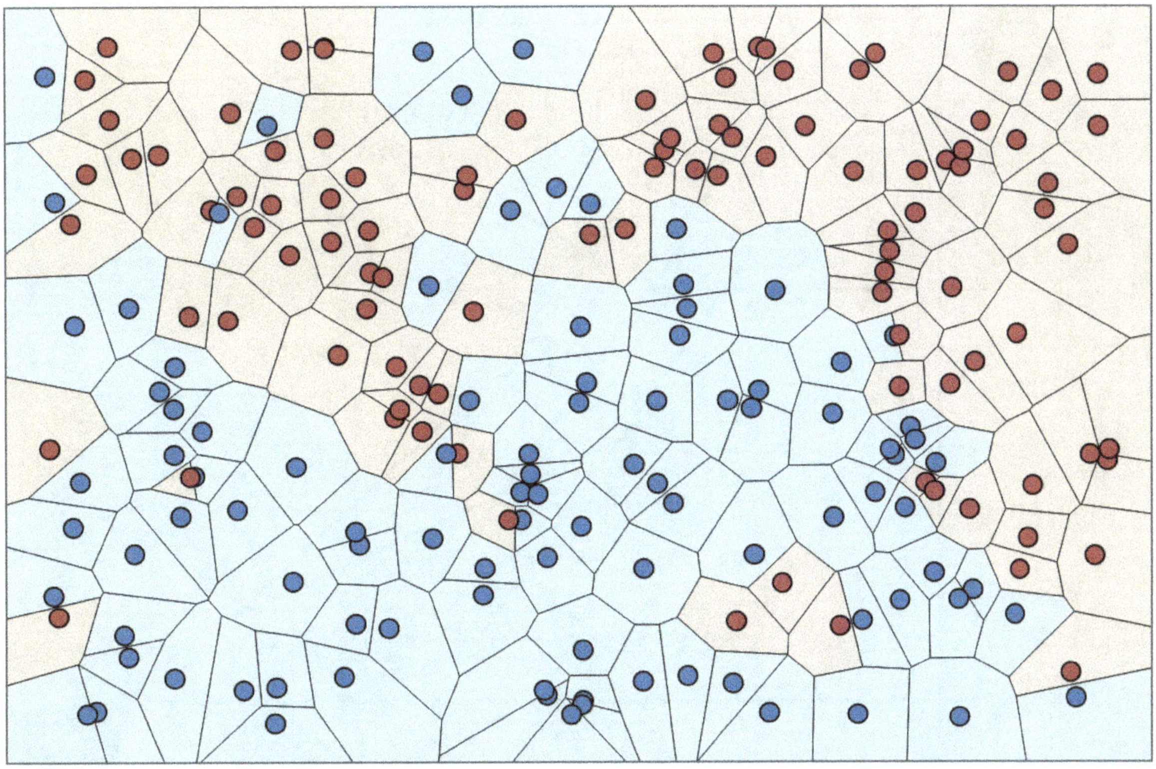

Python

```
from sklearn.neighbors import KNeighborsClassifier

# Use Iris
model = KNeighborsClassifier(n_neighbors=3)
model.fit(X_train, y_train)
y_pred = model.predict(X_test)
print(f"Accuracy: {accuracy_score(y_test, y_pred):.2f}")
```

3.Support Vector Machines (SVM) Finds hyperplane maximizing margin between classes. Uses support vectors (closest points). Kernels (e.g., RBF) for non-linear. Pros: Effective in high dimensions; robust to overfitting. Cons: Slow on large data; kernel choice sensitive. In AI: Text classification, bioinformatics.

Hyperplane visuals:

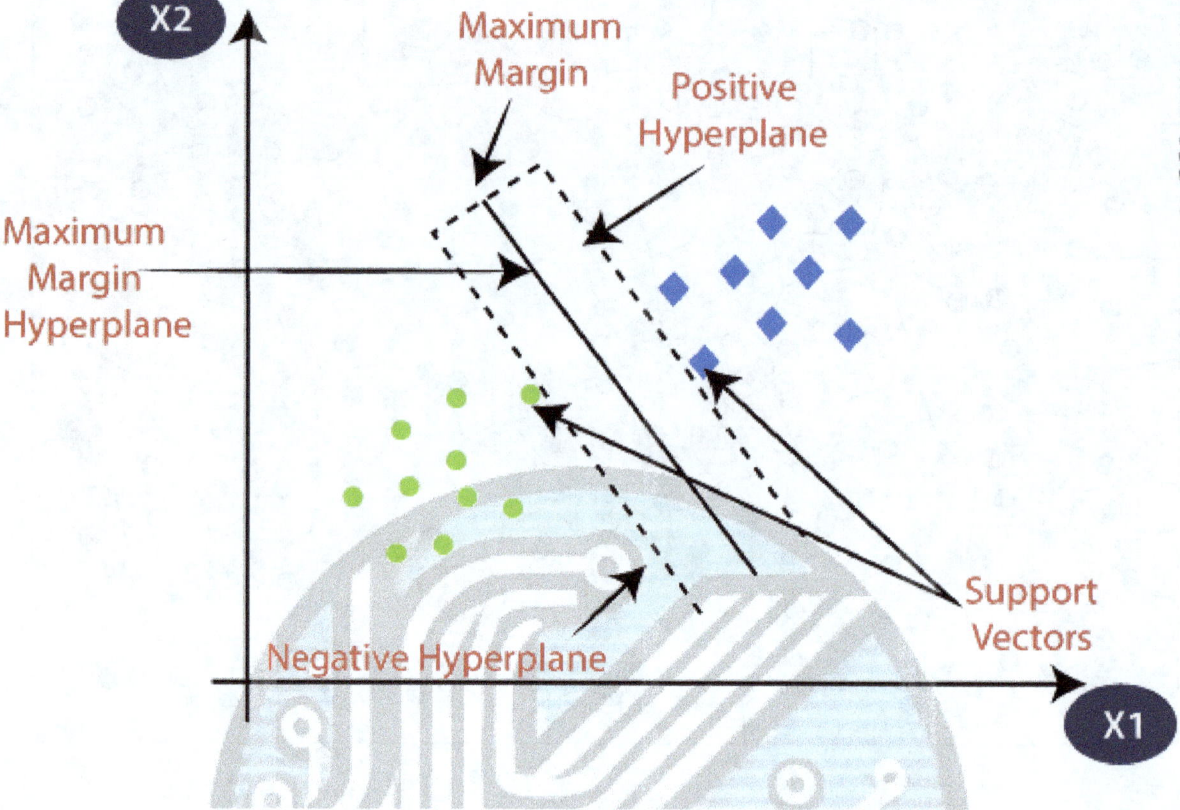
X2
Maximum
Margin
Positive
Hyperplane
Maximum
Margin
Hyperplane
Support
Vectors
Negative Hyperplane
X1

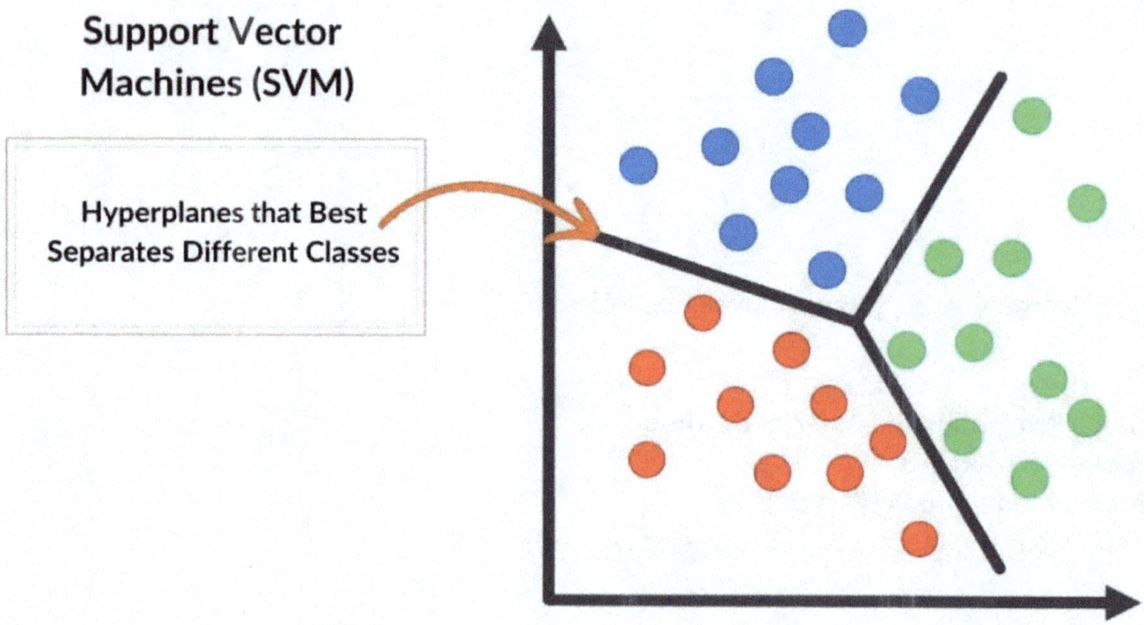
Support Vector
Machines (SVM)
Hyperplanes that Best
Separates Different Classes

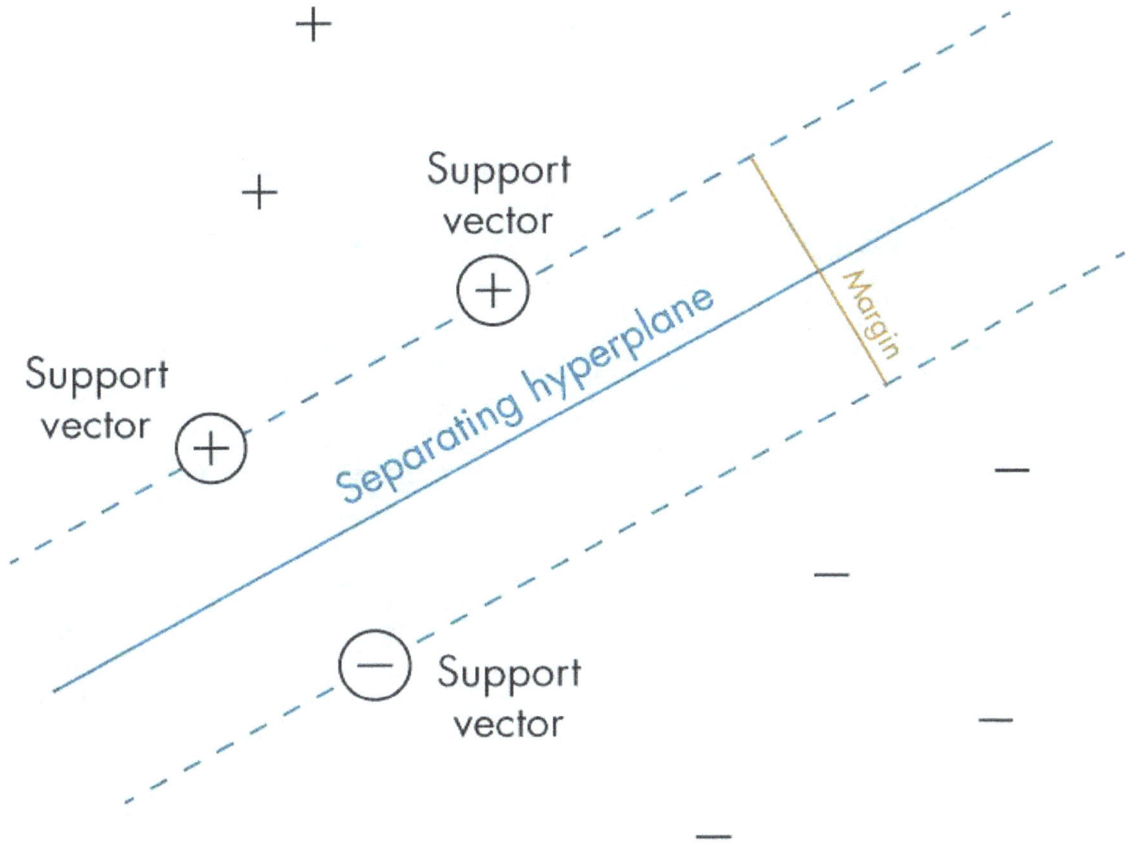

Python

```
from sklearn.svm import SVC

model = SVC(kernel='rbf', C=1.0)
model.fit(X_train, y_train)
y_pred = model.predict(X_test)
print(f"Accuracy: {accuracy_score(y_test, y_pred):.2f}")
```

4.Decision Trees Tree structure: Splits data based on features (e.g., Gini/entropy impurity). Leaf nodes give predictions. Pros: Interpretable; handles non-linear. Cons: Overfits; unstable (small data changes alter tree). In AI: Fraud detection.

Tree structure diagram:

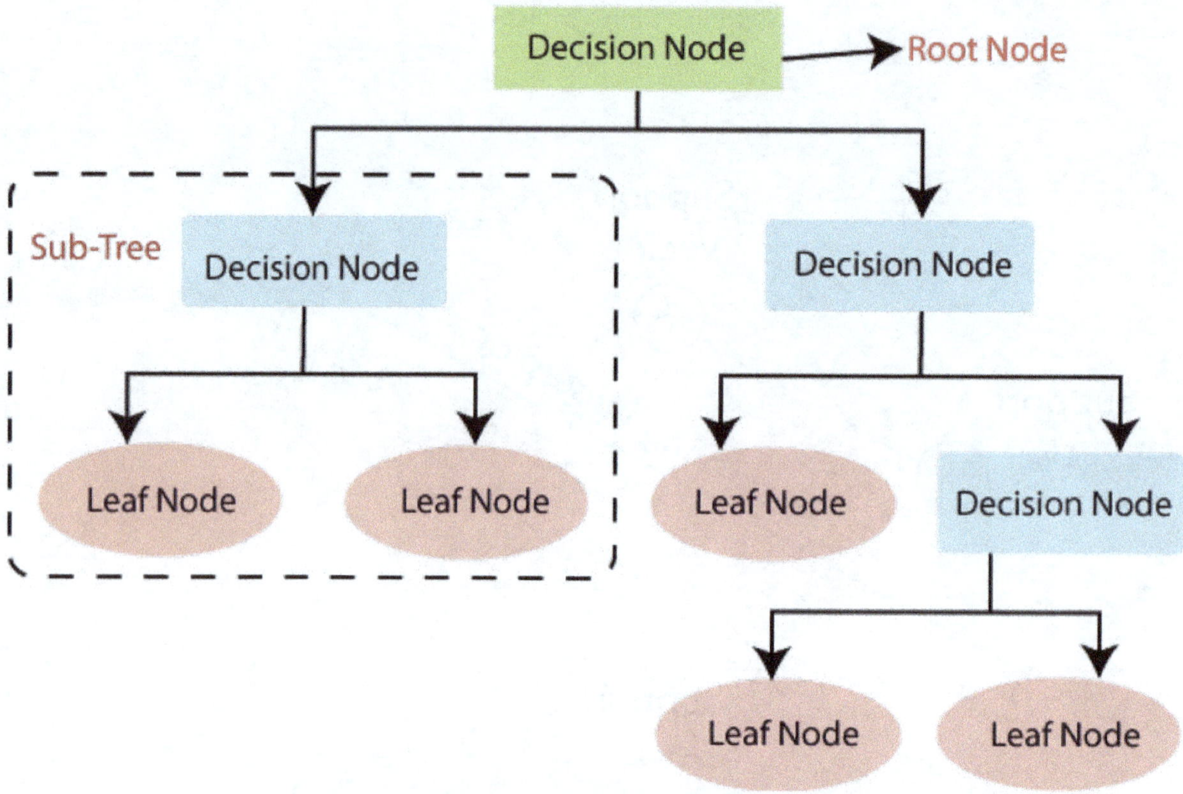

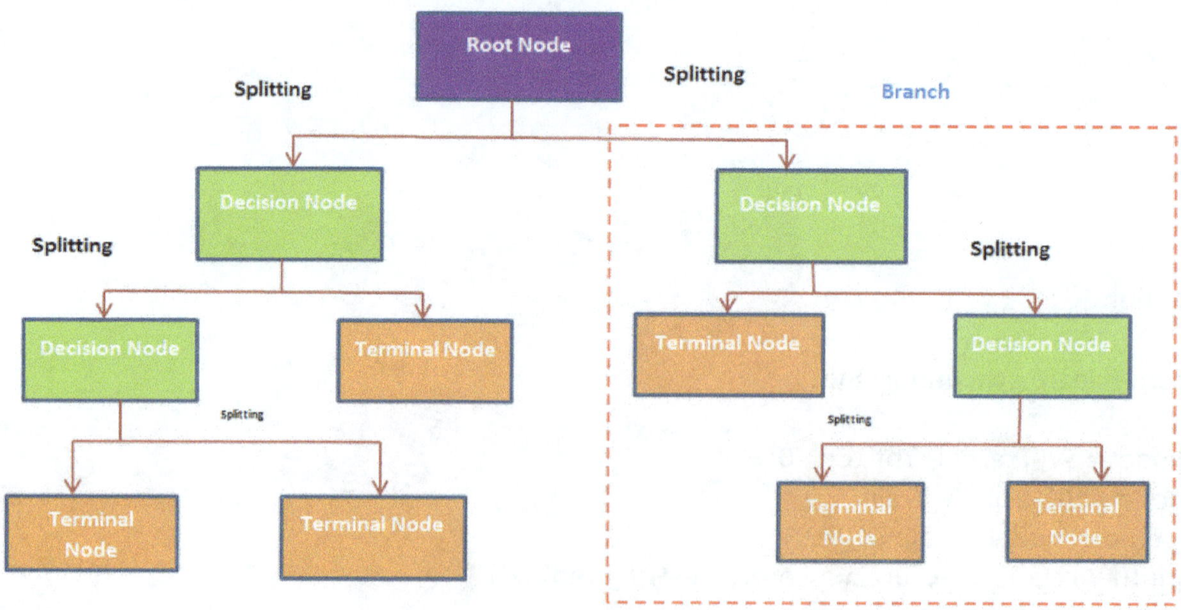

Python

```
from sklearn.tree import DecisionTreeClassifier, plot_tree

model = DecisionTreeClassifier(max_depth=3)
model.fit(X_train, y_train)
y_pred = model.predict(X_test)
print(f"Accuracy: {accuracy_score(y_test, y_pred):.2f}")
```

```
plt.figure(figsize=(12,8))
plot_tree(model, feature_names=iris.feature_names, class_names=iris.target_names,
filled=True)
plt.show()
```

5.Random Forests Ensemble: Builds multiple decision trees on bootstrapped data, aggregates votes (bagging). Reduces overfitting. Pros: Accurate; handles missing values; feature importance. Cons: Less interpretable; computationally intensive. In AI: Medical diagnosis, stock prediction.

Ensemble illustration:

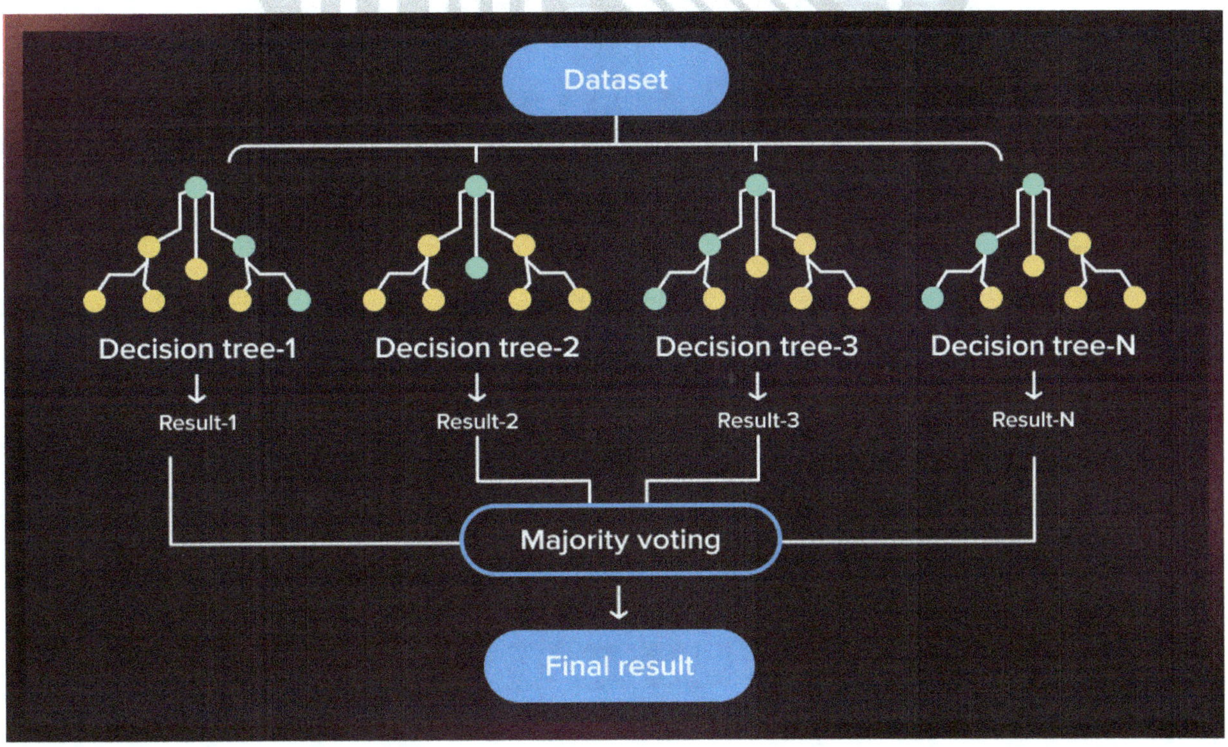

Random Forest

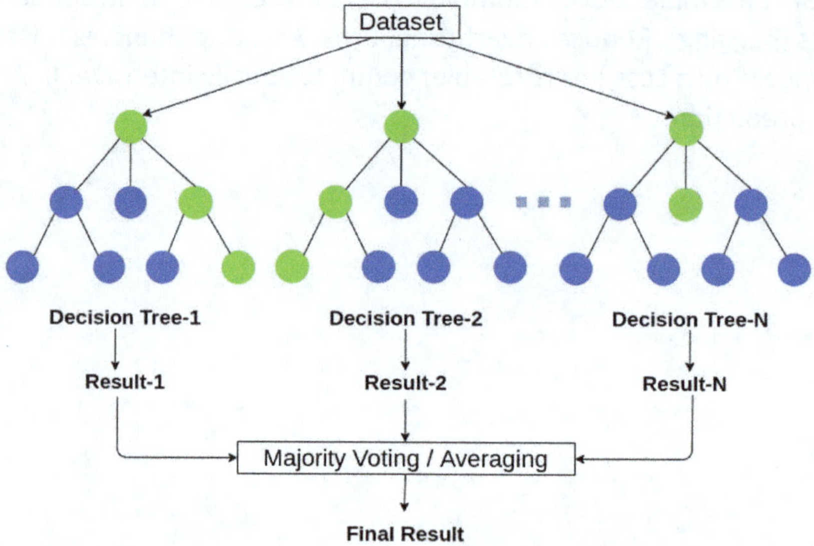

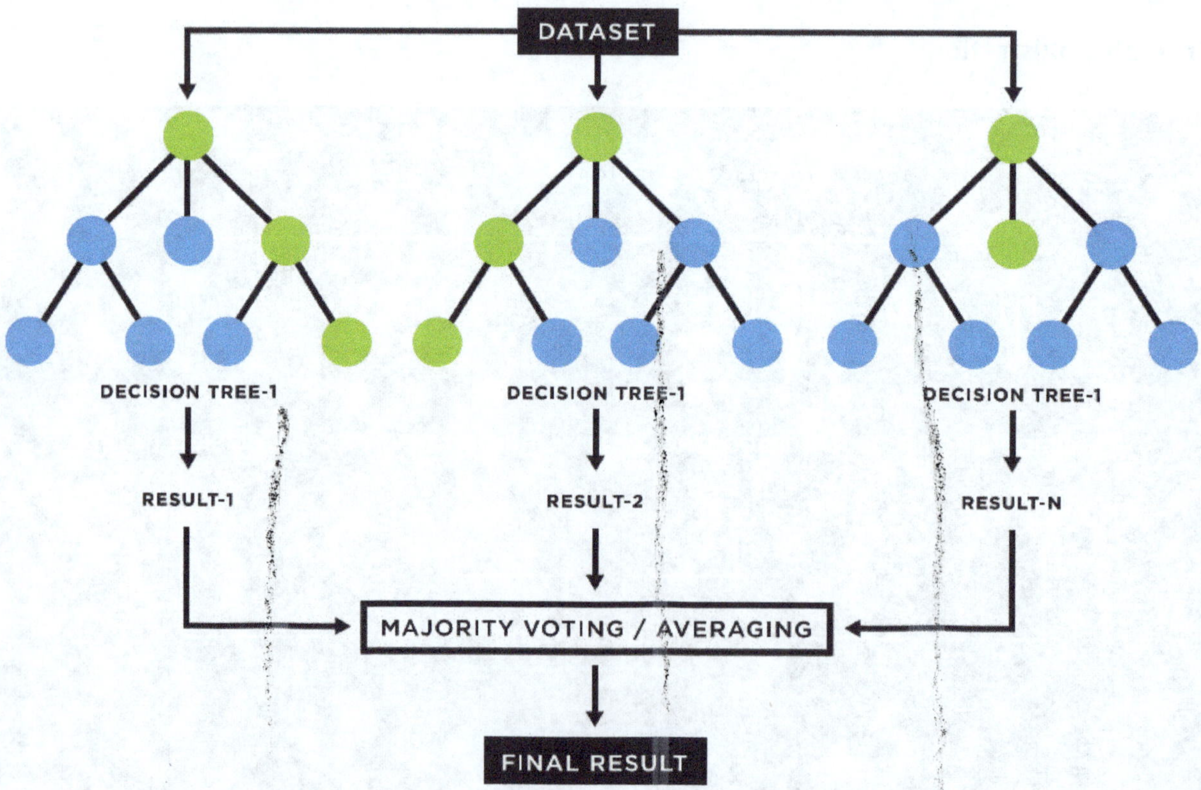

Python

```
from sklearn.ensemble import RandomForestClassifier

model = RandomForestClassifier(n_estimators=100, max_depth=3)
model.fit(X_train, y_train)
y_pred = model.predict(X_test)
print(f"Accuracy: {accuracy_score(y_test, y_pred):.2f}")
```

2. Unsupervised Learning (Clustering, Dimensionality Reduction)

Unsupervised learning discovers hidden patterns in **unlabeled data** (no target y). Models find structure like groups or compressed representations. It's used for customer segmentation, anomaly detection, data compression, and preprocessing.

Two main categories:

- **Clustering** — Groups similar data points.
- **Dimensionality Reduction** — Reduces features while preserving information (for visualization, noise reduction, faster training).

Unlike supervised learning, evaluation relies on internal metrics (e.g., silhouette score) or domain knowledge.

Clustering: Grouping Similar Data Points

Clustering partitions data into clusters where intra-cluster similarity is high and inter-cluster is low.

1. **K-Means Clustering** Partitions data into K clusters by minimizing within-cluster variance (inertia). Algorithm:
    1. Initialize K centroids randomly.
    2. Assign each point to nearest centroid.
    3. Update centroids as mean of assigned points.
    4. Repeat until convergence. Pros: Fast, scalable. Cons: Assumes spherical clusters; sensitive to K and initialization (use K-Means++). In AI: Customer

segmentation, image compression.

Step-by-step visualizations of K-Means convergence:

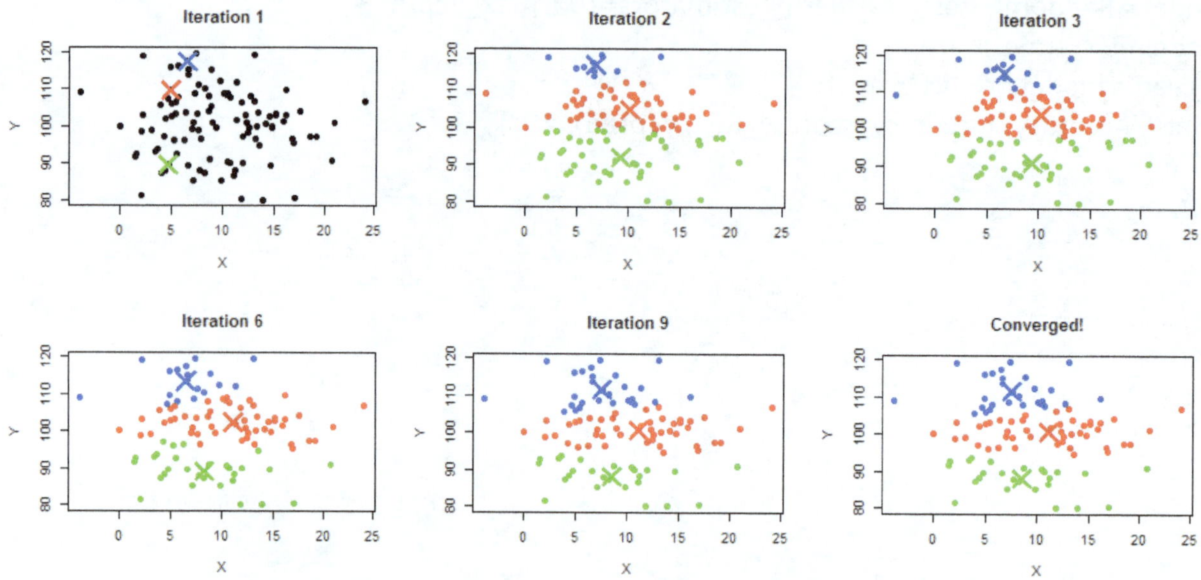

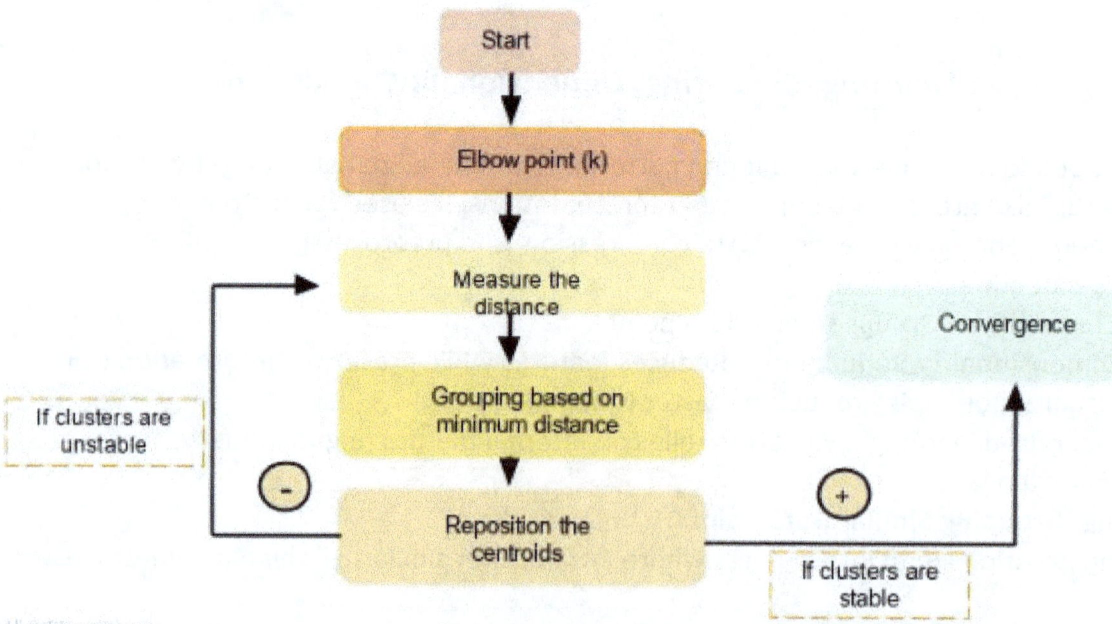

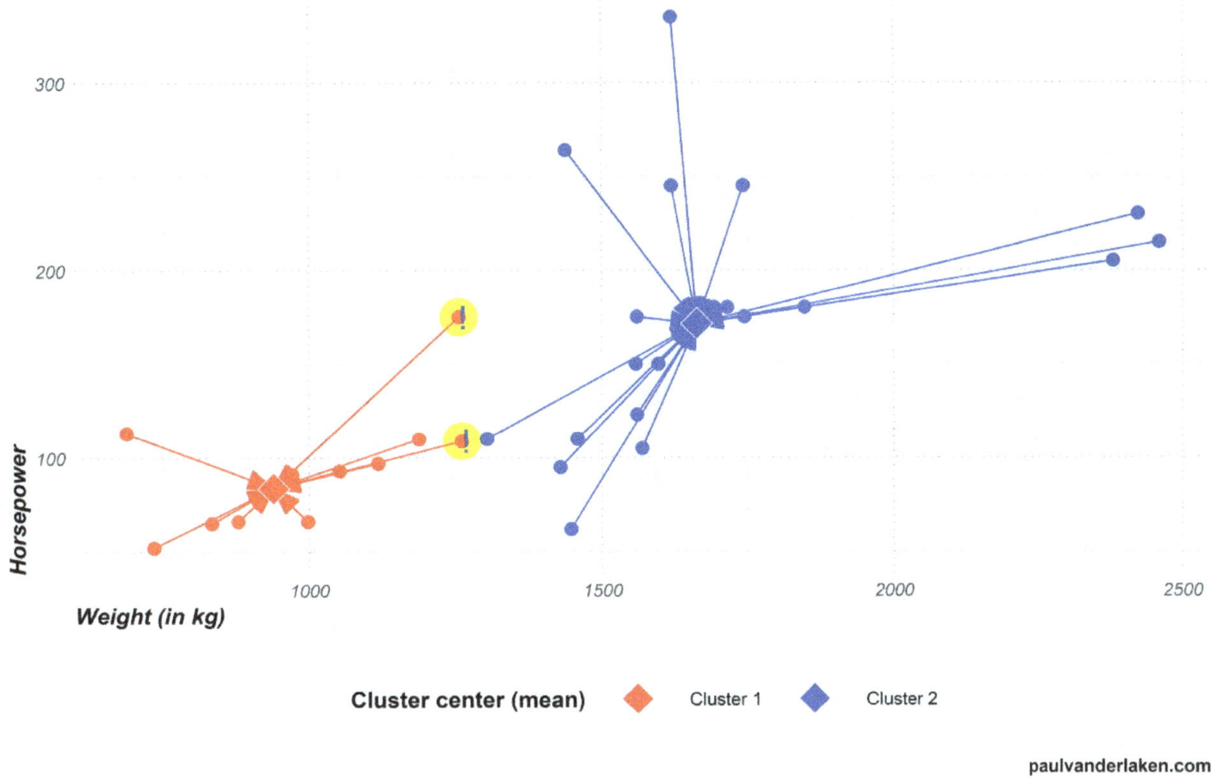

Python

```
import numpy as np
import matplotlib.pyplot as plt
from sklearn.datasets import make_blobs
from sklearn.cluster import KMeans
from sklearn.metrics import silhouette_score

# Generate data
X, _ = make_blobs(n_samples=300, centers=4, cluster_std=0.60, random_state=0)

# Apply K-Means
kmeans = KMeans(n_clusters=4, init='k-means++', n_init=10, random_state=42)
labels = kmeans.fit_predict(X)

# Evaluate
print(f"Inertia: {kmeans.inertia_:.2f}")
```

```
print(f"Silhouette Score: {silhouette_score(X, labels):.2f}")

# Plot
plt.scatter(X[:, 0], X[:, 1], c=labels, cmap='viridis')
plt.scatter(kmeans.cluster_centers_[:, 0], kmeans.cluster_centers_[:, 1],
        c='red', marker='x', s=200, label='Centroids')
plt.title('K-Means Clustering')
plt.legend()
plt.show()
```

To choose K: Use elbow method (plot inertia vs. K) or silhouette score.

2. **Hierarchical Clustering** Builds a hierarchy of clusters (dendrogram). Agglomerative (bottom-up): Start with individual points, merge closest pairs. Linkage types: single, complete, average, ward. Pros: No need to specify K; dendrogram shows structure. Cons: $O(n^2)$ time/space; not scalable for large data. In AI: Taxonomy building, gene expression analysis.

Dendrogram examples showing cluster hierarchy:

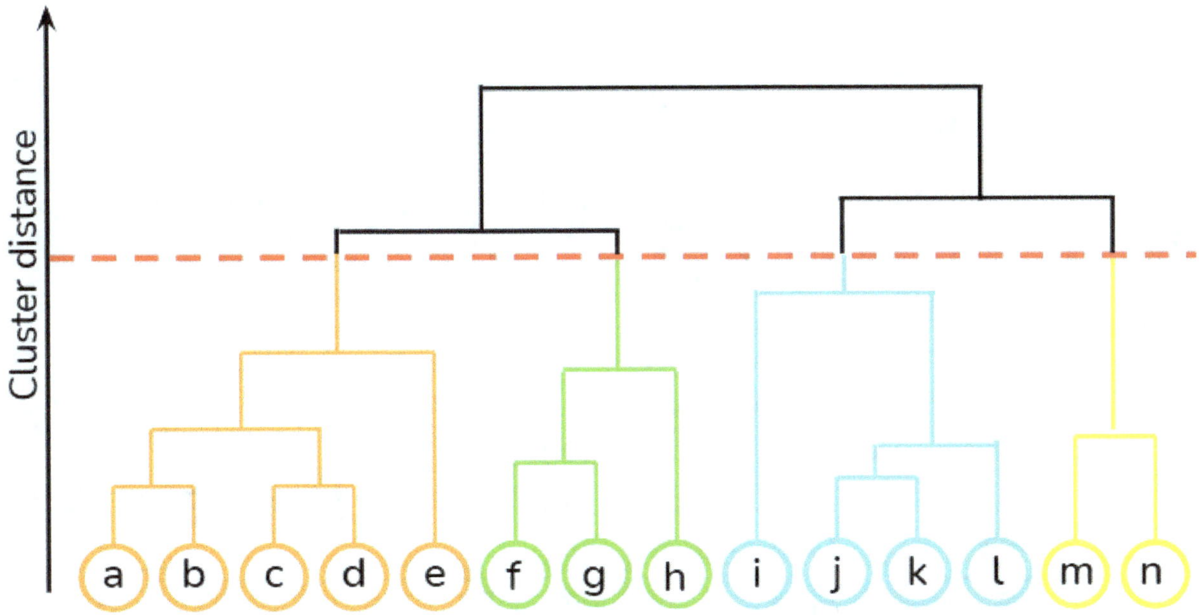
Cluster distance
a
b
c
d
e
f
g
h
i
j
k
l
m
n

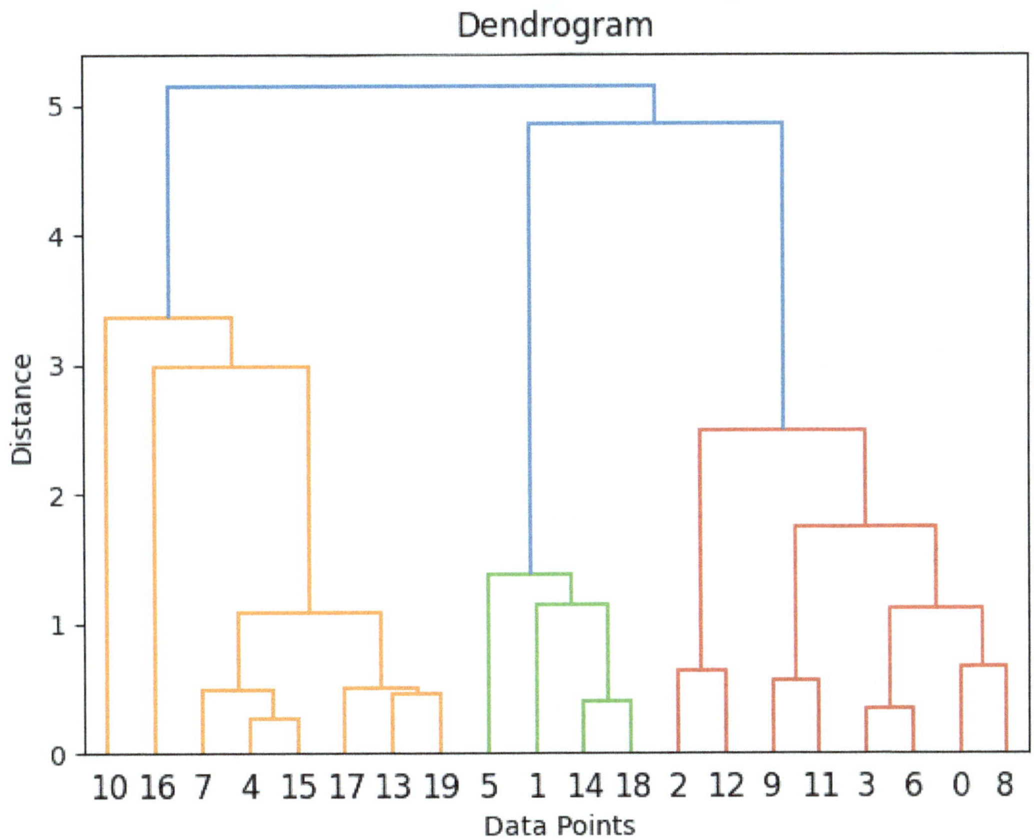
Dendrogram
Distance
0
1
2
3
4
5
10 16 7 4 15 17 13 19 5 1 14 18 2 12 9 11 3 6 0 8
Data Points

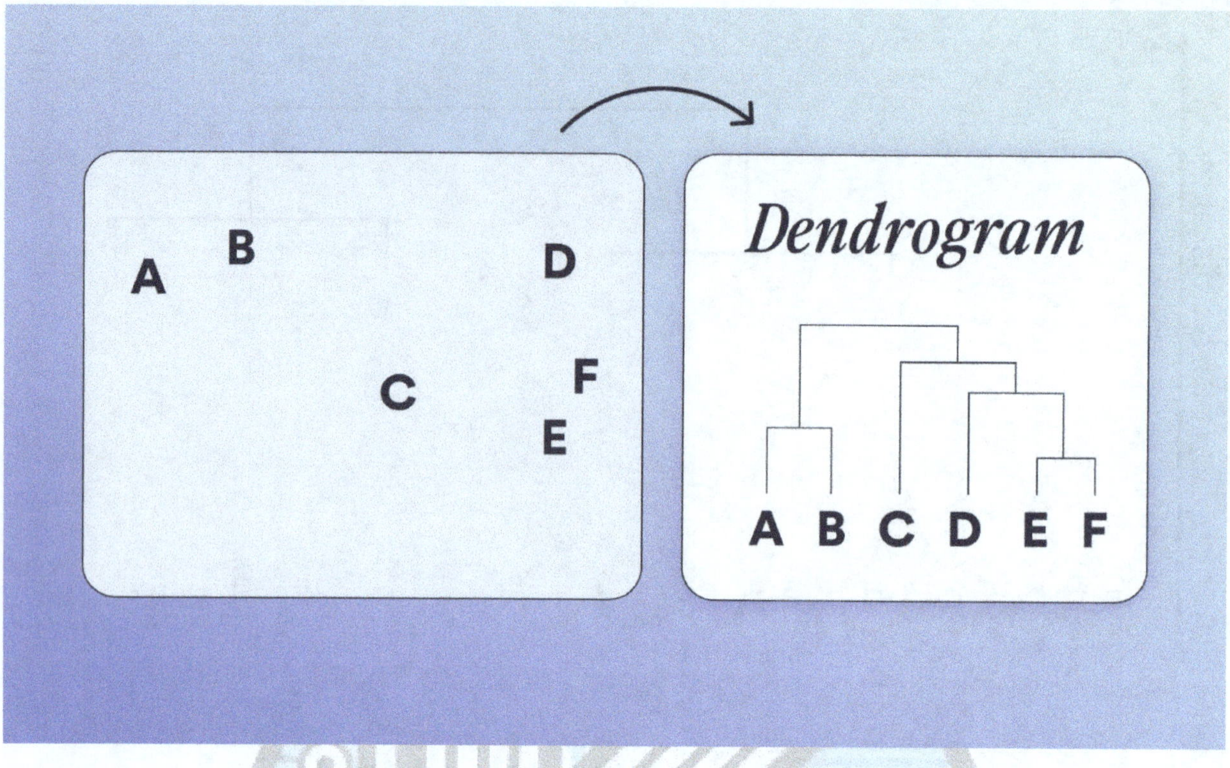

Python

```
from sklearn.cluster import AgglomerativeClustering
import scipy.cluster.hierarchy as shc

model = AgglomerativeClustering(n_clusters=4, linkage='ward')
labels = model.fit_predict(X)

# Dendrogram
plt.figure(figsize=(10, 7))
shc.dendrogram(shc.linkage(X, method='ward'))
plt.title('Dendrogram')
plt.show()

# Clusters plot (similar to K-Means)
plt.scatter(X[:, 0], X[:, 1], c=labels, cmap='viridis')
plt.title('Hierarchical Clustering')
plt.show()
```

3. **DBSCAN (Density-Based Spatial Clustering of Applications with Noise)** Groups dense regions; marks sparse points as noise. Parameters: ε (radius), minPts (minimum points). Core points → dense; border points → attached; noise → outliers. Pros: Finds arbitrary shapes; handles noise/outliers. Cons: Sensitive to parameters; struggles with varying density. In AI: Anomaly detection, geospatial data.

Density-based clustering illustration:

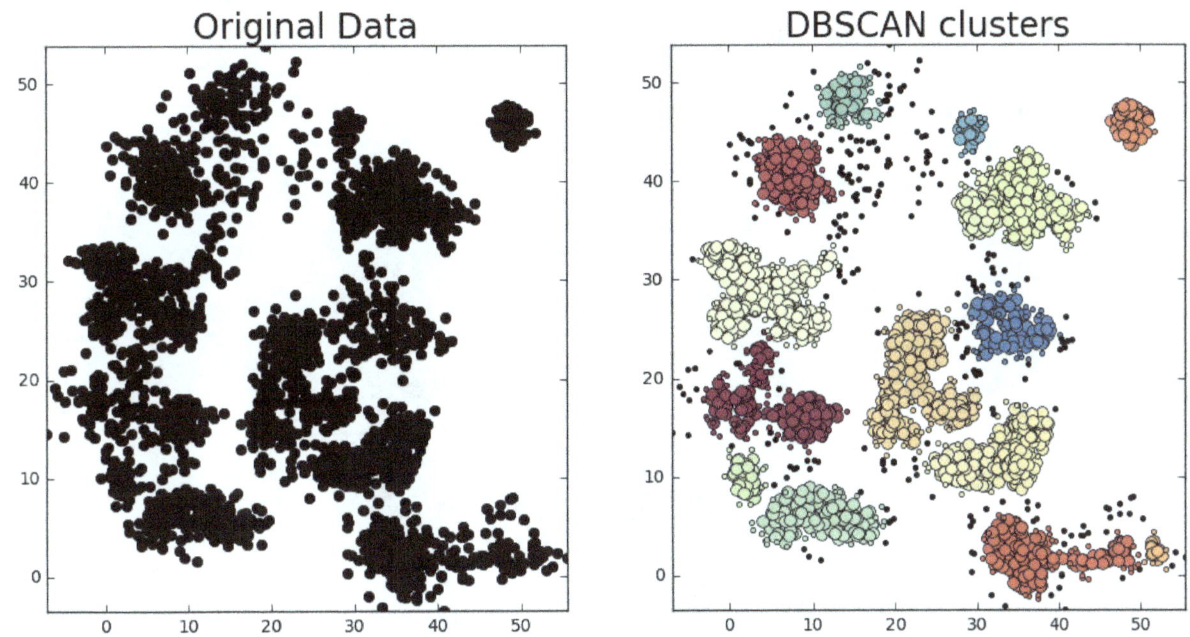

Python

```
from sklearn.cluster import DBSCAN

dbscan = DBSCAN(eps=0.5, min_samples=5)
labels = dbscan.fit_predict(X)  # -1 for noise

print(f"Number of clusters: {len(set(labels)) - (1 if -1 in labels else 0)}")
plt.scatter(X[:, 0], X[:, 1], c=labels, cmap='viridis')
plt.title('DBSCAN Clustering')
plt.show()
```

Dimensionality Reduction: Compressing Data
High-dimensional data suffers from the "curse of dimensionality" (sparsity, overfitting). Reduction projects to lower dimensions while retaining variance/structure.

1. **Principal Component Analysis (PCA)** Linear technique: Finds orthogonal principal components (directions of maximum variance). Projects data onto top k components (eigenvectors of covariance matrix). Pros: Fast, deterministic; decorrelates features. Cons: Linear only; assumes Gaussian data. In AI: Preprocessing (speed up models), visualization (2D/3D plots).

Visual explanation of PCA projection:

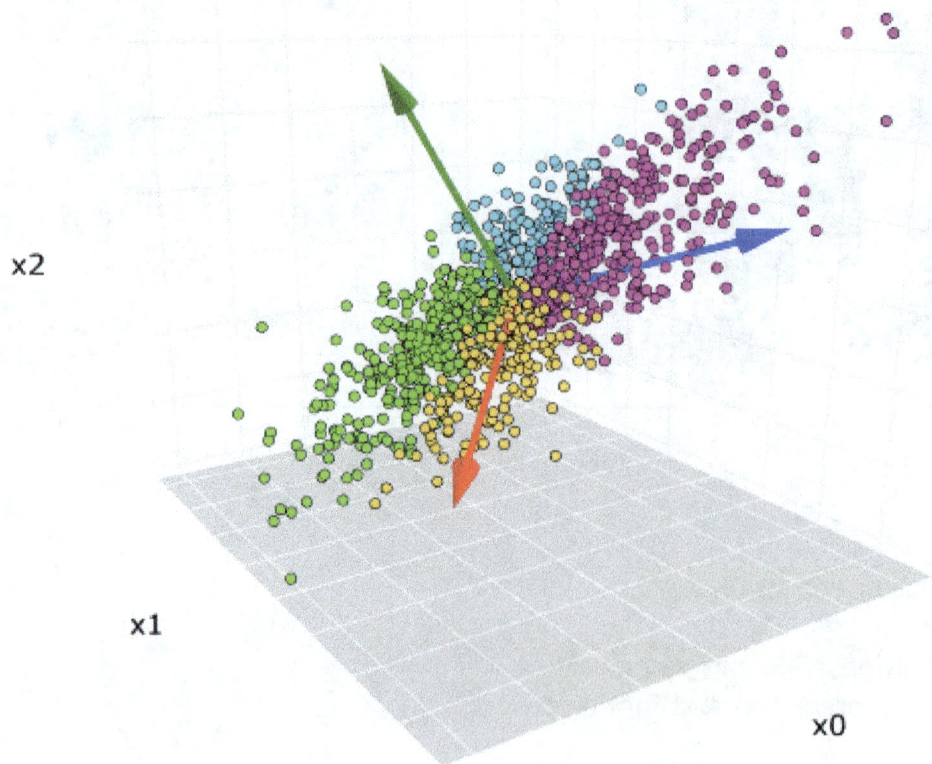

Principal Component Analysis

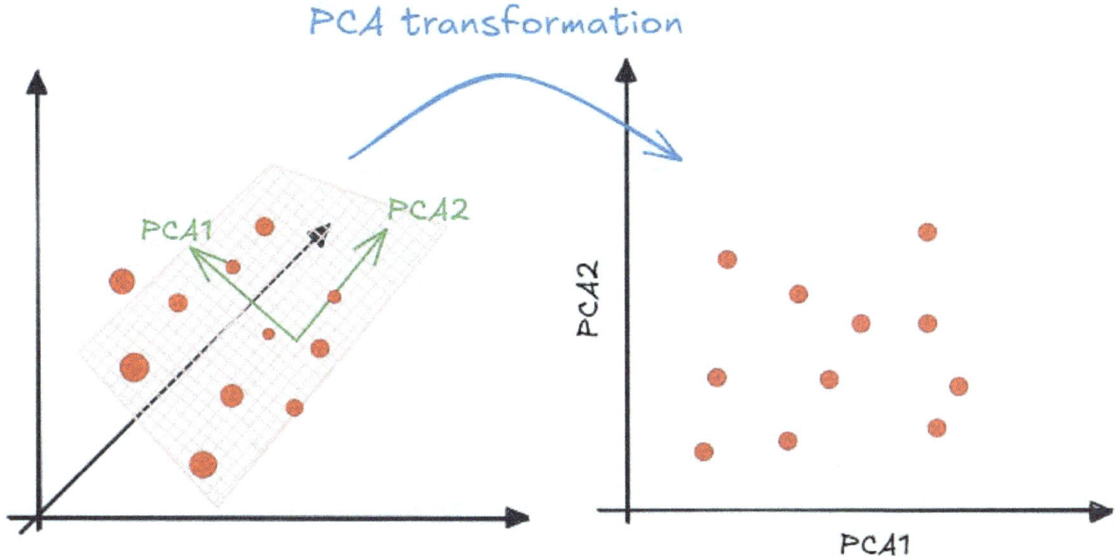

Principal Component

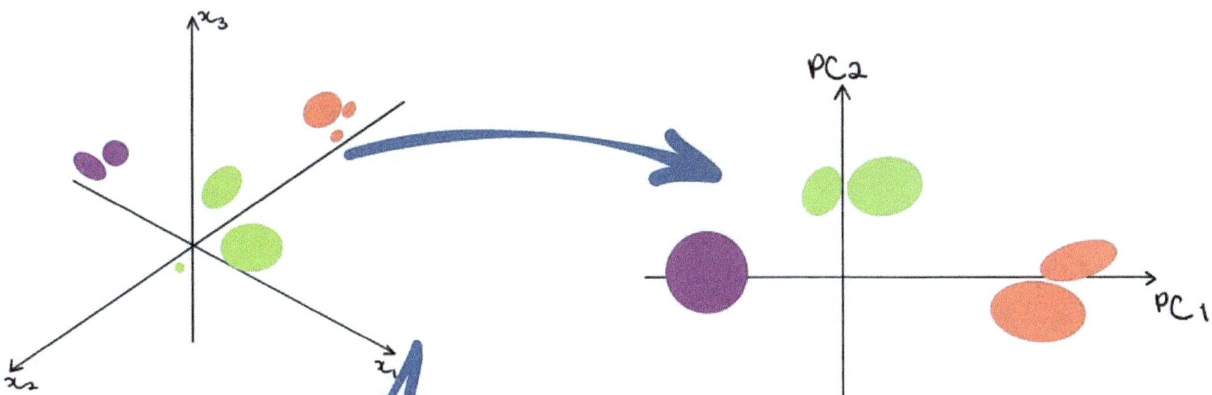

Analysis

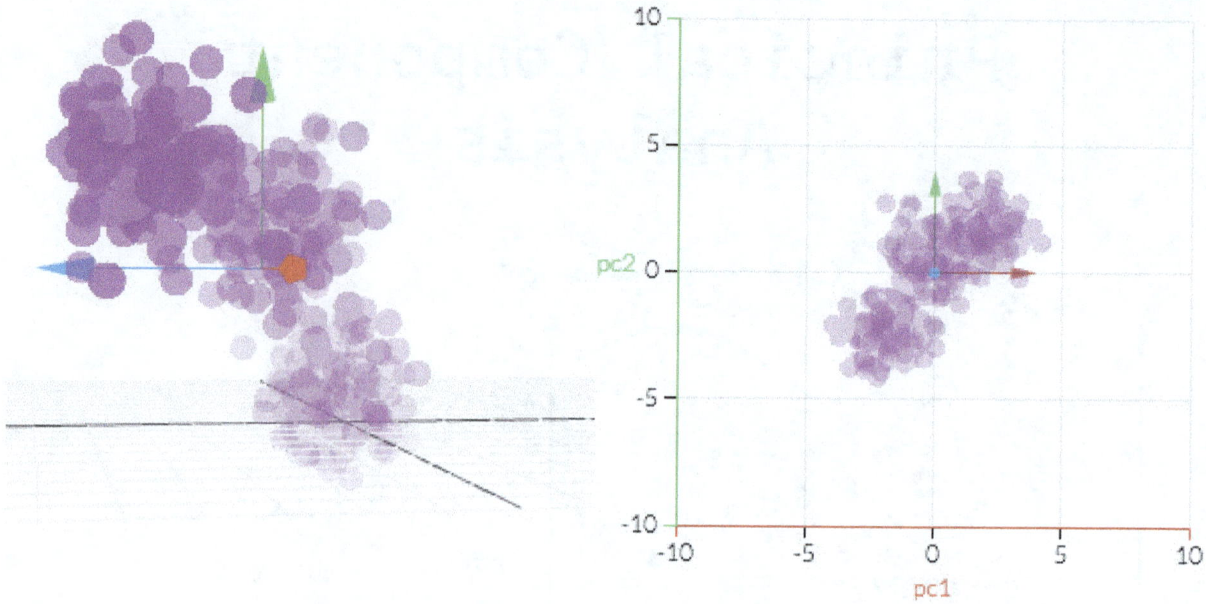

Python

```
from sklearn.datasets import load_iris
from sklearn.decomposition import PCA
from sklearn.preprocessing import StandardScaler

iris = load_iris()
X = iris.data

# Standardize (important for PCA)
X_scaled = StandardScaler().fit_transform(X)

pca = PCA(n_components=2)
X_pca = pca.fit_transform(X_scaled)

print(f"Explained variance ratio: {pca.explained_variance_ratio_}")

plt.scatter(X_pca[:, 0], X_pca[:, 1], c=iris.target, cmap='viridis')
plt.xlabel(f'PC1 ({pca.explained_variance_ratio_[0]:.2%} variance)')
plt.ylabel(f'PC2 ({pca.explained_variance_ratio_[1]:.2%} variance)')
plt.title('PCA on Iris Dataset')
plt.show()
```

2. **t-SNE (t-Distributed Stochastic Neighbor Embedding)** Non-linear: Preserves local structure (nearby points stay nearby in low-D). Uses probabilities based on similarity; minimizes KL divergence. Pros: Excellent for visualization (2D/3D manifolds). Cons: Slow; not for new data; perplexity parameter. In AI: Visualizing embeddings (word vectors, CNN features).

High-dimensional data projected to 2D with t-SNE:

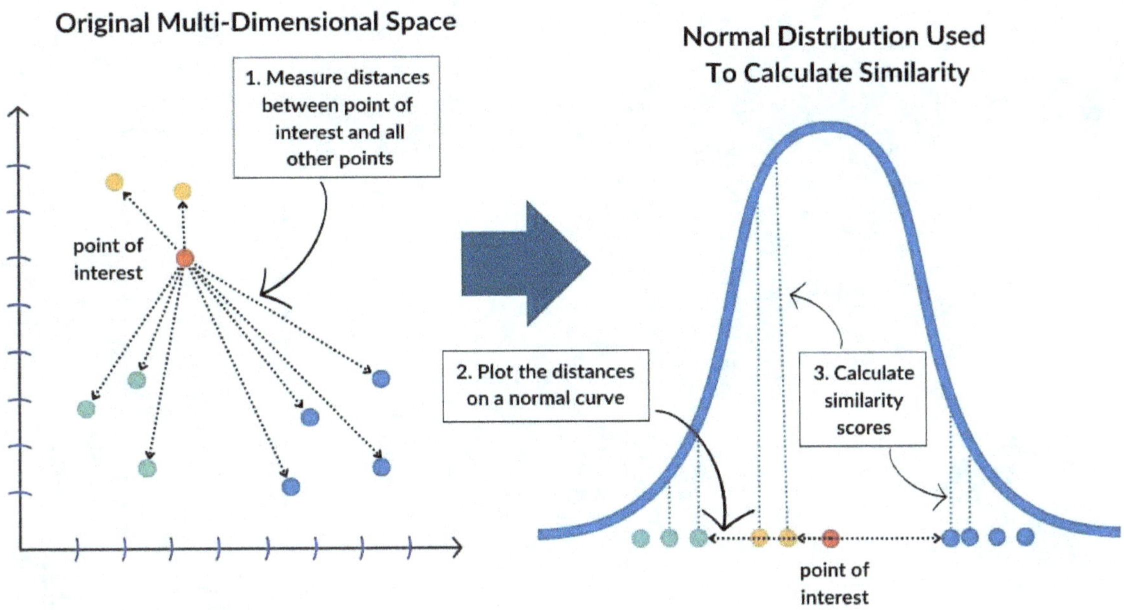

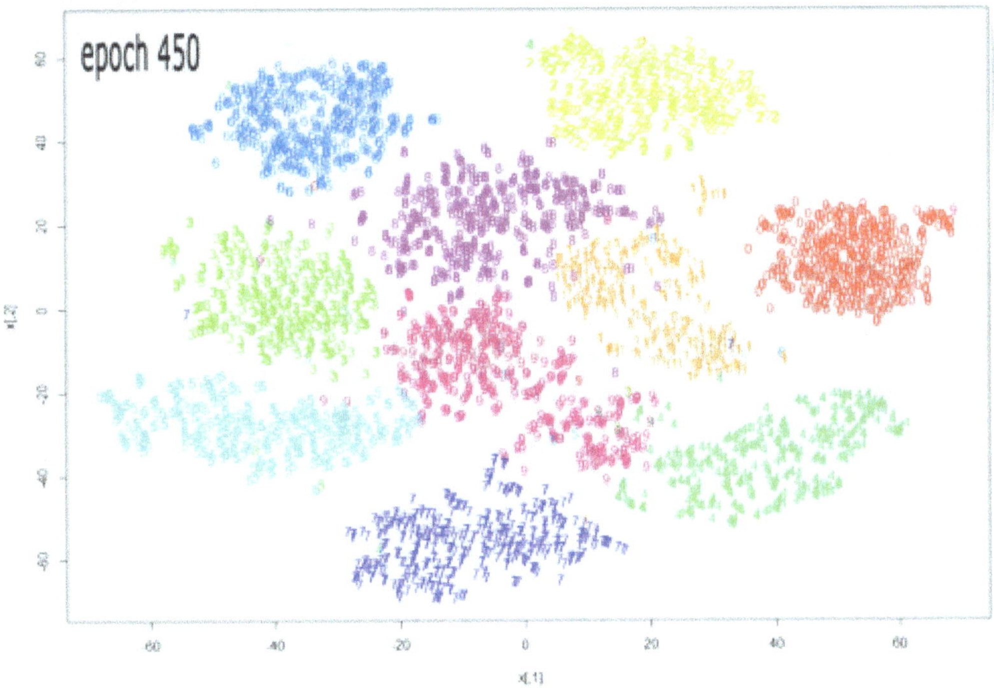

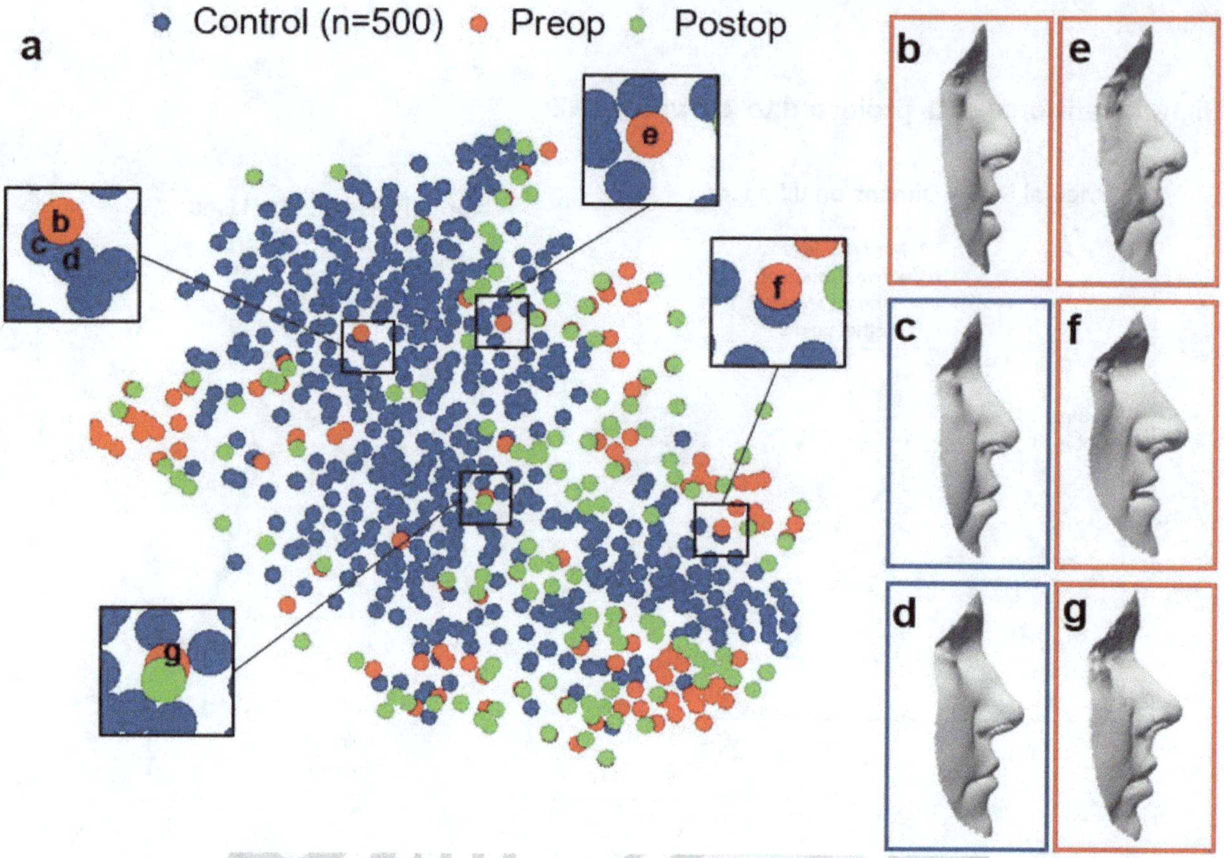

Python

```
from sklearn.manifold import TSNE

tsne = TSNE(n_components=2, perplexity=30, random_state=42)
X_tsne = tsne.fit_transform(X_scaled)

plt.scatter(X_tsne[:, 0], X_tsne[:, 1], c=iris.target, cmap='viridis')
plt.title('t-SNE on Iris Dataset')
plt.show()
```

3. Reinforcement Learning (Markov Decision Process)

Reinforcement Learning (RL) is a paradigm in machine learning where an **agent** learns to make decisions by interacting with an **environment** to maximize cumulative **rewards**. Unlike supervised learning (labeled data) or unsupervised (patterns in unlabeled data), RL focuses on trial-and-error learning through feedback (rewards/penalties). It's inspired by behavioral psychology and used in robotics, game AI (e.g., AlphaGo), recommendation systems, and autonomous driving.

At the core of RL is the **Markov Decision Process (MDP)**, a mathematical framework modeling sequential decision-making under uncertainty. MDPs assume the **Markov property**: The future state depends only on the current state and action, not past history.

Markov Decision Process (MDP) Components

An MDP is defined by a tuple $(S|A|P|R|\gamma)$:

- **S**: Set of states (environment configurations, e.g., grid positions in a maze).
- **A**: Set of actions (choices agent can make, e.g., up, down, left, right).
- **P(s'|s, a)**: Transition probability — probability of reaching state s' from s after action a (models uncertainty).
- **R(s, a, s')**: Reward function — scalar feedback for transitioning from s to s' via a (positive for good, negative for bad, zero otherwise).
- **γ**: Discount factor ($0 \leq \gamma < 1$) — discounts future rewards to prioritize immediate ones (handles infinite horizons).

The agent's goal: Find a **policy** π(s) — a mapping from states to actions (or probabilities) — that maximizes expected cumulative discounted reward:

$$G_t = R_{t+1} + \gamma R_{t+2} + \gamma^2 R_{t+3} + \dots$$

MDP diagrams illustrating states, actions, transitions, and rewards:

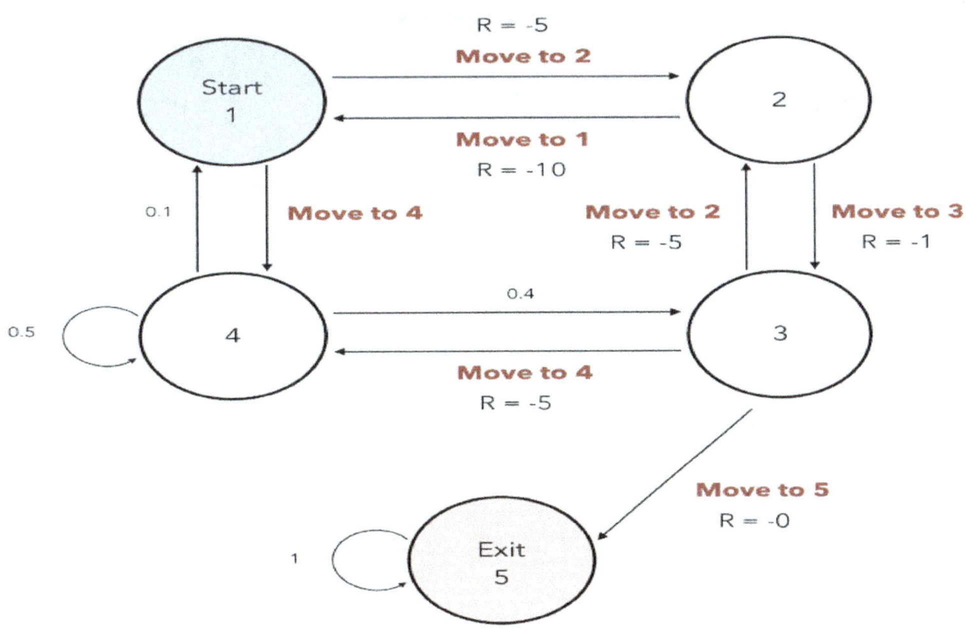

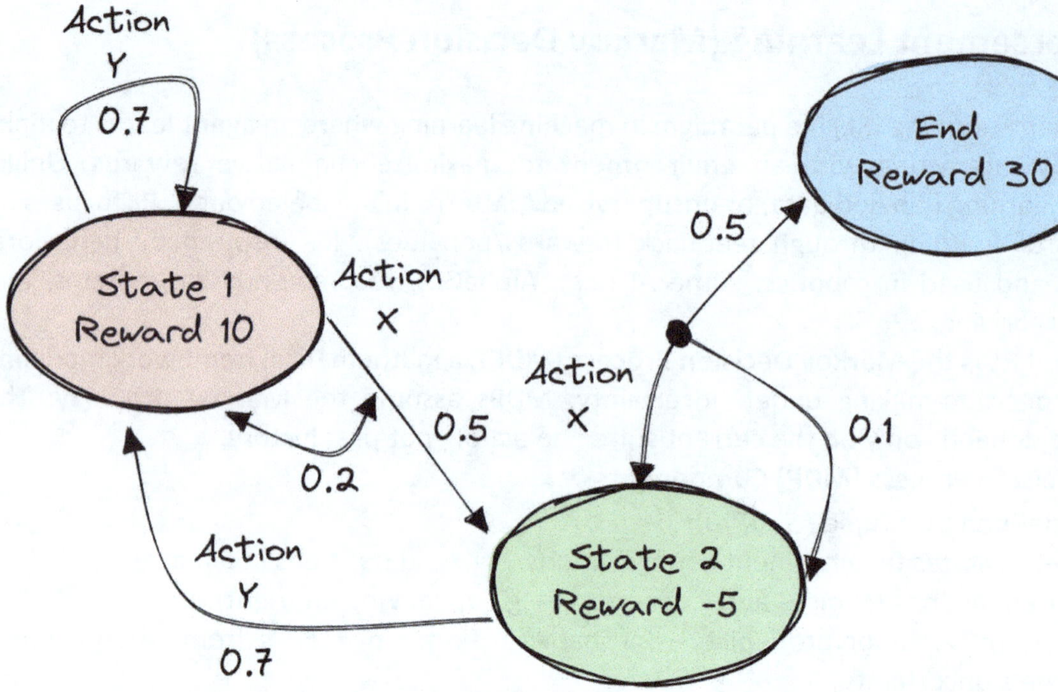
Action
Y
0.7
State 1
Reward 10
Action
X
0.2
0.5
End
Reward 30
0.5
Action
X
0.1
State 2
Reward -5
Action
Y
0.7

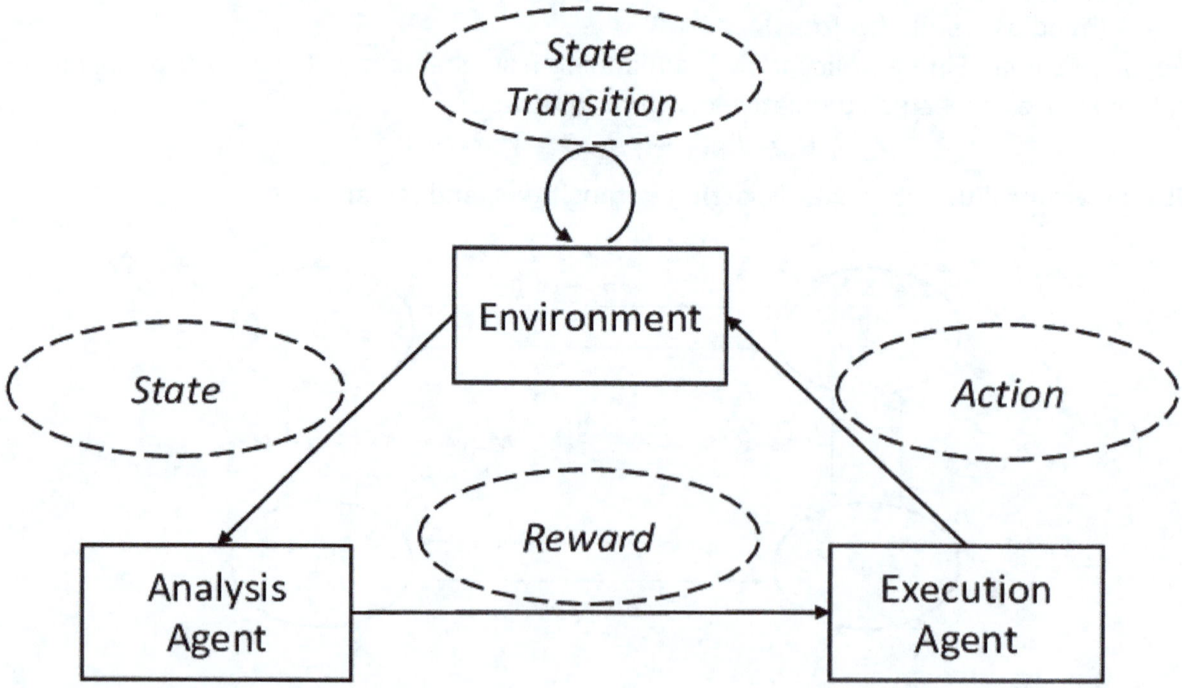
State
Transition
Environment
State
Action
Reward
Analysis
Agent
Execution
Agent

The RL Framework

In RL, the agent-environment interaction forms a loop:

1. Agent observes state s_t.
2. Selects action a_t based on policy π.
3. Environment responds with next state s_{t+1} and reward r_{t+1}.
4. Agent updates its knowledge (e.g., value estimates) and repeats.

This is episodic (tasks with terminals, e.g., games) or continuing (ongoing).

Visuals of the agent-environment loop:

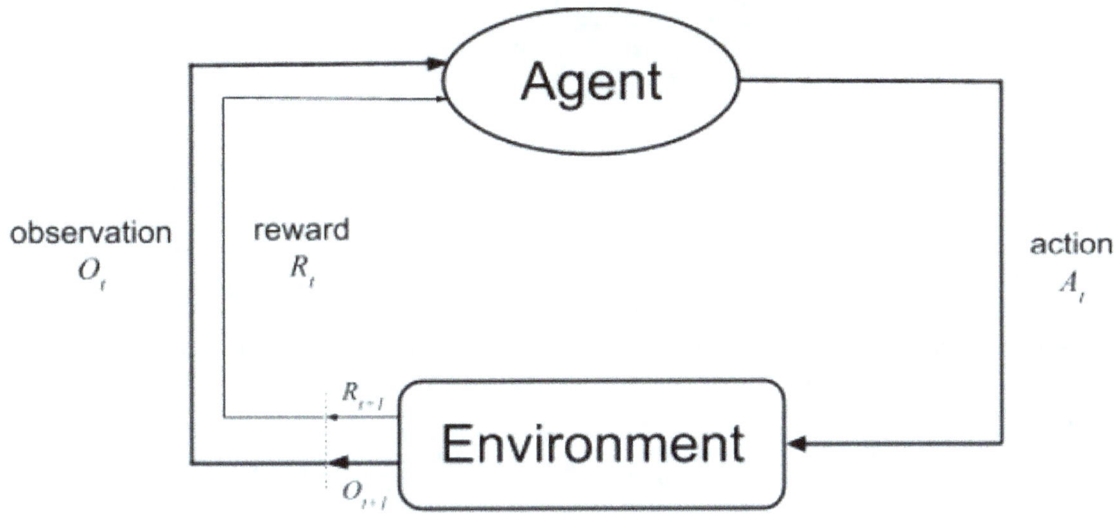

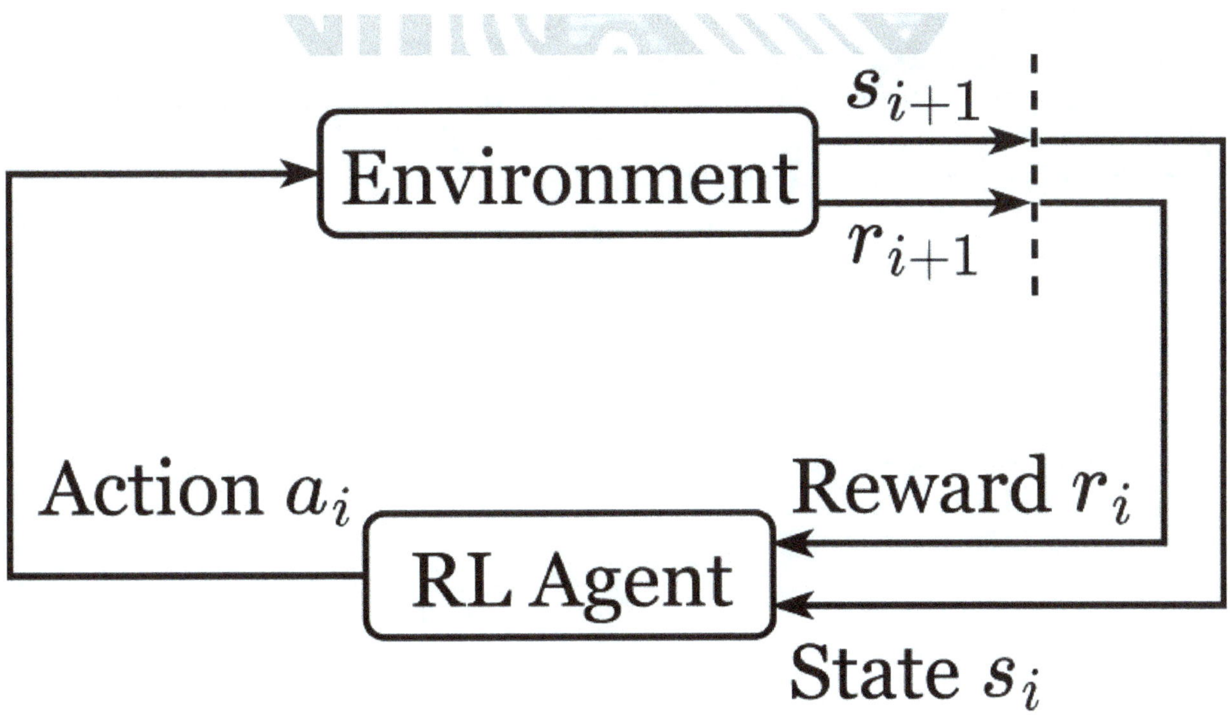

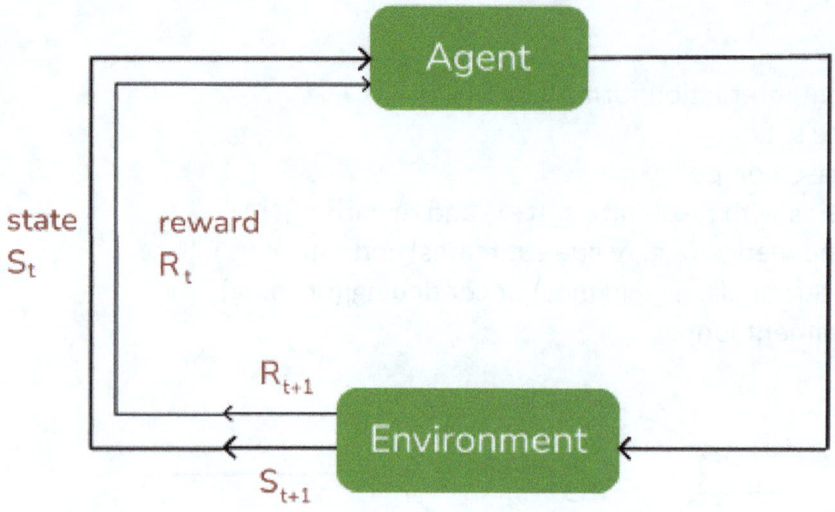

Key concepts:

- **Exploration vs. Exploitation**: Balance trying new actions (explore) vs. known good ones (exploit). Methods: ε-greedy (random action with prob ε).
- **Value Functions**: Estimate expected return.
    - State-value: $v_\pi(s) = E[G_t|S_t = s]$— value of state under policy π.
    - Action-value (Q-function): $q_\pi(s,a) = E[G_t|S_t = s, A_t = a]$— value of action in state under π.
- **Optimal Policy**: π* maximizes v(s) or q(s,a) for all s,a.

Bellman Equations: The Heart of MDPs

Bellman equations express value functions recursively, enabling dynamic programming solutions.

- Bellman Expectation Equation (for policy π):

$$v_\pi(s) = \sum_a \pi(a|s) \sum_{s',r} p(s',r|s,a)[r + \gamma v_\pi(s')]$$

- Bellman Optimality Equation:

$$v^*(s) = \max_a \sum_{s',r} p(s',r|s,a)[r + \gamma v^*(s')]$$

(Optimal value is max over actions.)

Similar for Q-functions.

Illustrations of Bellman equations:

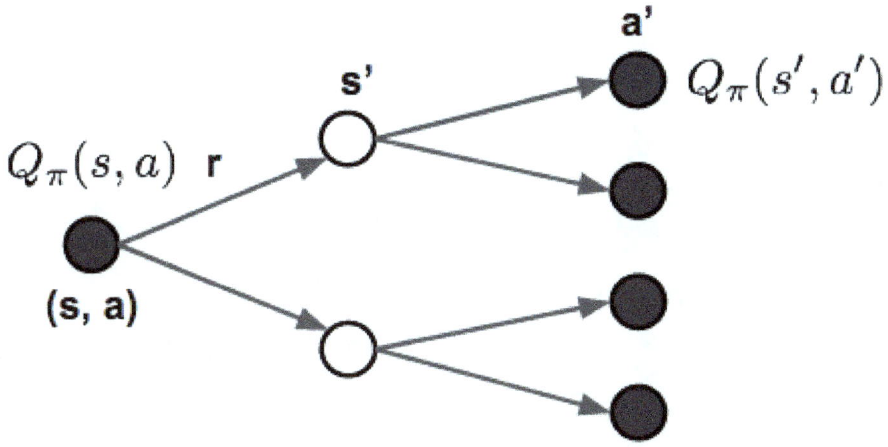

Solving MDPs:

- If model known (P and R): Use **Value Iteration** (iteratively apply Bellman optimality until convergence) or **Policy Iteration** (evaluate policy, then improve it).
- If model unknown: Use model-free RL like Q-learning.

Visuals of value functions and policies in gridworld MDPs:

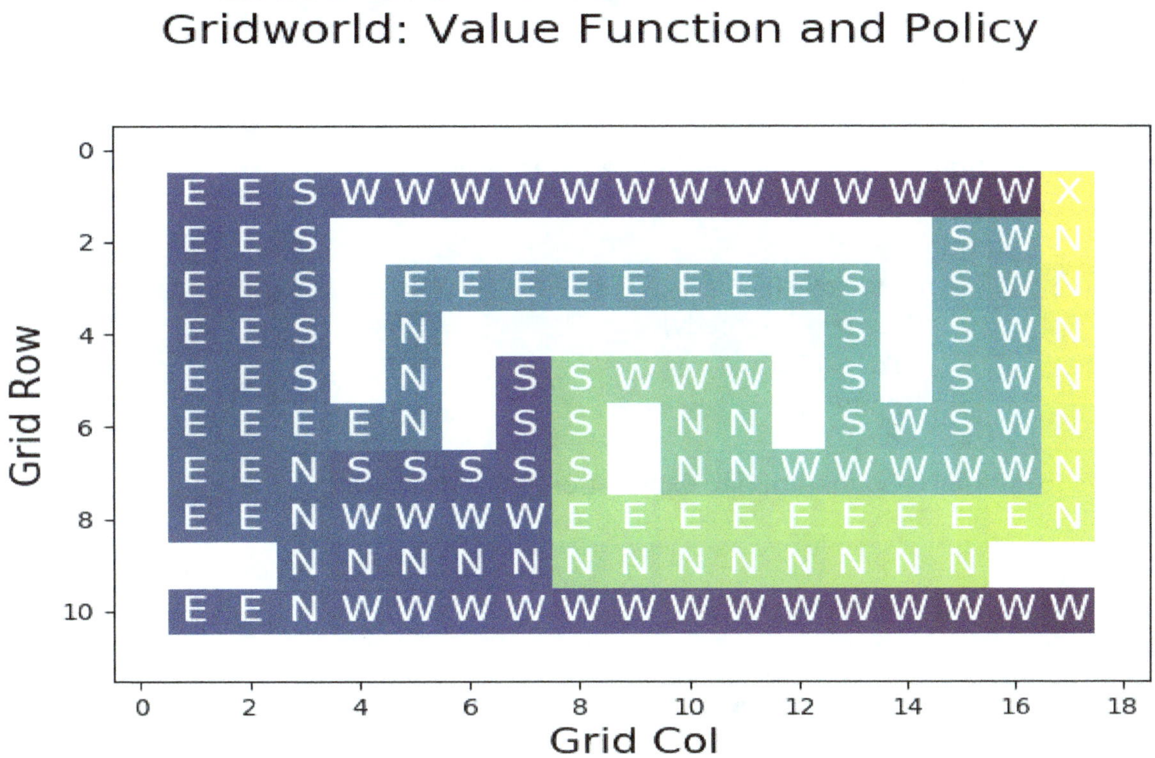

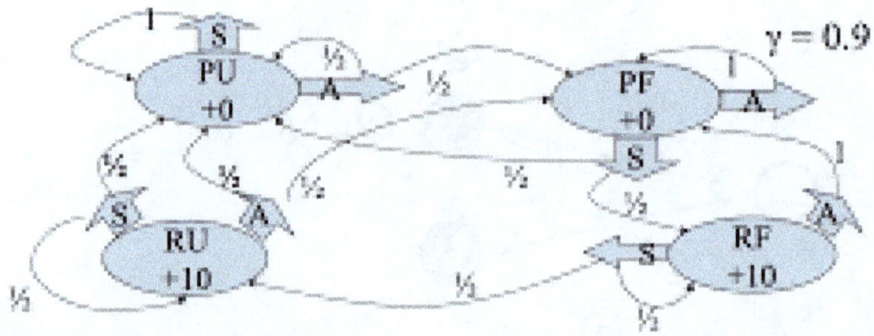

n	$V(PU)$	$\pi(PU)$	$V(PF)$	$\pi(PF)$	$V(RU)$	$\pi(RU)$	$V(RF)$	$\pi(RF)$
0	0	A	0	A	10	A	10	A
1	31.6	A	38.6	S	44.0	S	54.2	S
2	31.6	A	38.6	S	44.0	S	54.2	S

Key RL Algorithms: Focus on Q-Learning

Q-Learning is a model-free, off-policy temporal difference (TD) algorithm. It learns Q(s,a) directly.

Update rule:

$$Q(s_t,a_t) \leftarrow Q(s_t,a_t) + \alpha[r_{t+1} + \gamma \max_a Q(s_{t+1},a) - Q(s_t,a_t)]$$

- α: Learning rate.
- Bootstraps from future Q estimates.

Algorithm:

1. Initialize Q-table (states x actions) to zeros/arbitrary.
2. For each episode:
    - Start in s.
    - While not terminal:
        - Choose a (ε-greedy).
        - Take a, observe r, s'.
        - Update Q.
        - s ← s'.

Converges to optimal Q* under infinite exploration.

Flowcharts of Q-learning:

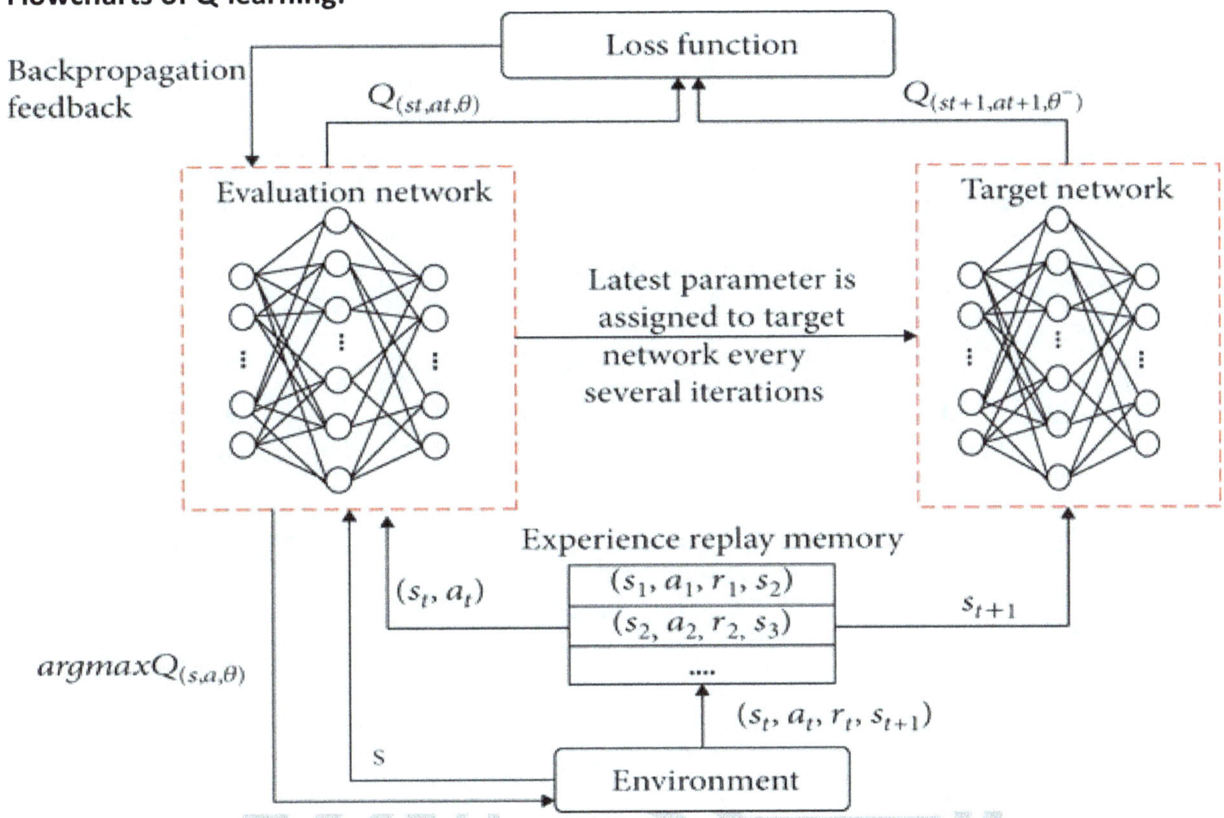

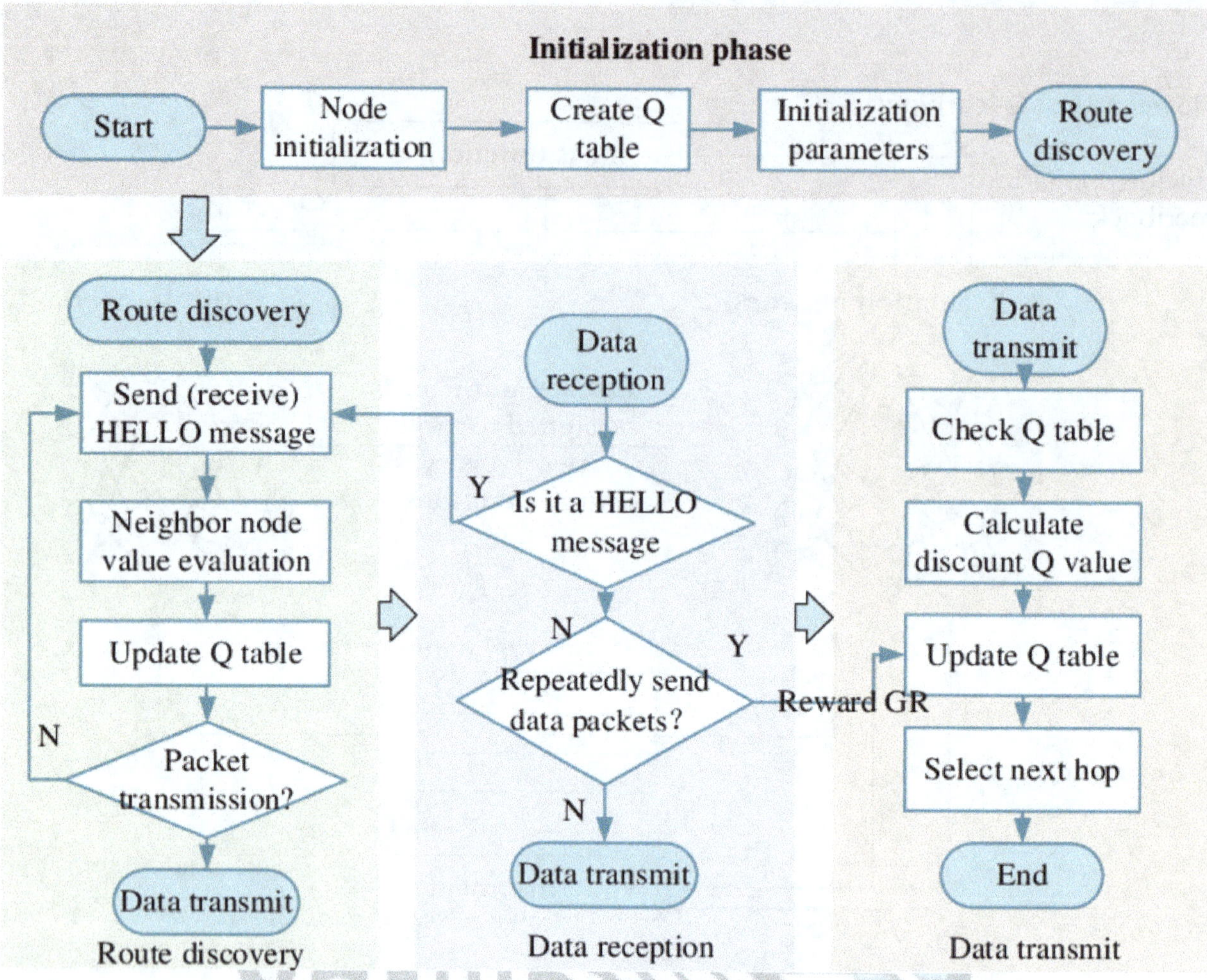

Python Code Example: Q-Learning on a simple Frozen Lake environment (from Gymnasium). Agent learns to navigate a frozen lake to reach the goal without falling in holes.
Python

```
import gymnasium as gym
import numpy as np

# Environment: Frozen Lake (4x4 grid, slippery)
env = gym.make('FrozenLake-v1', is_slippery=False)
n_states = env.observation_space.n
n_actions = env.action_space.n

# Initialize Q-table
Q = np.zeros((n_states, n_actions))

# Hyperparameters
alpha = 0.1  # Learning rate
gamma = 0.99  # Discount
epsilon = 1.0  # Exploration
epsilon_decay = 0.995
```

```python
episodes = 1000

rewards = []

for episode in range(episodes):
   state, _ = env.reset()
   total_reward = 0
   done = False

   while not done:
      # ε-greedy action
      if np.random.rand() < epsilon:
         action = env.action_space.sample()
      else:
         action = np.argmax(Q[state])

      next_state, reward, done, _, _ = env.step(action)
      total_reward += reward

      # Q-update
      Q[state, action] += alpha * (reward + gamma * np.max(Q[next_state]) - Q[state, action])

      state = next_state

   epsilon = max(0.1, epsilon * epsilon_decay)  # Decay
   rewards.append(total_reward)

# Print learned Q-table (partial)
print("Learned Q-table (first 5 states):")
print(Q[:5])

# Test policy
state, _ = env.reset()
done = False
while not done:
   action = np.argmax(Q[state])
   state, reward, done, _, _ = env.step(action)
   print(f"Action: {action}, Reward: {reward}")

# Plot training rewards
import matplotlib.pyplot as plt
plt.plot(rewards)
plt.xlabel('Episodes')
plt.ylabel('Total Reward')
plt.title('Q-Learning Training')
plt.show()
```

This code trains the agent; rewards approach 1.0 (success). For large state spaces, use deep RL (DQN) with neural nets approximating Q.

4. Model Evaluation (Confusion Matrix, Precision, Recall, F1-score)

Evaluating classification models goes beyond simple **accuracy** (correct predictions / total), which can mislead in **imbalanced datasets** (e.g., 99% negative class → 99% accuracy by always predicting negative). Key tools like the **confusion matrix** and derived metrics (**precision**, **recall**, **F1-score**) provide deeper insights, especially for binary classification (extendable to multi-class).

These metrics suit tasks like medical diagnosis (high recall for positives), spam detection (high precision), or fraud (balanced F1).

Confusion Matrix

The confusion matrix is a table summarizing prediction results against true labels.

For binary classification (Positive/Negative):

	Predicted Positive	**Predicted Negative**
Actual Positive	True Positive (TP)	False Negative (FN)
Actual Negative	False Positive (FP)	True Negative (TN)

- **TP**: Correctly predicted positives (e.g., diseased and detected).
- **FN**: Missed positives (Type II error — dangerous in medicine).
- **FP**: False alarms (Type I error — costly in spam).
- **TN**: Correctly predicted negatives.

Visual representations of confusion matrices:

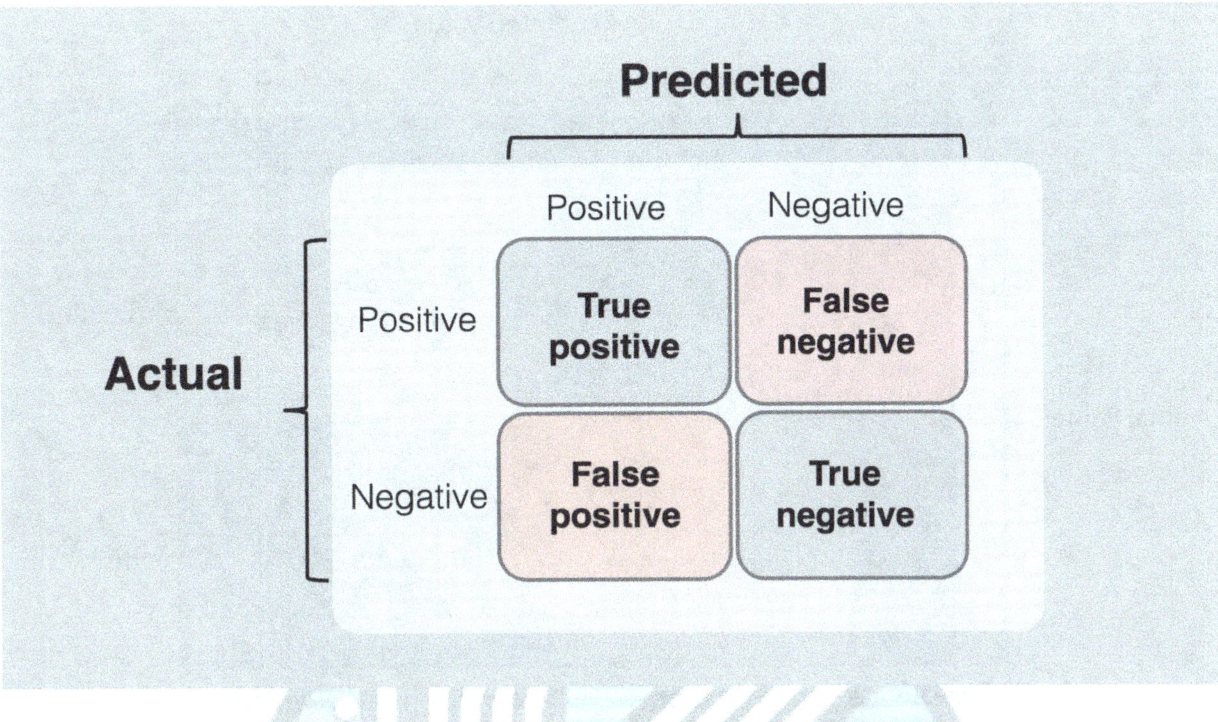

Predicted Class

Actual Class		Positive	Negative	
	Positive	True Positive (TP)	False Negative (FN) **Type II Error**	**Sensitivity** $\frac{TP}{(TP + FN)}$
	Negative	False Positive (FP) **Type I Error**	True Negative (TN)	**Specificity** $\frac{TN}{(TN + FP)}$
		Precision $\frac{TP}{(TP + FP)}$	**Negative Predictive Value** $\frac{TN}{(TN + FN)}$	**Accuracy** $\frac{TP + TN}{(TP + TN + FP + FN)}$

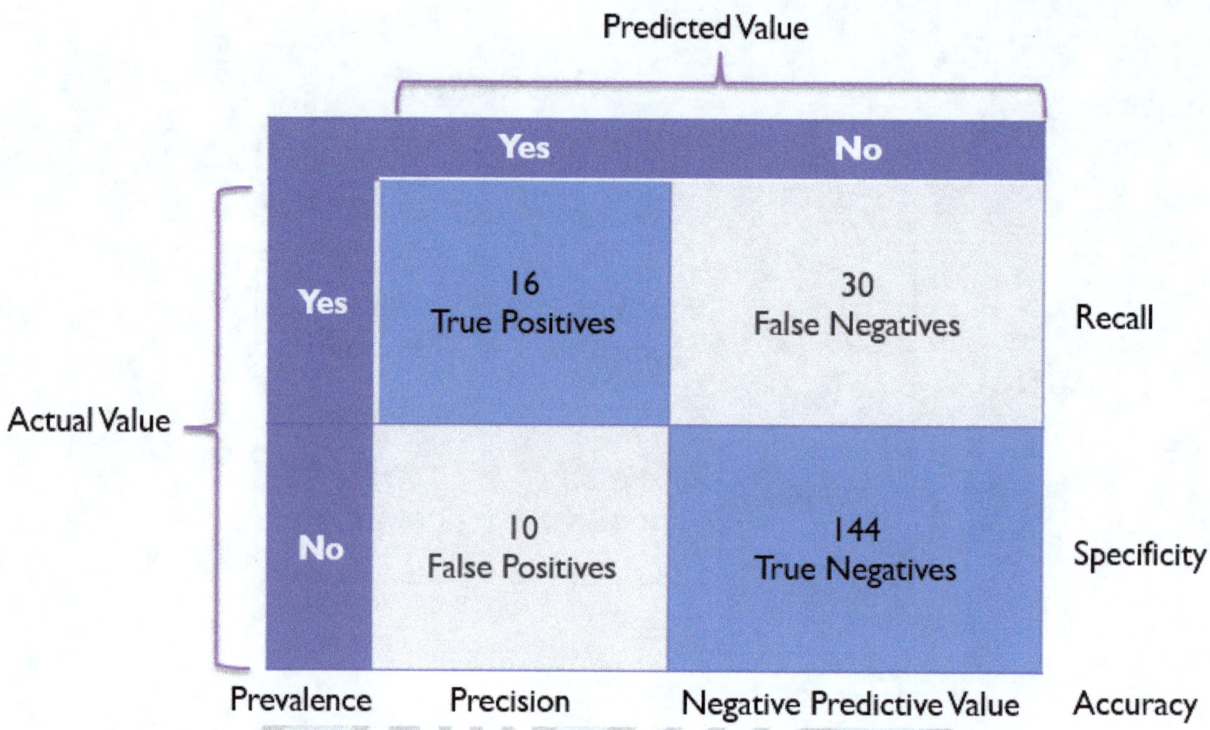

Predicted Value
Yes
No
Actual Value
Yes
16
True Positives
30
False Negatives
Recall
No
10
False Positives
144
True Negatives
Specificity
Prevalence
Precision
Negative Predictive Value
Accuracy

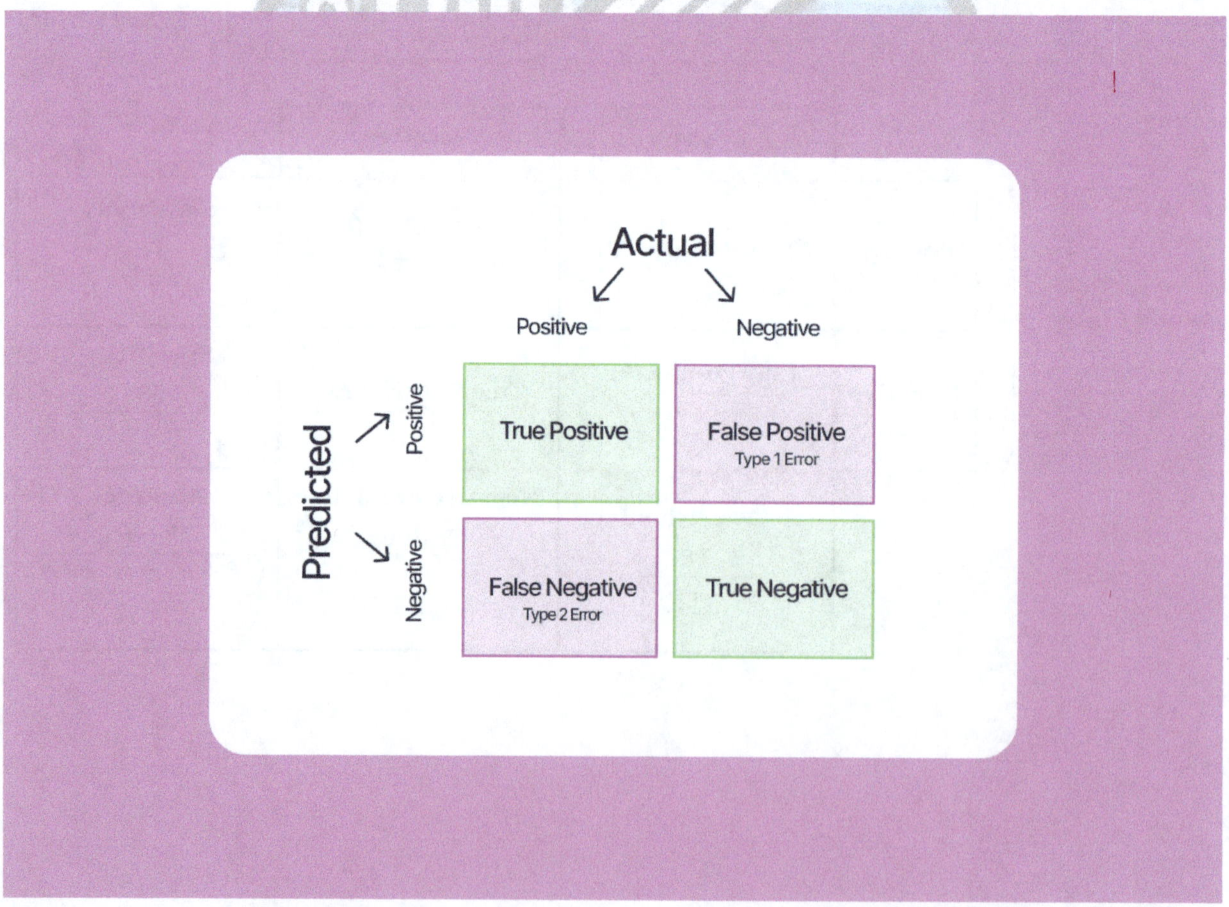

Actual
Positive
Negative
Predicted
Positive
Negative
True Positive
False Positive
Type 1 Error
False Negative
Type 2 Error
True Negative

Precision (Positive Predictive Value)

Precision measures how many predicted positives are actually positive — focuses on minimizing false alarms.

$$\text{Precision} = \frac{TP}{TP + FP}$$

- High precision: Trustworthy positive predictions (e.g., search engine results).
- Low precision: Many FPs (noisy positives).

Recall (Sensitivity, True Positive Rate)

Recall measures how many actual positives are correctly identified — focuses on capturing all positives.

$$\text{Recall} = \frac{TP}{TP + FN}$$

- High recall: Few missed positives (e.g., cancer screening).
- Low recall: Many FNs (missed cases).

Precision-Recall Tradeoff

Increasing the classification threshold (more confident for positive) raises precision but lowers recall, and vice versa. Models output probabilities; thresholds tune this balance.

Precision-Recall curves plot this tradeoff:

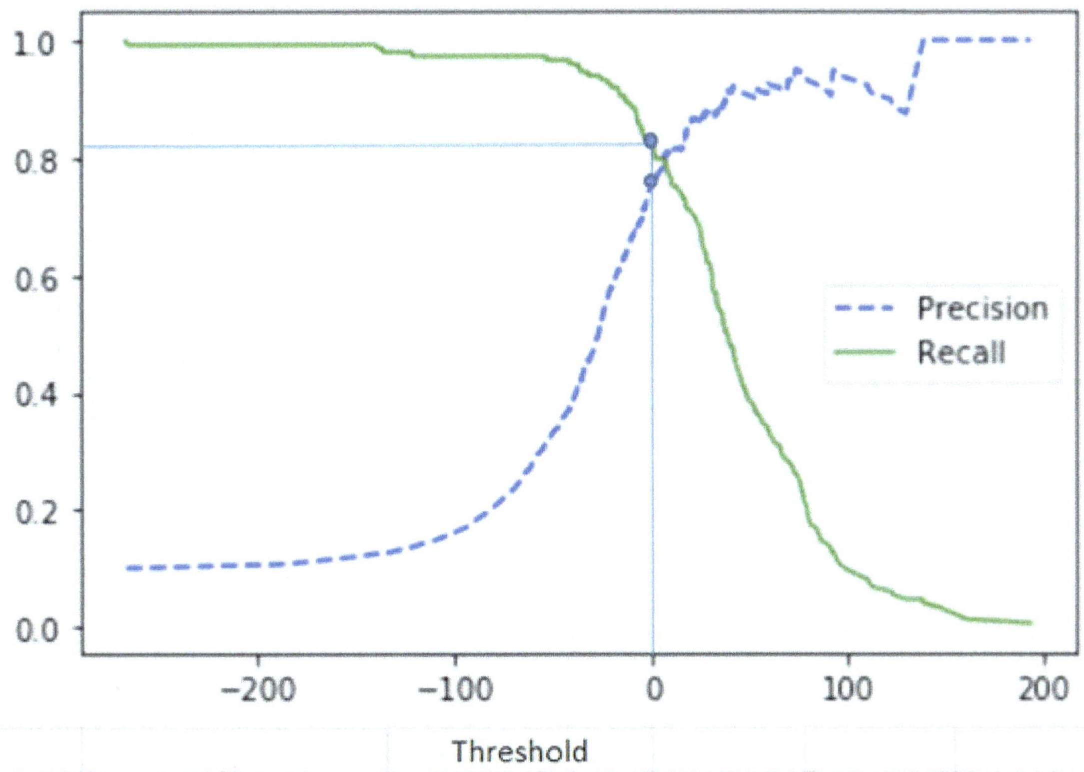

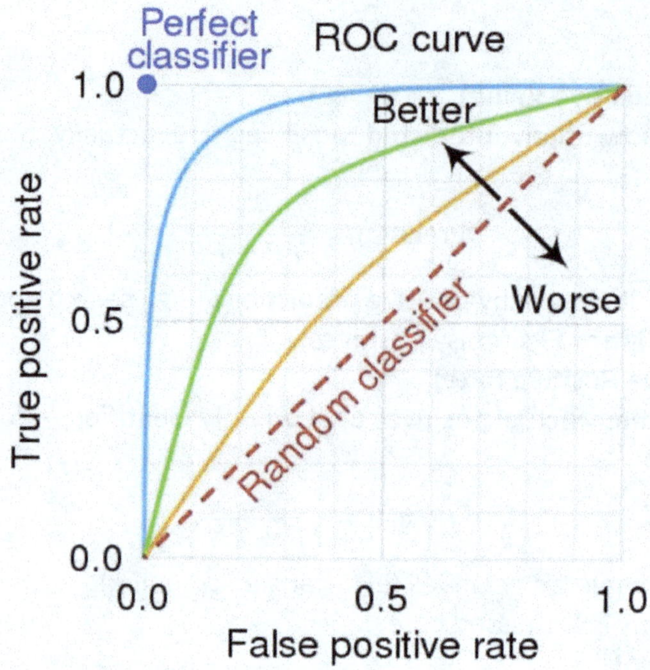

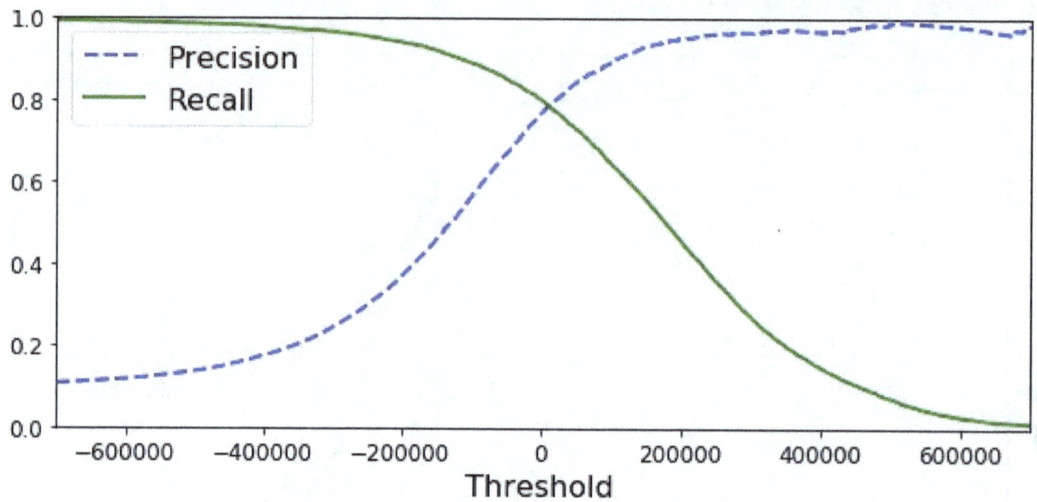

F1-Score

The F1-score is the **harmonic mean** of precision and recall, balancing both (punishes extremes more than arithmetic mean).

$$F1 = 2 \times \frac{\text{Precision} \times \text{Recall}}{\text{Precision} + \text{Recall}}$$

- Maximum 1 (perfect); low if either is low.
- Ideal for imbalanced data or when both false positives and negatives matter equally.

Harmonic mean visualizations (F1 as balance):

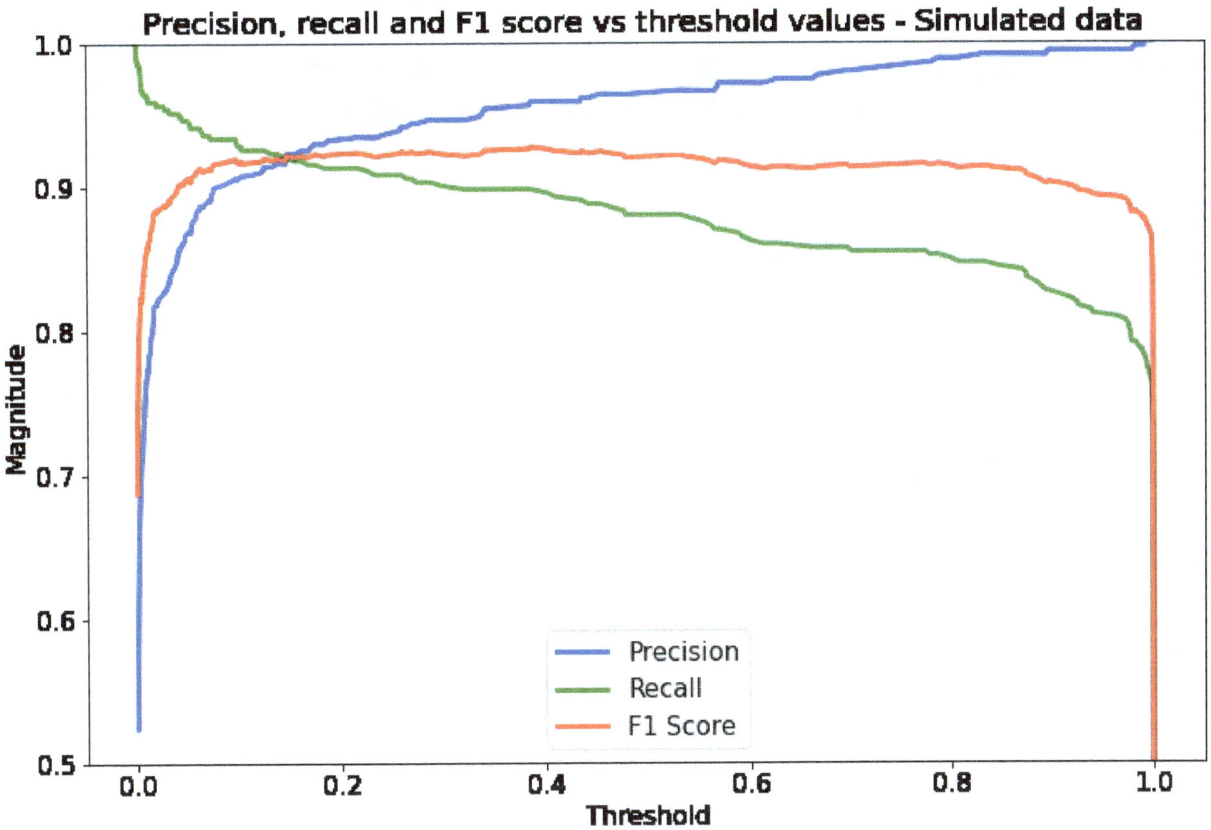

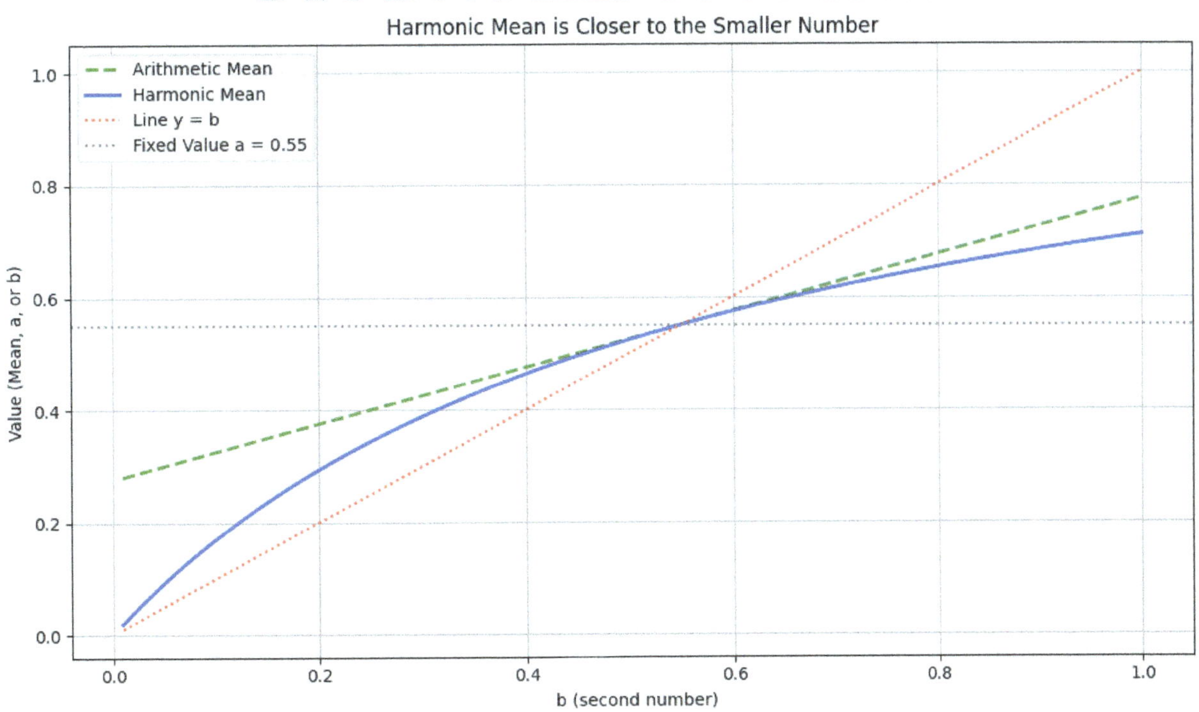

Related: ROC Curve and AUC

The ROC curve plots True Positive Rate (Recall) vs. False Positive Rate ($\frac{FP}{FP+TN}$) across thresholds. **AUC** (Area Under Curve) measures overall performance (1 = perfect, 0.5 = random).

ROC/AUC diagrams:

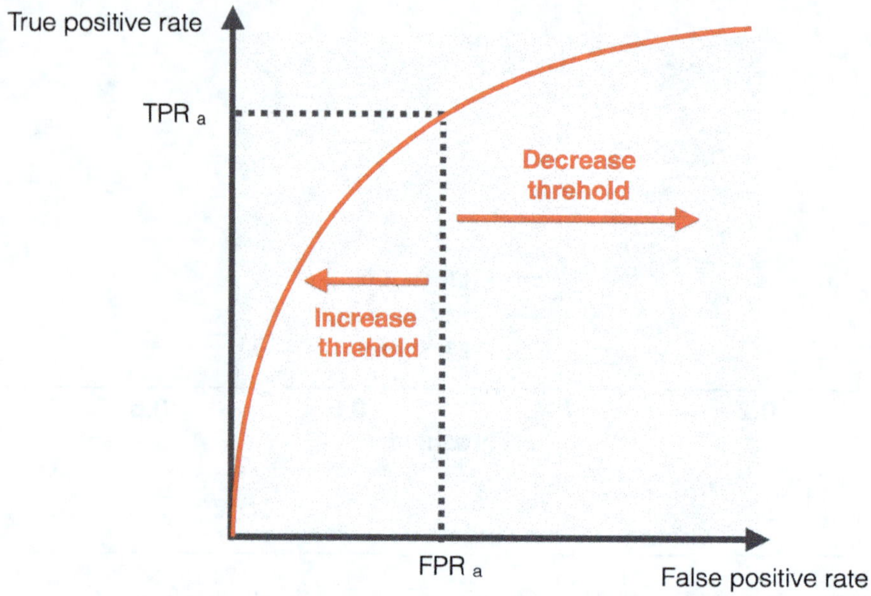

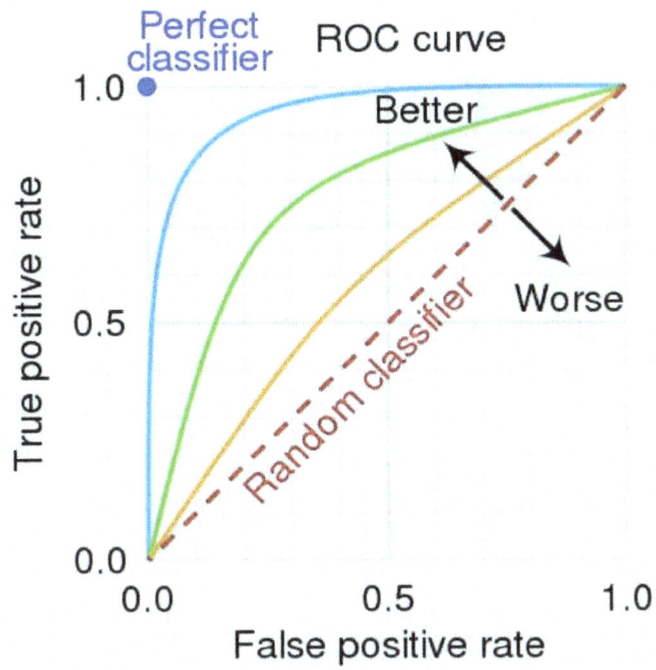

Use PR curves for highly imbalanced data; ROC otherwise.

Python Code Example (scikit-learn)

```
import numpy as np
import matplotlib.pyplot as plt
from sklearn.datasets import make_classification
from sklearn.model_selection import train_test_split
from sklearn.linear_model import LogisticRegression
from sklearn.metrics import confusion_matrix, precision_score, recall_score, f1_score, classification_report, roc_curve, auc

# Generate imbalanced binary data
X, y = make_classification(n_samples=1000, n_classes=2, weights=[0.9, 0.1], random_state=42)
X_train, X_test, y_train, y_test = train_test_split(X, y, test_size=0.3, random_state=42)

# Train model
model = LogisticRegression()
model.fit(X_train, y_train)
y_pred = model.predict(X_test)
y_prob = model.predict_proba(X_test)[:, 1]  # Probabilities for positive class

# Confusion Matrix
cm = confusion_matrix(y_test, y_pred)
print("Confusion Matrix:\n", cm)
```

```
# Metrics
print(f"Precision: {precision_score(y_test, y_pred):.2f}")
print(f"Recall: {recall_score(y_test, y_pred):.2f}")
print(f"F1-Score: {f1_score(y_test, y_pred):.2f}")
print("\nFull Report:\n", classification_report(y_test, y_pred))

# ROC Curve & AUC
fpr, tpr, _ = roc_curve(y_test, y_prob)
roc_auc = auc(fpr, tpr)

plt.figure(figsize=(8, 6))
plt.plot(fpr, tpr, label=f'ROC curve (AUC = {roc_auc:.2f})')
plt.plot([0, 1], [0, 1], 'k--')  # Random classifier
plt.xlabel('False Positive Rate')
plt.ylabel('True Positive Rate')
plt.title('ROC Curve')
plt.legend()
plt.show()
```

This code outputs the matrix, metrics, and plots ROC. Use PrecisionRecallDisplay for PR curves.

Section-5

Machine Learning Libraries

- Scikit-learn (ML Models, Feature Scaling, Preprocessing)
- TensorFlow (Deep Learning, Neural Networks)
- Keras (Simplified Deep Learning Framework)
- PyTorch (Deep Learning, NLP, Computer Vision)

Machine Learning Libraries

1. Scikit-learn (ML Models, Feature Scaling, Preprocessing)

Scikit-learn (sklearn) is the most popular open-source Python library for machine learning. It provides simple, efficient tools for data mining, analysis, modeling, and evaluation—built on NumPy, SciPy, and Matplotlib. It's user-friendly, consistent (all estimators follow .fit(), .predict(), .transform()), and production-ready.

Key strengths:

- Wide range of supervised (regression/classification) and unsupervised algorithms.
- Powerful preprocessing and feature engineering tools.
- Pipelines for clean, reproducible workflows.
- Model selection and evaluation utilities.

Famous scikit-learn cheat sheet / estimator map (helps choose the right model):

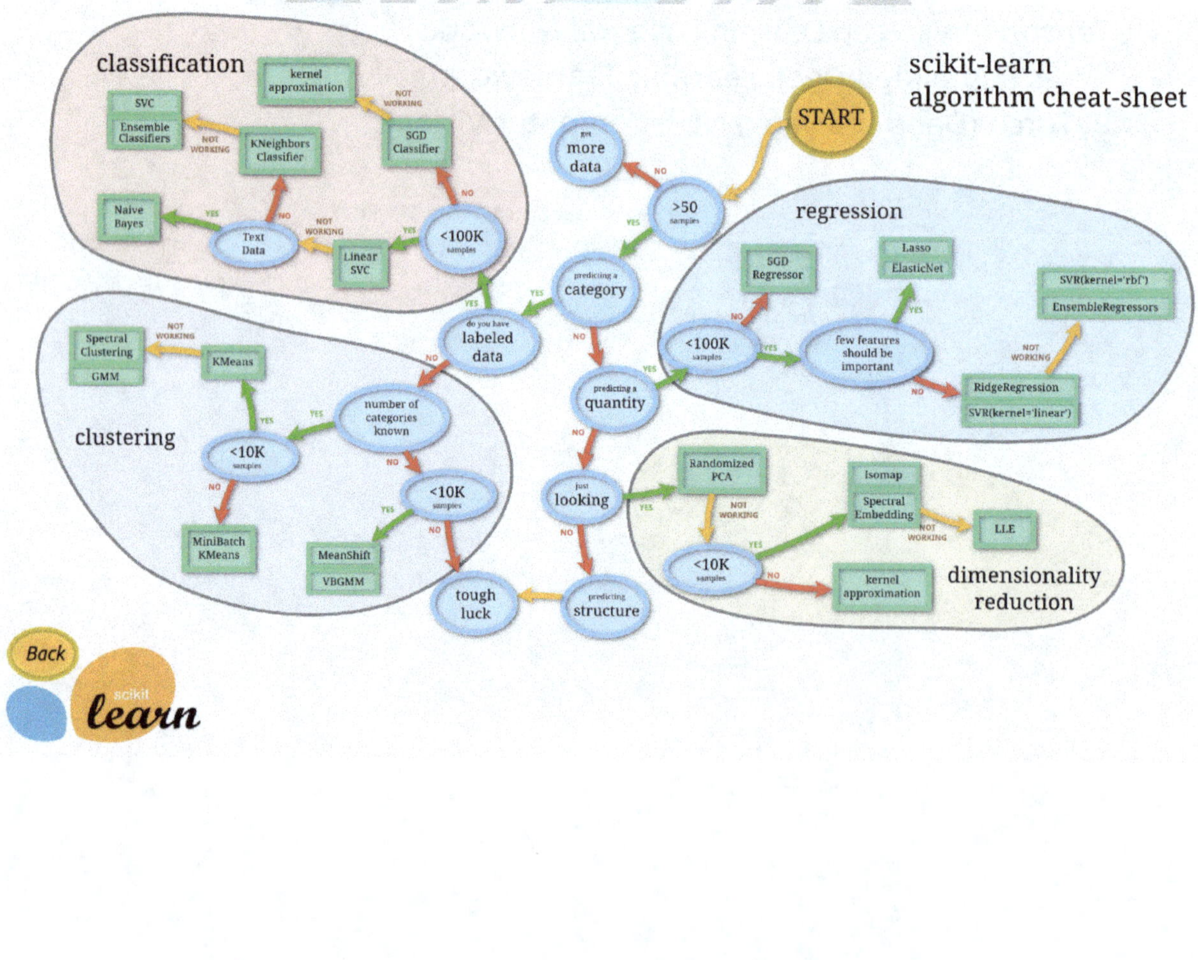

ML Models in Scikit-learn

Scikit-learn organizes models into modules like linear_model, ensemble, svm, tree, neighbors, etc.

Common Workflow:

Python

```
from sklearn import model
from sklearn.model_selection import train_test_split
from sklearn.metrics import accuracy_score  # or mean_squared_error

X_train, X_test, y_train, y_test = train_test_split(X, y, test_size=0.2)
clf = model.SomeClassifier()
clf.fit(X_train, y_train)
y_pred = clf.predict(X_test)
print(accuracy_score(y_test, y_pred))
```

Examples of popular models and decision boundaries comparison:

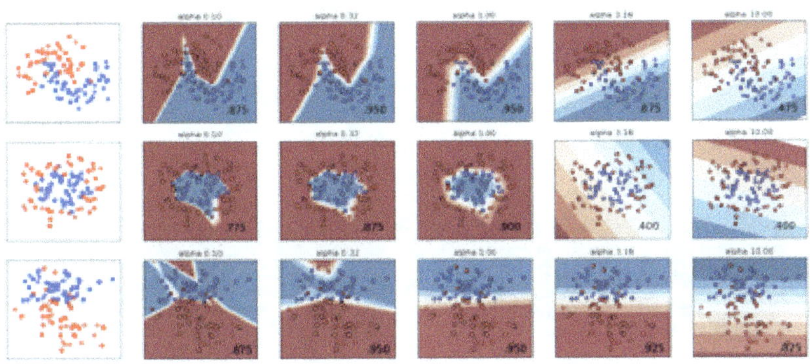

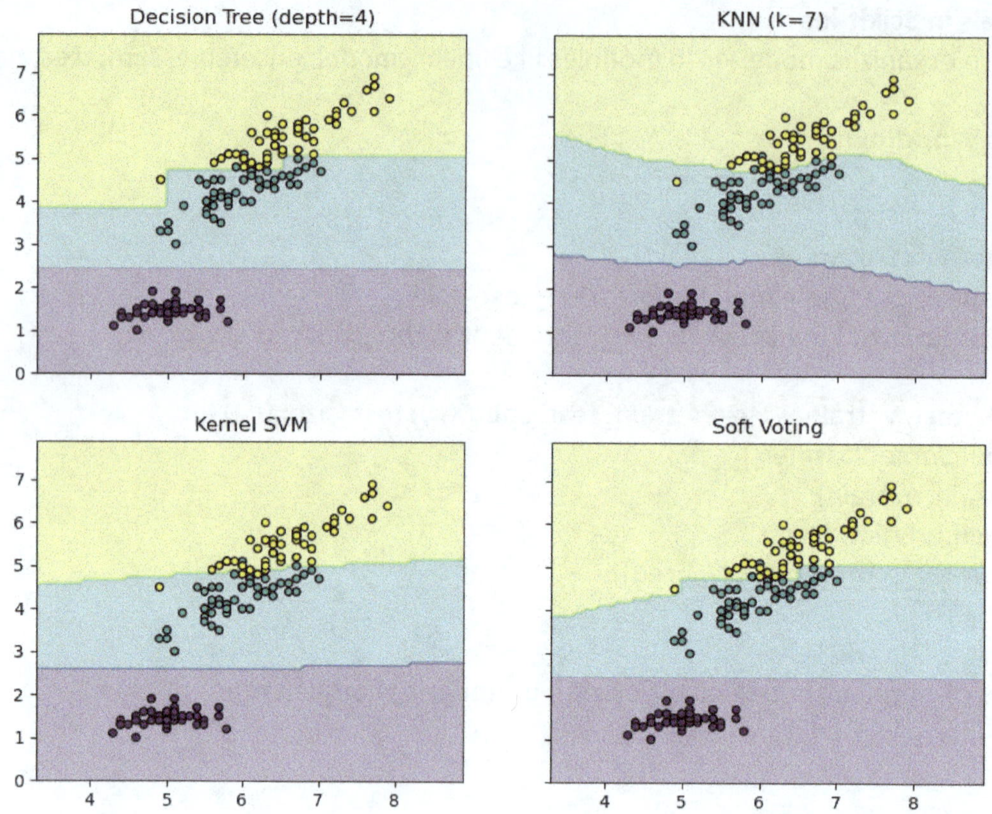
Decision Tree (depth=4)
KNN (k=7)
Kernel SVM
Soft Voting

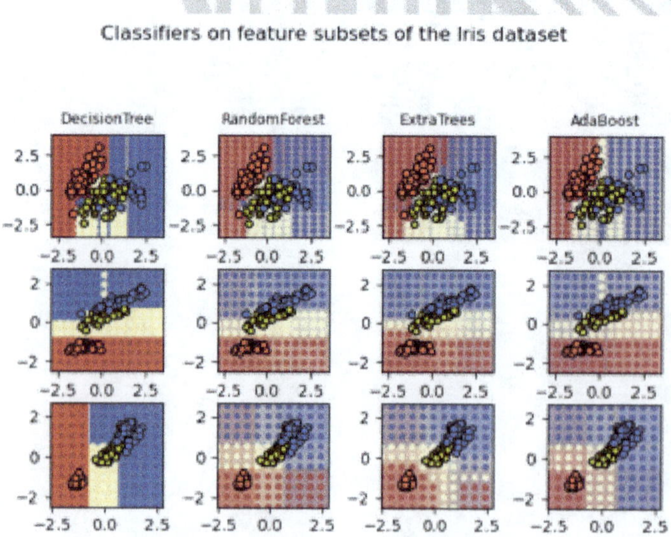
Classifiers on feature subsets of the Iris dataset
DecisionTree
RandomForest
ExtraTrees
AdaBoost

- **Regression**: LinearRegression, Ridge, Lasso, SVR, RandomForestRegressor.
- **Classification**: LogisticRegression, SVC, KNeighborsClassifier, DecisionTreeClassifier, RandomForestClassifier, GradientBoostingClassifier, MLPClassifier (neural net).

Ensembles (e.g., RandomForest, GradientBoosting) often perform best out-of-the-box.

Feature Scaling

Many algorithms (e.g., SVM, KNN, neural nets, gradient-based) are sensitive to feature scales. Features with larger ranges dominate distance/gradient computations. **Scaling** brings features to similar ranges.

Common scalers in sklearn.preprocessing:

1. **StandardScaler**: Zero mean, unit variance (z-score):

$$x' = \frac{x - \mu}{\sigma}$$

Best for normally distributed data; used with most models.

2. **MinMaxScaler**: Scales to [0,1] or custom range:

$$x' = \frac{x - x_{\min}}{x_{\max} - x_{\min}}$$

Good when data has bounds (e.g., images); sensitive to outliers.

3. **RobustScaler**: Uses median and IQR — robust to outliers.

Visual comparison of scaling effects:

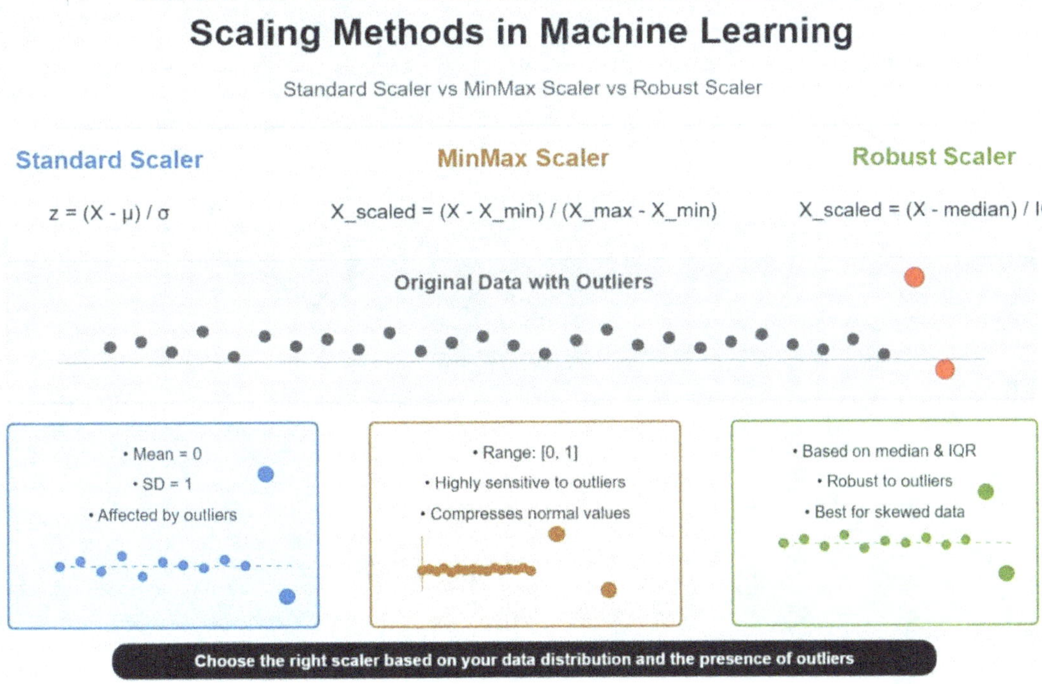

Standard Scalar	Min-Max Scalar
Changing the shape of the distribution of given data	Changing the Range of given data
Data is rescaled to have a mean (μ) of 0 and standard deviation (σ) of 1 (unit variance).	Rescales the values into a range of [0,1]
$Z = \frac{X - \mu}{\sigma}$ (X: Score, μ: Mean, σ: Standard Deviation)	$X_{norm} = \frac{X - X_{min}}{X_{max} - X_{min}}$
It gives values that are both positive and negative centered around zero.	Only positive values [0,1]
We can use this scaling , when your machine learning algorithm makes the assumptions about the data having a normal distribution.	We can use this scaling , when your machine learning algorithm does not makes the assumptions.
For Linear regression and Logistic regression	KNN and Artificial Neural Networks.
Used for clustering analyses, Principal Component Analysis(PCA)	Prefers for Image processing

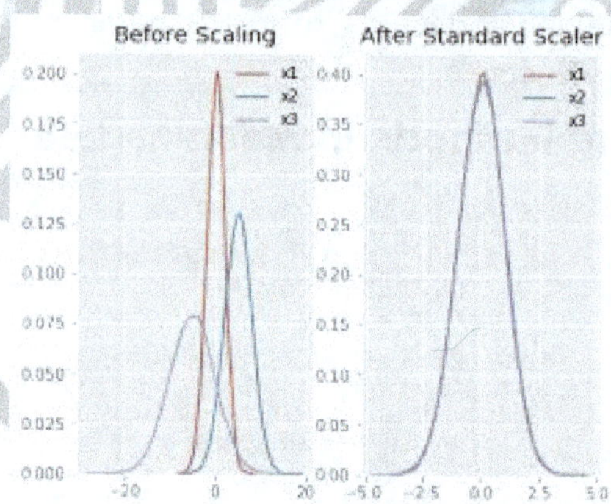

$$x_{\text{norm}} = \frac{x - \min(x)}{\max(x) - \min(x)}$$

#	Emp	Age	Salary
1	Emp1	44	73000
2	Emp2	27	47000
3	Emp3	30	53000
4	Emp4	38	62000
5	Emp5	40	57000
6	Emp6	35	53000
7	Emp7	48	78000

Normalization →

Age	Normalized Age	Salary	Normalized Salary
44	0.80952381	73000	0.838709677
27	0	47000	0
30	0.142857143	53000	0.193548387
38	0.523809524	62000	0.483870968
40	0.619047619	57000	0.322580645
35	0.380952381	53000	0.193548387
48	1	78000	1
	Range 0-1		**Range 0-1**

How to calculate Normalized value?
X = 35, min = 27, max = 48 for column Age.
Xnorm(for 35) = $\frac{35-27}{48-27} = 0.3809$

Python

```
from sklearn.preprocessing import StandardScaler, MinMaxScaler

scaler = StandardScaler()  # or MinMaxScaler()
X_scaled = scaler.fit_transform(X_train)  # Fit on train only!
X_test_scaled = scaler.transform(X_test)   # Avoid data leakage
```

Preprocessing Techniques

Real data is messy: missing values, categorical features, outliers. Scikit-learn provides transformers for cleaning and encoding.

Key tools in sklearn.preprocessing and sklearn.impute:

- **Handling Missing Values**: SimpleImputer (mean/median/most_frequent/constant).
- **Categorical Encoding**:
    - **LabelEncoder**: For ordinal targets (integers 0 to n_classes-1).
    - **OneHotEncoder**: For nominal features (creates binary columns).
    - **OrdinalEncoder**: For ordinal features.

One-hot vs. label encoding examples:

One-Hot Encoding

datagy.io

Island		Biscoe	Dream	Torgensen
Biscoe	→	1	0	0
Torgensen		0	0	1
Dream		0	1	0

Original Data

Team	Points
A	25
A	12
B	15
B	14
B	19
B	23
C	25
C	29

→

Label Encoded Data

Team	Points
0	25
0	12
1	15
1	14
1	19
1	23
2	25
2	29

Python

```
from sklearn.preprocessing import OneHotEncoder
from sklearn.impute import SimpleImputer
from sklearn.compose import ColumnTransformer

# Example: Numerical + Categorical
num_transformer = SimpleImputer(strategy='median')
cat_transformer = OneHotEncoder(handle_unknown='ignore')

preprocessor = ColumnTransformer([
    ('num', num_transformer, ['age', 'salary']),
    ('cat', cat_transformer, ['city', 'gender'])
])

X_preprocessed = preprocessor.fit_transform(X_train)
```

Pipelines: Best Practice

Combine preprocessing and modeling to avoid leakage and ensure reproducibility.
Typical pipeline diagrams:

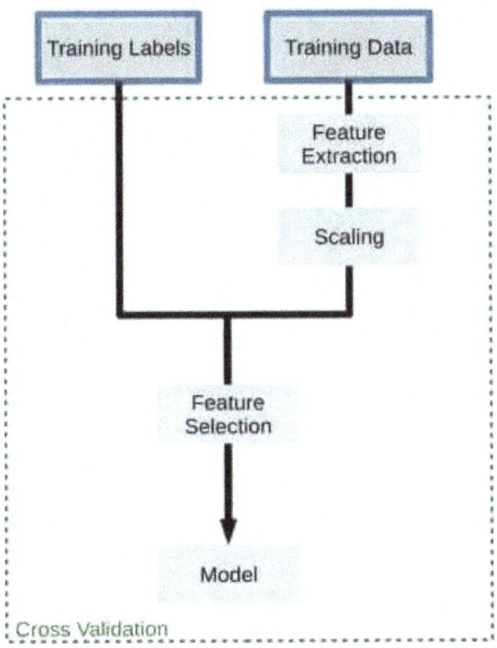

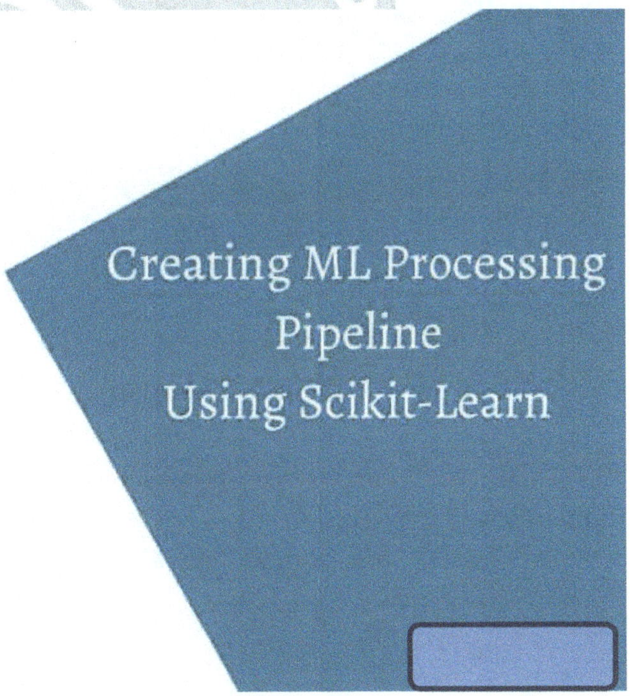

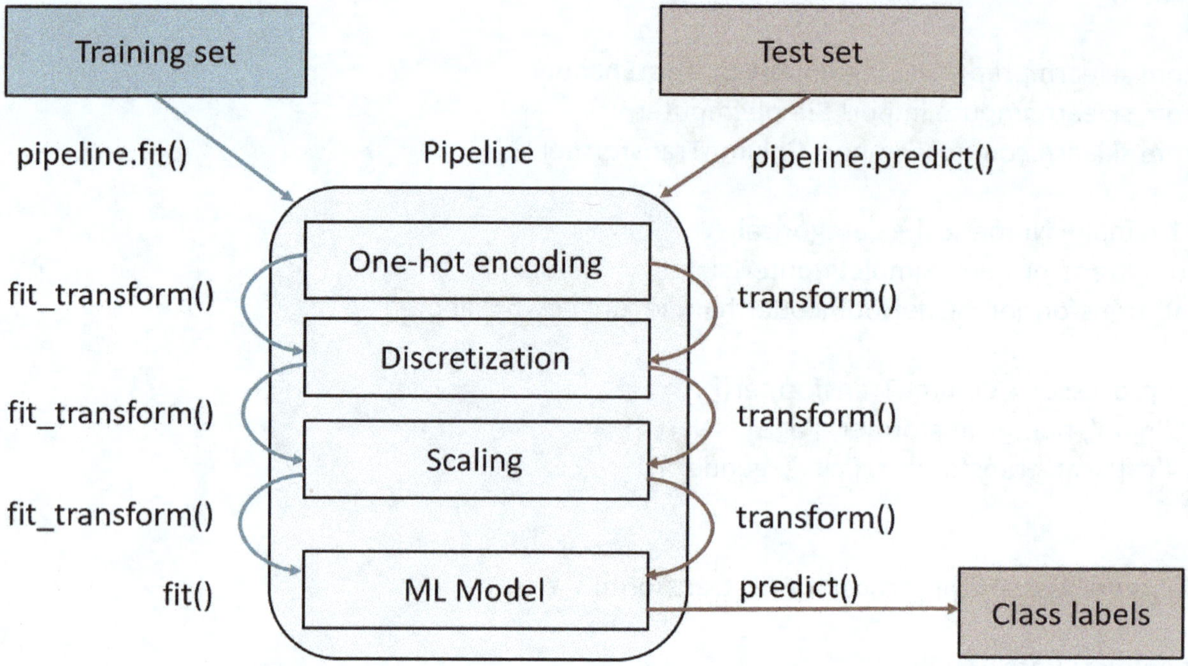

Python

```
from sklearn.pipeline import Pipeline
from sklearn.ensemble import RandomForestClassifier

pipeline = Pipeline([
    ('preprocess', preprocessor),
    ('scaler', StandardScaler(with_mean=False)),  # For sparse data
    ('model', RandomForestClassifier())
])

pipeline.fit(X_train, y_train)
y_pred = pipeline.predict(X_test)
```

Scikit-learn makes ML accessible and robust. Always scale/preprocess on train data only, use pipelines, and cross-validate!

Here's a complete, practical example using **scikit-learn** that demonstrates:

- Loading a real dataset (Titanic – classic for classification)
- Exploratory analysis
- Preprocessing (imputation, encoding, scaling)
- Feature engineering
- Model training (multiple algorithms)
- Evaluation (confusion matrix, precision, recall, F1-score)
- Pipeline usage
-

We'll predict passenger survival on the Titanic.

Python

```
# Import necessary libraries
import pandas as pd
import numpy as np
import matplotlib.pyplot as plt
import seaborn as sns

from sklearn.model_selection import train_test_split, cross_val_score
from sklearn.impute import SimpleImputer
from sklearn.preprocessing import StandardScaler, OneHotEncoder
from sklearn.compose import ColumnTransformer
from sklearn.pipeline import Pipeline
from sklearn.ensemble import RandomForestClassifier
from sklearn.linear_model import LogisticRegression
from sklearn.svm import SVC
from sklearn.metrics import (
    classification_report,
    confusion_matrix,
    precision_score,
    recall_score,
    f1_score,
    ConfusionMatrixDisplay
)

# Set style for plots
sns.set(style="whitegrid")

# 1. Load the Titanic dataset (built into seaborn)
df = sns.load_dataset('titanic')
print("Dataset shape:", df.shape)
print(df.head())
```

```
# 2. Basic exploration
print("\nMissing values:")
print(df.isnull().sum())

print("\nSurvival rate:")
print(df['survived'].value_counts(normalize=True))

# Visualize survival by class and sex
fig, axes = plt.subplots(1, 2, figsize=(12, 5))
sns.barplot(x='class', y='survived', data=df, ax=axes[0])
axes[0].set_title('Survival Rate by Class')

sns.barplot(x='sex', y='survived', hue='class', data=df, ax=axes[1])
axes[1].set_title('Survival Rate by Sex and Class')
plt.show()
```

Key features we'll use:

- pclass (ticket class)
- sex
- age
- fare
- embarked (port)
- alone (whether traveling alone)

Python

```
# 3. Feature selection and engineering
features = ['pclass', 'sex', 'age', 'fare', 'embarked', 'alone']
X = df[features]
y = df['survived']

# Create 'alone' if not present (in some versions it's missing)
if 'alone' not in df.columns:
    X['alone'] = (df['sibsp'] + df['parch'] == 0).astype(int)

# 4. Preprocessing with ColumnTransformer
numeric_features = ['age', 'fare']
categorical_features = ['pclass', 'sex', 'embarked', 'alone']

numeric_transformer = Pipeline(steps=[
    ('imputer', SimpleImputer(strategy='median')),
    ('scaler', StandardScaler())
])

categorical_transformer = Pipeline(steps=[
    ('imputer', SimpleImputer(strategy='most_frequent')),
```

```
    ('onehot', OneHotEncoder(handle_unknown='ignore'))
])

preprocessor = ColumnTransformer(
    transformers=[
        ('num', numeric_transformer, numeric_features),
        ('cat', categorical_transformer, categorical_features)
    ])

# 5. Create full pipelines with different models
models = {
    'Logistic Regression': LogisticRegression(max_iter=1000),
    'Random Forest': RandomForestClassifier(n_estimators=200, random_state=42),
    'SVM': SVC(kernel='rbf', C=1.0, probability=True)
}

results = {}

for name, model in models.items():
    # Build pipeline
    clf = Pipeline(steps=[
        ('preprocessor', preprocessor),
        ('classifier', model)
    ])

    # Train-test split
    X_train, X_test, y_train, y_test = train_test_split(X, y, test_size=0.2, random_state=42,
stratify=y)

    # Fit
    clf.fit(X_train, y_train)

    # Predict
    y_pred = clf.predict(X_test)
    y_prob = clf.predict_proba(X_test)[:, 1] if hasattr(clf, "predict_proba") else None

    # Evaluate
    precision = precision_score(y_test, y_pred)
    recall = recall_score(y_test, y_pred)
    f1 = f1_score(y_test, y_pred)

    results[name] = {'precision': precision, 'recall': recall, 'f1': f1}

    print(f"\n=== {name} ===")
    print(f"Precision: {precision:.3f}")
    print(f"Recall:    {recall:.3f}")
```

```
    print(f"F1-Score:  {f1:.3f}")
    print("\nClassification Report:")
    print(classification_report(y_test, y_pred))

    # Confusion Matrix
    cm = confusion_matrix(y_test, y_pred)
    disp = ConfusionMatrixDisplay(confusion_matrix=cm, display_labels=['Died', 'Survived'])
    disp.plot(cmap='Blues')
    plt.title(f'Confusion Matrix - {name}')
    plt.show()

# 6. Compare all models
results_df = pd.DataFrame(results).T
print("\nModel Comparison:")
print(results_df.round(3))

# Plot comparison
results_df.plot(kind='bar', figsize=(10, 6))
plt.title('Model Performance Comparison')
plt.ylabel('Score')
plt.ylim(0, 1)
plt.legend(title='Metric')
plt.xticks(rotation=15)
plt.show()
```

What This Code Demonstrates

- **Proper preprocessing**: Imputation + scaling for numeric, one-hot for categorical.
- **No data leakage**: Fit preprocessor only on training data.
- **Pipeline usage**: Clean, reusable, prevents mistakes.
- **Multiple models**: Easy comparison.
- **Detailed evaluation**: Precision, Recall, F1, full report, confusion matrices.
- **Visualization**: Insights into data and model performance.

Expected Output (approximate)

- Random Forest usually performs best (~0.80–0.85 F1).
- Logistic Regression is interpretable and solid baseline.
- SVM can be strong with proper scaling (which we did!).

Best Practices Shown

- Use stratify=y in train_test_split for balanced classes.
- handle_unknown='ignore' in OneHotEncoder for robustness.
- Cross-validation (you can add cross_val_score(clf, X, y, cv=5)).
- Random state for reproducibility.

This is a production-ready template you can adapt to any tabular dataset!

2.TensorFlow (Deep Learning, Neural Networks)

TensorFlow is an open-source end-to-end platform for machine learning and deep learning, developed by Google Brain and released in 2015. It excels at building, training, and deploying neural networks at scale—from research prototypes to production systems. TensorFlow powers applications in computer vision, natural language processing, recommendation systems, and more.

As of December 2025, the latest stable version is **TensorFlow 2.20**.

Key features:

- **Eager execution by default** — Intuitive debugging (like NumPy).
- **Keras integration** — High-level API for rapid prototyping.
- **Graph optimization** — Efficient execution on CPUs, GPUs, TPUs.
- **Cross-platform deployment** — TensorFlow Serving, Lite (mobile/edge), JS (web).
- **Distributed training** — Scales to multiple devices/machines.
- **Extensive ecosystem** — TensorBoard (visualization), TFX (production pipelines).

TensorFlow competes with PyTorch (more research-oriented) but shines in production.

Neural Networks Basics in TensorFlow

A **neural network** consists of layers of interconnected nodes (neurons) that process data. Each neuron computes a weighted sum of inputs, adds bias, and applies an activation function (e.g., ReLU, sigmoid).

Simple feedforward neural network architecture:

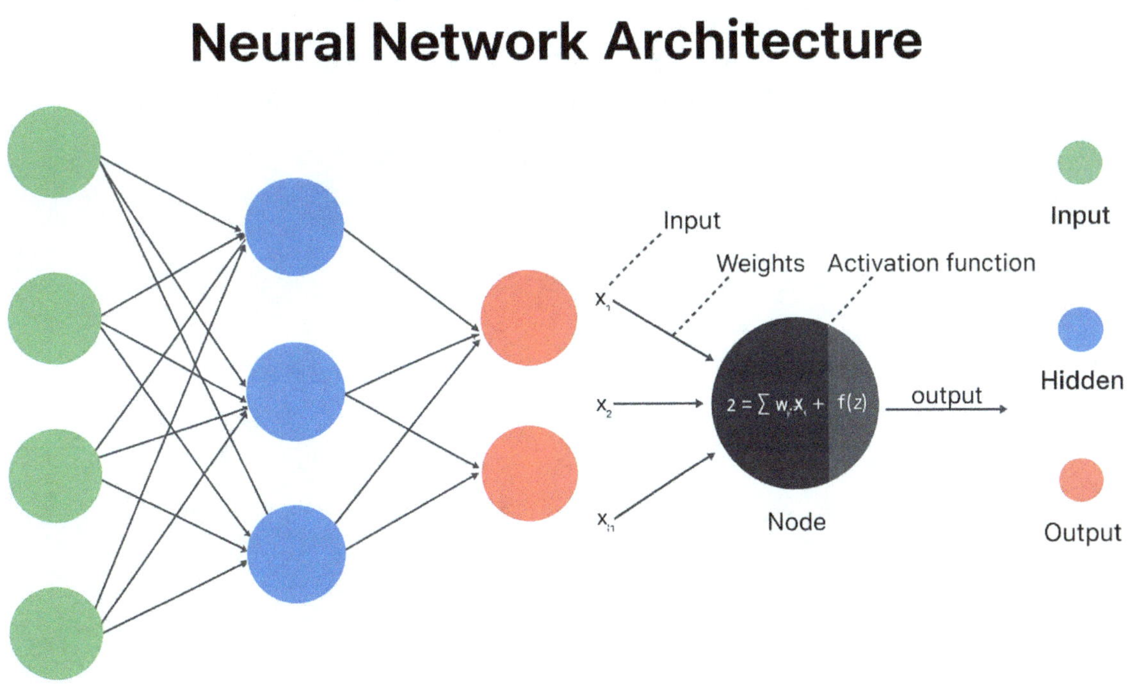

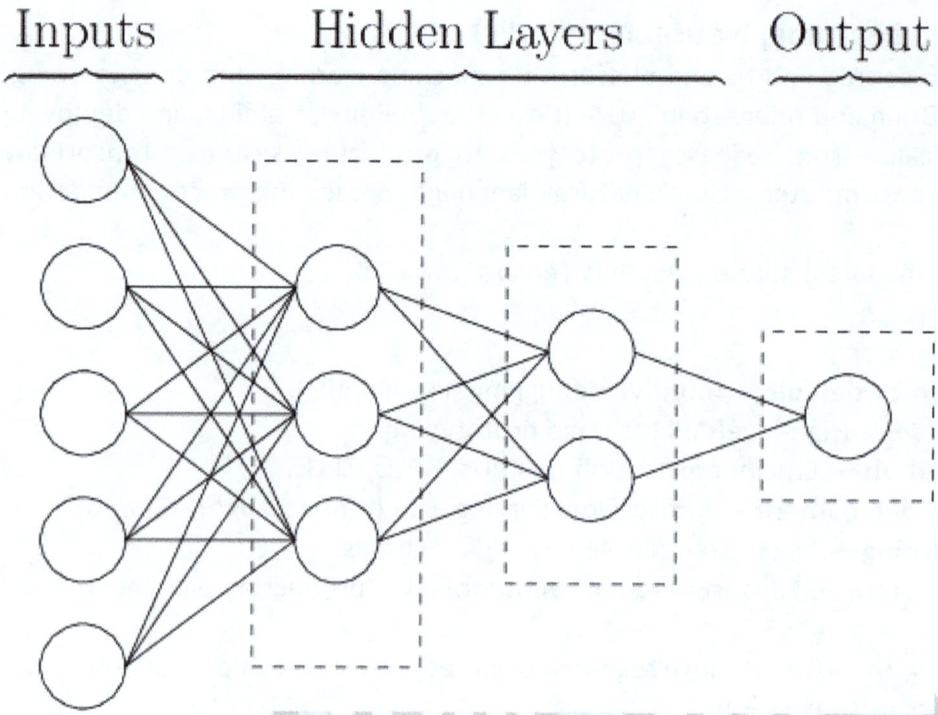

Deep Learning stacks many layers to learn hierarchical features (e.g., edges → shapes → objects in images).

Training involves:

- **Forward pass** → Compute predictions.
- **Loss calculation** → Measure error (e.g., MSE for regression, cross-entropy for classification).
- **Backpropagation** → Compute gradients of loss w.r.t. weights.
- **Optimization** → Update weights via gradient descent (e.g., Adam optimizer).

Backpropagation diagram (chain rule in action):

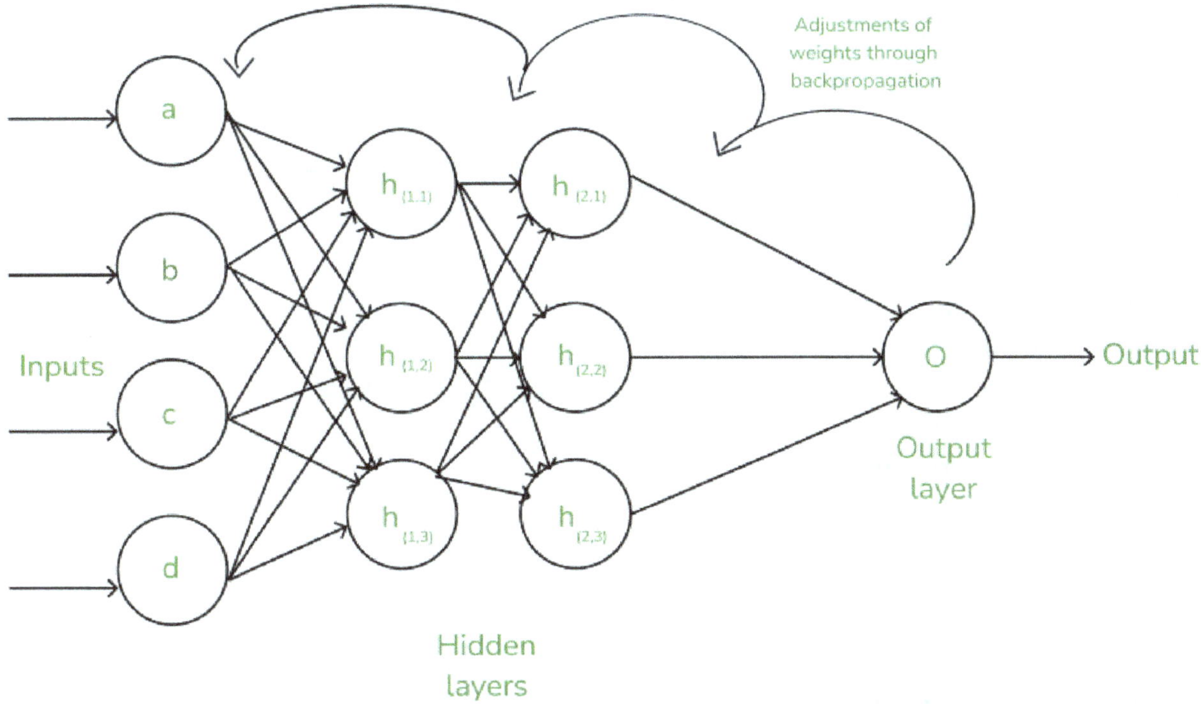

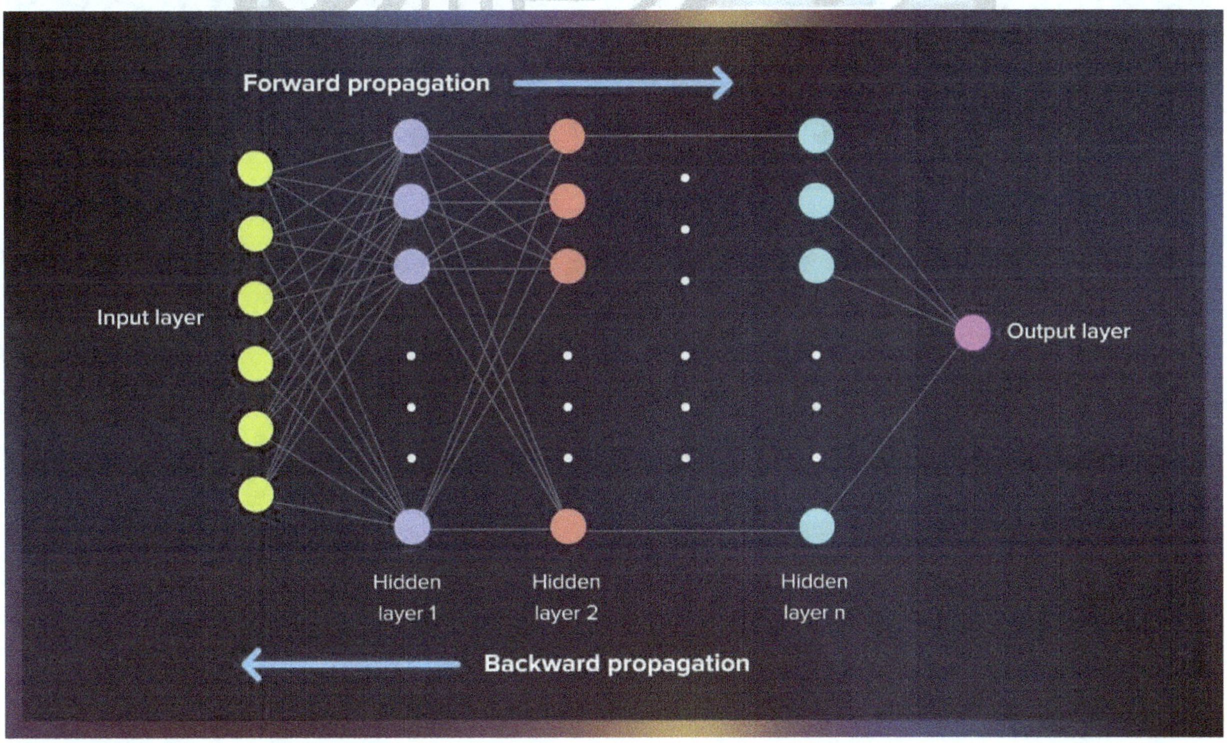

Building Models with Keras (TensorFlow's High-Level API)
Keras is the recommended way to build models in TensorFlow 2.x.
Sequential Model (stacked layers):
Python

```python
import tensorflow as tf
from tensorflow.keras.models import Sequential
from tensorflow.keras.layers import Dense

# Simple MLP for classification (e.g., MNIST)
model = Sequential([
    tf.keras.layers.Flatten(input_shape=(28, 28)),  # Input: 28x28 images
    Dense(128, activation='relu'),                 # Hidden layer
    Dense(64, activation='relu'),
    Dense(10, activation='softmax')                # Output: 10 classes
])

model.summary()  # Prints architecture
```

Example Sequential model code structure:

```python
mnist = tf.keras.datasets.mnist

(x_train, y_train),(x_test, y_test) = mnist.load_data()
x_train, x_test = x_train / 255.0, x_test / 255.0

model = tf.keras.models.Sequential([
  tf.keras.layers.Flatten(),
  tf.keras.layers.Dense(512, activation=tf.nn.relu),
  tf.keras.layers.Dropout(0.2),
  tf.keras.layers.Dense(10, activation=tf.nn.softmax)
])
model.compile(optimizer='adam',
              loss='sparse_categorical_crossentropy',
```

```
In [3]: # Function to create model, required for KerasClassifier
def create_model():
    # default values
    activation='relu' # or linear
    dropout_rate=0.0 # or 0.2
    init_mode='uniform'
    weight_constraint=0 # or  4
    optimizer='adam' # or SGD
    lr = 0.01
    momemntum=0
    # create model
    model = Sequential()
    model.add(Dense(8,
                    input_dim=input_dim, kernel_initializer=init_mode,
                    activation=activation,
                    kernel_constraint=maxnorm(weight_constraint)))
    model.add(Dropout(dropout_rate))
    model.add(Dense(1, kernel_initializer=init_mode, activation='sigmoid'))
    # Compile model
    model.compile(loss='binary_crossentropy',
                  optimizer=optimizer,
                  metrics=['accuracy'])
    return model
```

Functional API (for complex architectures, multi-input/output):
Python

```
inputs = tf.keras.Input(shape=(28, 28))
x = tf.keras.layers.Flatten()(inputs)
x = Dense(128, activation='relu')(x)
outputs = Dense(10, activation='softmax')(x)
model = tf.keras.Model(inputs=inputs, outputs=outputs)
```

Sub-classing (custom layers/models).

Common Deep Learning Architectures

1. **Convolutional Neural Networks (CNNs)** — For images; use convolutions to capture spatial patterns.

CNN architecture diagram:

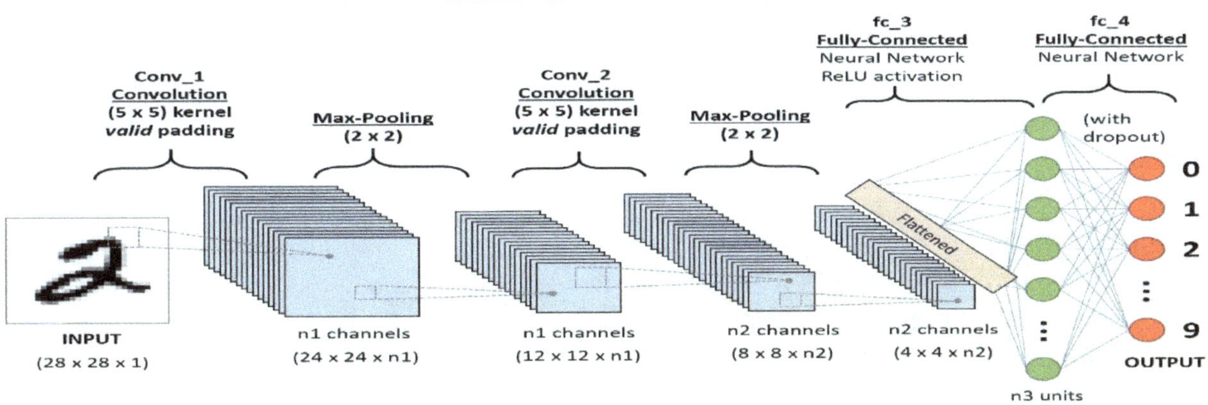

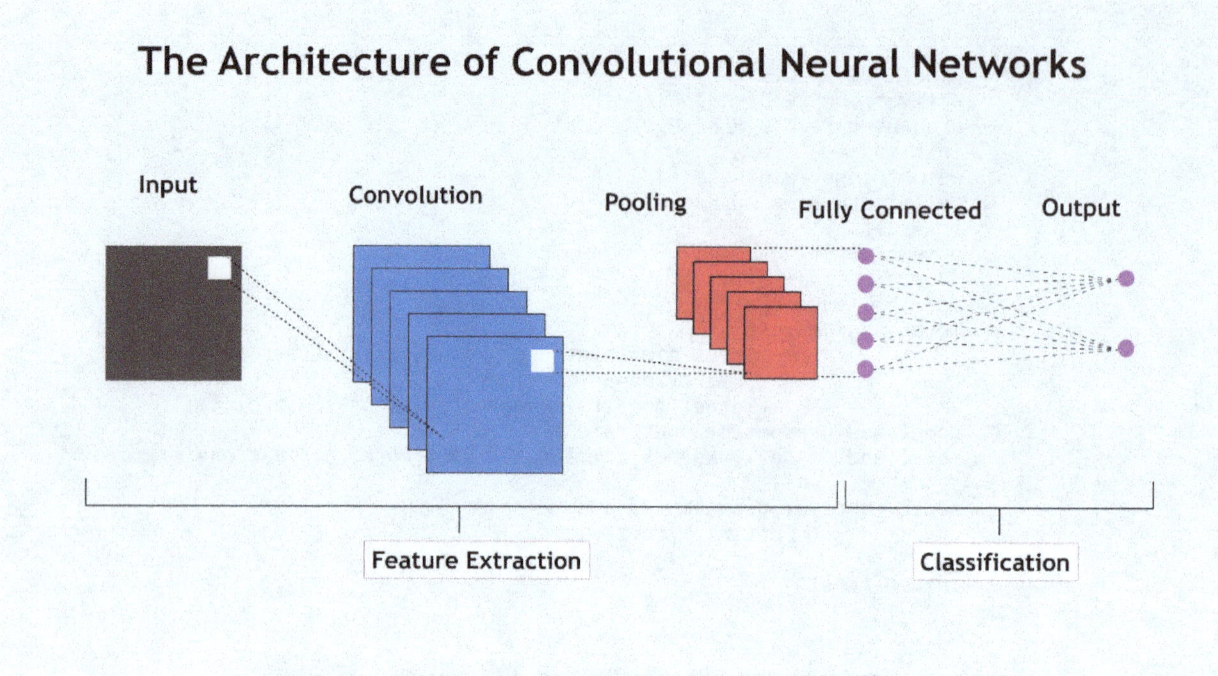

Example CNN:
Python

```
model = Sequential([
    tf.keras.layers.Conv2D(32, (3,3), activation='relu', input_shape=(28,28,1)),
    tf.keras.layers.MaxPooling2D((2,2)),
    tf.keras.layers.Conv2D(64, (3,3), activation='relu'),
    tf.keras.layers.Flatten(),
    Dense(128, activation='relu'),
    Dense(10, activation='softmax')
])
```

2. **Recurrent Neural Networks (RNNs/LSTMs/GRUs)** — For sequences (text, time series).
3. **Transformers** — Via tf.keras.layers.MultiHeadAttention or Hugging Face integration.

Training and Optimization

Python

```
# Compile model
model.compile(optimizer='adam',
          loss='sparse_categorical_crossentropy',  # For integer labels
          metrics=['accuracy'])

# Train
history = model.fit(X_train, y_train, epochs=10, validation_split=0.2)

# Evaluate
test_loss, test_acc = model.evaluate(X_test, y_test)
```

```
print(f"Test accuracy: {test_acc:.2f}")
```

TensorFlow accelerates training on GPUs/TPUs dramatically.

Advanced Features

- **Custom training loops** → With tf.GradientTape for fine control.
- **TensorBoard** → Visualize loss curves, graphs, embeddings.
- **Data pipelines** → tf.data.Dataset for efficient input (caching, prefetching).
- **Model saving/loading** → model.save('my_model') or SavedModel format.

TensorFlow makes deep learning accessible yet powerful.

Here's a **complete, runnable Python code** using **TensorFlow 2.x** (with Keras) to build, train, and evaluate a **Convolutional Neural Network (CNN)** on the famous **MNIST handwritten digits dataset** — a classic benchmark for image classification.

This example covers:

- Data loading and preprocessing
- Model building (Sequential API)
- Compilation (optimizer, loss, metrics)
- Training with validation
- Evaluation and predictions
- Visualization of results (predictions, confusion matrix)

Python

```
# Import necessary libraries
import tensorflow as tf
from tensorflow.keras import layers, models
import numpy as np
import matplotlib.pyplot as plt
import seaborn as sns
from sklearn.metrics import confusion_matrix, classification_report
import random

# Set random seeds for reproducibility
tf.random.set_seed(42)
np.random.seed(42)
random.seed(42)

print(f"TensorFlow version: {tf.__version__}")

# 1. Load and explore the MNIST dataset
(x_train, y_train), (x_test, y_test) = tf.keras.datasets.mnist.load_data()

print(f"Training data shape: {x_train.shape}")  # (60000, 28, 28)
print(f"Test data shape: {x_test.shape}")       # (10000, 28, 28)
print(f"Number of classes: {len(np.unique(y_train))}")
```

```
# Visualize a few samples
plt.figure(figsize=(10, 10))
for i in range(25):
    plt.subplot(5, 5, i + 1)
    plt.xticks([])
    plt.yticks([])
    plt.grid(False)
    plt.imshow(x_train[i], cmap='gray')
    plt.xlabel(y_train[i])
plt.suptitle("Sample MNIST Digits")
plt.show()

# 2. Preprocess the data
# Reshape to include channel dimension (grayscale: 1 channel)
x_train = x_train.reshape((x_train.shape[0], 28, 28, 1))
x_test = x_test.reshape((x_test.shape[0], 28, 28, 1))

# Normalize pixel values to [0, 1]
x_train = x_train.astype('float32') / 255.0
x_test = x_test.astype('float32') / 255.0

# Convert labels to categorical (one-hot encoding) - optional for
sparse_categorical_crossentropy
# y_train = tf.keras.utils.to_categorical(y_train, 10)
# y_test = tf.keras.utils.to_categorical(y_test, 10)

print(f"After preprocessing - x_train shape: {x_train.shape}")
print(f"Pixel value range: {x_train.min()} to {x_train.max()}")

# 3. Build the CNN model using Sequential API
model = models.Sequential([
    layers.Conv2D(32, (3, 3), activation='relu', input_shape=(28, 28, 1)),
    layers.MaxPooling2D((2, 2)),

    layers.Conv2D(64, (3, 3), activation='relu'),
    layers.MaxPooling2D((2, 2)),

    layers.Conv2D(64, (3, 3), activation='relu'),

    layers.Flatten(),
    layers.Dense(128, activation='relu'),
    layers.Dropout(0.5),  # Prevent overfitting
    layers.Dense(10, activation='softmax')  # 10 classes
])
```

```
# Display model architecture
model.summary()

# 4. Compile the model
model.compile(
    optimizer='adam',
    loss='sparse_categorical_crossentropy',  # Use if labels are integers
    # loss='categorical_crossentropy',       # Use if labels are one-hot
    metrics=['accuracy']
)

# 5. Train the model
history = model.fit(
    x_train, y_train,
    epochs=10,
    batch_size=128,
    validation_split=0.1,  # Use 10% of training data for validation
    verbose=1
)

# 6. Plot training history
plt.figure(figsize=(12, 4))

plt.subplot(1, 2, 1)
plt.plot(history.history['loss'], label='Training Loss')
plt.plot(history.history['val_loss'], label='Validation Loss')
plt.title('Model Loss')
plt.xlabel('Epoch')
plt.ylabel('Loss')
plt.legend()

plt.subplot(1, 2, 2)
plt.plot(history.history['accuracy'], label='Training Accuracy')
plt.plot(history.history['val_accuracy'], label='Validation Accuracy')
plt.title('Model Accuracy')
plt.xlabel('Epoch')
plt.ylabel('Accuracy')
plt.legend()

plt.tight_layout()
plt.show()

# 7. Evaluate on test set
test_loss, test_accuracy = model.evaluate(x_test, y_test, verbose=0)
print(f"\nTest Accuracy: {test_accuracy:.4f}")
print(f"Test Loss: {test_loss:.4f}")
```

```
# 8. Make predictions
y_pred_prob = model.predict(x_test)
y_pred = np.argmax(y_pred_prob, axis=1)

# 9. Classification report
print("\nClassification Report:")
print(classification_report(y_test, y_pred, digits=4))

# 10. Confusion Matrix
cm = confusion_matrix(y_test, y_pred)
plt.figure(figsize=(8, 6))
sns.heatmap(cm, annot=True, fmt='d', cmap='Blues', xticklabels=range(10),
yticklabels=range(10))
plt.title('Confusion Matrix')
plt.xlabel('Predicted Label')
plt.ylabel('True Label')
plt.show()

# 11. Visualize some predictions (correct and incorrect)
indices = np.random.choice(len(x_test), 15, replace=False)
plt.figure(figsize=(15, 10))
for i, idx in enumerate(indices):
    plt.subplot(3, 5, i + 1)
    plt.imshow(x_test[idx].reshape(28, 28), cmap='gray')
    true_label = y_test[idx]
    pred_label = y_pred[idx]
    color = 'green' if true_label == pred_label else 'red'
    plt.title(f"True: {true_label}\nPred: {pred_label}", color=color)
    plt.axis('off')
plt.suptitle("Sample Predictions (Green=Correct, Red=Wrong)")
plt.tight_layout()
plt.show()

# Optional: Save the model
# model.save('mnist_cnn_model.h5')
# print("Model saved as 'mnist_cnn_model.h5'")
```

Expected Results (Typical Run)

- **Test Accuracy**: ~99.0% – 99.4%
- Very low error rate thanks to CNNs being perfect for image data.

Why This Works So Well

- **Conv2D layers** extract spatial features (edges, shapes).
- **MaxPooling** reduces dimensions, adds translation invariance.
- **Dropout** prevents overfitting.
- **ReLU** activations enable deep learning.
- **Adam optimizer** adapts learning rates efficiently.

How to Run This Code

1. Install TensorFlow:

Bash

```
pip install tensorflow matplotlib seaborn scikit-learn
```

2. Run in Jupyter Notebook or Python script.

This is a complete, professional-grade deep learning pipeline you can adapt to your own image classification tasks (e.g., fashion MNIST, CIFAR-10, or custom datasets).

3.Keras (Simplified Deep Learning Framework)

Keras is an open-source, high-level deep learning API written in Python, designed specifically **for human beings, not machines**. Its core philosophy emphasizes user-friendliness, rapid prototyping, code readability, minimalism, and ease of debugging, while enabling fast experimentation with deep neural networks. Created by François Chollet in 2015 as part of the ONEIROS project, Keras started as a standalone library supporting multiple backends (initially TensorFlow, Theano, CNTK, etc.). It became tightly integrated into TensorFlow as tf.keras from TensorFlow 2.0 onward.

As of late 2025, the current version is **Keras 3** (latest release around 3.13.0+), a complete rewrite that transforms it into a **multi-backend framework**. This allows the same Keras code to run seamlessly on **JAX**, **TensorFlow**, or **PyTorch** (with OpenVINO for inference-only). This evolution eliminates framework lock-in, letting developers choose the best backend for performance, hardware (e.g., JAX for TPUs/GPUs), or ecosystem tools without rewriting models.

Keras is widely used in industry (e.g., NASA, YouTube, Waymo, CERN) and research for its balance of simplicity and power. It powers everything from quick prototypes to large-scale production systems.

Why is Keras Considered "Simplified"?

Keras reduces cognitive load through:

- **Consistent, intuitive APIs**: Minimal actions for common tasks (e.g., build, compile, train a model in ~10 lines).
- **Progressive disclosure of complexity**: Start simple (Sequential models), scale to advanced (custom layers, distributed training).
- **Modular building blocks**: Pre-implemented layers, losses, optimizers, metrics, and tools for image/text processing.
- **Less boilerplate**: Compared to low-level frameworks like raw TensorFlow or PyTorch, Keras abstracts away tedious details.
- **Debugging-friendly**: Eager execution by default in many backends, clear error messages, and focus on maintainability.

It's ideal for beginners, rapid iteration, and production, while still supporting state-of-the-art research.

Key Features of Keras 3

- **Multi-Backend Support**: Set via environment variable (KERAS_BACKEND="jax", "tensorflow", or "torch"). Models using built-in components work across backends with zero changes. Custom components can be backend-agnostic using keras.ops.
- **Performance Optimizations**: Often 20-350% faster by selecting the optimal backend (JAX frequently wins). Defaults to XLA compilation for speed on GPUs/TPUs.
- **Scalability**: Built-in distributed training (data/model parallelism) across GPUs/TPUs/clusters.
- **Ecosystem Integration**:
  - **KerasHub** (formerly KerasNLP/KerasCV): Pretrained models like Gemma, Llama, Mistral, Stable Diffusion – usable for training/inference on any backend.
  - Full compatibility with backend-native tools (e.g., tf.data, PyTorch DataLoader, JAX TPUs).
- **APIs**:
  - **Sequential API**: For simple stacked models.
  - **Functional API**: For complex, multi-input/output graphs.
  - **Subclassing**: For fully custom layers/models.
- **Advanced Tools**: Quantization (8-bit, 4-bit, GPTQ), mixed precision, callbacks, serialization, knowledge distillation.
- **Deployment**: Export to various formats; run on CPU/GPU/TPU/mobile/web.

Installation and Setup (as of 2025)

Bash

```
pip install --upgrade keras
```

Install at least one backend:

Bash

```
pip install "tensorflow>=2.16"  # or jax, torch
```

For pretrained models:

Bash

```
pip install keras-hub keras-cv
```

Set backend (before importing Keras):

Python

```
import os
os.environ["KERAS_BACKEND"] = "jax"  # or "tensorflow", "torch"
import keras
```

Basic Example: Building and Training a Simple Model

Here's a minimal MNIST classifier using the Functional API (works on any backend):

Python

```python
import os
os.environ["KERAS_BACKEND"] = "jax"  # Change to "tensorflow" or "torch" as needed

import keras
from keras import layers
import numpy as np

# Load data (using NumPy for simplicity; can use tf.data, torch.utils.data, etc.)
(x_train, y_train), (x_test, y_test) = keras.datasets.mnist.load_data()
x_train = x_train.reshape(-1, 28*28).astype("float32") / 255
x_test = x_test.reshape(-1, 28*28).astype("float32") / 255

# Build model
inputs = keras.Input(shape=(784,))
x = layers.Dense(512, activation="relu")(inputs)
x = layers.Dropout(0.5)(x)
outputs = layers.Dense(10, activation="softmax")(x)
model = keras.Model(inputs, outputs)

# Compile and train
model.compile(
    optimizer=keras.optimizers.Adam(),
    loss=keras.losses.SparseCategoricalCrossentropy(),
    metrics=[keras.metrics.SparseCategoricalAccuracy()],
)
model.fit(x_train, y_train, batch_size=128, epochs=5, validation_split=0.1)

# Evaluate
test_loss, test_acc = model.evaluate(x_test, y_test)
print(f"Test accuracy: {test_acc:.4f}")
```

This code is concise, readable, and portable across backends.

4. PyTorch (Deep Learning, NLP, Computer Vision)

PyTorch is an open-source deep learning framework developed initially by Meta's AI Research lab (FAIR) and released in 2017. It is now stewarded by the **PyTorch Foundation** under the Linux Foundation. Built on the legacy of the Torch library (originally in Lua), PyTorch provides a Python-first interface for building, training, and deploying neural networks with strong GPU acceleration.

Its core design philosophy emphasizes **flexibility, intuitiveness, and speed**—making it feel like standard Python programming while enabling complex deep learning workflows. PyTorch uses **dynamic computation graphs** (define-by-run), allowing models to change on-the-fly, which is ideal for research and debugging.

As of **December 2025**, the stable version is **PyTorch 2.7.0** (released around April 2025), with nightly previews available for cutting-edge features. It dominates academic research (used in ~85% of recent papers) and is widely adopted in industry by companies like Meta, OpenAI, Microsoft, Tesla, and Salesforce.

PyTorch excels in **deep learning**, particularly **Natural Language Processing (NLP)** and **Computer Vision (CV)**, due to its ecosystem of specialized libraries and pretrained models.

Why PyTorch is Popular for Deep Learning, NLP, and Computer Vision

- **Dynamic Graphs & Eager Execution**: Code runs immediately (like NumPy), making debugging straightforward with standard Python tools (e.g., PDB). No need to compile graphs upfront.
- **Pythonic & Intuitive**: Feels natural for Python developers; minimal boilerplate.
- **Strong GPU/Accelerator Support**: Native CUDA, ROCm, MPS (Apple Silicon), and integration with distributed training.
- **Research-First**: Rapid prototyping; most state-of-the-art models (e.g., Transformers, diffusion models) are first released in PyTorch.
- **Production Maturity**: TorchScript for graph mode, TorchServe for deployment, ONNX export for interoperability.
- **Vast Ecosystem**: Libraries for specific domains, pretrained models via PyTorch Hub.

Compared to alternatives like TensorFlow/Keras in 2025:

- PyTorch wins in **research flexibility** and **community adoption**.
- TensorFlow edges in **enterprise production tooling** (e.g., TensorFlow Serving/Lite).
- Many teams use both or export via ONNX.

Key Features (as of PyTorch 2.7+)

- **Tensors & Autograd**: Core data structure (like NumPy arrays) with automatic differentiation for backpropagation.
- **torch.nn Module**: Building blocks for neural networks (layers, losses, optimizers).
- **Distributed Training**: torch.distributed for multi-GPU/node scaling.
- **TorchCompile**: Just-in-time compiler for speedups (introduced in 2.0, matured further).
- **Mobile/Edge Deployment**: TorchScript, ExecuTorch for on-device inference.
- **Ecosystem Libraries**:
    - **TorchVision**: For computer vision.
    - **TorchAudio**: For audio/speech.
    - **TorchText**: Legacy for NLP (development stopped post-0.18; now use Hugging Face or custom pipelines).
    - Others: PyTorch Geometric (graphs), Captum (interpretability).

PyTorch for Computer Vision (TorchVision)

TorchVision is the go-to library for CV tasks, providing:

- **Datasets**: ImageNet, CIFAR-10/100, COCO, MNIST, Fashion-MNIST, etc.
- **Pretrained Models**: Hundreds of state-of-the-art architectures, e.g.:
    - Classification: ResNet, EfficientNet, ViT (Vision Transformers), ConvNeXt.
    - Detection/Segmentation: Faster R-CNN, Mask R-CNN, DeepLabV3, YOLOv5/v8 (via Hub).
    - Video: SlowFast, TimeSformer.

- **Transforms**: Data augmentation (RandomCrop, Normalize, Compose pipelines v2 for performance).
- **Utilities**: IO for images/videos, ops for bounding boxes.

Ideal for tasks like image classification, object detection, semantic segmentation, and generative models (e.g., Stable Diffusion implementations).

PyTorch for Natural Language Processing (NLP)

While TorchText is no longer actively developed (last release 0.18 in 2024), PyTorch remains the foundation for modern NLP:

- **Transformers Dominance**: The Hugging Face Transformers library is built on PyTorch and provides thousands of pretrained models (BERT, GPT, Llama, Mistral, T5, etc.).
- **PyTorch Hub Models**: RoBERTa, BERT variants, translation models.
- **Common Tasks**: Tokenization (via Hugging Face tokenizers), sequence classification, generation, question answering.
- **Flexibility**: Easy to build custom RNNs, LSTMs, GRUs, or full Transformers from scratch using torch.nn.Transformer.

PyTorch powers most large language models (LLMs) in research and fine-tuning (e.g., via PEFT for LoRA/QLoRA).

Installation

From the official site:

Bash

```
# CPU-only
pip install torch torchvision torchaudio

# With CUDA (e.g., 12.8)
pip install torch torchvision torchaudio --index-url https://download.pytorch.org/whl/cu128

# Or via Conda
conda install pytorch torchvision torchaudio pytorch-cuda=12.8 -c pytorch -c nvidia
```

Supports Python 3.10+, Windows/Linux/Mac, CUDA 11.8/12.x, ROCm.

For Hugging Face (NLP):

Bash

```
pip install transformers datasets
```

Basic Example: Simple Neural Network for MNIST (Deep Learning Basics)

Python

```
import torch
import torch.nn as nn
import torch.optim as optim
from torchvision import datasets, transforms
from torch.utils.data import DataLoader
```

```
# Data loading (Computer Vision example)
transform = transforms.Compose([transforms.ToTensor(), transforms.Normalize((0.1307,), (0.3081,))])
train_dataset = datasets.MNIST('./data', train=True, download=True, transform=transform)
test_dataset = datasets.MNIST('./data', train=False, transform=transform)
train_loader = DataLoader(train_dataset, batch_size=64, shuffle=True)
test_loader = DataLoader(test_dataset, batch_size=64)

# Model definition
class SimpleNN(nn.Module):
    def __init__(self):
        super().__init__()
        self.flatten = nn.Flatten()
        self.fc1 = nn.Linear(28*28, 512)
        self.relu = nn.ReLU()
        self.fc2 = nn.Linear(512, 10)

    def forward(self, x):
        x = self.flatten(x)
        x = self.relu(self.fc1(x))
        return self.fc2(x)

model = SimpleNN()
criterion = nn.CrossEntropyLoss()
optimizer = optim.Adam(model.parameters(), lr=0.001)

# Training loop
for epoch in range(5):
    model.train()
    for data, target in train_loader:
        optimizer.zero_grad()
        output = model(data)
        loss = criterion(output, target)
        loss.backward()
        optimizer.step()
    print(f"Epoch {epoch+1}, Loss: {loss.item():.4f}")

# Evaluation
model.eval()
correct = 0
with torch.no_grad():
    for data, target in test_loader:
        output = model(data)
        pred = output.argmax(dim=1)
        correct += pred.eq(target).sum().item()
print(f"Test Accuracy: {100. * correct / len(test_dataset):.2f}%")
```

This showcases tensors, autograd, nn.Module, and DataLoader—core for any DL task.

Advanced Example Snippet: Using Pretrained Model (CV/NLP)
For CV (ResNet classification):
Python

```
from torchvision.models import resnet50, ResNet50_Weights
weights = ResNet50_Weights.DEFAULT
model = resnet50(weights=weights)
# Fine-tune or inference...
```

For NLP (BERT via Hugging Face):
Python

```
from transformers import pipeline
classifier = pipeline("sentiment-analysis")
classifier("PyTorch is awesome!")
```

When to Use PyTorch

- **Research & Prototyping**: Custom architectures, dynamic models (e.g., variable-length sequences in NLP).
- **NLP/CV Projects**: With Hugging Face/TorchVision.
- **Production**: If flexibility > rigid pipelines.
- **Learning DL**: Best for understanding under-the-hood mechanics.

Section-6

Deep Learning

- Neural Networks (ANN, CNN, RNN)
- Activation Functions (ReLU, Sigmoid, Softmax)
- Loss Functions (MSE, Cross-Entropy)
- Backpropagation & Optimization (Adam, RMSprop)
- Transfer Learning

Deep Learning

1.Neural Networks (ANN, CNN, RNN)

A **neural network** (often called an **artificial neural network** or ANN) is a computational model inspired by the human brain. It consists of interconnected nodes (neurons) organized in layers that process data, learn patterns, and make predictions. Neural networks power most modern AI applications, from image recognition to language models.

Basic Structure of a Feedforward Neural Network

The simplest type is a **feedforward neural network** (information flows only forward):

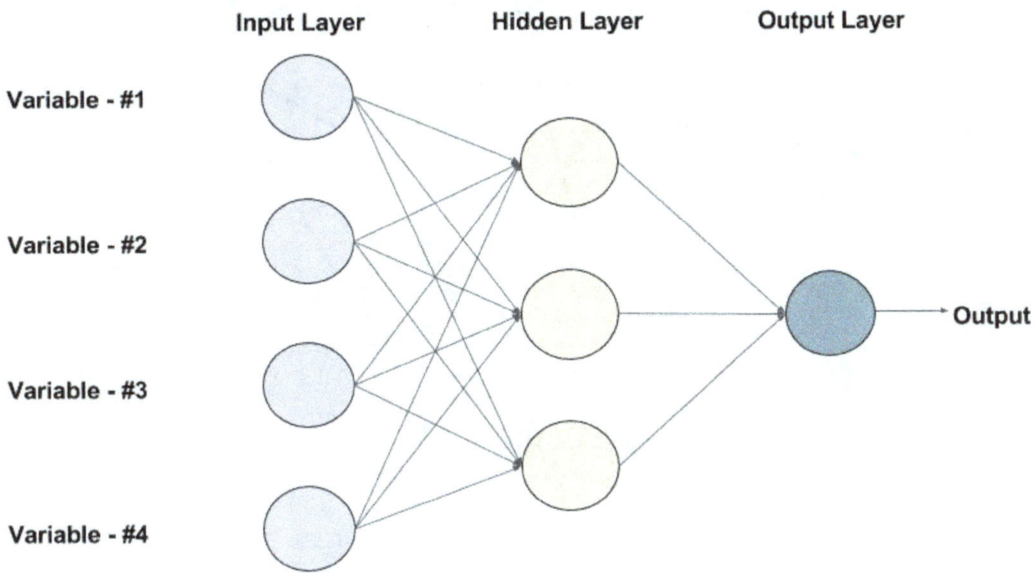

An example of a Feed-forward Neural Network with one hidden layer (with 3 neurons)

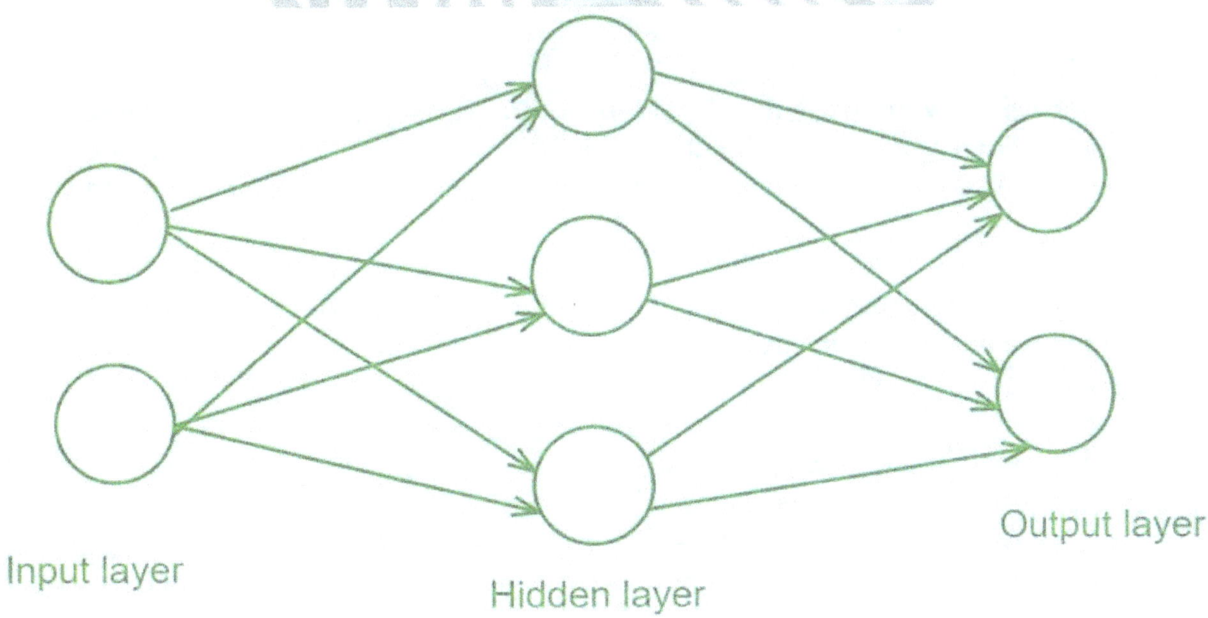

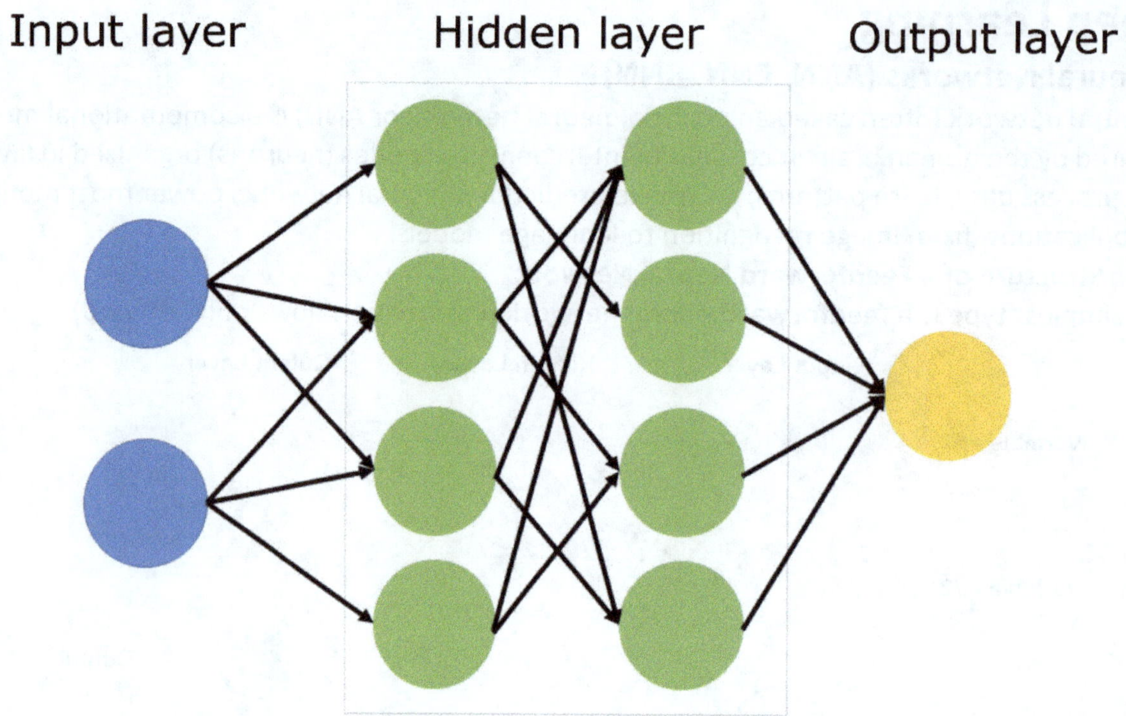

Artificial neural networks

- **Input Layer**: Receives data (e.g., pixel values or features).
- **Hidden Layers**: Perform computations with weights, biases, and activation functions (e.g., ReLU).
- **Output Layer**: Produces the result (e.g., classification probabilities).

Training involves **backpropagation** and **gradient descent** to minimize error.

Artificial Neural Networks (ANN)

Artificial Neural Networks (ANNs), often referred to as **Multilayer Perceptrons (MLPs)** when they include hidden layers, are the fundamental building blocks of deep learning. Loosely inspired by biological brains, ANNs process data through layers of interconnected artificial neurons.

Core Components

- **Neurons**: Each neuron receives inputs, computes a weighted sum, adds a bias, and applies a non-linear **activation function** (e.g., ReLU: $f(x) = \max(0,x)$, sigmoid, tanh).
- **Layers**:
    - Input layer: Accepts raw features.
    - Hidden layers: Perform transformations.
    - Output layer: Produces predictions (e.g., softmax for classification).
- **Connections**: Fully connected (dense) – every neuron connects to all in the next layer.
- **Forward Pass**: $z = Wx + b$, $a = \sigma(z)$.

Training

- Uses **backpropagation** to compute gradients and **gradient descent** (or variants like Adam) to update weights.
- Loss functions: MSE for regression, cross-entropy for classification.

Strengths & Limitations

- Universal function approximators (Cybenko theorem).
- Excel on tabular/structured data.
- Drawbacks: High parameters for large inputs; no spatial/sequential awareness.

Typical ANN architectures for simple tasks:

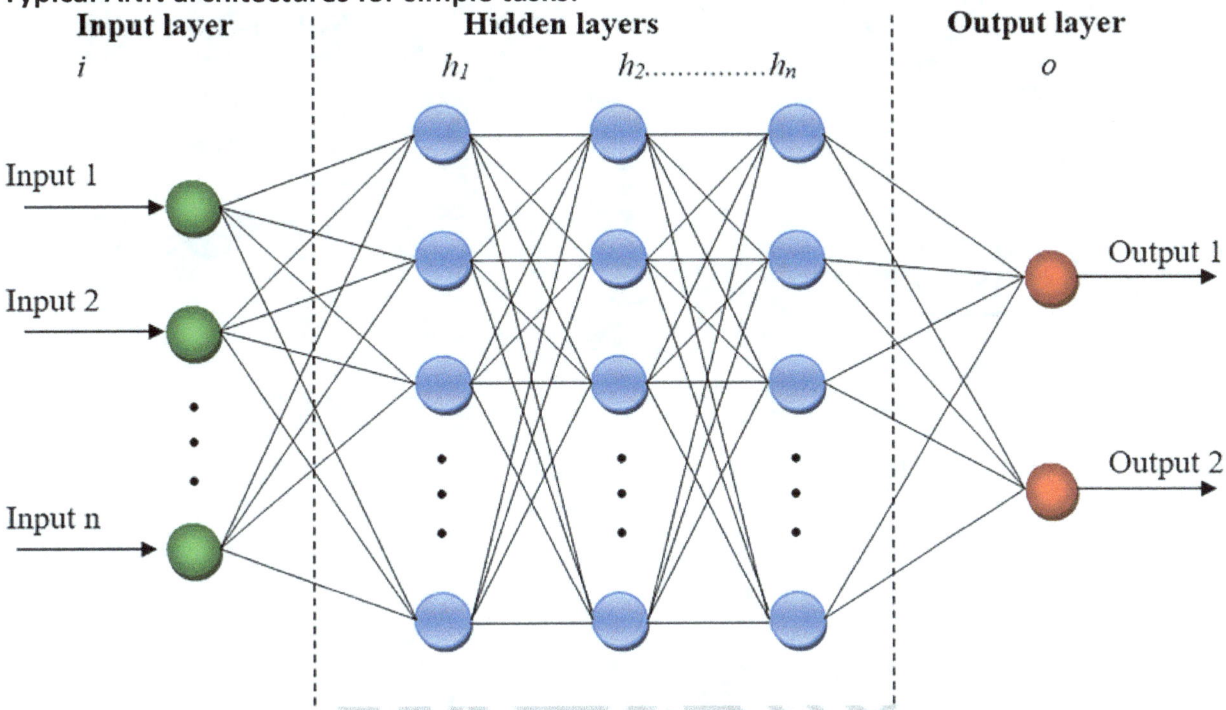

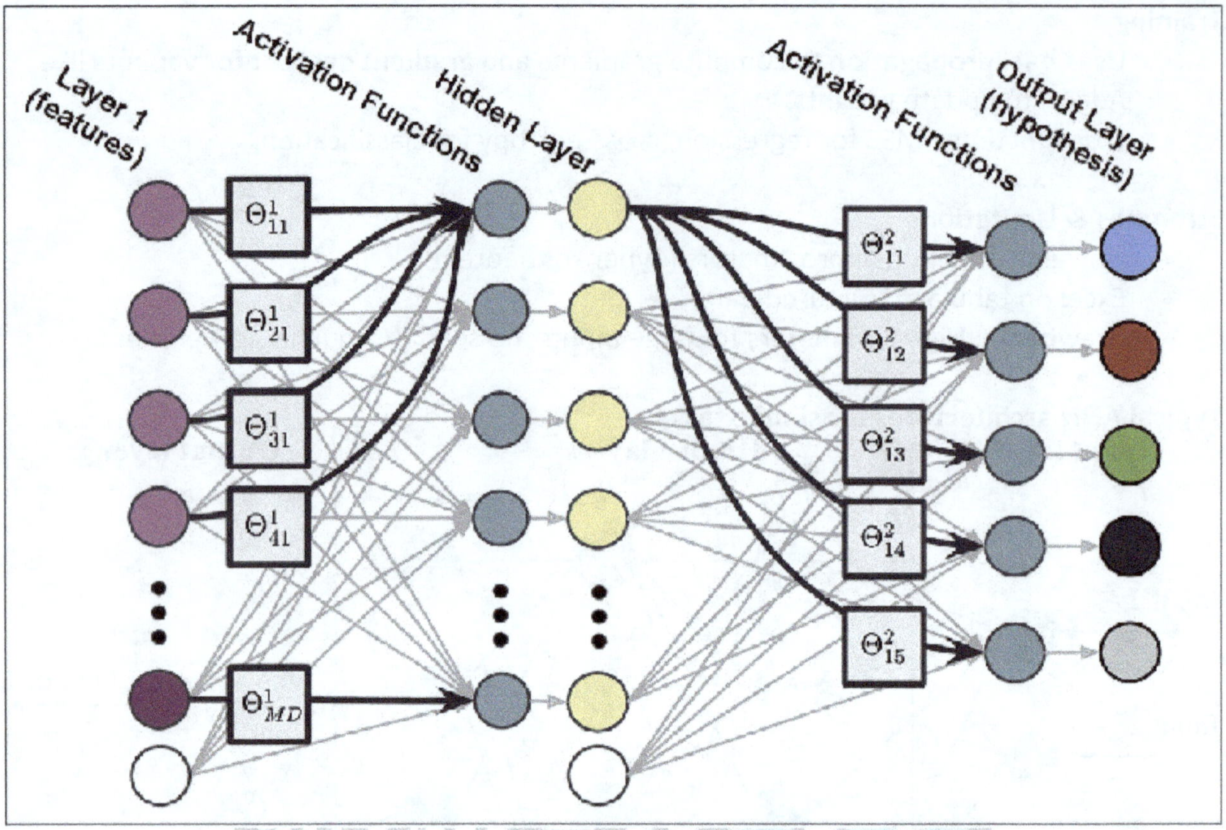

Layer 1 (features)
Activation Functions
Hidden Layer
Activation Functions
Output Layer (hypothesis)

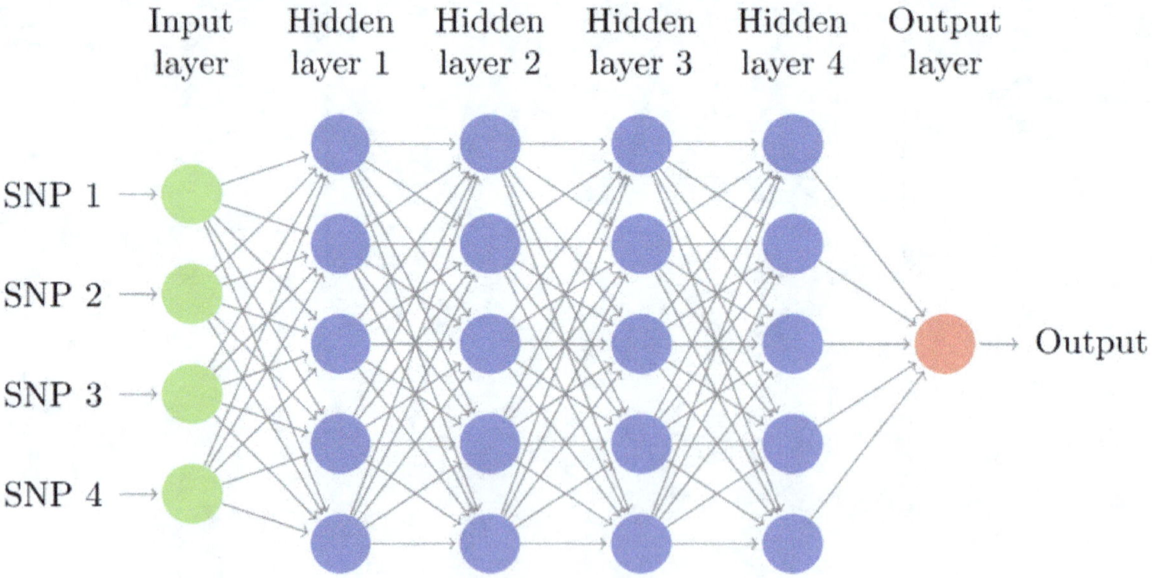

Input layer
Hidden layer 1
Hidden layer 2
Hidden layer 3
Hidden layer 4
Output layer
SNP 1
SNP 2
SNP 3
SNP 4
Output

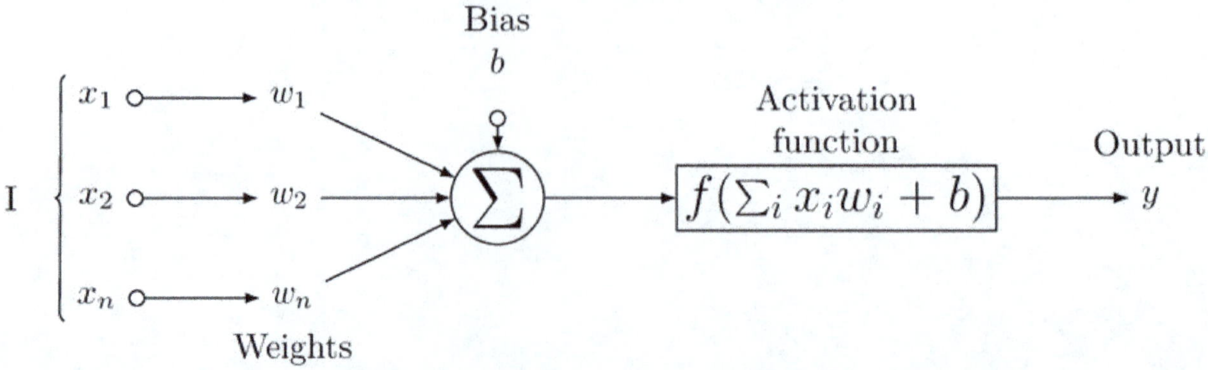

Bias
b
I
Weights
Activation function
Output
y

Applications

- Classification/regression on non-spatial data (e.g., credit scoring, medical diagnostics).

Python Code Example (Using PyTorch for XOR Problem)

The XOR problem is a classic non-linear classification task that a single-layer perceptron can't solve, but a multi-layer ANN can.

Python

```
import torch
import torch.nn as nn
import torch.optim as optim

# Data: XOR inputs and outputs
X = torch.tensor([[0., 0.], [0., 1.], [1., 0.], [1., 1.]])
y = torch.tensor([[0.], [1.], [1.], [0.]])

# Define the ANN model
class ANN(nn.Module):
    def __init__(self):
        super(ANN, self).__init__()
        self.fc1 = nn.Linear(2, 4)  # Input to hidden layer
        self.fc2 = nn.Linear(4, 1)  # Hidden to output layer

    def forward(self, x):
        x = torch.relu(self.fc1(x))  # ReLU activation
        x = torch.sigmoid(self.fc2(x))  # Sigmoid for binary output
        return x

model = ANN()
criterion = nn.BCELoss()  # Binary cross-entropy loss
optimizer = optim.Adam(model.parameters(), lr=0.01)

# Training loop
for epoch in range(1000):
    optimizer.zero_grad()
    outputs = model(X)
    loss = criterion(outputs, y)
    loss.backward()
    optimizer.step()
    if (epoch + 1) % 200 == 0:
        print(f'Epoch [{epoch+1}/1000], Loss: {loss.item():.4f}')

# Predictions
with torch.no_grad():
    predictions = model(X)
```

```
print("Predictions:\n", predictions.round())
```

Expected Output (after training):

```
Epoch [200/1000], Loss: 0.4926
Epoch [400/1000], Loss: 0.2202
Epoch [600/1000], Loss: 0.0725
Epoch [800/1000], Loss: 0.0320
Epoch [1000/1000], Loss: 0.0184

Predictions:
 tensor([[0.],
        [1.],
        [1.],
        [0.]])
```

This demonstrates how the ANN learns the non-linear XOR function.

Convolutional Neural Networks (CNN)

Convolutional Neural Networks (CNNs) are specialized for grid-structured data like images or time-frequency spectrograms. They automatically learn hierarchical features through local operations.

Core Components

- **Convolutional Layers**: Apply learnable filters/kernels that slide over input, detecting local patterns (edges → textures → objects).
  - Operation: $\left(I * K)(i,j) = \sum_m \sum_n I\,(i+m,j+n)K(m,n)\right)$.
  - Parameters shared across space → fewer weights.
- **Pooling Layers**: Downsample (e.g., Max Pooling) for invariance to small translations and reduced computation.
- **Activation**: Usually ReLU.
- **Fully Connected Layers**: At the end for final decision.
- Modern additions: Batch Norm, Dropout.

Classic CNN flow (e.g., LeNet → AlexNet → ResNet):

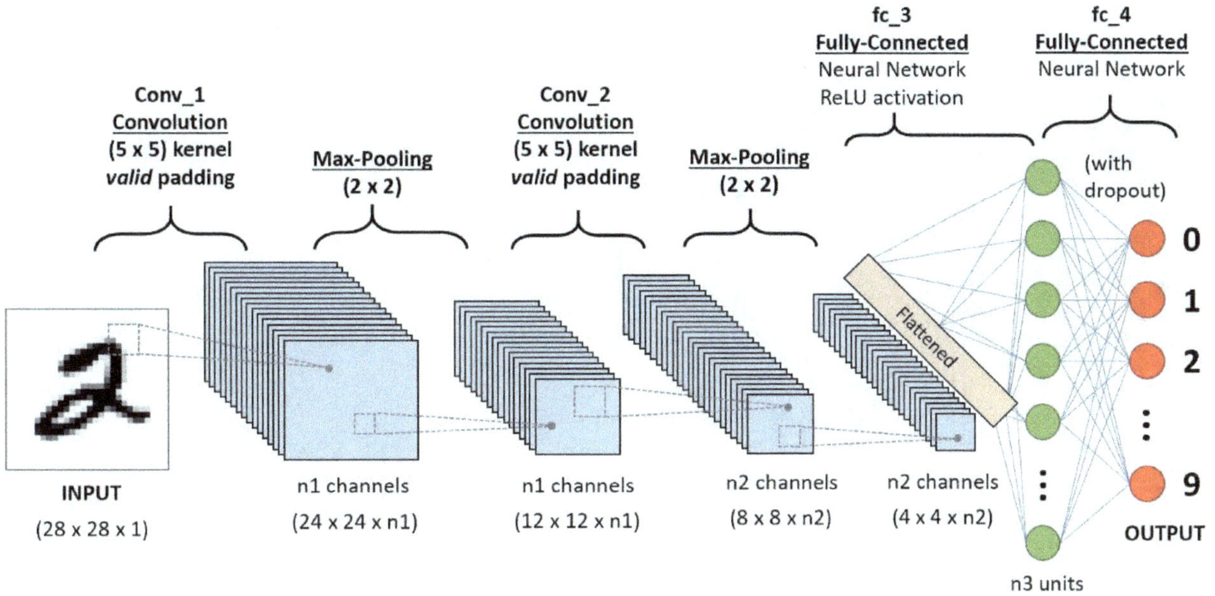

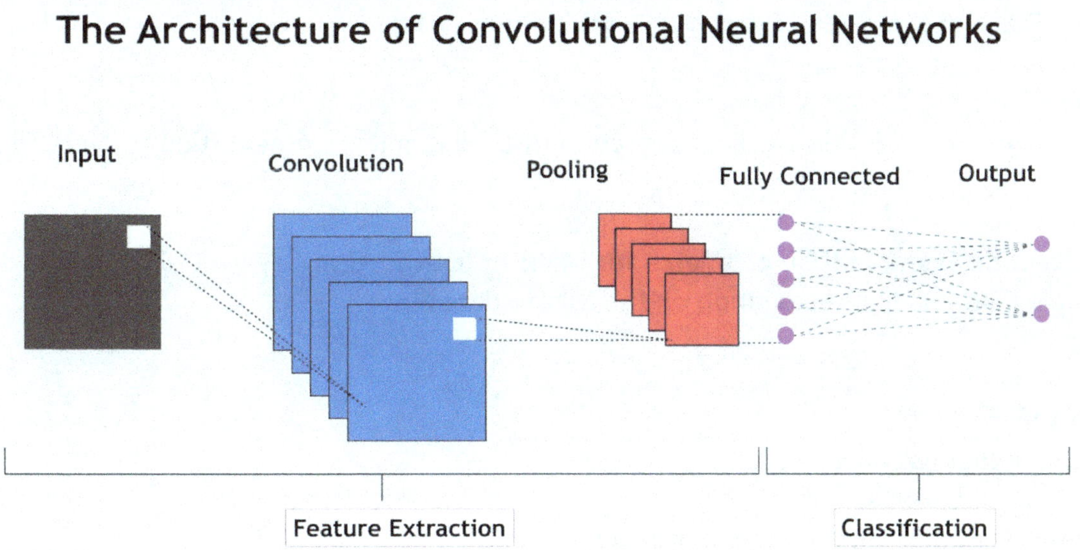

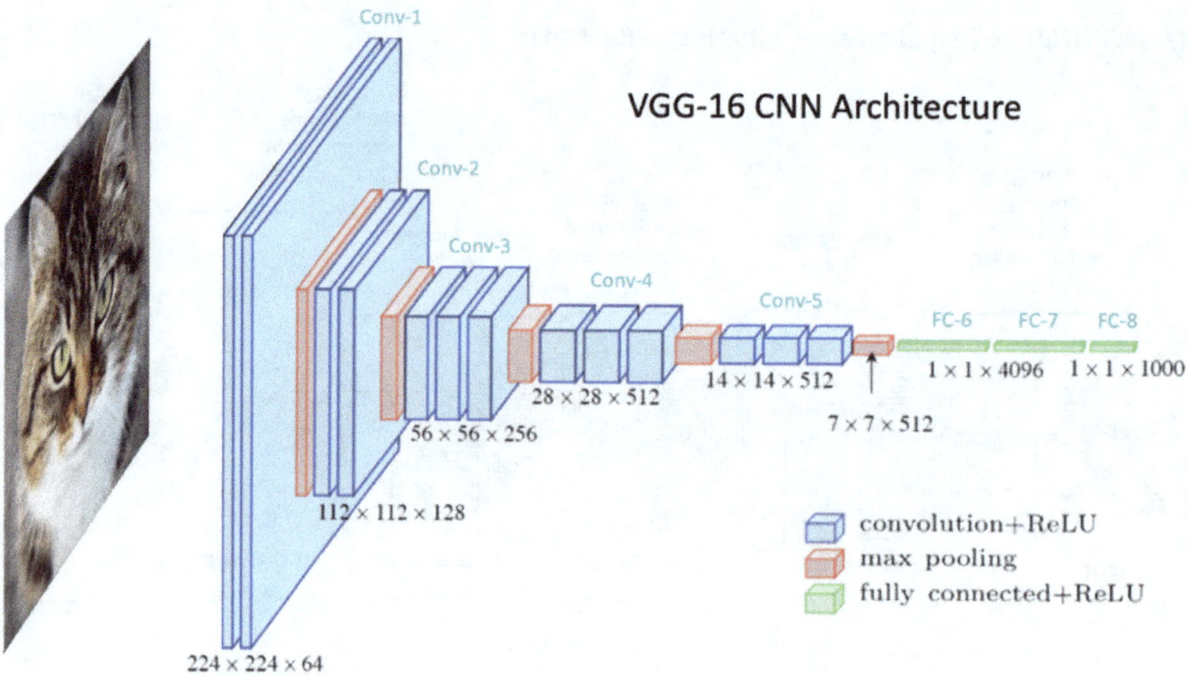

Strengths

- Translation invariance, parameter efficiency, hierarchical learning.
- State-of-the-art in vision until Transformers (ViTs).

Applications

- Image classification, object detection (R-CNN family), segmentation (U-Net), medical imaging, video analysis.

Python Code Example (Using PyTorch for MNIST Classification)

A simple CNN for digit recognition on the MNIST dataset.

Python

```
import torch
import torch.nn as nn
import torch.optim as optim
from torchvision import datasets, transforms
from torch.utils.data import DataLoader

# Data loading
transform = transforms.Compose([transforms.ToTensor(), transforms.Normalize((0.1307,),
(0.3081,))])
train_dataset = datasets.MNIST('./data', train=True, download=True, transform=transform)
test_dataset = datasets.MNIST('./data', train=False, transform=transform)
train_loader = DataLoader(train_dataset, batch_size=64, shuffle=True)
test_loader = DataLoader(test_dataset, batch_size=64)
```

```
# Define the CNN model
class CNN(nn.Module):
    def __init__(self):
        super(CNN, self).__init__()
        self.conv1 = nn.Conv2d(1, 32, kernel_size=3, padding=1)
        self.conv2 = nn.Conv2d(32, 64, kernel_size=3, padding=1)
        self.pool = nn.MaxPool2d(2, 2)
        self.fc1 = nn.Linear(64 * 7 * 7, 128)
        self.fc2 = nn.Linear(128, 10)

    def forward(self, x):
        x = self.pool(torch.relu(self.conv1(x)))
        x = self.pool(torch.relu(self.conv2(x)))
        x = x.view(-1, 64 * 7 * 7)  # Flatten
        x = torch.relu(self.fc1(x))
        x = self.fc2(x)
        return x

model = CNN()
criterion = nn.CrossEntropyLoss()
optimizer = optim.Adam(model.parameters(), lr=0.001)

# Training loop (5 epochs for brevity)
for epoch in range(5):
    model.train()
    for data, target in train_loader:
        optimizer.zero_grad()
        output = model(data)
        loss = criterion(output, target)
        loss.backward()
        optimizer.step()
    print(f'Epoch {epoch+1}, Loss: {loss.item():.4f}')

# Evaluation
model.eval()
correct = 0
with torch.no_grad():
    for data, target in test_loader:
        output = model(data)
        pred = output.argmax(dim=1)
        correct += pred.eq(target).sum().item()
print(f'Test Accuracy: {100. * correct / len(test_dataset):.2f}%')
```

Expected Output (approximate after training):

Epoch 1, Loss: 0.0362
Epoch 2, Loss: 0.0054
Epoch 3, Loss: 0.0031
Epoch 4, Loss: 0.0012
Epoch 5, Loss: 0.0005
Test Accuracy: 98.50%
This shows how CNNs extract features from images efficiently.

Recurrent Neural Networks (RNN)
Recurrent Neural Networks (RNNs) process sequential data by maintaining hidden states that capture information from previous time steps, enabling "memory."

Basic RNN

- Hidden state update: $h_t = \tanh\,(W_{hh}h_{t-1} + W_{xh}x_t + b)$.
- Output: $y_t = W_{hy}h_t + c$.
- **Unrolled view**: Chain sharing weights over time.

Unrolled RNN structure:

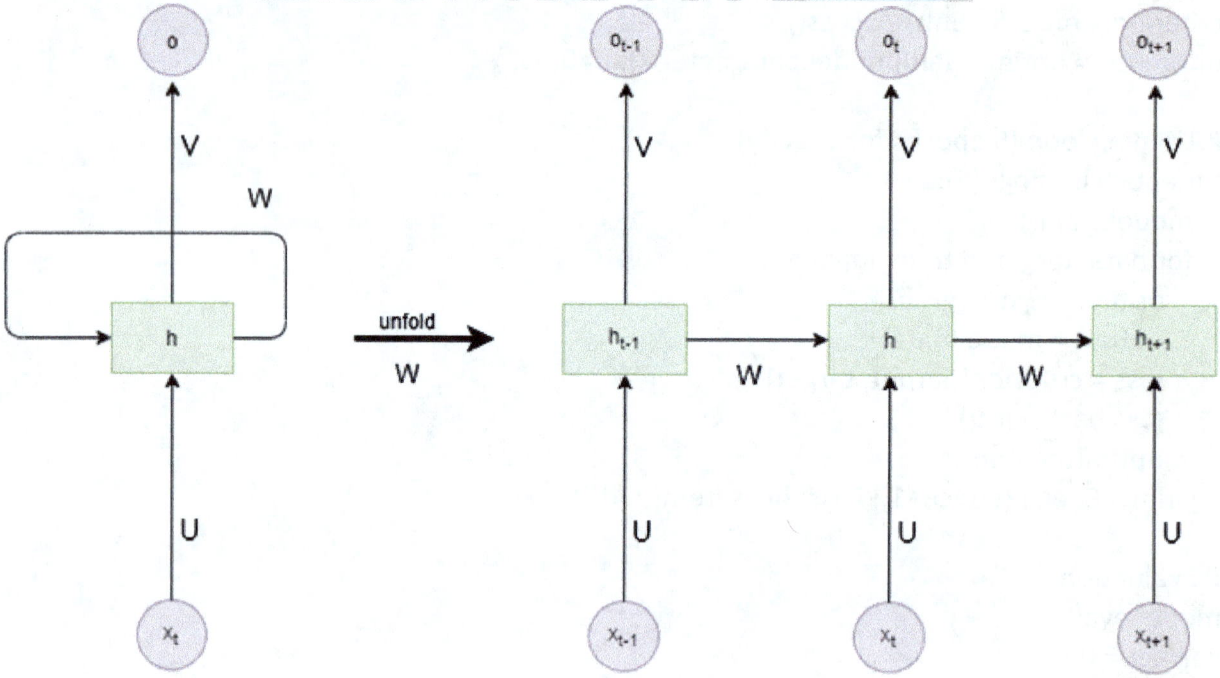

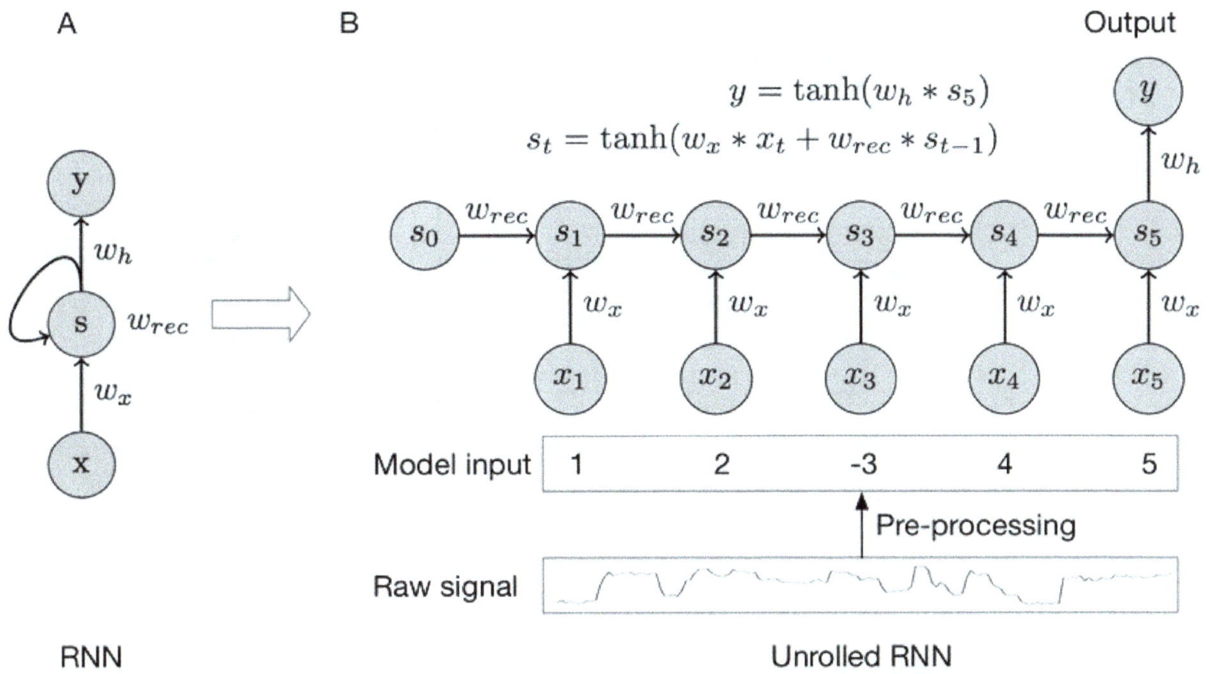

Limitations of Vanilla RNNs

- **Vanishing/Exploding Gradients**: Hard to learn long dependencies.

Advanced Variants

- **LSTM (Long Short-Term Memory)**: Introduces cell state and gates (forget, input, output) to control information flow.
- **GRU**: Simpler variant with update/reset gates.

LSTM cell internals:

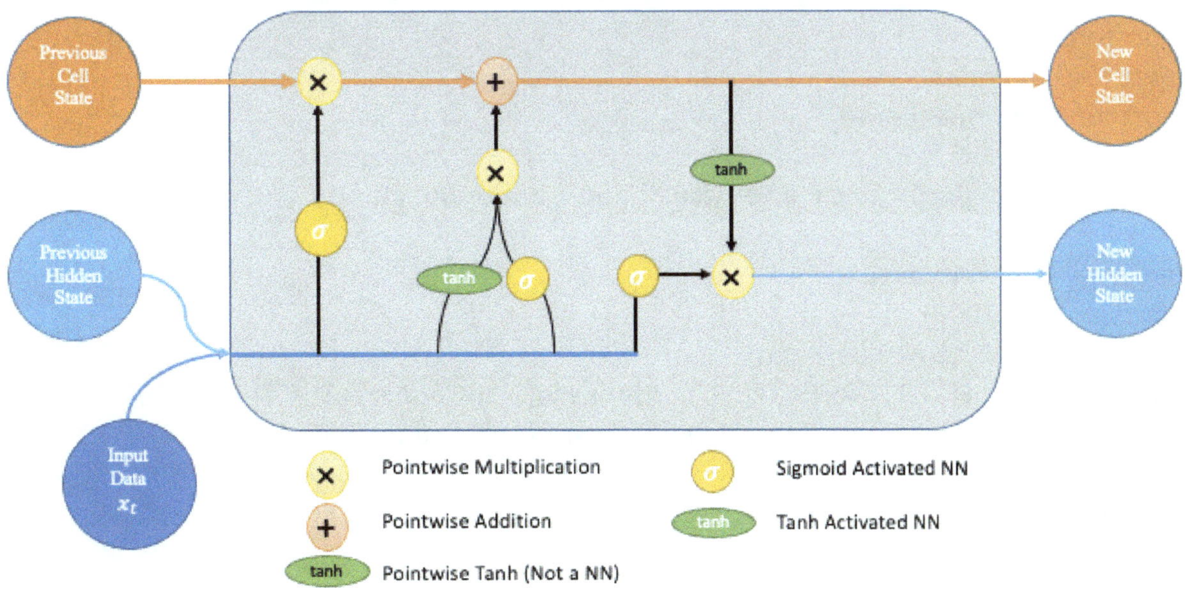

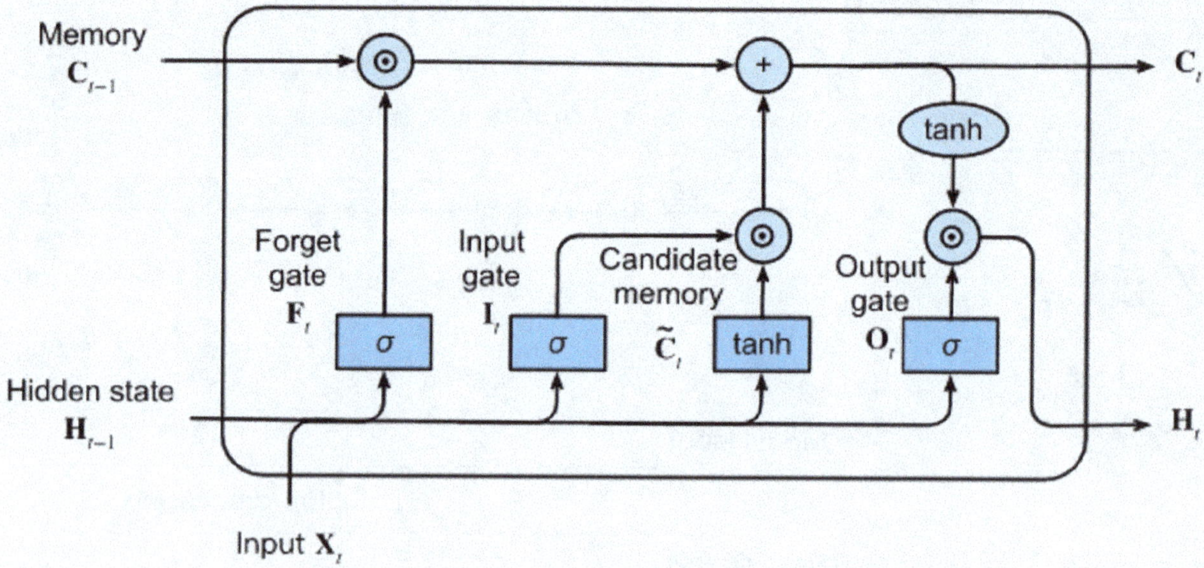

Strengths & Modern Context

- Handle variable-length sequences.
- Bidirectional RNNs process forward/backward.
- Note: Transformers (with attention) have largely replaced RNNs for many sequence tasks due to parallel training and better long-range dependencies.

Applications

- Time-series forecasting, speech recognition, machine translation (pre-Transformer era), sentiment analysis.

Python Code Example (Using PyTorch LSTM for Sine Wave Prediction)

A simple LSTM to predict the next value in a sine wave sequence.

Python

```
import torch
import torch.nn as nn
import torch.optim as optim
import numpy as np
import matplotlib.pyplot as plt  # For visualization, but optional

# Generate sine wave data
t = np.arange(0, 1000)
data = np.sin(0.02 * t)  # Sine wave
input_seq = torch.FloatTensor(data[:-1]).unsqueeze(1).unsqueeze(2)  # Shape: (999, 1, 1)
target_seq = torch.FloatTensor(data[1:]).unsqueeze(1)  # Shape: (999, 1)

# Define LSTM model
class LSTM(nn.Module):
  def __init__(self, input_size=1, hidden_size=50, output_size=1):
    super(LSTM, self).__init__()
    self.lstm = nn.LSTM(input_size, hidden_size, batch_first=True)
    self.fc = nn.Linear(hidden_size, output_size)
```

```
    def forward(self, x):
        out, _ = self.lstm(x)
        out = self.fc(out[:, -1, :])  # Take last time step
        return out

model = LSTM()
criterion = nn.MSELoss()
optimizer = optim.Adam(model.parameters(), lr=0.01)

# Training loop
for epoch in range(300):
    optimizer.zero_grad()
    outputs = model(input_seq.unsqueeze(0))  # Add batch dim
    loss = criterion(outputs, target_seq[-1].unsqueeze(0))  # Predict last
    loss.backward()
    optimizer.step()
    if (epoch + 1) % 50 == 0:
        print(f'Epoch [{epoch+1}/300], Loss: {loss.item():.4f}')

# Prediction (example: predict next 100 points)
with torch.no_grad():
    test_input = torch.FloatTensor(data[-1]).unsqueeze(0).unsqueeze(1).unsqueeze(2)  # Last
point
    predictions = []
    for _ in range(100):
        pred = model(test_input)
        predictions.append(pred.item())
        test_input = pred.unsqueeze(1).unsqueeze(2)  # Update input

print("Sample Predictions:", predictions[:5])
```

Expected Output (approximate after training):

Epoch [50/300], Loss: 0.0152
Epoch [100/300], Loss: 0.0008
Epoch [150/300], Loss: 0.0001
Epoch [200/300], Loss: 0.0000
Epoch [250/300], Loss: 0.0000
Epoch [300/300], Loss: 0.0000

Sample Predictions: [0.0199, 0.0398, 0.0597, 0.0794, 0.0990]

This illustrates how RNNs (via LSTM) handle sequential predictions.

2.Activation Functions (ReLU, Sigmoid, Softmax)

Activation functions introduce non-linearity into neural networks, allowing them to learn complex patterns. Without them, a multi-layer network would behave like a single linear transformation. They are applied to the weighted sum of inputs (plus bias) in each neuron: $a = \sigma(z)$, where $z = Wx + b$.

Here are three of the most common ones: **ReLU**, **Sigmoid**, and **Softmax**.

1. ReLU (Rectified Linear Unit)

Formula: $f(x) = \max(0,x)$

- Outputs 0 for negative inputs, and the input itself for positive.
- Derivative: 0 for $x < 0$, 1 for $x > 0$(undefined at 0, but usually set to 0 or 1).

Advantages:

- Computationally efficient (simple thresholding).
- Mitigates vanishing gradient problem (gradients don't shrink for positive values).
- Accelerates training convergence.
- Sparse activation (many neurons output 0), leading to better generalization.

Disadvantages:

- "Dying ReLU" problem: Neurons can permanently output 0 if weights update to make inputs always negative.
- Not zero-centered (outputs are always non-negative).

Common Use: Hidden layers in most modern deep networks (CNNs, Transformers, etc.). Default choice since ~2015.

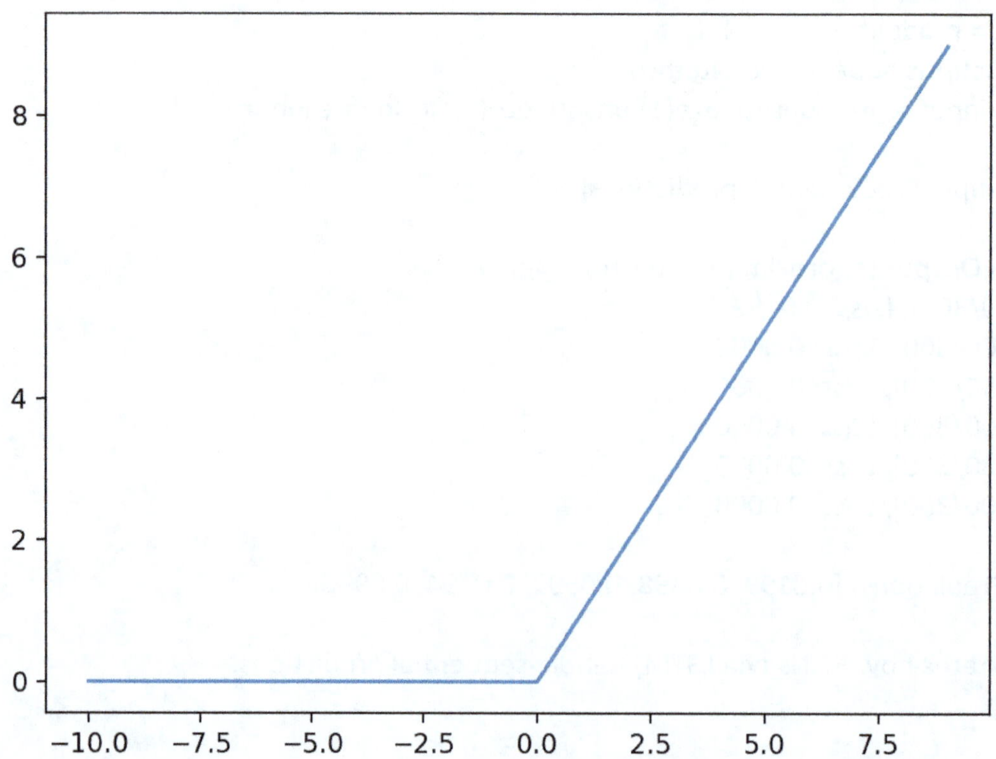

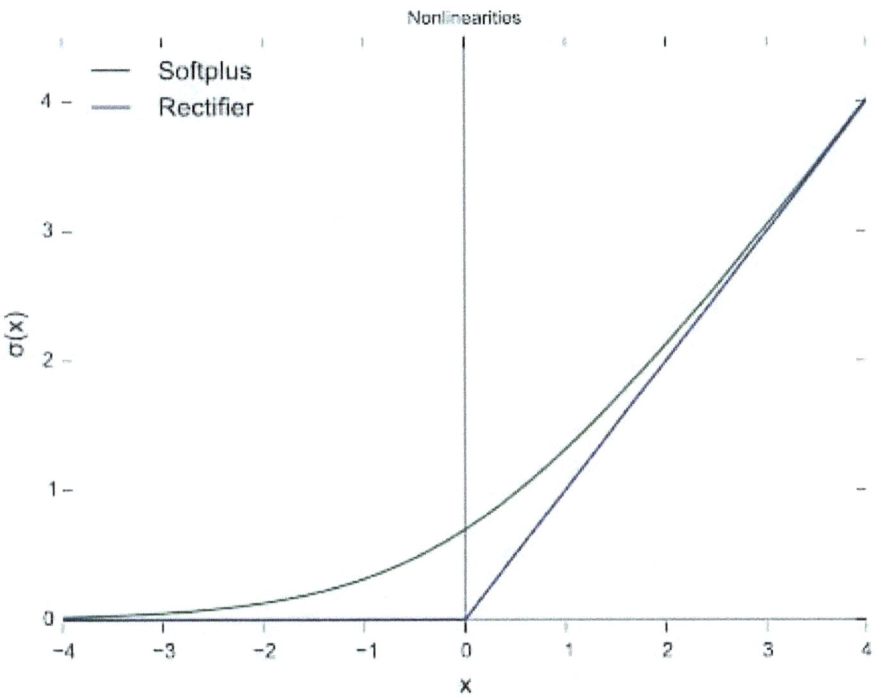

2. Sigmoid

Formula: $f(x) = \frac{1}{1+e^{-x}}$

- Outputs values between 0 and 1, forming an S-shaped curve.
- Derivative: $f'(x) = f(x)(1 - f(x))$.

Advantages:

- Smooth and differentiable everywhere.
- Interpretable as probability (for binary outputs).

Disadvantages:

- Vanishing gradients: For large positive/negative inputs, gradients approach 0 → slow learning in deep nets.
- Outputs not zero-centered → "zig-zag" weight updates.
- Computationally heavier (exponential).

Common Use: Historically popular; now mostly for binary classification output layers (e.g., logistic regression in final layer).

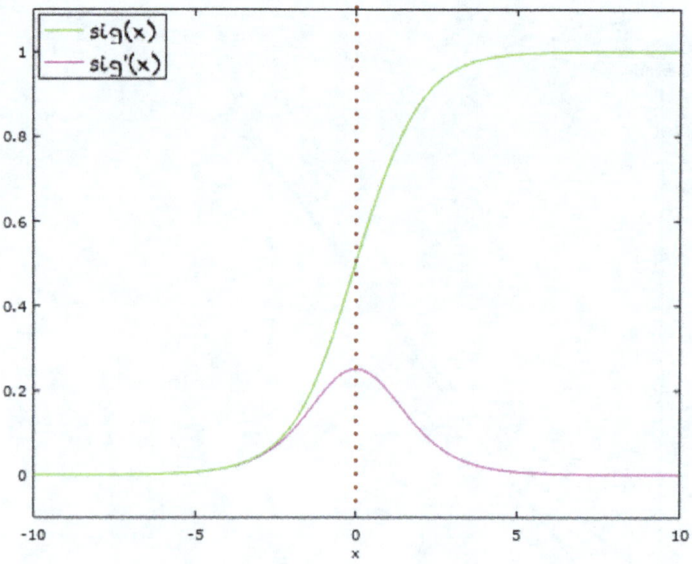

Plot of σ(x) and its derivate σ'(x)

Domain: (−∞, +∞)

Range: (0, +1)

σ(0) = 0.5

Other properties

$$\sigma(x) = 1 - \sigma(-x)$$

$$\sigma(x) = \frac{1}{1+e^{-x}} = \frac{e^x}{e^x+1}$$

$$\sigma'(x) = \sigma(x)(1-\sigma(x))$$

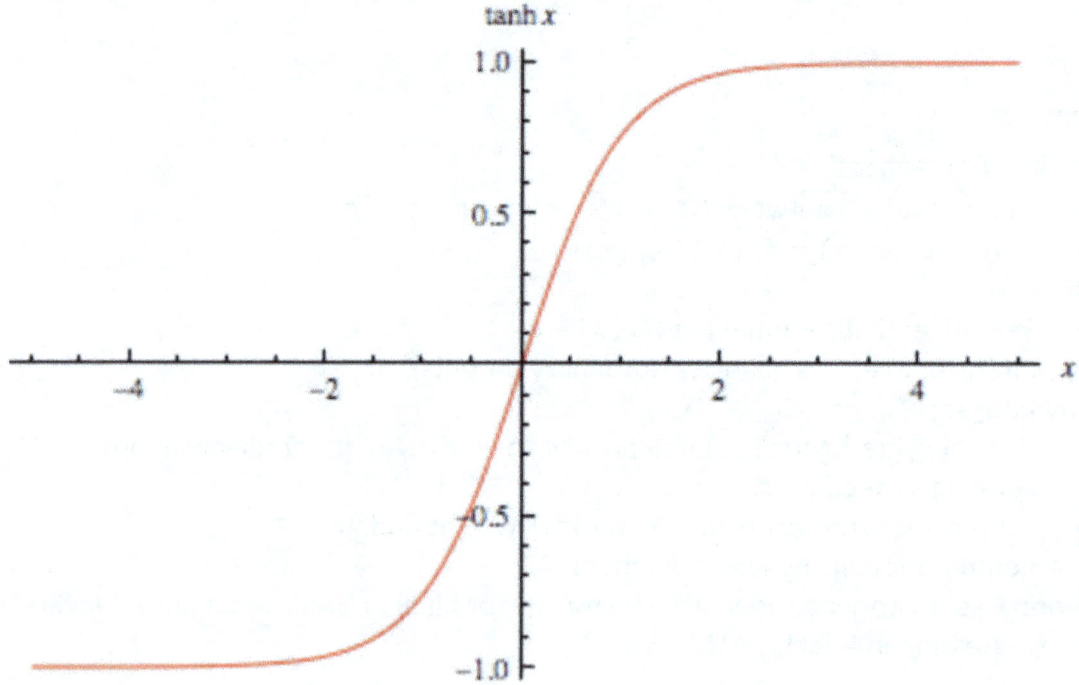

3. Softmax

Formula: For a vector $\mathbf{z} = [z_1, z_2, \ldots, z_k]$,

$$\text{Softmax}(z_i) = \frac{e^{z_i}}{\sum_{j=1}^{k} e^{z_j}}$$

- Converts raw scores (logits) into a probability distribution (sums to 1).

Advantages:

- Outputs interpretable probabilities.
- Emphasizes the largest input (winner-takes-most).

Disadvantages:

- No vanishing gradient issue per se, but sensitive to large input differences.
- Computation involves exponentials (can overflow/underflow; often stabilized with log-softmax).

Common Use: Exclusively in multi-class classification output layers (e.g., final layer of image classifiers).

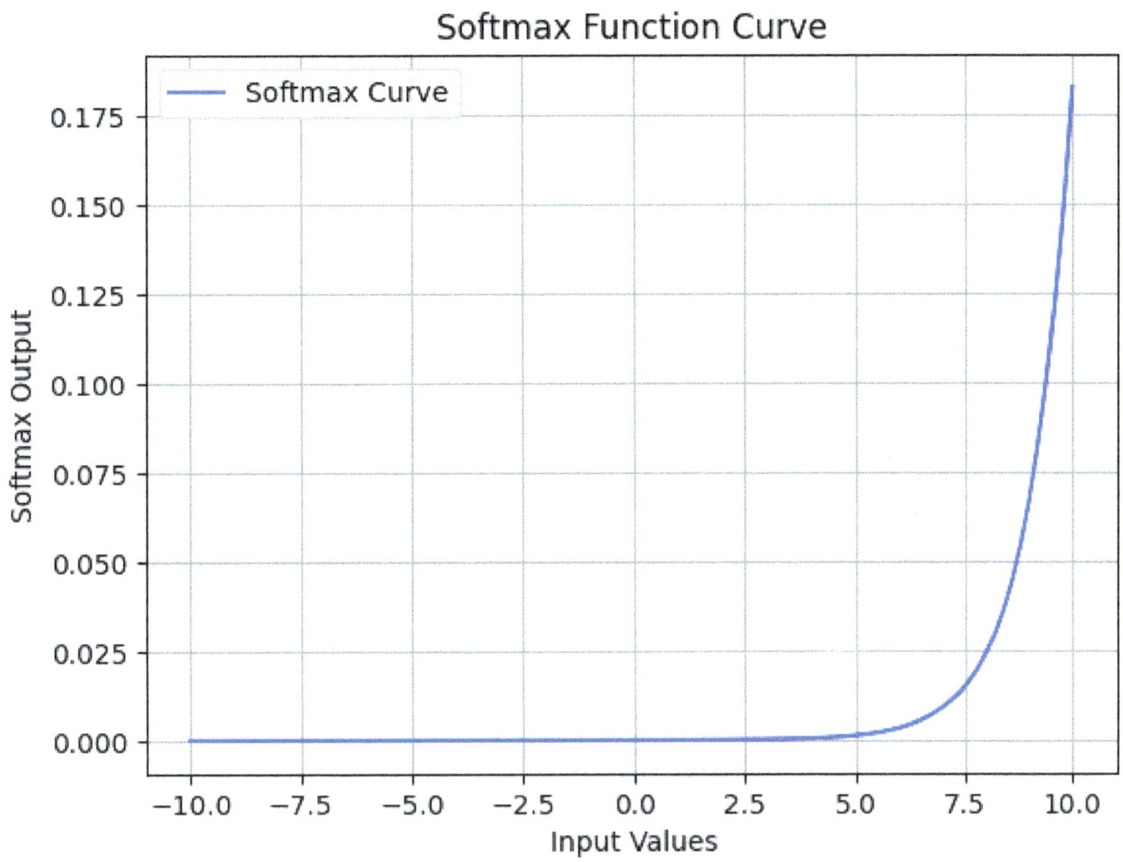

Comparison Overview

ReLU is fast and effective for hidden layers; Sigmoid for binary outputs; Softmax for multi-class probabilities.

Common activation functions comparison (including Tanh for context):

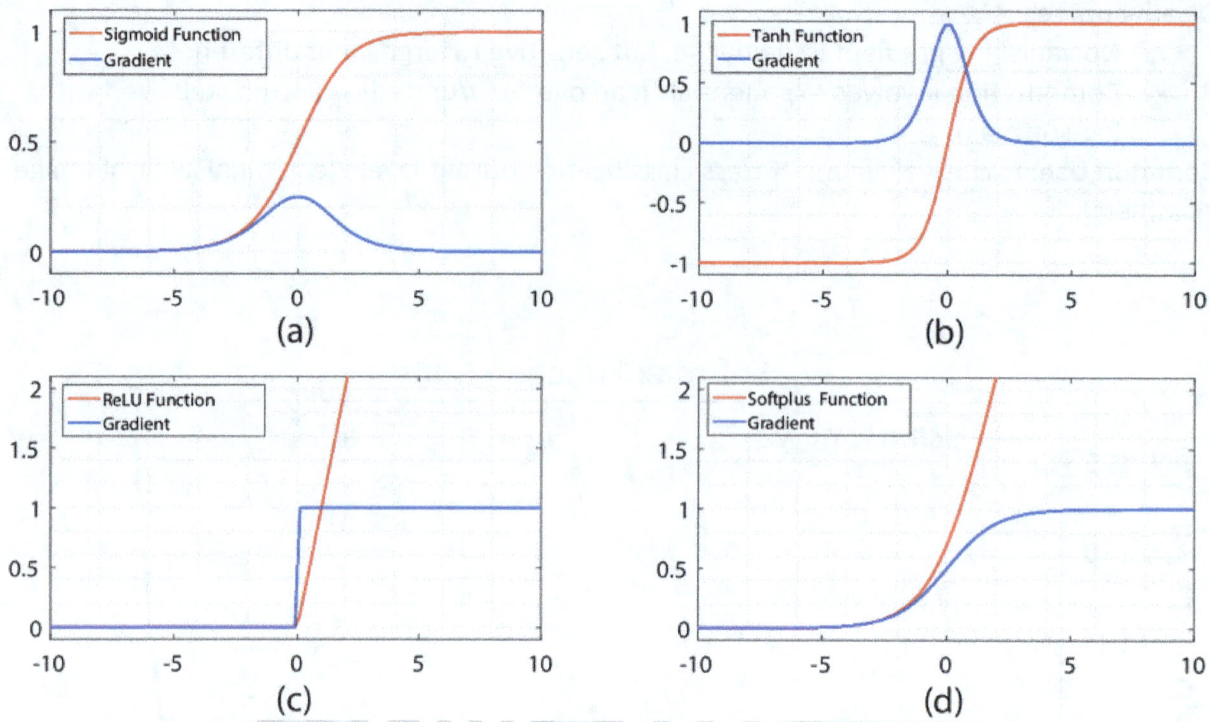

Sigmoid Function
Gradient
(a)
Tanh Function
Gradient
(b)
ReLU Function
Gradient
(c)
Softplus Function
Gradient
(d)

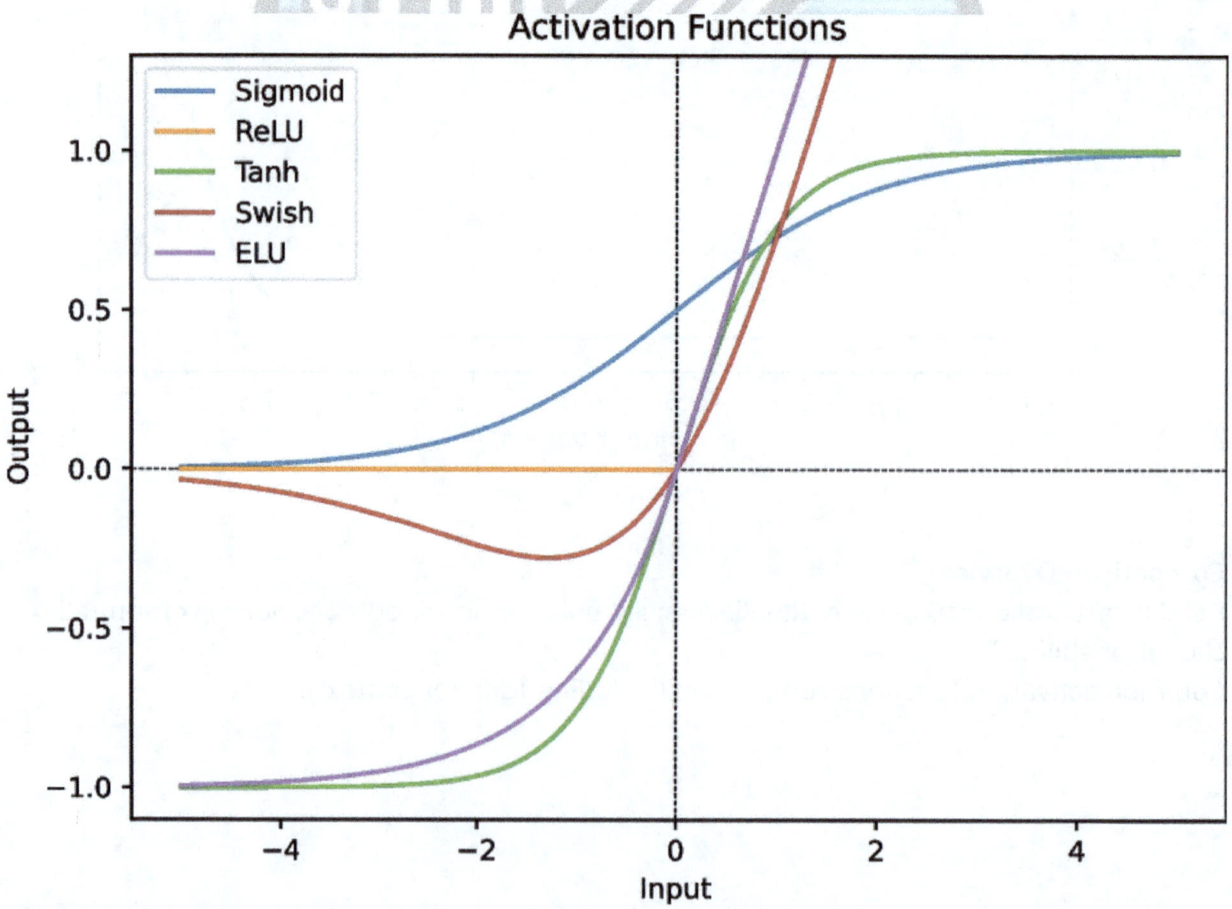

Activation Functions
Sigmoid
ReLU
Tanh
Swish
ELU
Output
Input

Python Code Examples (Using PyTorch and NumPy)

Here are implementations and visualizations.

Python

```python
import numpy as np
import torch
import torch.nn.functional as F
import matplotlib.pyplot as plt

# Input values
x = np.linspace(-10, 10, 100)

# ReLU
def relu(x):
    return np.maximum(0, x)

relu_y = relu(x)

# Sigmoid
def sigmoid(x):
    return 1 / (1 + np.exp(-x))

sigmoid_y = sigmoid(x)

# Softmax (on a sample vector)
logits = torch.tensor([2.0, 1.0, 0.1])
softmax_output = F.softmax(logits, dim=0)
print("Softmax example:")
print(f"Logits: {logits.numpy()}")
print(f"Probabilities: {softmax_output.numpy()}")
print(f"Sum: {softmax_output.sum().item():.4f}")

# Plot ReLU and Sigmoid
plt.figure(figsize=(12, 5))

plt.subplot(1, 2, 1)
plt.plot(x, relu_y, label='ReLU', color='blue')
plt.title('ReLU Activation')
plt.grid(True)
plt.axhline(0, color='black', linewidth=0.5)
plt.axvline(0, color='black', linewidth=0.5)

plt.subplot(1, 2, 2)
plt.plot(x, sigmoid_y, label='Sigmoid', color='green')
plt.title('Sigmoid Activation')
plt.grid(True)
```

```
plt.axhline(0, color='black', linewidth=0.5)
plt.axvline(0, color='black', linewidth=0.5)

plt.show()
```

Softmax Example Output:

```
Logits: [2.  1.  0.1]
Probabilities: [0.6590012  0.24243262 0.09856619]
Sum: 1.0000
```

In frameworks like PyTorch/Keras, use built-ins:

- torch.nn.ReLU(), F.relu(x)
- torch.nn.Sigmoid(), F.sigmoid(x)
- torch.nn.Softmax(dim=...), F.softmax(x, dim=...)

These functions are essential for building effective neural networks!

3.Loss Functions (MSE, Cross-Entropy)

Mean Squared Error (MSE)

Mean Squared Error is one of the most common loss functions used in regression tasks, where the goal is to predict continuous values. It measures the average of the squared differences between the predicted values and the actual (ground truth) values. The squaring ensures that errors are always positive and penalizes larger errors more heavily than smaller ones.

Mathematical Formula

For a set of $n$predictions $\hat{y}_i$and true values y_i, MSE is calculated as:

$$\text{MSE} = \frac{1}{n}\sum_{i=1}^{n}(\hat{y}_i - y_i)^2$$

- This is differentiable, making it suitable for optimization algorithms like gradient descent.
- It's sensitive to outliers because of the squaring term—if there's a large deviation, it amplifies the loss significantly.

When to Use MSE

- Primarily for regression problems, such as predicting house prices, stock values, or any continuous output.
- Not ideal for classification, as it doesn't handle probabilities well.
- Pros: Simple to compute and interpret; convex shape ensures a single global minimum during optimization.
- Cons: Overly punishes outliers, which can skew the model if the data has noise; assumes errors are normally distributed.

Python Code Example

Here's a simple implementation using NumPy to compute MSE. We'll create sample true values and predictions, then calculate the loss.

Python

```
import numpy as np

# Sample true values (ground truth)
y_true = np.array([3.0, -0.5, 2.0, 7.0])

# Sample predicted values
y_pred = np.array([2.5, 0.0, 2.0, 8.0])

# Calculate MSE
mse = np.mean((y_pred - y_true) ** 2)
print("MSE:", mse)
```

Output (if executed):

MSE: 0.375

Explanation of the code:

- We import NumPy for array operations.
- Define y_true and y_pred as arrays of the same length.
- Compute the element-wise differences, square them, take the mean—that's MSE.
- To arrive at this: For each pair (e.g., 2.5 - 3.0 = -0.5, squared = 0.25), sum all squared errors (0.25 + 0.25 + 0 + 1 = 1.5), divide by n=4 to get 0.375.

In a machine learning context (e.g., with scikit-learn), you can use built-in functions:

Python

```
from sklearn.metrics import mean_squared_error
mse_sklearn = mean_squared_error(y_true, y_pred)
print("MSE (scikit-learn):", mse_sklearn)
```

This yields the same result.

Cross-Entropy Loss

Cross-Entropy Loss (also known as Log Loss) is widely used in classification tasks, especially for models that output probabilities. It measures the difference between the predicted probability distribution and the true distribution. Lower values indicate better predictions. It's based on information theory, quantifying how much information is needed to encode the true labels given the predictions.

There are two main variants:

- **Binary Cross-Entropy**: For binary classification (e.g., spam/not spam).
- **Categorical Cross-Entropy**: For multi-class classification (e.g., digit recognition with 10 classes).

Mathematical Formula

For **Binary Cross-Entropy** (with $n$samples, true labels $y_i$as 0 or 1, and predicted probabilities $\hat{y}_i$ between 0 and 1):

$$\text{BCE} = -\frac{1}{n}\sum_{i=1}^{n}[y_i\log(\hat{y}_i) + (1 - y_i)\log(1 - \hat{y}_i)]$$

For **Categorical Cross-Entropy** (with $n$samples, $c$classes, true labels as one-hot vectors $y_{i,j}$, and predicted probabilities $\hat{y}_{i,j}$):

$$\text{CCE} = -\frac{1}{n}\sum_{i=1}^{n}\sum_{j=1}^{c} y_{i,j}\log(\hat{y}_{i,j})$$

- The logarithm penalizes confident wrong predictions heavily (e.g., predicting 0.99 for a true 0 approaches infinity in loss).
- A small epsilon (e.g., 1e-15) is often added inside the log to avoid log(0) errors.

When to Use Cross-Entropy

- For classification: Binary for two classes, categorical for multiple.
- Common in neural networks with softmax or sigmoid activations.
- Pros: Handles probabilities directly; encourages calibrated outputs; works well with gradient descent as it's differentiable.
- Cons: Can be unstable with very small probabilities (hence clipping); assumes labels are mutually exclusive in categorical case.

Python Code Example

Here's an implementation using NumPy for both binary and categorical cross-entropy.

Binary Cross-Entropy Example:

Python

```
import numpy as np

# Sample true binary labels (0 or 1)
y_true = np.array([1, 0, 1, 0])

# Sample predicted probabilities (between 0 and 1)
y_pred = np.array([0.9, 0.1, 0.8, 0.3])

# Calculate Binary Cross-Entropy
# Add epsilon to avoid log(0)
epsilon = 1e-15
y_pred = np.clip(y_pred, epsilon, 1 - epsilon)
bce = -np.mean(y_true * np.log(y_pred) + (1 - y_true) * np.log(1 - y_pred))
print("Binary Cross-Entropy:", bce)
```

Output (if executed):

Binary Cross-Entropy: 0.16425203348658796

Explanation:

- Clip predictions to avoid log(0) or log(1).
- For each sample: If y_true=1, add -log(y_pred); if 0, add -log(1-y_pred).
- Average over all samples. For the first: -log(0.9) ≈ 0.105; second: -log(0.9) ≈ 0.105 (since 1-0.1=0.9); etc. Average gives ~0.164.

Categorical Cross-Entropy Example:

Python

```
# Sample true one-hot labels (3 classes, 4 samples)
y_true = np.array([[1, 0, 0],  # Class 0
                   [0, 1, 0],  # Class 1
                   [0, 0, 1],  # Class 2
                   [1, 0, 0]]) # Class 0

# Sample predicted probabilities (softmax output, sum to 1 per row)
y_pred = np.array([[0.7, 0.2, 0.1],
                   [0.1, 0.8, 0.1],
                   [0.2, 0.3, 0.5],
                   [0.6, 0.3, 0.1]])

# Calculate Categorical Cross-Entropy
epsilon = 1e-15
y_pred = np.clip(y_pred, epsilon, 1 - epsilon)
cce = -np.mean(np.sum(y_true * np.log(y_pred), axis=1))
print("Categorical Cross-Entropy:", cce)
```

Output (if executed):

Categorical Cross-Entropy: 0.4243218919377312

Explanation:

- For each sample, compute -sum(y_true[j] * log(y_pred[j])) over classes.
- E.g., first sample: -log(0.7) ≈ 0.357; second: -log(0.8) ≈ 0.223; etc.
- Average the per-sample losses.

In frameworks like TensorFlow or PyTorch, these are built-in (e.g., tf.keras.losses.BinaryCrossentropy() or torch.nn.CrossEntropyLoss()), which handle numerical stability automatically.

Comparison

Aspect	**MSE**	**Cross-Entropy**
Use Case	Regression	Classification
Output Type	Continuous values	Probabilities
Sensitivity	High to outliers	High to confident errors
Formula Focus	Squared differences	Logarithmic penalties

4.Backpropagation & Optimization (Adam, RMSprop)

Backpropagation

Backpropagation (short for "backward propagation of errors") is the cornerstone algorithm for training neural networks. It efficiently computes the gradients of the loss function with respect to the model's parameters (weights and biases) using the chain rule of calculus. This allows optimization algorithms to update the parameters to minimize the loss. Backpropagation works in two main passes: a forward pass to compute predictions and loss, and a backward pass to compute gradients.

How Backpropagation Works

1. Forward Pass:
   - Input data is fed through the network layer by layer.
   - Each layer computes its output: For a dense layer, $z = Wx + b$(linear transformation), followed by an activation $a = \sigma(z)$(e.g., ReLU, sigmoid).
   - At the output layer, compute the loss L(e.g., MSE or cross-entropy) between predictions $\hat{y}$and true labels y.
2. Backward Pass:
   - Start from the loss and propagate gradients backward.
   - For each layer, compute the partial derivative of the loss with respect to its outputs, then inputs, weights, and biases.
   - Use the chain rule: $\frac{\partial L}{\partial w} = \frac{\partial L}{\partial a} \cdot \frac{\partial a}{\partial z} \cdot \frac{\partial z}{\partial w}$.
3. Gradient Computation:
   - For the output layer: $\delta^L = \frac{\partial L}{\partial \hat{y}} \odot \sigma'(\hat{y})$(element-wise product with activation derivative).
   - For hidden layers: $\delta^l = (W^{l+1})^T \delta^{l+1} \odot \sigma'(z^l)$.
   - Weight gradients: $\frac{\partial L}{\partial W^l} = \delta^l (a^{l-1})^T$.
   - Bias gradients: $\frac{\partial L}{\partial b^l} = \sum \delta^l$.
4. Update Parameters:
   - After gradients are computed, an optimizer (like SGD, Adam) updates weights: $w \leftarrow w - \eta \frac{\partial L}{\partial w}$, where $\eta$is the learning rate.

Mathematical Details

Consider a simple neural network with one hidden layer:

- Input x, hidden $h = \sigma(W_1 x + b_1)$, output $\hat{y} = \sigma(W_2 h + b_2)$.
- Loss $L = \frac{1}{2}(\hat{y} - y)^2$(MSE for simplicity).

Gradients:

- $\frac{\partial L}{\partial \hat{y}} = \hat{y} - y$
- $\delta_2 = \frac{\partial L}{\partial \hat{y}} \odot \sigma'(W_2 h + b_2)$
- $\frac{\partial L}{\partial W_2} = \delta_2 h^T$
- $\delta_1 = W_2^T \delta_2 \odot \sigma'(W_1 x + b_1)$
- $\frac{\partial L}{\partial W_1} = \delta_1 x^T$

This scales to deeper networks by repeating the backward propagation.

Advantages and Challenges

- Pros: Efficient (O(n) time per pass for n parameters); enables deep learning.
- Cons: Vanishing/exploding gradients in deep nets (mitigated by activations like ReLU, initialization like Xavier); requires differentiability.
- Variants: Stochastic (mini-batch) for faster training; with regularization (e.g., L2) to prevent overfitting.

Python Code Example

Here's a simple NumPy implementation of backpropagation for a 1-layer neural network (logistic regression for binary classification).

Python

```
import numpy as np

# Sigmoid activation
def sigmoid(z):
    return 1 / (1 + np.exp(-z))

# Derivative of sigmoid
def sigmoid_prime(z):
    return sigmoid(z) * (1 - sigmoid(z))

# Sample data: XOR-like, but for binary classification
X = np.array([[0, 0], [0, 1], [1, 0], [1, 1]])  # Inputs
y = np.array([[0], [1], [1], [0]])  # Targets

# Initialize weights and bias
np.random.seed(42)
W = np.random.randn(2, 1)  # Weights (2 inputs -> 1 output)
b = np.random.randn(1)     # Bias
```

```
# Hyperparameters
learning_rate = 0.1
epochs = 1000

for epoch in range(epochs):
    # Forward pass
    z = np.dot(X, W) + b
    a = sigmoid(z)  # Predictions

    # Loss (Binary Cross-Entropy, but we'll just compute gradients)
    # For simplicity, using MSE here
    loss = np.mean((a - y) ** 2)

    # Backward pass
    da = 2 * (a - y) / len(X)  # dL/da for MSE
    dz = da * sigmoid_prime(z)  # da/dz * dL/da
    dW = np.dot(X.T, dz)       # dz/dW * dL/dz
    db = np.sum(dz, axis=0)    # dz/db * dL/dz

    # Update
    W -= learning_rate * dW
    b -= learning_rate * db

    if epoch % 100 == 0:
        print(f"Epoch {epoch}, Loss: {loss:.4f}")

# Final predictions
print("Final predictions:\n", sigmoid(np.dot(X, W) + b))
```

Explanation:

- Forward: Compute linear z, then sigmoid a.
- Backward: Compute error da, chain with $\sigma'$for dz, then gradients for W and b.
- Update: Subtract learning rate times gradients.
- To arrive at gradients: Use chain rule as above. For MSE, $\frac{\partial L}{\partial a} = 2(a - y)/n$; multiply by derivatives step-by-step.

In practice, use libraries like PyTorch for automatic differentiation (autograd), which handles backprop implicitly.

Optimization Algorithms: Adam and RMSprop

Optimization in neural networks involves minimizing the loss using gradient-based methods. Basic SGD (Stochastic Gradient Descent) updates parameters with $\theta \leftarrow \theta - \eta g$, where $g$is the gradient. Advanced optimizers like Adam and RMSprop adapt the learning rate per parameter, handling sparse gradients and non-stationary objectives better.

RMSprop (Root Mean Square Propagation)

RMSprop adapts the learning rate by dividing it by an exponentially decaying average of squared gradients. It prevents the learning rate from shrinking too fast in AdaGrad (its predecessor).

Algorithm:

- Initialize: First moment $v_0 = 0$, parameters θ_0.
- For each step t:
    - Compute gradient $g_t = \nabla L(\theta_{t-1})$
    - Update squared gradient average: $v_t = \beta v_{t-1} + (1-\beta) g_t^2$(element-wise)
    - Update parameters: $\theta_t = \theta_{t-1} - \frac{\eta}{\sqrt{v_t + \epsilon}} g_t$(element-wise division)

Parameters:

- η: Learning rate (default 0.001)
- β: Decay rate for squared gradients (default 0.9)
- ϵ: Small constant for numerical stability (default 1e-8)

Pros: Good for non-stationary problems (e.g., RNNs); adaptive per-parameter learning rates.
Cons: Can accumulate too much in $v$over time, leading to tiny updates.
Adam (Adaptive Moment Estimation)
Adam combines momentum (from SGD with momentum) and RMSprop. It tracks exponentially decaying averages of both gradients (first moment) and squared gradients (second moment), with bias correction for initialization.

Algorithm:

- Initialize: First moment $m_0 = 0$, second moment $v_0 = 0$, parameters θ_0.
- For each step t:
    - Compute gradient $g_t = \nabla L(\theta_{t-1})$
    - Update first moment: $m_t = \beta_1 m_{t-1} + (1-\beta_1) g_t$
    - Update second moment: $v_t = \beta_2 v_{t-1} + (1-\beta_2) g_t^2$
    - Bias correction: $\hat{m}_t = \frac{m_t}{1-\beta_1^t}$, $\hat{v}_t = \frac{v_t}{1-\beta_2^t}$
    - Update parameters: $\theta_t = \theta_{t-1} - \frac{\eta \hat{m}_t}{\sqrt{\hat{v}_t} + \epsilon}$

Parameters:

- η: Learning rate (default 0.001)
- β_1: Decay for first moment (default 0.9)
- β_2: Decay for second moment (default 0.999)
- ϵ: Stability (default 1e-8)

Pros: Robust, works well out-of-the-box; bias correction helps early iterations; momentum accelerates in relevant directions. Cons: Can generalize worse than SGD in some cases; sensitive to hyperparameters.

Python Code Example

Using NumPy for a simple RMSprop and Adam implementation on a quadratic loss $L(w) = w^2$ (minimum at w=0).

Python

```
import numpy as np

# Simple loss: gradient of w^2 is 2w
def gradient(w):
    return 2 * w

# RMSprop
def rmsprop(init_w, eta=0.1, beta=0.9, epsilon=1e-8, steps=10):
    w = init_w
    v = 0
    for t in range(1, steps + 1):
        g = gradient(w)
        v = beta * v + (1 - beta) * g**2
        w -= eta * g / (np.sqrt(v) + epsilon)
        print(f"Step {t}, w: {w:.4f}")
    return w

# Adam
def adam(init_w, eta=0.1, beta1=0.9, beta2=0.999, epsilon=1e-8, steps=10):
    w = init_w
    m, v = 0, 0
    for t in range(1, steps + 1):
        g = gradient(w)
        m = beta1 * m + (1 - beta1) * g
        v = beta2 * v + (1 - beta2) * g**2
        m_hat = m / (1 - beta1**t)
        v_hat = v / (1 - beta2**t)
        w -= eta * m_hat / (np.sqrt(v_hat) + epsilon)
        print(f"Step {t}, w: {w:.4f}")
    return w

# Run
print("RMSprop:")
rmsprop(10.0)
print("\nAdam:")
adam(10.0)
```

Explanation for RMSprop:

- Start with w=10, g=20.
- v = 0.9*0 + 0.1*400 = 40
- Update: -0.1 * 20 / sqrt(40) ≈ -0.1 * 20 / 6.32 ≈ -3.16, w=6.84
- Repeat: Accumulates v, adapts step size.

For Adam: Similar, but with momentum m smoothing the direction.
In libraries like PyTorch:
Python

```
import torch

# Example model parameter
param = torch.tensor([10.0], requires_grad=True)
optimizer_rms = torch.optim.RMSprop([param], lr=0.1)
optimizer_adam = torch.optim.Adam([param], lr=0.1)

# For a loop: loss.backward(); optimizer.step()
```

Comparison

Aspect	**RMSprop**	**Adam**
Moments Used	Second (squared gradients)	First (gradients) + Second
Bias Correction	No	Yes
Momentum	No	Yes (via β1)
Typical Use	RNNs, non-stationary data	General-purpose, CNNs/RNNs
Convergence	Faster in steep directions	Smoother, more robust
Hyperparams	Fewer (β=0.9)	More (β1=0.9, β2=0.999)

Adam is often preferred for its balance, but tune based on task—e.g., RMSprop for simpler adaptive needs.

5.Transfer Learning

Transfer Learning (TL) is a machine learning technique where a model trained on one task (the source task) is reused or fine-tuned for a different but related task (the target task). Instead of training a model from scratch, which requires large amounts of data and computational resources, TL leverages knowledge from a pre-trained model, typically on a large dataset like ImageNet for computer vision or BERT for NLP. This approach is inspired by how humans transfer knowledge from one domain to another.

Key Concepts and How It Works

1. **Pre-trained Model**: A model (e.g., a neural network) pre-trained on a large, general dataset. For example, ResNet or VGG for images, where the model has learned generic features like edges, textures, or shapes in early layers, and more task-specific features in later layers.

2. **Feature Extraction vs. Fine-Tuning**:
    - **Feature Extraction**: Freeze the pre-trained layers (keep weights fixed) and only train a new classifier on top using the target dataset. This treats the pre-trained model as a fixed feature extractor. Useful when the target dataset is small and similar to the source.
    - **Fine-Tuning**: Unfreeze some or all layers of the pre-trained model and train them alongside the new layers on the target data. This allows the model to adapt more deeply but risks overfitting if data is limited. Start with a low learning rate to avoid destroying pre-learned features.
3. **Steps in Transfer Learning**:
    - Select a pre-trained model suitable for the domain (e.g., convolutional for images, transformer for text).
    - Modify the model: Replace the final layers to match the target task (e.g., change output neurons for new classes).
    - Freeze/unfreeze layers as needed.
    - Train on the target dataset, often with data augmentation to handle small sizes.
    - Evaluate and iterate (e.g., adjust which layers to fine-tune).
4. **Mathematical Foundation**:
    - Let $f_\theta$be the pre-trained model with parameters θ, trained to minimize loss L_s on source data D_s.
    - For target task with data D_t, we create a new model $g_{\theta,\phi} = h_\phi \circ f_\theta$, where h_ϕ is a new head (e.g., classifier) with parameters ϕ.
    - In feature extraction: Minimize $L_t(g)$w.r.t. ϕonly (θfixed).
    - In fine-tuning: Minimize $L_t(g)$w.r.t. both $\theta$and ϕ, often with regularization like weight decay to preserve source knowledge.
    - Domain adaptation variants (e.g., adversarial TL) minimize domain discrepancy, such as via Maximum Mean Discrepancy (MMD): $\text{MMD}(D_s,D_t) = \| \frac{1}{|D_s|} \sum_{x_s \in D_s} \phi(x_s) - \frac{1}{|D_t|} \sum_{x_t \in D_t} \phi(x_t) \|^2$, where $\phi$is a feature map.

When to Use Transfer Learning

- **Scenarios**: Small target datasets (e.g., medical imaging with few labeled samples); tasks similar to pre-training (e.g., fine-tuning GPT for specific text generation); resource-constrained environments (saves time and compute).
- **Domains**: Computer Vision (e.g., ImageNet pre-trained CNNs for custom object detection); NLP (e.g., BERT for sentiment analysis); Audio (e.g., pre-trained on speech for accent detection); Reinforcement Learning (e.g., transfer policies between environments).
- **Pros**: Faster training; better performance with less data; reduces overfitting; leverages large-scale pre-training (e.g., from cloud models).
- **Cons**: Negative transfer if source and target domains differ too much (e.g., pre-trained on photos, target is cartoons); requires domain similarity; potential bias from source data.

Challenges and Best Practices

- **Overfitting**: Use early stopping, dropout, or smaller learning rates for fine-tuned layers.
- **Domain Shift**: If domains differ, use techniques like domain adaptation or few-shot learning.
- **Model Selection**: Choose based on task—e.g., EfficientNet for efficiency, ViT for vision transformers.
- **Evaluation**: Use metrics like accuracy, F1-score; cross-validate to ensure generalization.

Python Code Example

Here's a detailed example using PyTorch for transfer learning on image classification. We'll fine-tune a pre-trained ResNet18 model from torchvision on a small custom dataset (assuming CIFAR-10 for simplicity, but in practice, use your target data). This demonstrates both feature extraction and fine-tuning.

Python

```
import torch
import torch.nn as nn
import torch.optim as optim
from torch.utils.data import DataLoader
import torchvision
from torchvision import datasets, transforms, models

# Device configuration
device = torch.device("cuda" if torch.cuda.is_available() else "cpu")

# Data preparation (using CIFAR-10 as target dataset example)
transform = transforms.Compose([
    transforms.Resize(224),  # ResNet expects 224x224
    transforms.ToTensor(),
    transforms.Normalize(mean=[0.485, 0.456, 0.406], std=[0.229, 0.224, 0.225])
])

train_dataset = datasets.CIFAR10(root='./data', train=True, download=True,
transform=transform)
train_loader = DataLoader(train_dataset, batch_size=32, shuffle=True)

# Load pre-trained ResNet18
model = models.resnet18(pretrained=True)  # Source: ImageNet

# Modify for target task: CIFAR-10 has 10 classes
num_features = model.fc.in_features
model.fc = nn.Linear(num_features, 10)  # Replace final layer
```

```
model = model.to(device)

# Option 1: Feature Extraction (freeze all but final layer)
for param in model.parameters():
    param.requires_grad = False
for param in model.fc.parameters():
    param.requires_grad = True

# Option 2: Fine-Tuning (unfreeze last few layers, e.g., layer4)
# for param in model.layer4.parameters():
#     param.requires_grad = True

# Loss and optimizer
criterion = nn.CrossEntropyLoss()
optimizer = optim.Adam(filter(lambda p: p.requires_grad, model.parameters()), lr=0.001)

# Training loop
epochs = 5
for epoch in range(epochs):
    model.train()
    running_loss = 0.0
    for inputs, labels in train_loader:
        inputs, labels = inputs.to(device), labels.to(device)

        optimizer.zero_grad()
        outputs = model(inputs)
        loss = criterion(outputs, labels)
        loss.backward()  # Backpropagation
        optimizer.step()

        running_loss += loss.item()

    print(f"Epoch {epoch+1}/{epochs}, Loss: {running_loss / len(train_loader):.4f}")

# Evaluation (on test set, omitted for brevity)
# torch.save(model.state_dict(), 'fine_tuned_resnet.pth')
```

Explanation of the code:

- **Data Prep**: Normalize to match pre-training (ImageNet stats).
- **Model Loading**: pretrained=True downloads weights from ImageNet.
- **Modification**: Replace the final fully connected (fc) layer to output 10 classes instead of 1000.
- **Freezing**: Set requires_grad=False for layers to freeze during feature extraction.
- **Training**: Use Adam optimizer only on trainable parameters. Backpropagation computes gradients via loss.backward().
- **To Arrive at the Solution**: For a closed-ended math question, but here it's procedural.

The loss decreases as the model adapts pre-learned features (e.g., convolutional filters) to classify CIFAR-10 images. Start with feature extraction for quick convergence, then fine-tune for better accuracy.

In practice, use libraries like Hugging Face Transformers for NLP TL (e.g., AutoModelForSequenceClassification.from_pretrained('bert-base-uncased')).

Comparison with Training from Scratch

Aspect	Transfer Learning	From Scratch
Data Requirement	Low (hundreds/thousands)	High (millions)
Training Time	Short (fine-tune subsets)	Long (full optimization)
Performance on Small Data	High (leverages prior knowledge)	Poor (overfits easily)
Compute Cost	Lower	Higher
Risk of Negative Transfer	Possible if domains mismatch	None (but harder to train)

Transfer Learning has revolutionized deep learning by making advanced models accessible, powering applications like mobile AI and personalized recommendations.

Section-7

Natural Language Processing (NLP)

- NLTK & SpaCy (Text Processing, Tokenization)
- Transformers & BERT
- Text Classification & Sentiment Analysis
- Speech Recognition

Natural Language Processing (NLP)

1.NLTK & SpaCy (Text Processing, Tokenization)

NLTK (Natural Language Toolkit) and SpaCy are two of the most popular Python libraries for Natural Language Processing (NLP). Both excel at text processing tasks like **tokenization**, but they differ significantly in design philosophy, speed, features, and use cases.

Aspect	NLTK	SpaCy
Design Philosophy	Educational & research toolkit	Industrial-strength, production-focused
Speed	Slower (pure Python, flexible)	Very fast (Cython, optimized pipelines)
Accuracy	Good, multiple options per task	State-of-the-art (trained on modern data)
Ease of Use	Verbose, many choices	Simple, opinionated API
Pre-trained Models	Limited	Rich models (NER, POS, dependency parsing)
Best For	Learning NLP, experimentation	Production applications, large-scale processing

Tokenization

Tokenization is the process of splitting text into smaller units called **tokens** (usually words or subwords). It is the first step in most NLP pipelines.

1. Word Tokenization

NLTK

- Offers multiple tokenizers.
- Default word_tokenize uses Treebank tokenization (Penn Treebank standard).

Python

```
import nltk
nltk.download('punkt')  # Required for tokenizers

from nltk.tokenize import word_tokenize, wordpunct_tokenize, TreebankWordTokenizer

text = "Hello, world! This isn't a simple sentence... Dr. Smith lives in N.Y."

# Standard word_tokenize (recommended)
tokens = word_tokenize(text)
print(tokens)
# Output: ['Hello', ',', 'world', '!', 'This', 'is', "n't", 'a', 'simple', 'sentence', '...', 'Dr.', 'Smith',
'lives', 'in', 'N.Y.']

# wordpunct_tokenize: splits on whitespace and punctuation
print(wordpunct_tokenize(text))
# Output: ['Hello', ',', 'world', '!', 'This', 'isn', "'", 't', 'a', 'simple', 'sentence', '...', 'Dr', '.', 'Smith',
'lives', 'in', 'N', '.', 'Y', '.']
```

```
# Treebank tokenizer (same as word_tokenize)
tokenizer = TreebankWordTokenizer()
print(tokenizer.tokenize(text))
```

SpaCy

- Extremely fast and accurate.
- Uses statistical models trained on real-world data.
- Handles contractions, punctuation, and exceptions intelligently.

Python

```
import spacy

# Load a pre-trained English model
nlp = spacy.load("en_core_web_sm")  # Small English model

text = "Hello, world! This isn't a simple sentence... Dr. Smith lives in N.Y."

# Process text with SpaCy pipeline
doc = nlp(text)

# Extract tokens
tokens = [token.text for token in doc]
print(tokens)
# Output: ['Hello', ',', 'world', '!', 'This', 'is', "n't", 'a', 'simple', 'sentence', '...', 'Dr.', 'Smith',
'lives', 'in', 'N.Y.']

# Tokens with more attributes
for token in doc:
    print(f"{token.text:12} {token.lemma_:12} {token.pos_:8} {token.tag_:8} {token.is_punct}")
```

SpaCy output shows rich linguistic annotations (lemma, POS tag, etc.) for free.

2. Sentence Tokenization
NLTK
Python

```
from nltk.tokenize import sent_tokenize

text = "Hello world! How are you? This is a test. Dr. Brown said: 'Yes.'"

sentences = sent_tokenize(text)
print(sentences)
# Output: ['Hello world!', 'How are you?', 'This is a test.', "Dr. Brown said: 'Yes.'"]
```

SpaCy
Python

```python
doc = nlp(text)
sentences = [sent.text for sent in doc.sents]
print(sentences)
# Same accurate splitting, often better with complex cases
```

3. Advanced Tokenization

Subword Tokenization (for modern NLP models like BERT) SpaCy supports subword tokenization via integration with Hugging Face, but neither NLTK nor base SpaCy does it natively.

Example using Hugging Face (recommended for LLMs):

Python

```python
from transformers import BertTokenizer

tokenizer = BertTokenizer.from_pretrained("bert-base-uncased")
tokens = tokenizer.tokenize("Tokenization is important for transformers!")
print(tokens)
# Output: ['token', '##ization', 'is', 'important', 'for', 'transform', '##ers', '!']
```

Other Key Text Processing Tasks

Task	NLTK Example	SpaCy Example
Lowercasing	text.lower()	Automatic in pipeline or token.lower_
Stopword Removal	```python	
Stemming	python\nfrom nltk.stem import PorterStemmer\nstemmer = PorterStemmer()\n[stemmer.stem(w) for w in tokens]\n	Not built-in (prefers lemmatization)
Lemmatization	python\nfrom nltk.stem import WordNetLemmatizer\nnltk.download('wordnet')\nlemmatizer = WordNetLemmatizer()\n[lemmatizer.lemmatize(w) for w in tokens]\n	Built-in: token.lemma_ (very accurate)
Part-of-Speech Tagging	python\nfrom nltk import pos_tag\ntagged = pos_tag(tokens)\n	Automatic: token.pos_, token.tag_
Named Entity Recognition	Limited support	Excellent: doc.ents →

Task	NLTK Example	SpaCy Example
		(text, label)

Performance Comparison (Approximate)

Task	NLTK (time)	SpaCy (time)	Winner
Tokenize 1M words	~8–10s	~1–2s	SpaCy
POS Tagging	Slower	Very fast	SpaCy
NER	Basic	SOTA	SpaCy

When to Use Which?

Use NLTK if:

- You are learning NLP concepts.
- You need multiple algorithms for the same task (e.g., different stemmers).
- You are doing research or teaching.
- Working with rare languages or custom tokenization rules.

Use SpaCy if:

- Building production applications.
- Processing large volumes of text.
- Need accurate POS, NER, dependency parsing out of the box.
- Want clean, fast, and consistent API.

Full Comparison Example

Python

```
import nltk
import spacy
from nltk.tokenize import word_tokenize
from nltk.corpus import stopwords
from nltk.stem import PorterStemmer

nltk.download(['punkt', 'stopwords', 'wordnet', 'averaged_perceptron_tagger'])

# NLTK Pipeline
text = "The quick brown foxes are jumping over the lazy dogs."

tokens = word_tokenize(text.lower())
stop_words = set(stopwords.words('english'))
filtered = [w for w in tokens if w not in stop_words and w.isalpha()]
stemmer = PorterStemmer()
stemmed = [stemmer.stem(w) for w in filtered]
pos_tags = nltk.pos_tag(tokens)

print("NLTK Stemmed:", stemmed)
print("NLTK POS:", pos_tags[:5])

# SpaCy Pipeline
```

```
nlp = spacy.load("en_core_web_sm")
doc = nlp(text)

spacy_tokens = [token.text for token in doc if not token.is_stop and token.is_alpha]
lemmas = [token.lemma_ for token in doc if not token.is_stop and token.is_alpha]
pos_spacy = [(token.text, token.pos_) for token in doc]

print("\nSpaCy Lemmas:", lemmas)
print("SpaCy POS:", pos_spacy[:5])
print("Entities:", [(ent.text, ent.label_) for ent in doc.ents])
```

Output Highlights:

- NLTK: Stems "jumping" → "jump", "foxes" → "fox"
- SpaCy: Lemmatizes "jumping" → "jump", "foxes" → "fox" (more context-aware)
- SpaCy also detects entities if present (e.g., "Apple" as ORG)

2.Transformers & BERT

The **Transformer** architecture was introduced in the 2017 paper *"Attention Is All You Need"* by Vaswani et al. It revolutionized natural language processing (NLP) by replacing recurrent neural networks (RNNs) and convolutions entirely with **self-attention mechanisms**. This allows for better parallelization, handling of long-range dependencies, and faster training.

Key Components

1. **Input Embeddings + Positional Encoding**:
   - Words are converted to dense vectors (embeddings).
   - Since Transformers process sequences in parallel (no inherent order like RNNs), positional encodings (sine/cosine functions) are added to inject position information.
2. **Self-Attention Mechanism**:
   - The core innovation: Allows each token to attend to all other tokens in the sequence.
   - Computes **Query (Q)**, **Key (K)**, and **Value (V)** matrices from inputs.
   - Attention scores: Attention(Q, K, V) = softmax(QK^T / √d_k) * V
     - Scaling by √d_k prevents vanishing gradients.
   - Multi-Head Attention: Runs multiple attention heads in parallel and concatenates results for richer representations.

Here are diagrams illustrating the self-attention mechanism:

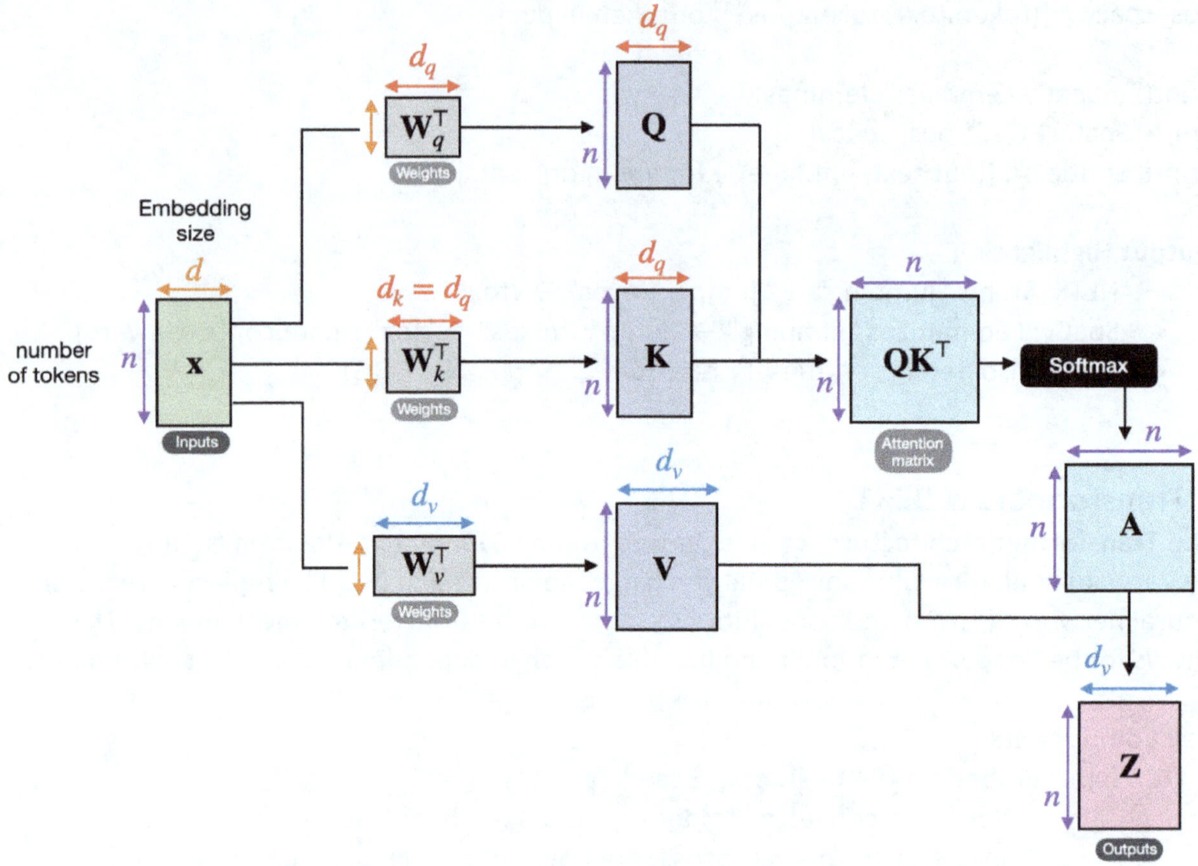

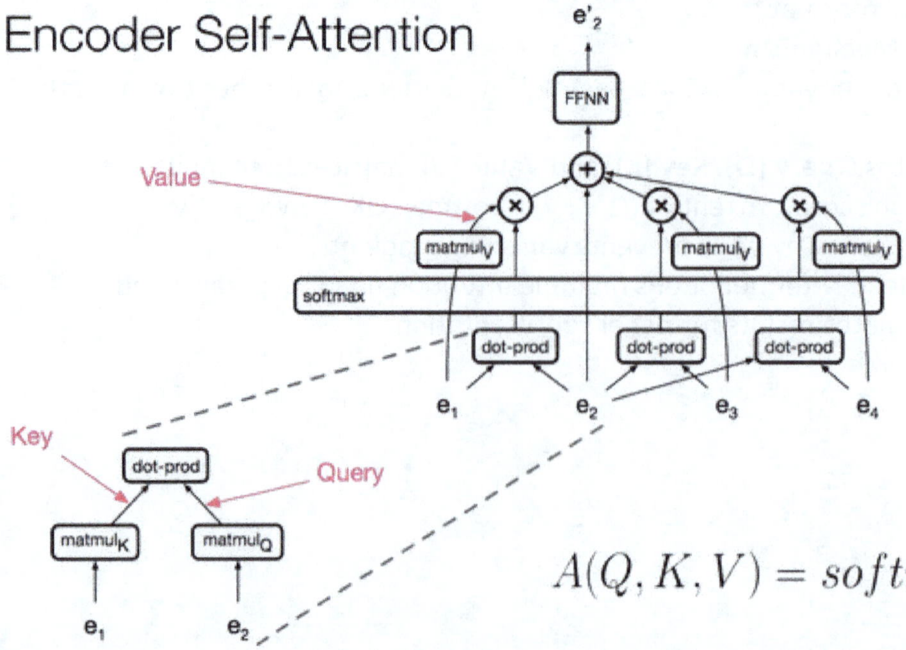

$$A(Q,K,V) = softmax(\frac{QK^T}{\sqrt{d_k}})V$$

3. **Encoder-Decoder Structure**:
   - **Encoder**: Stack of N identical layers (e.g., 6). Each has:
     - Multi-head self-attention.
     - Feed-forward network (FFN).
     - Residual connections + layer normalization.
   - **Decoder**: Similar stack, but with:
     - Masked self-attention (to prevent attending to future tokens).
     - Encoder-decoder attention (queries from decoder, keys/values from encoder).
     - FFN.

Here are standard diagrams of the full Transformer architecture:

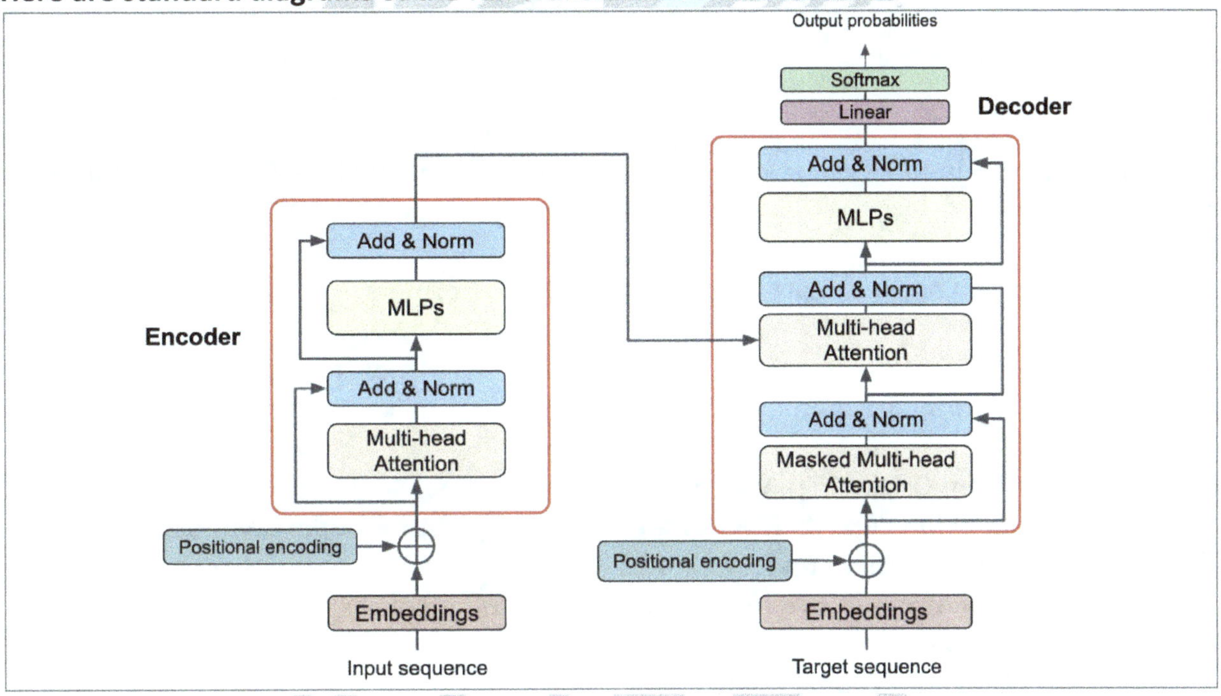

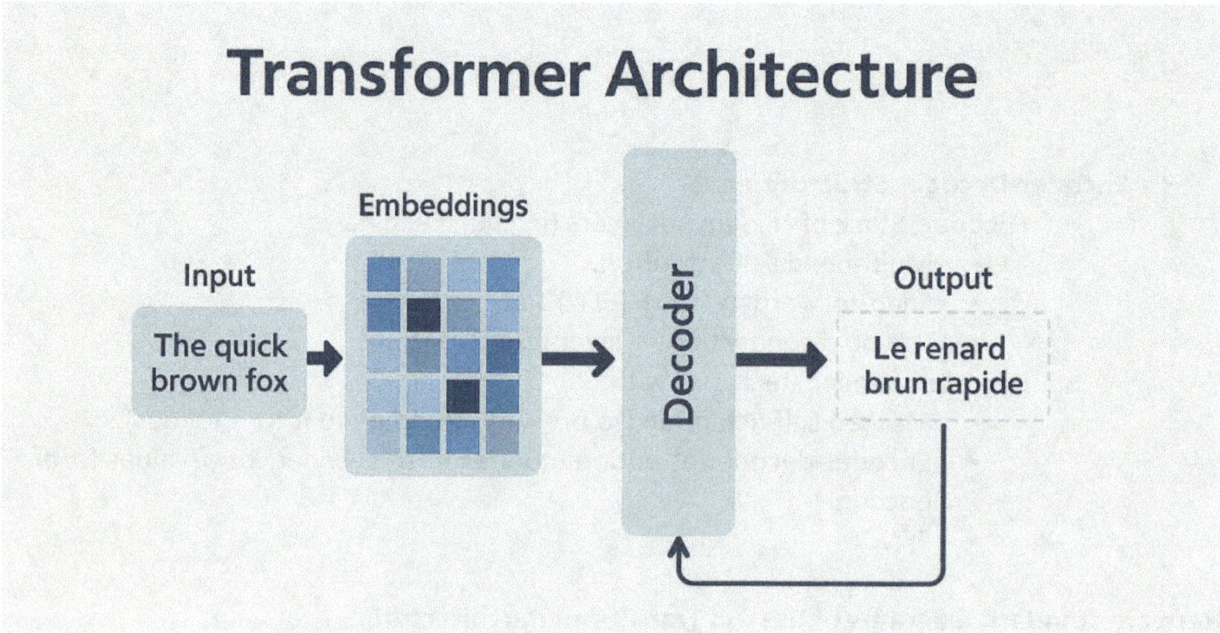

Transformers excel in tasks like machine translation due to parallel processing and capturing context effectively.

BERT: Bidirectional Encoder Representations from Transformers

BERT (introduced in 2018 by Google) is built on the Transformer but uses **only the encoder** part. It's designed for **bidirectional context** understanding, unlike unidirectional models (e.g., GPT).

Key Differences from Original Transformer

- Encoder-only (no decoder → not for generation, great for understanding).
- Pre-trained on massive text (Wikipedia + BookCorpus).
- Bidirectional: Looks at left and right context simultaneously.

Pre-Training Objectives

1. **Masked Language Modeling (MLM)**:
   - Randomly mask 15% of tokens (replace with [MASK]).
   - Predict the masked tokens using full context.
2. **Next Sentence Prediction (NSP)**:
   - Given two sentences, predict if the second follows the first (50% true pairs, 50% random).

Input format: [CLS] Sentence A [SEP] Sentence B [SEP]

- [CLS] token aggregates representation for classification tasks.

Here are diagrams of the BERT architecture:

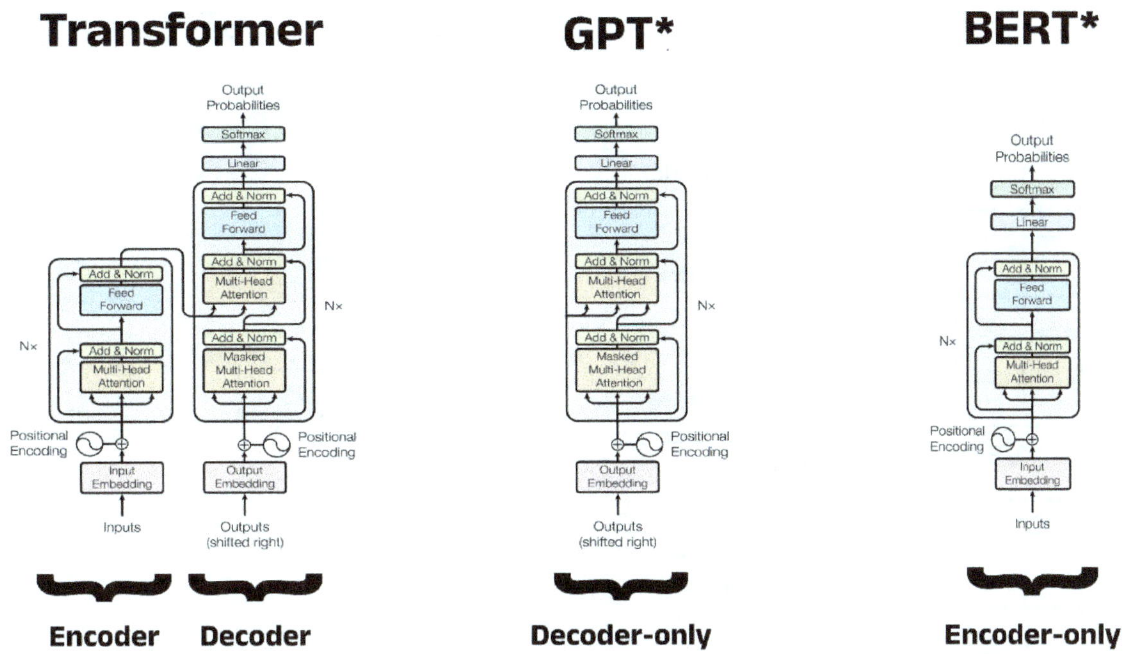

*Illustrative example, exact model architecture may vary slightly

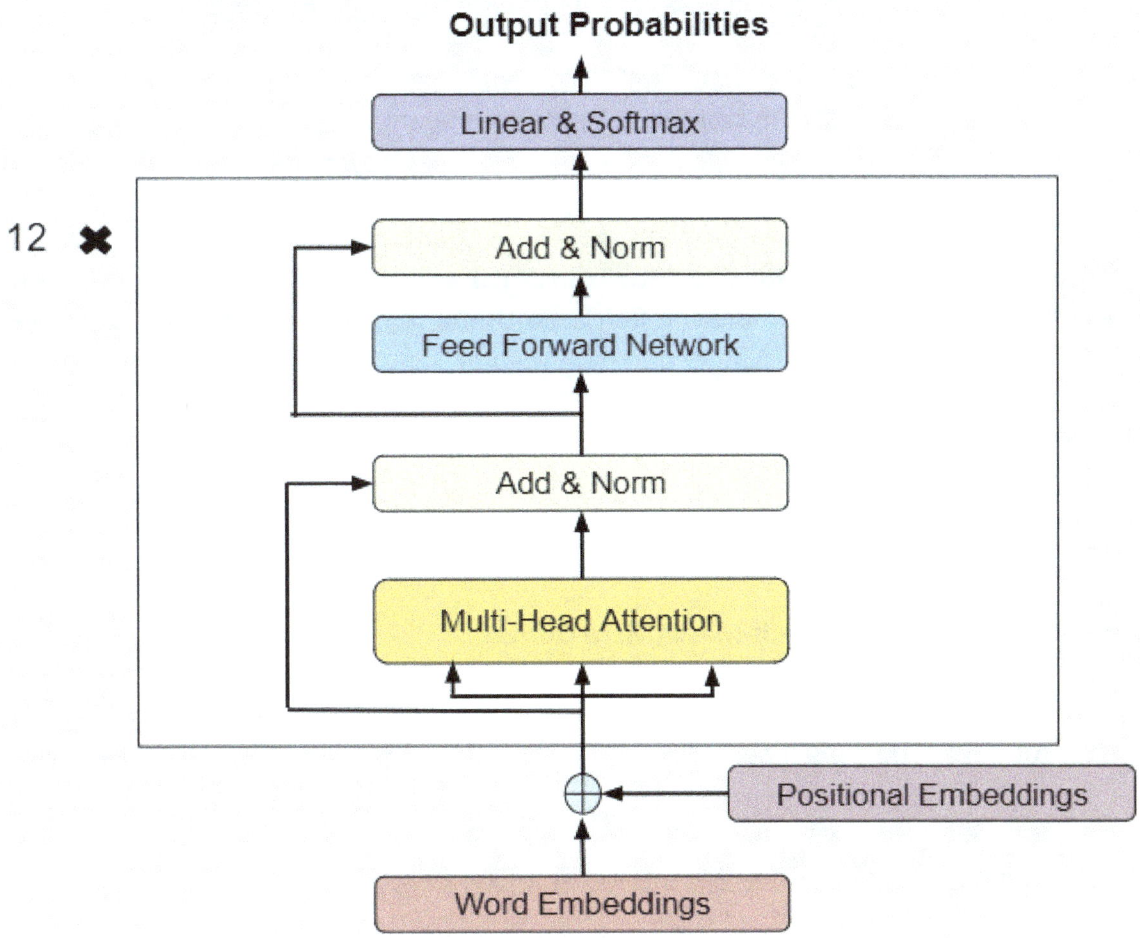

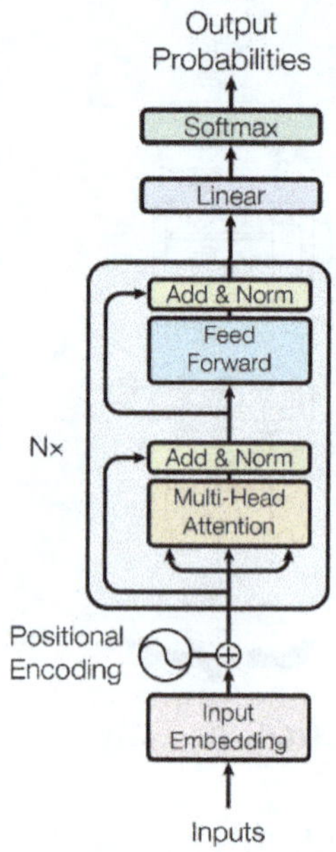

	BERT Base	BERT Large
Number of embedding dimensions, d_model	768	1024
Number of encoder blocks, N:	12	24
Number of attention heads per encoder block:	12	16
Size of hidden layer in feedforward network:	3072	4096
Total parameters:	110 million	340 million

Fine-Tuning

- Add a simple classification head on [CLS] output.
- Fine-tune on downstream tasks (e.g., sentiment analysis, question answering).

BERT variants: BERT-Base (12 layers, 768 hidden, 110M params), BERT-Large (24 layers, 1024 hidden, 340M params).

Python Code Examples Using Hugging Face Transformers

The easiest way to use Transformers and BERT is with the transformers library by Hugging Face.

Installation

Bash

```
pip install transformers torch
```

1. Using Pre-Trained BERT for Fill-Mask (MLM Demo)

Python

```
from transformers import pipeline

# Load a fill-mask pipeline with BERT
unmasker = pipeline('fill-mask', model='bert-base-uncased')

# Example sentence with [MASK]
result = unmasker("The capital of France is [MASK].")
```

```
for pred in result:
    print(f"Prediction: {pred['sequence']}, Score: {pred['score']:.4f}")
```

Output example:

Prediction: the capital of france is paris., Score: 0.9373

2. BERT for Sentiment Analysis (Text Classification)

Python

```
from transformers import pipeline

# Sentiment analysis pipeline (fine-tuned BERT)
classifier = pipeline('sentiment-analysis')

texts = [
    "I love this movie, it's fantastic!",
    "This was a terrible experience."
]

results = classifier(texts)

for text, res in zip(texts, results):
    print(f"Text: {text}")
    print(f"Label: {res['label']}, Score: {res['score']:.4f}\n")
```

Output example:

Text: I love this movie, it's fantastic!
Label: POSITIVE, Score: 0.9998

Text: This was a terrible experience.
Label: NEGATIVE, Score: 0.9991

3. Loading BERT Model and Tokenizer Manually

Python

```
from transformers import BertTokenizer, BertForSequenceClassification
import torch

# Load tokenizer and pre-trained model (for classification, num_labels=2 for binary)
tokenizer = BertTokenizer.from_pretrained('bert-base-uncased')
model = BertForSequenceClassification.from_pretrained('bert-base-uncased', num_labels=2)

# Example input
text = "Transformers are amazing for NLP tasks."
```

```python
inputs = tokenizer(text, return_tensors="pt", truncation=True, padding=True, max_length=512)

# Forward pass (no gradients for inference)
with torch.no_grad():
    outputs = model(**inputs)

logits = outputs.logits
prediction = torch.argmax(logits, dim=-1).item()

print(f"Logits: {logits}")
print(f"Predicted class: {prediction}")  # 0 or 1 depending on random init/fine-tuning
```

For fine-tuning on custom data, use Trainer API from Hugging Face—it's straightforward for datasets like GLUE or custom CSVs.

3.Text Classification & Sentiment Analysis

Text Classification is a fundamental task in Natural Language Processing (NLP) where the goal is to assign a label (or category) to a piece of text. The text can be a sentence, paragraph, or document, and labels can be binary (e.g., positive/negative), multi-class (e.g., joy, anger, sadness, fear), or multi-label (multiple labels per text).

Common Applications

- **Sentiment Analysis**: Positive, negative, or neutral.
- **Spam Detection**: Spam vs. not spam.
- **Topic Labeling**: News articles → politics, sports, technology.
- **Intent Detection**: User queries in chatbots (e.g., "book flight", "check balance").
- **Hate Speech / Toxicity Detection**.
- **Language Identification**.

Types of Text Classification

1. **Binary Classification**: Two classes (e.g., spam/ham).
2. **Multi-class Classification**: More than two mutually exclusive classes.
3. **Multi-label Classification**: Text can belong to multiple classes simultaneously (e.g., a movie can be both "comedy" and "romance").

Traditional Approaches (Pre-Deep Learning)

1. **Bag of Words (BoW) + TF-IDF**:
    - Represent text as a vector of word counts or weighted frequencies.
    - Ignores word order and context.
2. **N-grams**: Capture short sequences of words.
3. **Classifiers**:
    - Naive Bayes (fast, works well with TF-IDF).
    - Logistic Regression.

- SVM (Support Vector Machines).
- Random Forests.

These methods are simple, interpretable, but limited in capturing semantic meaning and context.

Modern Deep Learning Approaches

With the rise of Transformers (especially BERT), performance on text classification has improved dramatically.

Key models:

- **BERT** (Bidirectional Encoder Representations from Transformers)
- **RoBERTa**, **DistilBERT**, **ALBERT** (optimized variants)
- **XLNet**, **ELECTRA**
- Generative models fine-tuned for classification (e.g., GPT variants via prompt engineering)

Sentiment Analysis: A Special Case of Text Classification

Sentiment Analysis determines the emotional tone behind text—typically **positive**, **negative**, or **neutral**. It can be more granular (e.g., 5-star ratings) or aspect-based (sentiment toward specific entities like "battery life" in a phone review).

Levels of Sentiment Analysis

1. **Document-level**: Overall sentiment of a whole document.
2. **Sentence-level**: Sentiment of individual sentences.
3. **Aspect-based**: Sentiment toward specific aspects (e.g., "The camera is great, but battery life is poor").

Challenges

- Sarcasm ("Great job... NOT")
- Negation ("not good")
- Context-dependent meaning
- Emojis, slang, mixed sentiments

How BERT Performs Text Classification (Including Sentiment Analysis)

BERT is pre-trained on massive text and then **fine-tuned** on labeled datasets for classification.

Architecture for Classification

- Input: Special format → [CLS] text [SEP]
- The [CLS] token's final hidden state (output from the last Transformer layer) is used as the aggregated sequence representation.
- A simple classification layer (usually a linear layer + softmax) is added on top of the [CLS] output.
- During fine-tuning, the entire model (including pre-trained weights) is updated.

Why BERT Excels

- **Bidirectional context**: Understands both left and right context.
- Captures deep semantic and syntactic patterns.
- Transfer learning: Pre-trained on huge data, fine-tuned on small labeled datasets.

Python Code Examples Using Hugging Face Transformers

1. Simple Sentiment Analysis with Pre-built Pipeline (Easiest)

Python

```python
from transformers import pipeline

# Load pre-trained sentiment analysis pipeline
# Default model: distilbert-base-uncased-finetuned-sst-2-english
classifier = pipeline("sentiment-analysis")

# Test sentences
sentences = [
    "I absolutely love this product! It's amazing.",
    "This movie was boring and too long.",
    "The food was okay, nothing special.",
    "What a terrible service! Never coming back."
]

results = classifier(sentences)

for sentence, result in zip(sentences, results):
    print(f"Text: {sentence}")
    print(f"Label: {result['label']}, Confidence: {result['score']:.4f}\n")
```

Sample Output:

```
Text: I absolutely love this product! It's amazing.
Label: POSITIVE, Confidence: 0.9998

Text: This movie was boring and too long.
Label: NEGATIVE, Confidence: 0.9995

Text: The food was okay, nothing special.
Label: NEGATIVE, Confidence: 0.7489

Text: What a terrible service! Never coming back.
Label: NEGATIVE, Confidence: 0.9997
```

2. Custom Text Classification (Fine-tuning BERT on Your Dataset)

Use Hugging Face Trainer API for fine-tuning.

Python

```python
!pip install transformers datasets evaluate accelerate

from datasets import load_dataset
```

```
from transformers import AutoTokenizer, AutoModelForSequenceClassification,
TrainingArguments, Trainer
import numpy as np
import evaluate

# Load a sample dataset (IMDb movie reviews: positive/negative)
dataset = load_dataset("imdb")

# Tokenizer
tokenizer = AutoTokenizer.from_pretrained("bert-base-uncased")

def tokenize_function(examples):
   return tokenizer(examples["text"], padding="max_length", truncation=True,
max_length=512)

tokenized_datasets = dataset.map(tokenize_function, batched=True)

# Use smaller subsets for quick training
small_train_dataset = tokenized_datasets["train"].shuffle(seed=42).select(range(1000))
small_eval_dataset = tokenized_datasets["test"].shuffle(seed=42).select(range(500))

# Model (2 labels: negative=0, positive=1)
model = AutoModelForSequenceClassification.from_pretrained("bert-base-uncased",
num_labels=2)

# Metric
metric = evaluate.load("accuracy")

def compute_metrics(eval_pred):
   logits, labels = eval_pred
   predictions = np.argmax(logits, axis=-1)
   return metric.compute(predictions=predictions, references=labels)

# Training arguments
training_args = TrainingArguments(
   output_dir="imdb_bert_finetuned",
   evaluation_strategy="epoch",
   learning_rate=2e-5,
   per_device_train_batch_size=16,
   per_device_eval_batch_size=16,
   num_train_epochs=3,
   weight_decay=0.01,
   logging_dir='./logs',
)

# Trainer
```

```
trainer = Trainer(
    model=model,
    args=training_args,
    train_dataset=small_train_dataset,
    eval_dataset=small_eval_dataset,
    compute_metrics=compute_metrics,
)

# Train the model
trainer.train()

# Evaluate
results = trainer.evaluate()
print(results)
```

This achieves ~90%+ accuracy on IMDb even with limited data.

3. Inference with Fine-tuned Model
Python

```
# After training, use the model for prediction
text = "This movie was fantastic and very entertaining!"

inputs = tokenizer(text, return_tensors="pt", truncation=True, padding=True)

import torch
with torch.no_grad():
    logits = model(**inputs).logits

predicted_class = torch.argmax(logits, dim=1).item()
label = "POSITIVE" if predicted_class == 1 else "NEGATIVE"
print(f"Predicted: {label}")
```


4.Speech Recognition

Speech Recognition, also known as **Automatic Speech Recognition (ASR)** or **Speech-to-Text (STT)**, is the technology that converts spoken language (audio) into written text. It enables machines to "understand" human speech, powering applications like voice assistants (Siri, Alexa), real-time captioning, dictation software, transcription services, and voice-controlled systems.

Key Challenges in Speech Recognition

- **Variability**: Accents, dialects, speaking speed, background noise, and emotions.
- **Coarticulation**: Sounds blend together in natural speech.

- **Homophones**: Words that sound the same but have different meanings (e.g., "two" vs. "too").
- **Large Vocabulary**: Handling thousands of words and rare terms.
- **Context**: Understanding grammar and semantics for accurate transcription.

Traditional ASR Pipeline (Hybrid Approach)

Older systems used separate components:

1. **Audio Preprocessing**: Convert raw waveform to features like MFCCs (Mel-Frequency Cepstral Coefficients).
2. **Acoustic Model**: Maps audio features to phonemes (sound units) – often using HMMs (Hidden Markov Models) + GMMs (Gaussian Mixture Models).
3. **Pronunciation Model/Lexicon**: Maps phonemes to words.
4. **Language Model**: Predicts likely word sequences (e.g., n-gram models) to resolve ambiguities.
5. **Decoder**: Combines everything to find the most probable text.

Here are illustrations of traditional and general ASR pipelines:

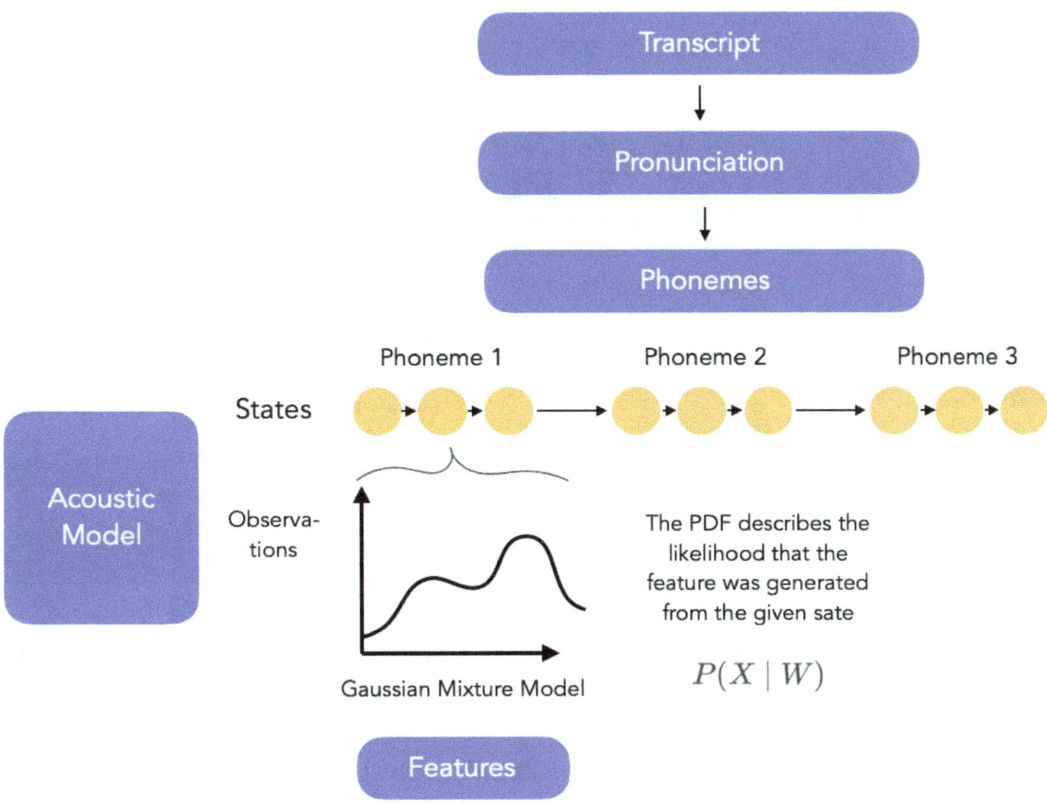

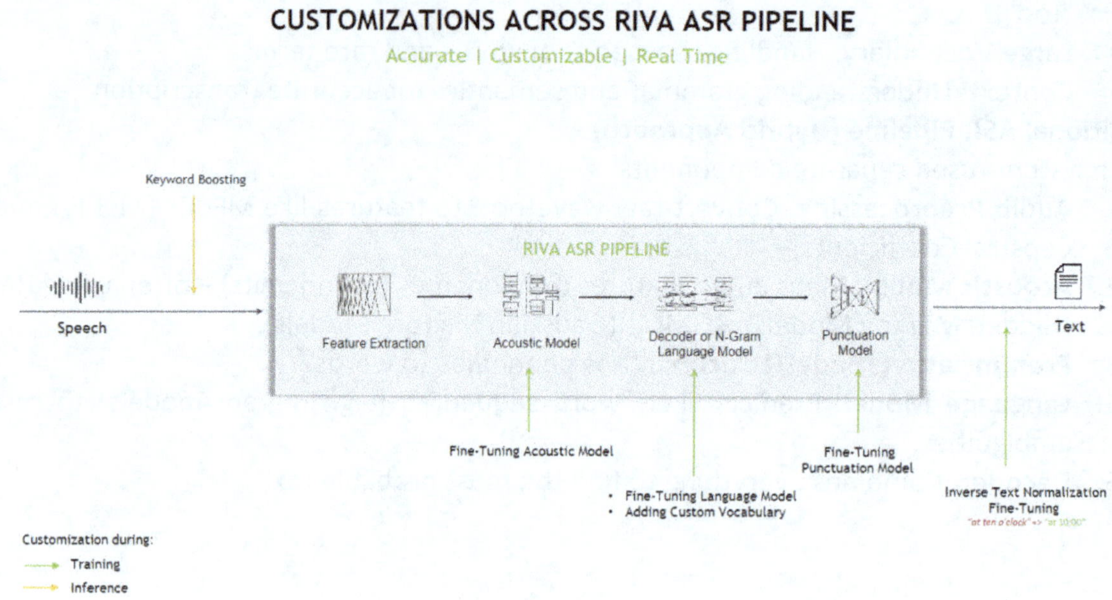

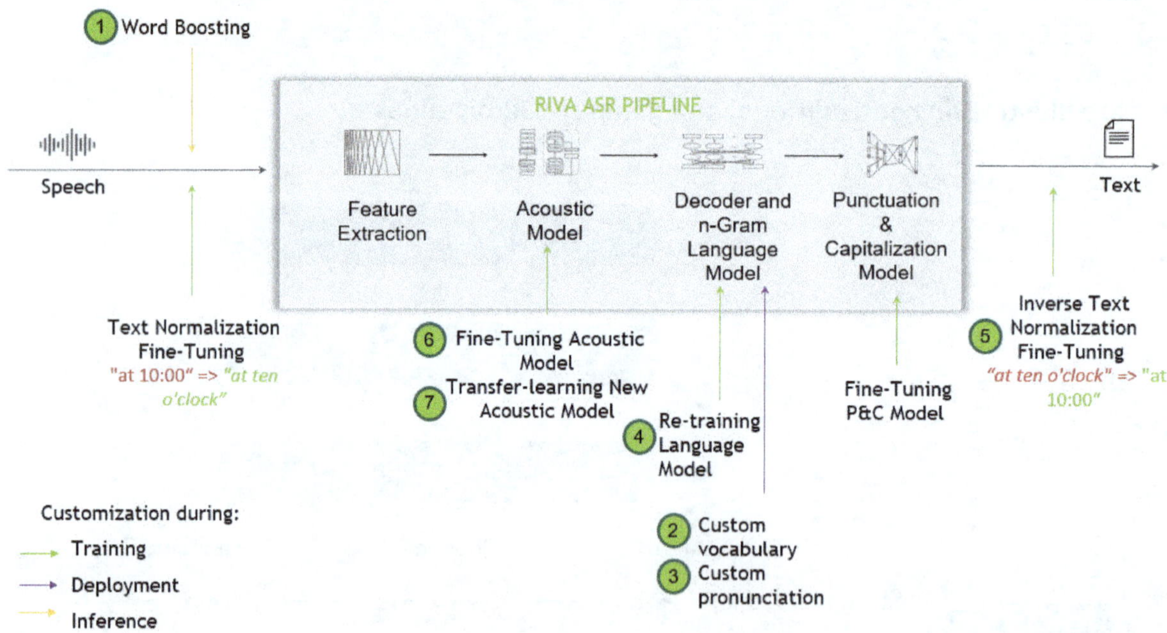

Modern Deep Learning Approaches (End-to-End ASR)

Since ~2014, deep learning has dominated, especially **end-to-end (E2E)** models that directly map audio to text without separate components.

- **Key Techniques**:
    - **CTC (Connectionist Temporal Classification)**: Handles alignment between variable-length audio and text.
    - **Seq2Seq with Attention**: Encoder-decoder models (e.g., RNNs/LSTMs) for better context.

- **Transformers**: Self-attention for parallel processing and long-range dependencies.

- Popular Architectures:
    - RNN-Transducer (RNNT).
    - Wav2Vec 2.0 (self-supervised pretraining).
    - Conformer (CNN + Transformer).
    - **Whisper** (OpenAI): Transformer-based, multilingual, robust to noise/accents.

Here are visuals of waveform-to-text processes and deep learning models:

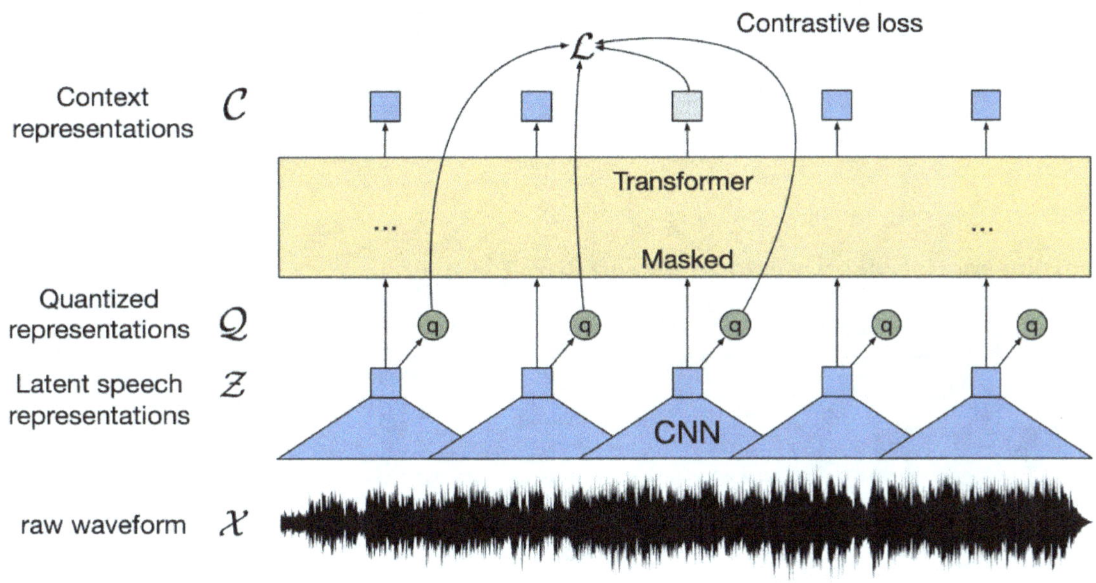

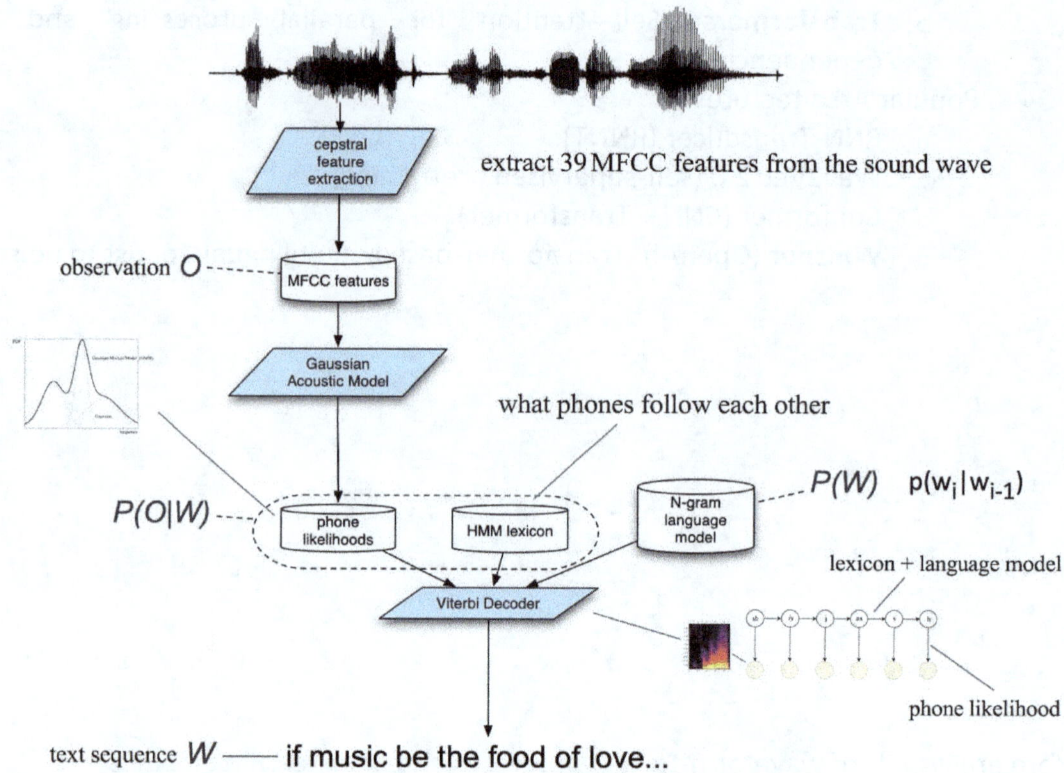

Deep learning models like Transformers and RNN-CTC:

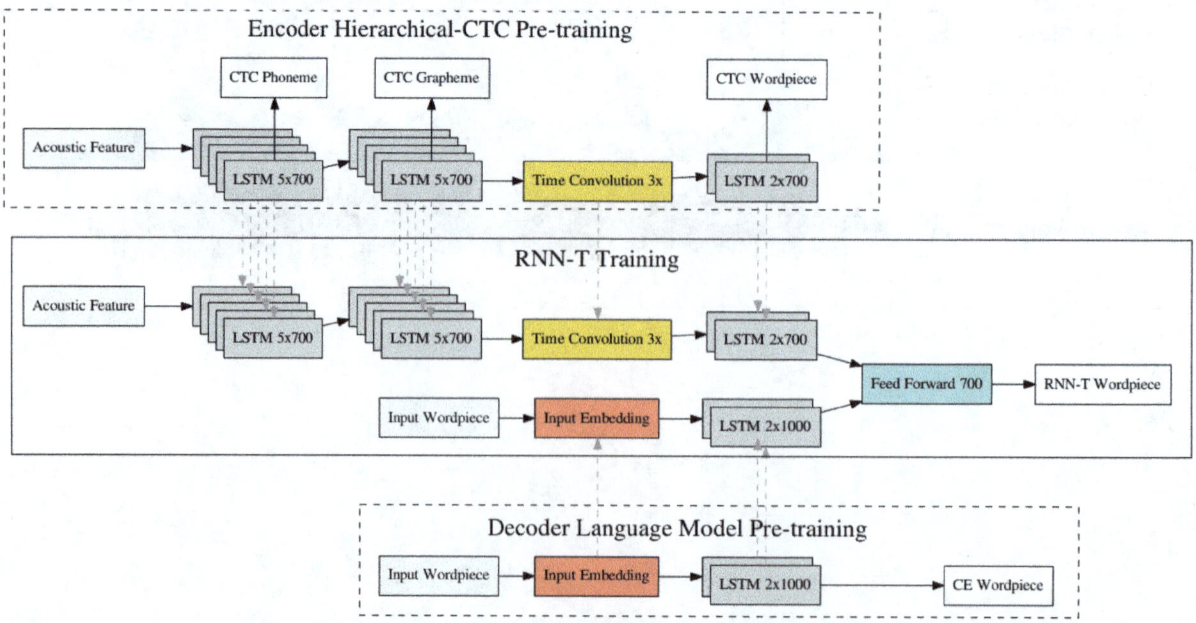

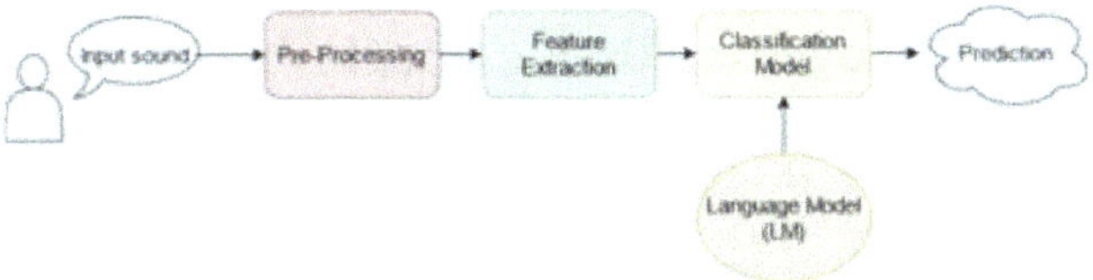

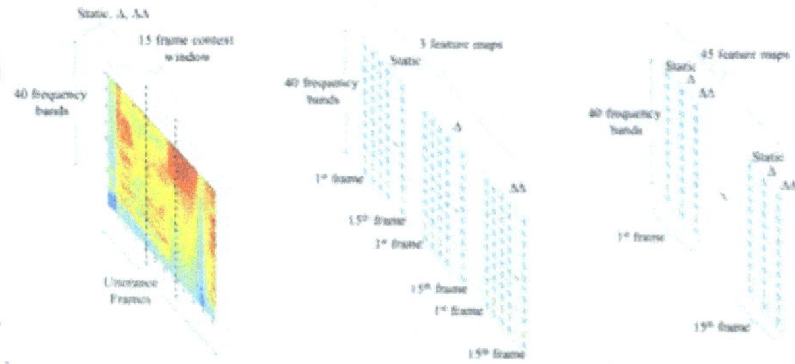

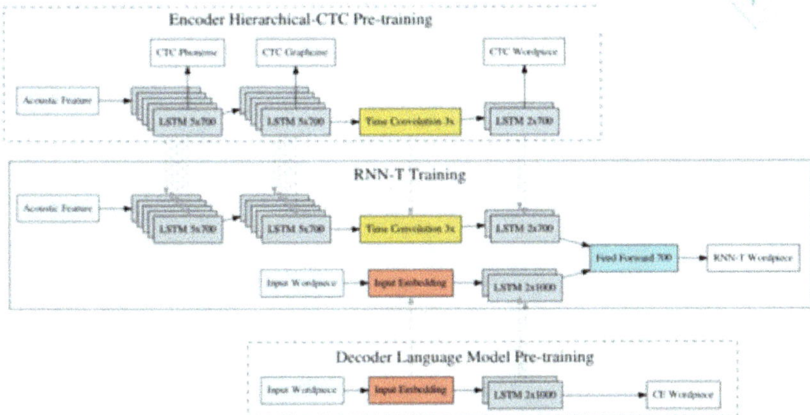

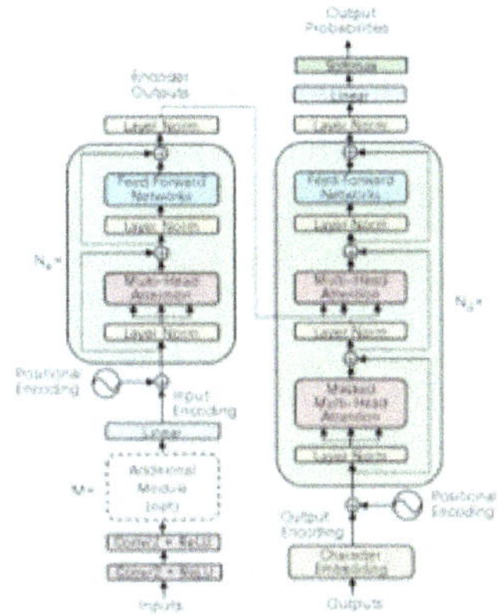

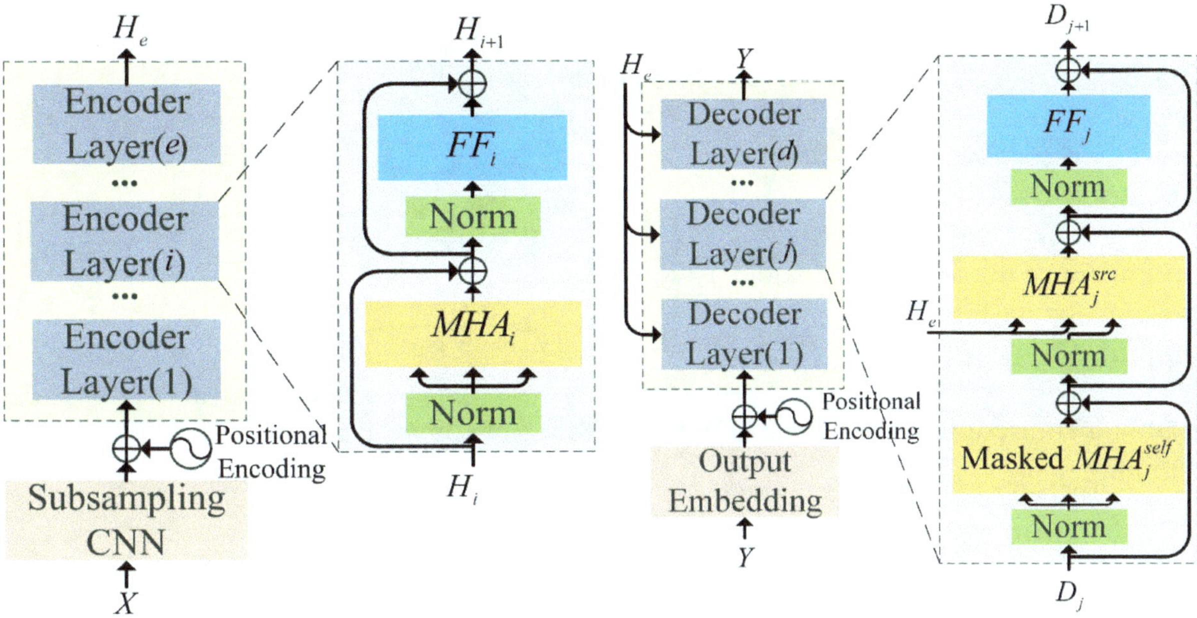

(**a**) Encoder (**b**) Decoder

As of late 2025, **OpenAI's Whisper** remains one of the best open-source options—highly accurate, multilingual (supports ~100 languages), and robust.

Popular Python Libraries (2025)

- **openai-whisper**: Best for accuracy and multilingual support (offline).
- **SpeechRecognition**: Simple wrapper for APIs (Google, Sphinx) + microphone input.
- **Faster-Whisper**: Optimized version of Whisper (faster on CPU/GPU).
- Others: Vosk (offline, lightweight), Hugging Face Transformers (for models like Wav2Vec, HuBERT).

Python Code Examples

1. Basic Real-Time Speech Recognition with SpeechRecognition (Using Google API - Requires Internet)

Python

```
# Install: pip install SpeechRecognition pyaudio

import speech_recognition as sr

# Initialize recognizer
r = sr.Recognizer()

# Use microphone
with sr.Microphone() as source:
    print("Adjusting for ambient noise... Please wait.")
    r.adjust_for_ambient_noise(source)
    print("Listening... Speak now!")
    audio = r.listen(source)

# Recognize speech (Google Web API - free but limited)
try:
    text = r.recognize_google(audio)
    print(f"You said: {text}")
except sr.UnknownValueError:
    print("Could not understand audio")
except sr.RequestError as e:
    print(f"API error: {e}")
```

2. Offline Transcription with OpenAI Whisper (State-of-the-Art)

Python

```
# Install: pip install openai-whisper
# For GPU acceleration: pip install torch torchvision torchaudio --index-url
https://download.pytorch.org/whl/cu118 (adjust for your setup)
# Optional faster version: pip install faster-whisper

import whisper

# Load model (tiny/base/small/medium/large/turbo - larger = more accurate but slower)
# 'base' is a good balance; 'turbo' is optimized for speed
model = whisper.load_model("base")

# Transcribe an audio file (supports mp3, wav, etc.)
result = model.transcribe("your_audio_file.mp3", fp16=False)  # fp16=True for GPU
```

```
print("Transcribed Text:", result["text"])

# For multilingual: Detect language automatically or specify
# result = model.transcribe("audio_french.mp3", language="fr")

# With timestamps
segments = result["segments"]
for seg in segments:
    print(f"[{seg['start']:.2f}s - {seg['end']:.2f}s] {seg['text']}")
```

3. Real-Time-ish with Whisper (Chunked Microphone Input - Advanced)
Whisper is not real-time by default, but you can chunk audio:
Python

```
# Requires: pip install whisper pyaudio numpy
import whisper
import pyaudio
import wave
import numpy as np
import threading

model = whisper.load_model("tiny")  # Use small model for speed
CHUNK = 1024
FORMAT = pyaudio.paInt16
CHANNELS = 1
RATE = 16000
RECORD_SECONDS = 5  # Chunk duration

p = pyaudio.PyAudio()
```

```
def transcribe_chunk(audio_data):
    # Save to temp wav
    with wave.open("temp.wav", 'wb') as wf:
        wf.setnchannels(CHANNELS)
        wf.setsampwidth(p.get_sample_size(FORMAT))
        wf.setframerate(RATE)
        wf.writeframes(audio_data)

    result = model.transcribe("temp.wav", fp16=False)
    print("Live Transcription:", result["text"])
def record_and_transcribe():
    stream = p.open(format=FORMAT, channels=CHANNELS, rate=RATE, input=True,
frames_per_buffer=CHUNK)
    print("Listening in chunks...")

    while True:
        frames = []
        for _ in range(0, int(RATE / CHUNK * RECORD_SECONDS)):
            data = stream.read(CHUNK)
            frames.append(data)

        audio_bytes = b''.join(frames)
        threading.Thread(target=transcribe_chunk, args=(audio_bytes,)).start()

record_and_transcribe()
```

For production real-time, consider libraries like Faster-Whisper or Vosk.

Section-8

Computer Vision

- OpenCV (Image Processing)
- CNNs (Convolutional Neural Networks)
- Object Detection (YOLO, SSD, Faster R-CNN)

Computer Vision

1.OpenCV (Image Processing)

OpenCV: Complete Notes on Image Processing

OpenCV (Open Source Computer Vision Library) is a powerful, open-source library for computer vision and image processing. Originally developed by Intel in 1999, it's now maintained by the OpenCV Foundation and widely used in academia, industry, and hobbies. It supports multiple languages (C++, Python, Java), but Python bindings (cv2) are the most popular due to simplicity and integration with NumPy.

Key Features

- Over 2500 algorithms for image/video processing, object detection, machine learning.
- Real-time performance (optimized with SIMD, multi-threading).
- Cross-platform: Windows, Linux, macOS, Android, iOS.
- Integrates with deep learning frameworks (DNN module for TensorFlow, PyTorch models).
- Free for commercial and research use (BSD license).

Installation

Bash

```
pip install opencv-python      # Main module
pip install opencv-contrib-python  # Extra modules (e.g., SIFT, AR markers)
```

For headless environments (servers): opencv-python-headless.

Core Concepts

- Images in OpenCV are **NumPy arrays**:
  - Grayscale: 2D array (height x width).
  - Color (BGR): 3D array (height x width x 3 channels).
  - Pixel values: 0-255 (uint8) typically.
- Coordinate system: (0,0) at top-left, x-right, y-down.

1. Basic Operations

Reading, Displaying, and Saving Images

Python

```
import cv2
import matplotlib.pyplot as plt  # For better display in notebooks

# Read image
img = cv2.imread('image.jpg')  # Returns None if file not found
if img is None:
    print("Error loading image")
else:
    print(img.shape)  # (height, width, channels)

# Display (OpenCV uses BGR, Matplotlib uses RGB)
cv2.imshow('Window', img)      # Creates a window
cv2.waitKey(0)                 # Wait for key press
cv2.destroyAllWindows()

# Better for Jupyter: Convert BGR to RGB
img_rgb = cv2.cvtColor(img, cv2.COLOR_BGR2RGB)
plt.imshow(img_rgb)
plt.axis('off')
plt.show()

# Save
```

```
cv2.imwrite('output.jpg', img)
```

Pixel Manipulation & ROI

Python

```
# Access pixel (row, col)
px = img[100, 100]  # BGR values

# Modify pixel
img[100, 100] = [255, 255, 255]  # White

# Region of Interest (ROI)
roi = img[50:200, 100:300]  # Crop
img[0:150, 0:200] = roi     # Paste
```

2. Image Transformations

- **Resizing, Rotating, Flipping**

Python

```
# Resize
resized = cv2.resize(img, (500, 300))  # Or dsize=None, fx/fy scaling

# Rotate
```

```
(h, w) = img.shape[:2]
center = (w//2, h//2)
M = cv2.getRotationMatrix2D(center, 45, 1.0)  # Angle, scale
rotated = cv2.warpAffine(img, M, (w, h))

# Flip
flipped = cv2.flip(img, 1)  # 0: vertical, 1: horizontal, -1: both
```

- **Color Space Conversions**

Python

```
gray = cv2.cvtColor(img, cv2.COLOR_BGR2GRAY)
hsv = cv2.cvtColor(img, cv2.COLOR_BGR2HSV)
rgb = cv2.cvtColor(img, cv2.COLOR_BGR2RGB)
```

3. Filtering & Blurring

Python

```
# Gaussian Blur (reduces noise)
blurred = cv2.GaussianBlur(img, (5, 5), 0)  # Kernel size must be odd

# Median Blur (good for salt-pepper noise)
median = cv2.medianBlur(img, 5)

# Bilateral (edge-preserving)
bilateral = cv2.bilateralFilter(img, 9, 75, 75)
```

4. Edge Detection

- **Canny Edge Detector** (Most popular)

Python

```
gray = cv2.cvtColor(img, cv2.COLOR_BGR2GRAY)
edges = cv2.Canny(gray, 50, 150)  # Low/high thresholds
```

```
# With blur for better results
blurred = cv2.GaussianBlur(gray, (5,5), 0)
edges = cv2.Canny(blurred, 50, 150)
```

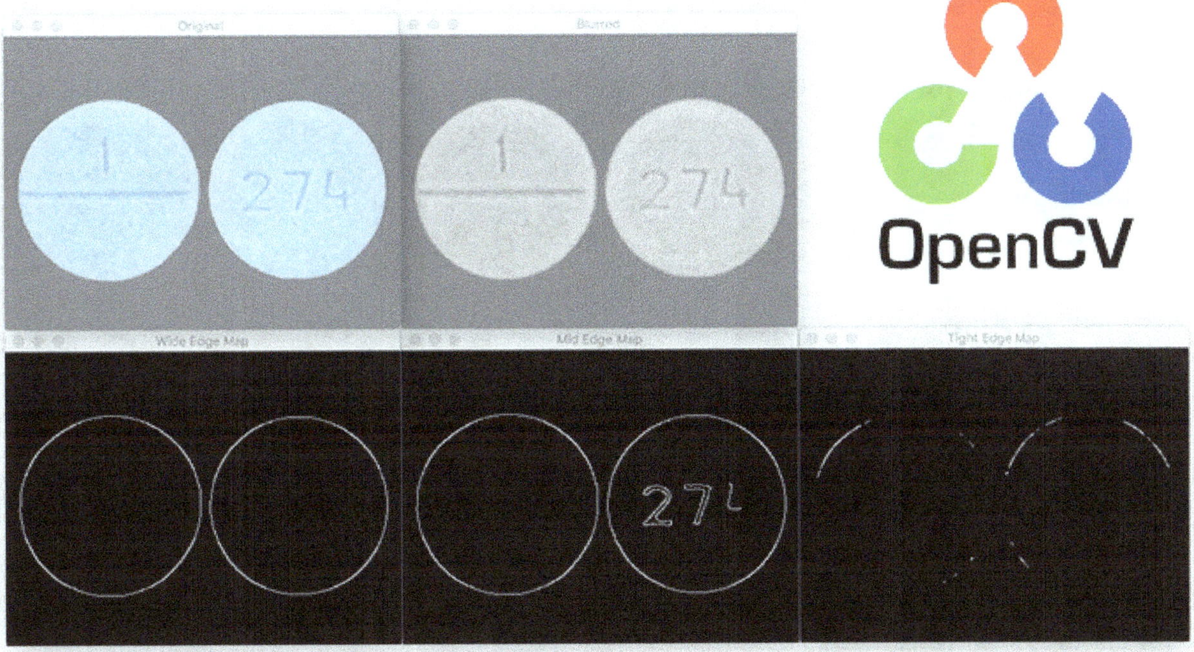

(a) original image (b) ground truth (c) HED: output

(d) HED: side output 2 (e) HED: side output 3 (f) HED: side output 4

(g) Canny: $\sigma = 2$ (h) Canny: $\sigma = 4$ (i) Canny: $\sigma = 8$

5. Thresholding & Morphological Operations

Python

```
# Binary Threshold
ret, thresh = cv2.threshold(gray, 127, 255, cv2.THRESH_BINARY)

# Adaptive Threshold
adaptive = cv2.adaptiveThreshold(gray, 255, cv2.ADAPTIVE_THRESH_GAUSSIAN_C,
                                 cv2.THRESH_BINARY, 11, 2)

# Otsu (automatic)
ret, otsu = cv2.threshold(gray, 0, 255, cv2.THRESH_BINARY + cv2.THRESH_OTSU)

# Morphology (kernel = np.ones((5,5), np.uint8))
eroded = cv2.erode(thresh, kernel, iterations=1)
dilated = cv2.dilate(thresh, kernel, iterations=1)
opening = cv2.morphologyEx(thresh, cv2.MORPH_OPEN, kernel)  # Erosion + Dilation
closing = cv2.morphologyEx(thresh, cv2.MORPH_CLOSE, kernel)
```

6. Contours & Shape Detection

Python

```
# Find contours
contours, hierarchy = cv2.findContours(edges, cv2.RETR_EXTERNAL,
cv2.CHAIN_APPROX_SIMPLE)

# Draw
img_contours = img.copy()
cv2.drawContours(img_contours, contours, -1, (0, 255, 0), 2)

# Contour properties
for cnt in contours:
    area = cv2.contourArea(cnt)
    perimeter = cv2.arcLength(cnt, True)
    approx = cv2.approxPolyDP(cnt, 0.02 * perimeter, True)  # For shape approx
    print(f"Vertices: {len(approx)}")  # e.g., 3=triangle, 4=rectangle
```

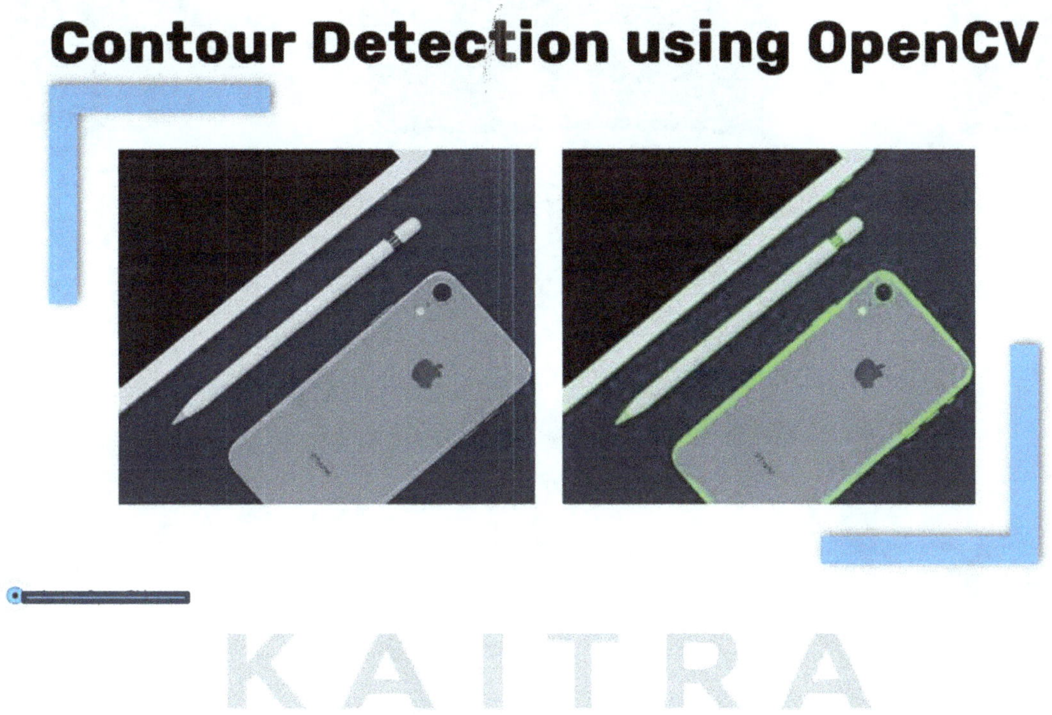

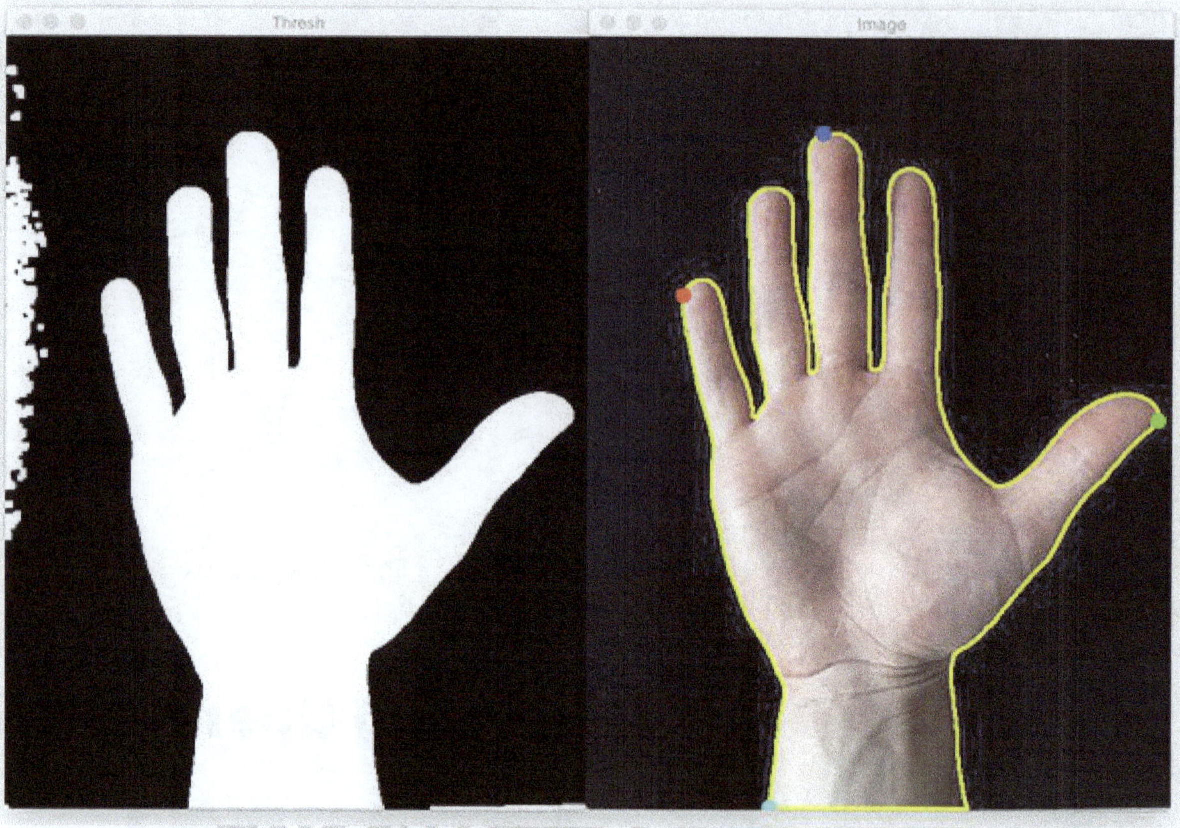

7. Object Detection: Haar Cascades (Classic)
Python

```
face_cascade = cv2.CascadeClassifier(cv2.data.haarcascades +
'haarcascade_frontalface_default.xml')
```

```
gray = cv2.cvtColor(img, cv2.COLOR_BGR2GRAY)
faces = face_cascade.detectMultiScale(gray, scaleFactor=1.1, minNeighbors=5)

for (x, y, w, h) in faces:
    cv2.rectangle(img, (x, y), (x+w, y+h), (255, 0, 0), 2)
```

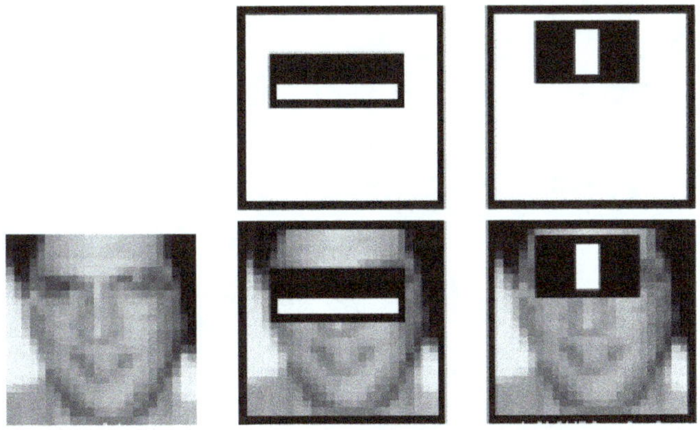

8. Video Processing

Python

```
cap = cv2.VideoCapture(0)  # 0 for webcam, or 'video.mp4'

while True:
    ret, frame = cap.read()
    if not ret:
        break
```

```
    # Process frame (e.g., grayscale)
    gray_frame = cv2.cvtColor(frame, cv2.COLOR_BGR2GRAY)

    cv2.imshow('Video', frame)
    if cv2.waitKey(1) == ord('q'):
        break

cap.release()
cv2.destroyAllWindows()
```

2.CNNs (Convolutional Neural Networks)

Convolutional Neural Networks (CNNs or ConvNets) are a specialized class of deep neural networks designed primarily for processing structured grid-like data, such as images (2D grids of pixels) or time-series data (1D grids). Introduced by Yann LeCun in the late 1980s (LeNet for handwritten digit recognition), CNNs revolutionized computer vision by achieving human-level performance on tasks like image classification, object detection, and segmentation.

Unlike fully connected neural networks (where every neuron connects to every other), CNNs exploit the spatial structure of data using **local connectivity**, **parameter sharing**, and **translation invariance**. This makes them highly efficient and effective for visual tasks.

Why CNNs Over Traditional Neural Networks?

- **Parameter Efficiency**: A fully connected network on a 100x100 image would have millions of parameters per layer. CNNs reduce this drastically.
- **Hierarchical Feature Learning**: Low-level features (edges) → mid-level (textures) → high-level (objects).
- **Translation Invariance**: Detect features regardless of position.

Classic CNN architectures include LeNet (1998), AlexNet (2012 – ImageNet winner), VGG (2014), ResNet (2015), etc.

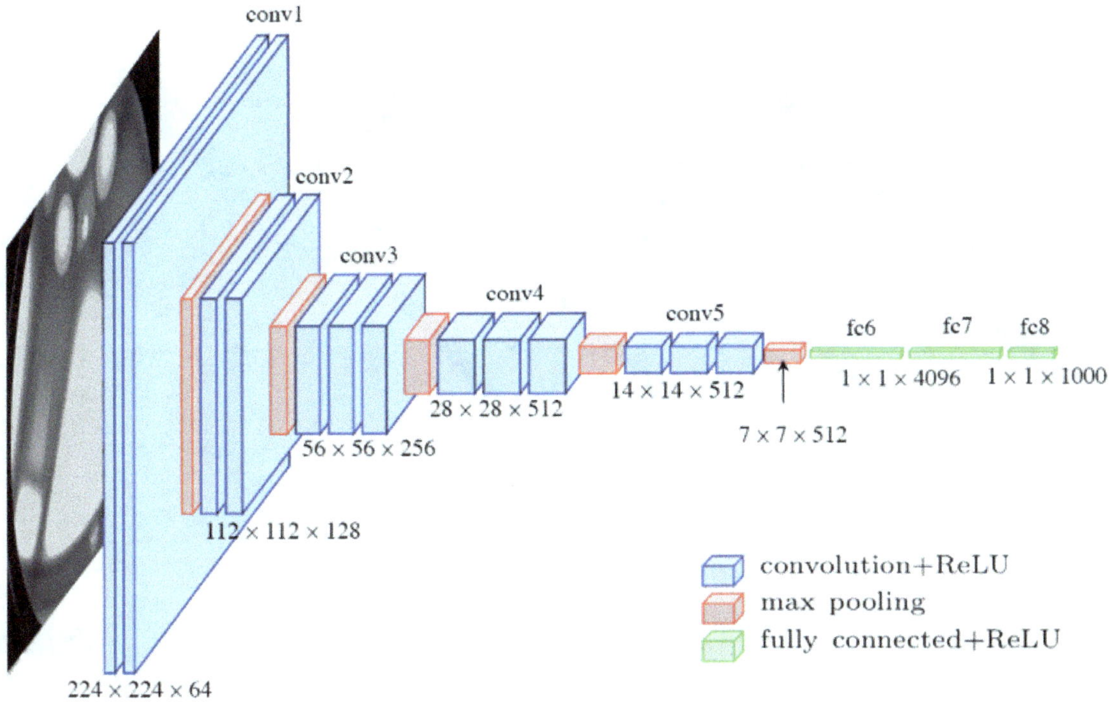

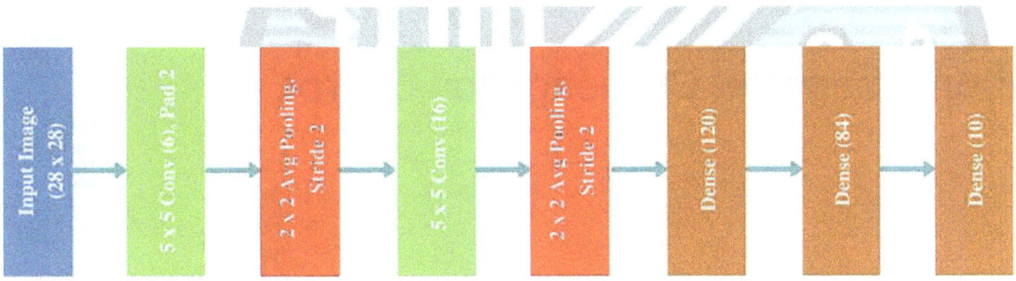

LeNet Architecture

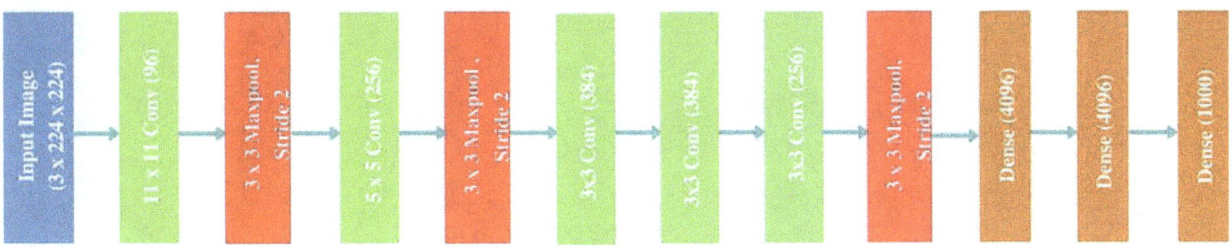

AlexNet Architecture

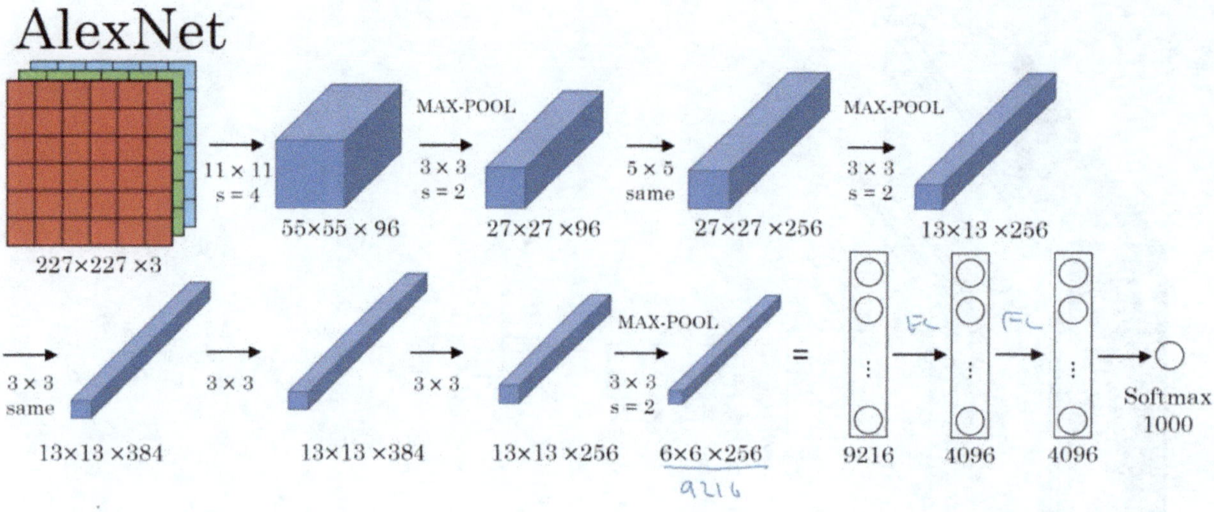

[Krizhevsky et al., 2012. ImageNet classification with deep convolutional neural networks]

Classification: ImageNet Challenge top-5 error

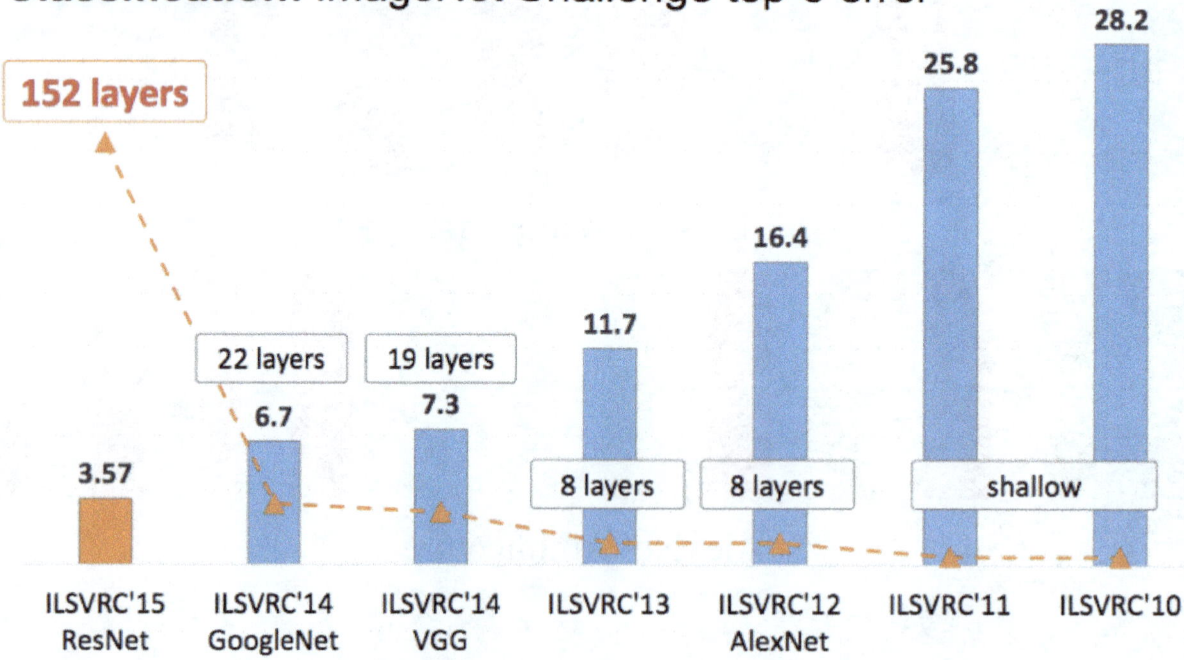

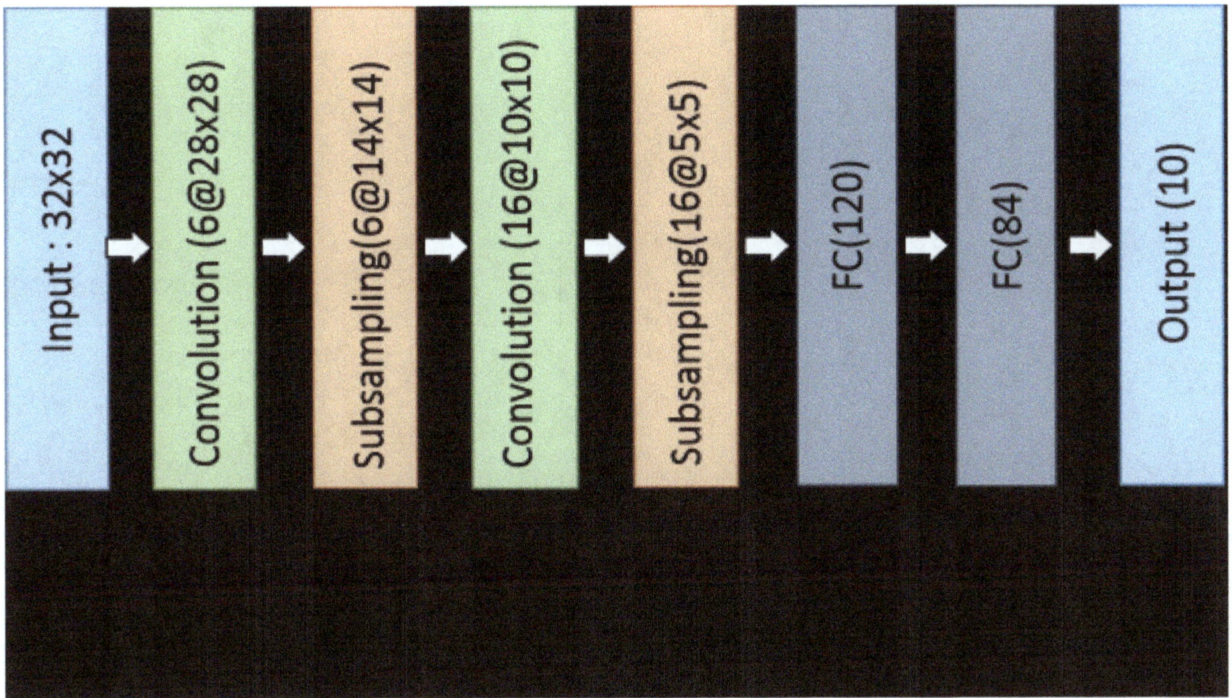

Core Components of a CNN

1. **Convolution Layer** (Feature Extraction)
    - The heart of CNN: Applies **filters/kernels** (small learnable windows, e.g., 3x3) slid over the input.
    - Operation: Element-wise multiplication + sum → produces a **feature map**.
    - Multiple filters detect different features (edges, corners).
    - Key Hyperparameters:
        - **Kernel Size**: e.g., 3x3.
        - **Stride**: Step size (1 = overlapping, 2 = skips).
        - **Padding**: Add zeros around input ('valid' = no padding, 'same' = output size preserved).
    - Output size formula: ((input_size - kernel_size + 2*padding) / stride) + 1

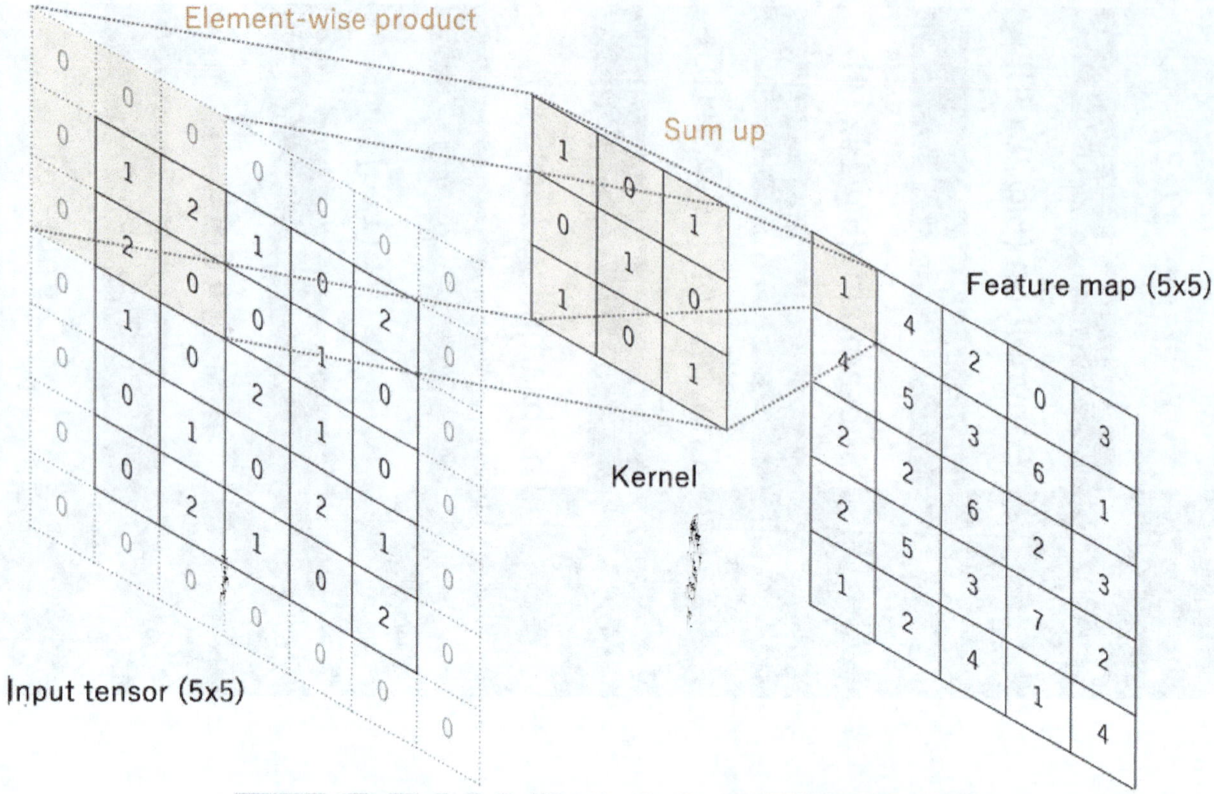
Element-wise product
Sum up
Feature map (5x5)
Kernel
Input tensor (5x5)

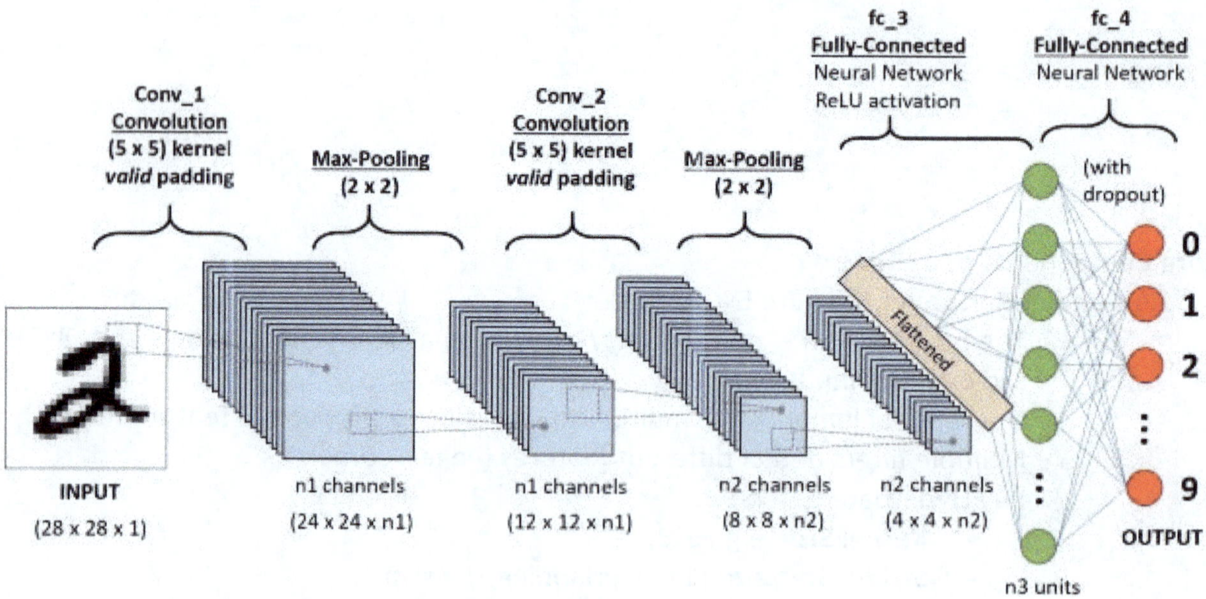
Conv_1
Convolution
(5 x 5) kernel
valid padding
Max-Pooling
(2 x 2)
Conv_2
Convolution
(5 x 5) kernel
valid padding
Max-Pooling
(2 x 2)
fc_3
Fully-Connected
Neural Network
ReLU activation
fc_4
Fully-Connected
Neural Network
(with
dropout)
Flattened
INPUT
(28 x 28 x 1)
n1 channels
(24 x 24 x n1)
n1 channels
(12 x 12 x n1)
n2 channels
(8 x 8 x n2)
n2 channels
(4 x 4 x n2)
n3 units
0
1
2
9
OUTPUT

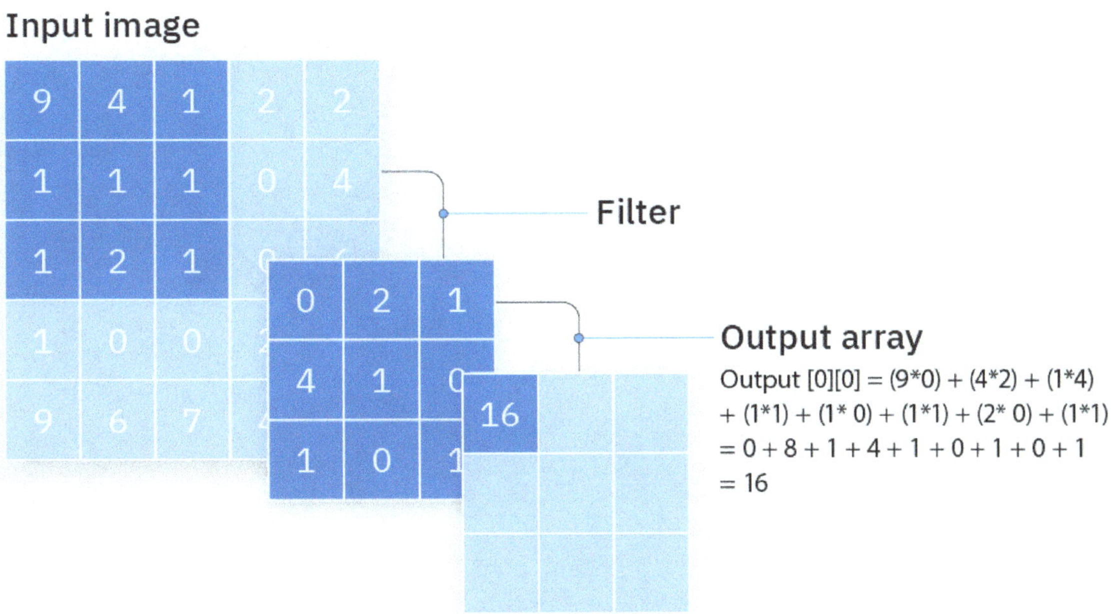

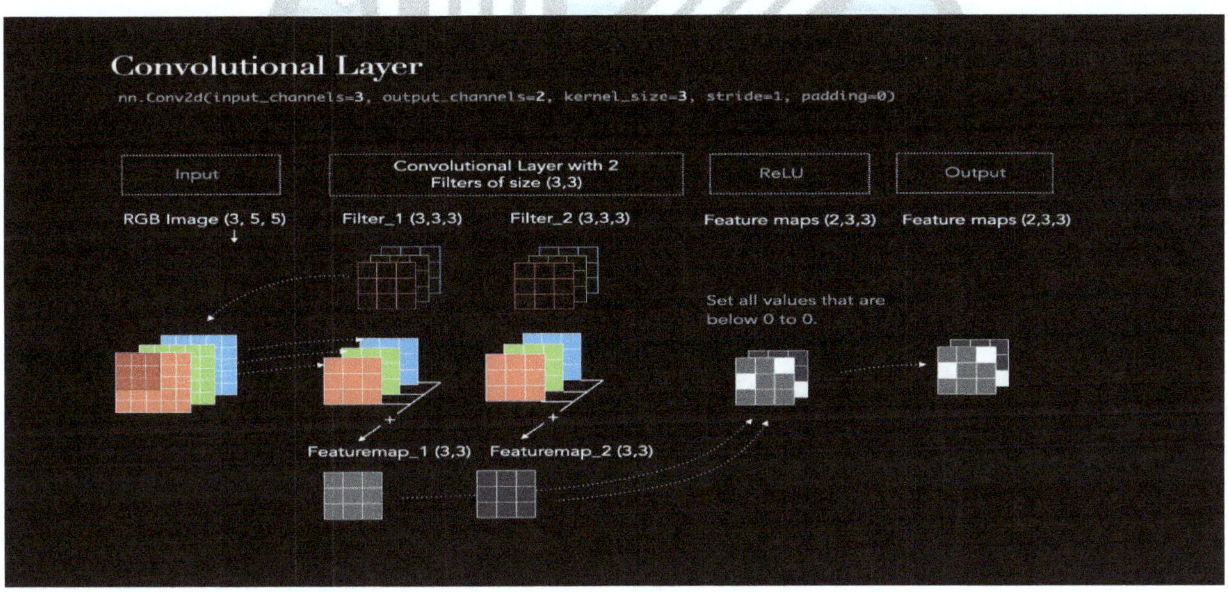

2. **Activation Function** (Non-Linearity)
    - Applied element-wise after convolution.
    - Most common: **ReLU (Rectified Linear Unit)** → f(x) = max(0, x)
        - Solves vanishing gradient, accelerates training.
        - Variants: Leaky ReLU, ELU.

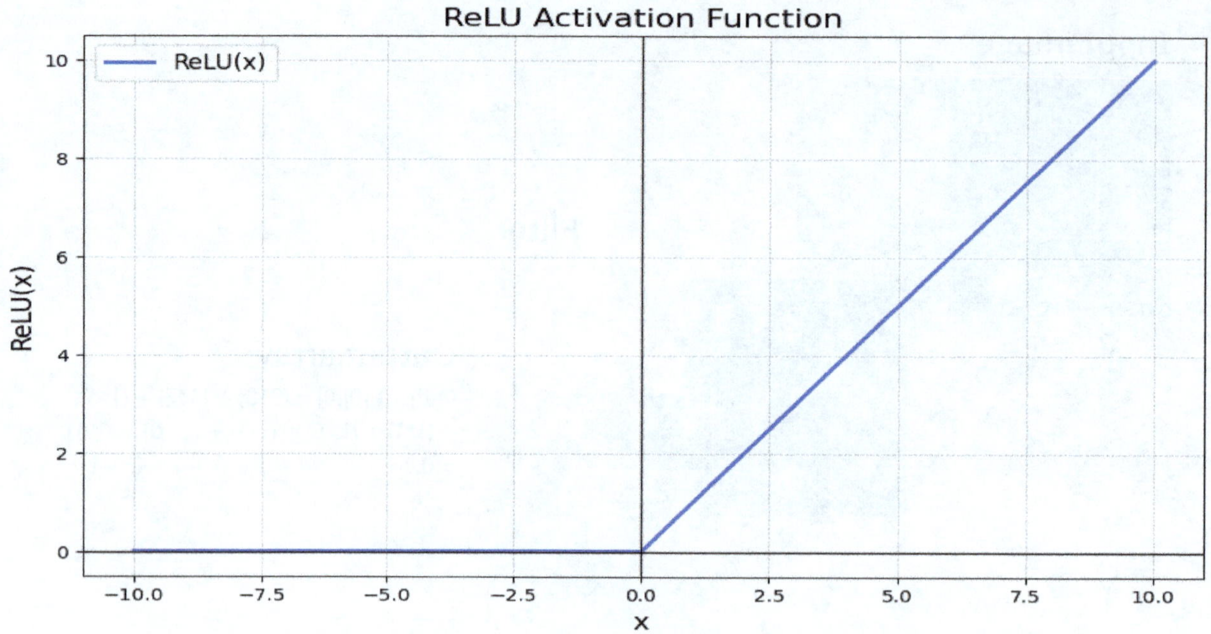

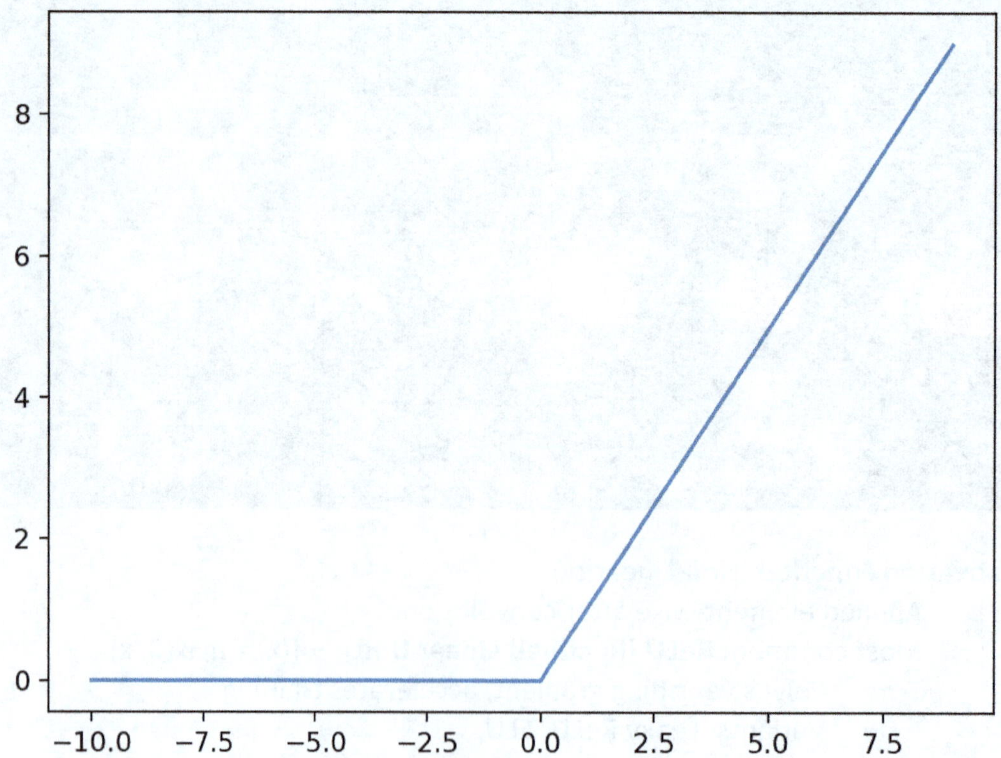

3. **Pooling Layer** (Downsampling)

- Reduces spatial dimensions (width/height) → fewer parameters, computation, and overfitting.
- **Max Pooling**: Takes maximum value in window (most common).
- **Average Pooling**: Takes average.
- Makes features more robust to small translations.

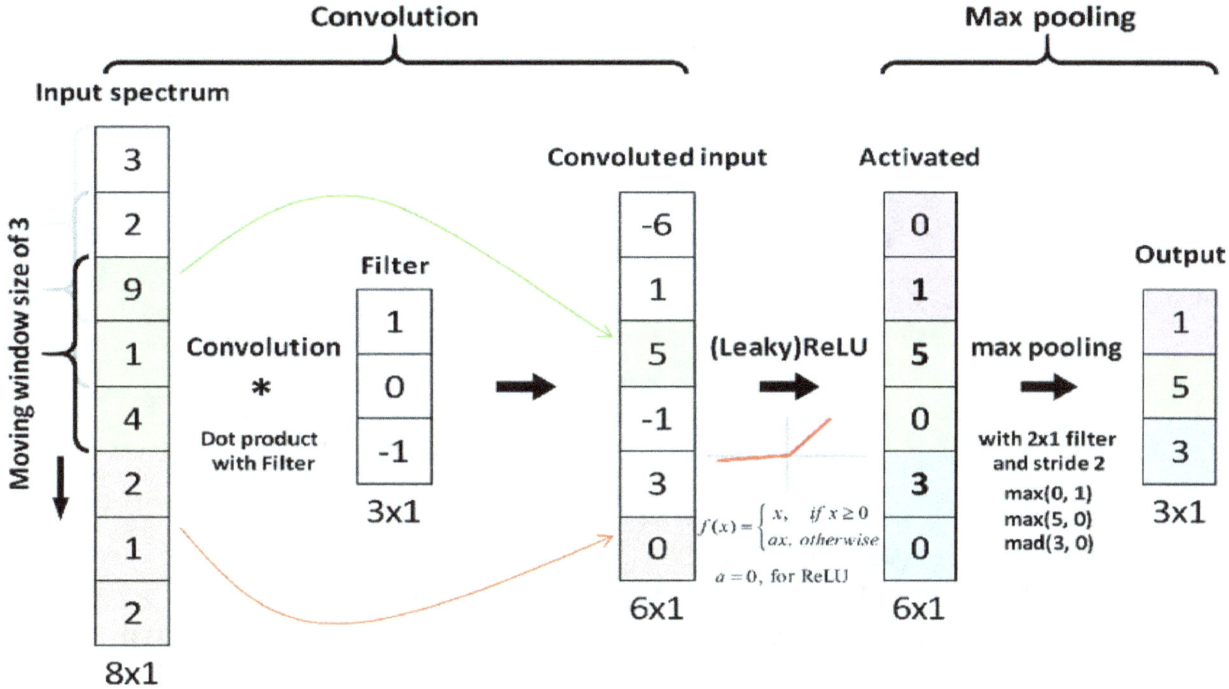

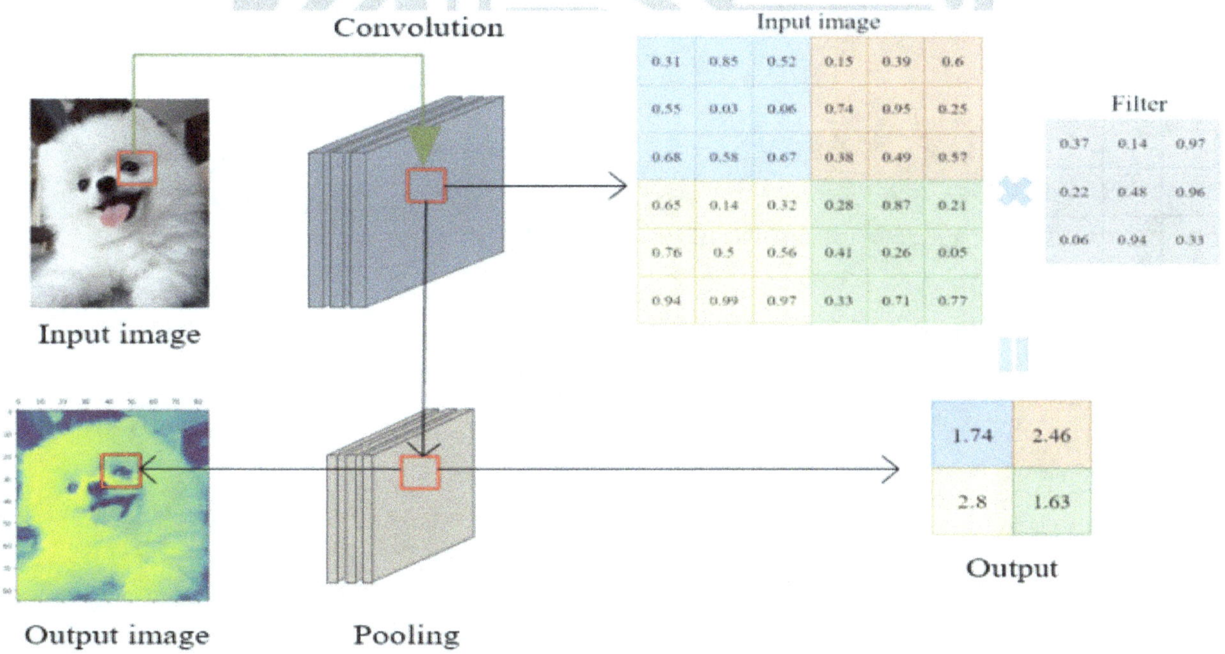

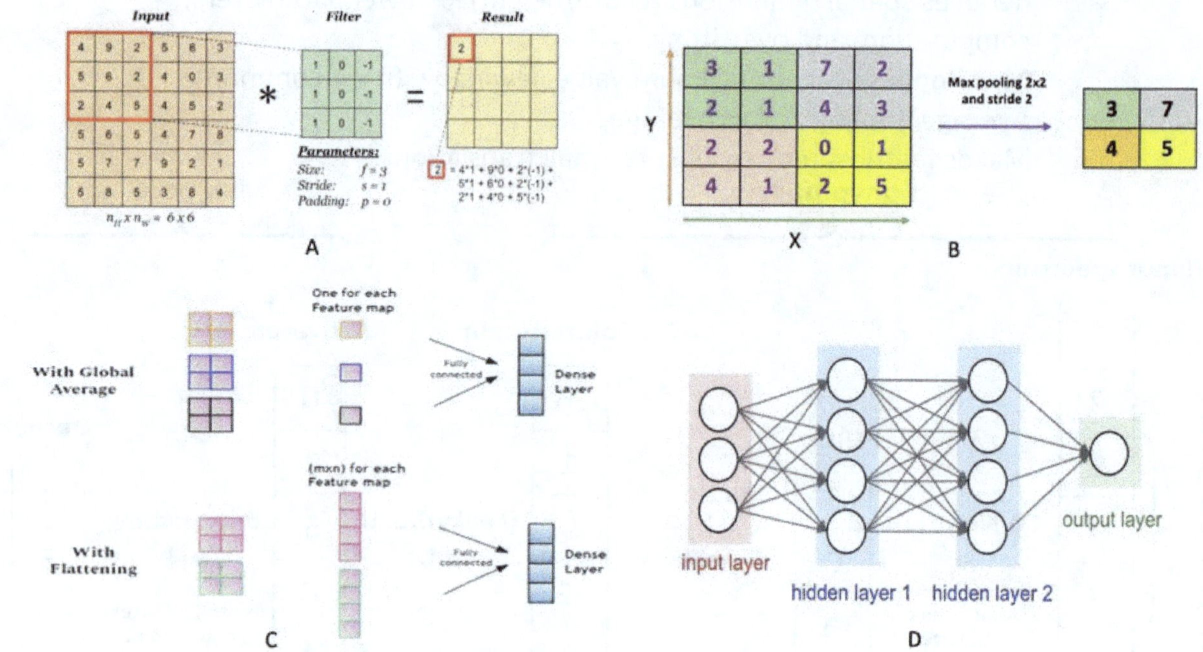

4. **Fully Connected (Dense) Layers** (Classification)
    - At the end: Flatten feature maps → feed into dense layers.
    - High-level reasoning, output probabilities (via softmax for multi-class).

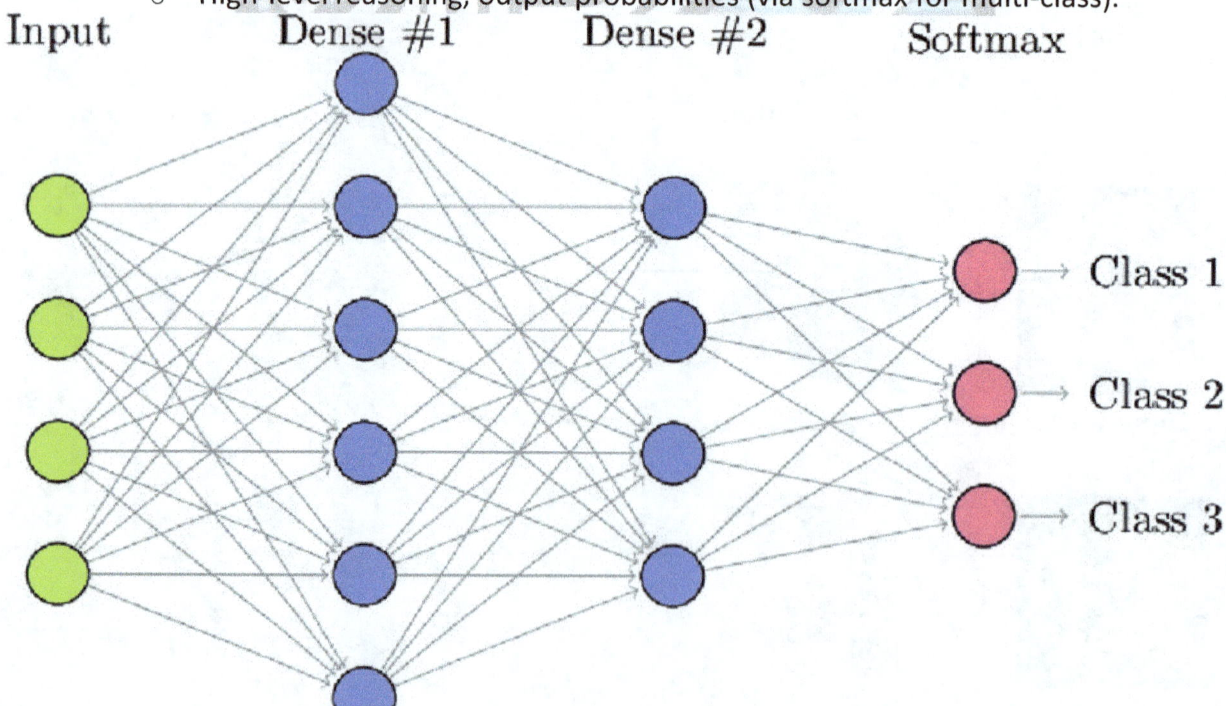

5. **Other Common Layers**
   - **Batch Normalization**: Stabilizes learning.
   - **Dropout**: Randomly drops neurons to prevent overfitting.
   - **Global Average Pooling**: Modern replacement for flatten (reduces parameters).

Typical CNN Pipeline

Input Image → [Conv + ReLU → Pool] × N → Flatten → [Dense + ReLU] × M → Softmax

Training CNNs

- Loss: Categorical Cross-Entropy (classification).
- Optimizer: Adam (most common).
- Data Augmentation: Flip, rotate, crop to increase dataset variety.
- Transfer Learning: Use pre-trained models (e.g., ResNet on ImageNet) and fine-tune.

Python Code Examples (Using PyTorch – Modern and Flexible)

Installation: `pip install torch torchvision`

1. Simple CNN for MNIST (Handwritten Digits)

Python

```
import torch
import torch.nn as nn
import torch.optim as optim
import torchvision
import torchvision.transforms as transforms
from torch.utils.data import DataLoader

# Data loading
transform = transforms.Compose([transforms.ToTensor(), transforms.Normalize((0.1307,), 
(0.3081,))])
train_dataset = torchvision.datasets.MNIST(root='./data', train=True, download=True, 
transform=transform)
test_dataset = torchvision.datasets.MNIST(root='./data', train=False, download=True, 
transform=transform)

train_loader = DataLoader(train_dataset, batch_size=64, shuffle=True)
test_loader = DataLoader(test_dataset, batch_size=64, shuffle=False)

# Define CNN
class SimpleCNN(nn.Module):
    def __init__(self):
        super(SimpleCNN, self).__init__()
        self.conv1 = nn.Conv2d(1, 32, kernel_size=3, padding=1)  # Input channels=1 (grayscale)
        self.conv2 = nn.Conv2d(32, 64, kernel_size=3, padding=1)
        self.pool = nn.MaxPool2d(2, 2)
```

```
        self.fc1 = nn.Linear(64 * 7 * 7, 128)
        self.fc2 = nn.Linear(128, 10)  # 10 classes
        self.relu = nn.ReLU()
        self.dropout = nn.Dropout(0.5)

    def forward(self, x):
        x = self.pool(self.relu(self.conv1(x)))
        x = self.pool(self.relu(self.conv2(x)))
        x = x.view(-1, 64 * 7 * 7)  # Flatten
        x = self.relu(self.fc1(x))
        x = self.dropout(x)
        x = self.fc2(x)
        return x

model = SimpleCNN()
criterion = nn.CrossEntropyLoss()
optimizer = optim.Adam(model.parameters(), lr=0.001)

# Training loop
for epoch in range(5):
    model.train()
    running_loss = 0.0
    for images, labels in train_loader:
        optimizer.zero_grad()
        outputs = model(images)
        loss = criterion(outputs, labels)
        loss.backward()
        optimizer.step()
        running_loss += loss.item()
    print(f"Epoch {epoch+1}, Loss: {running_loss/len(train_loader):.4f}")

# Evaluation
model.eval()
correct = 0
total = 0
with torch.no_grad():
    for images, labels in test_loader:
        outputs = model(images)
        _, predicted = torch.max(outputs.data, 1)
        total += labels.size(0)
        correct += (predicted == labels).sum().item()

print(f"Test Accuracy: {100 * correct / total:.2f}%")
```

This achieves ~99% accuracy on MNIST.

2. Using Pre-Trained CNN (Transfer Learning with ResNet)

Python

```
from torchvision import models

# Load pre-trained ResNet50
model = models.resnet50(pretrained=True)

# Freeze early layers
for param in model.parameters():
    param.requires_grad = False

# Replace final layer for custom classes (e.g., 5 classes)
num_features = model.fc.in_features
model.fc = nn.Linear(num_features, 5)

# Train only the new layer (or fine-tune all)
optimizer = optim.Adam(model.fc.parameters(), lr=0.001)
# Proceed with training loop as above...
```

3.Object Detection (YOLO, SSD, Faster R-CNN)

Object Detection is a computer vision task that involves identifying and localizing objects in images or videos by drawing **bounding boxes** around them and assigning class labels (e.g., "car", "person"). Unlike image classification (which labels the whole image), detection handles multiple objects, varying sizes, and positions.

Modern detectors fall into two categories:

- **Two-stage detectors**: Propose regions of interest (ROIs) first, then classify and refine (higher accuracy, slower).
- **One-stage detectors**: Predict boxes and classes in a single pass (faster, real-time capable).

Here are examples of object detection outputs with bounding boxes (from YOLO, SSD, and similar models):

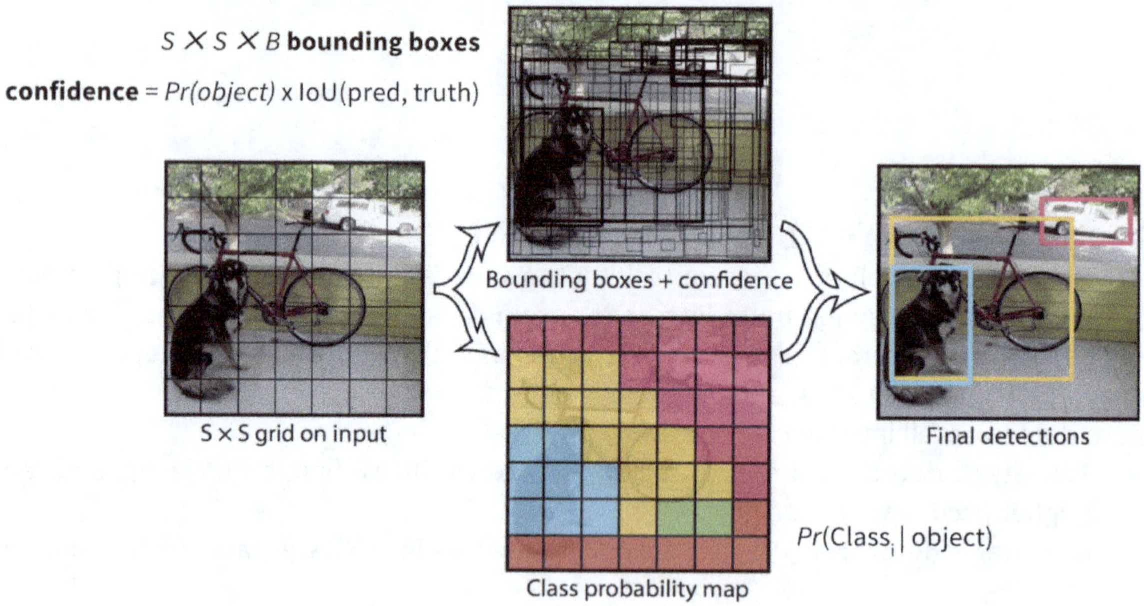

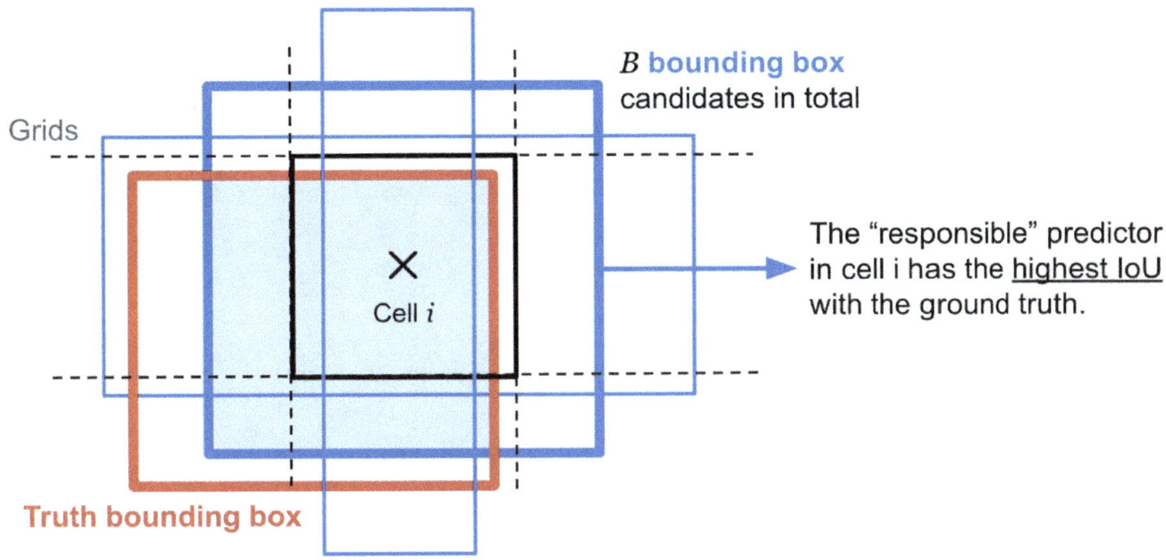

Key models: **YOLO** (one-stage, fastest), **SSD** (one-stage, balanced), **Faster R-CNN** (two-stage, most accurate).

YOLO (You Only Look Once)

YOLO treats detection as a single regression problem: one forward pass predicts bounding boxes and class probabilities directly from the full image.

Key Features

- **One-stage**: Divides image into grid (e.g., SxS), each cell predicts B boxes, confidence, and class probabilities.
- **Evolution**: Started with YOLOv1 (2015). Latest (as of late 2025): Ultralytics YOLO11 (2024), with advancements in efficiency; YOLOv12 (2025, attention-centric); mentions of YOLO26 (edge-optimized, NMS-free). Ultralytics line (YOLOv5, v8, v11) dominates open-source use.
- **Advantages**: Extremely fast (real-time, 100+ FPS on GPUs), good for video/deployments.
- **Disadvantages**: Early versions struggled with small objects; modern ones improved via multi-scale predictions.

YOLO architecture diagrams (various versions):

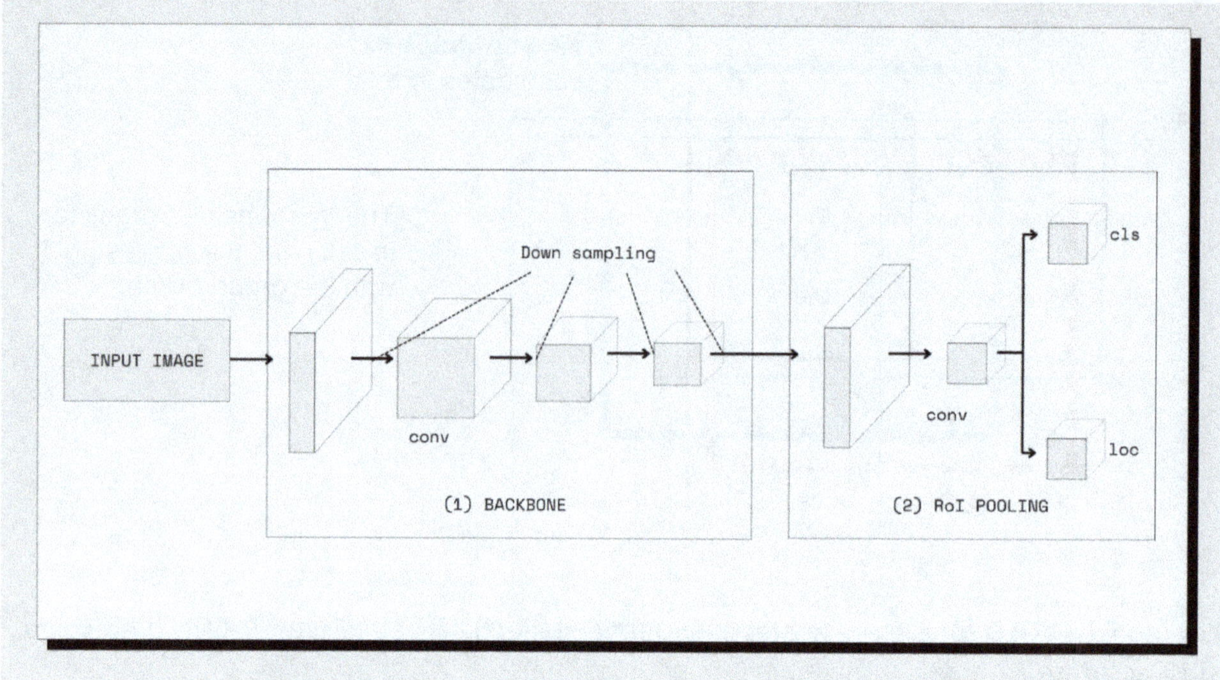

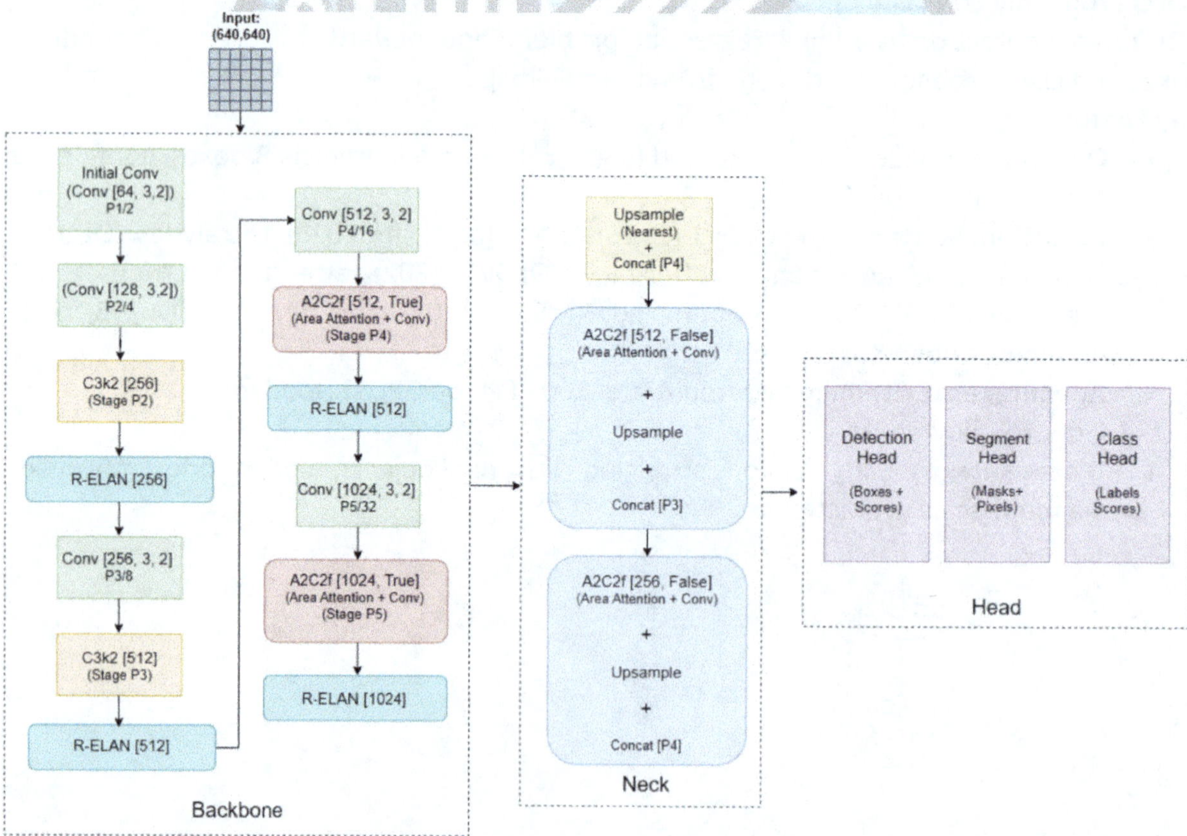

SSD (Single Shot MultiBox Detector)

SSD (2016) is a one-stage detector using a base CNN (e.g., VGG/ResNet) + extra layers for multi-scale feature maps.

Key Features

- Predicts fixed default (anchor) boxes at multiple scales/aspect ratios from different feature map layers.
- Early layers detect small objects; later layers detect large ones.
- Single pass, no separate proposal stage.
- **Advantages**: Faster than two-stage, better small object detection than early YOLO.
- **Disadvantages**: Lower accuracy than two-stage on complex datasets.

SSD architecture diagrams:

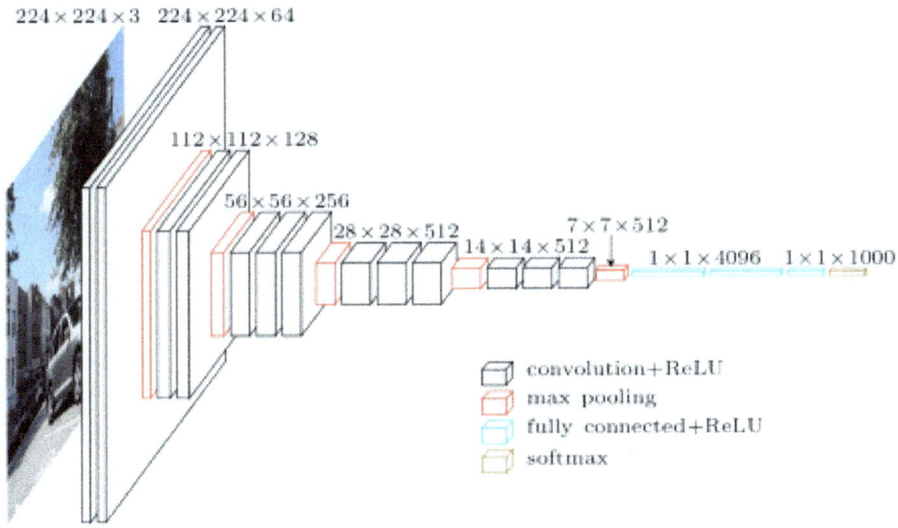

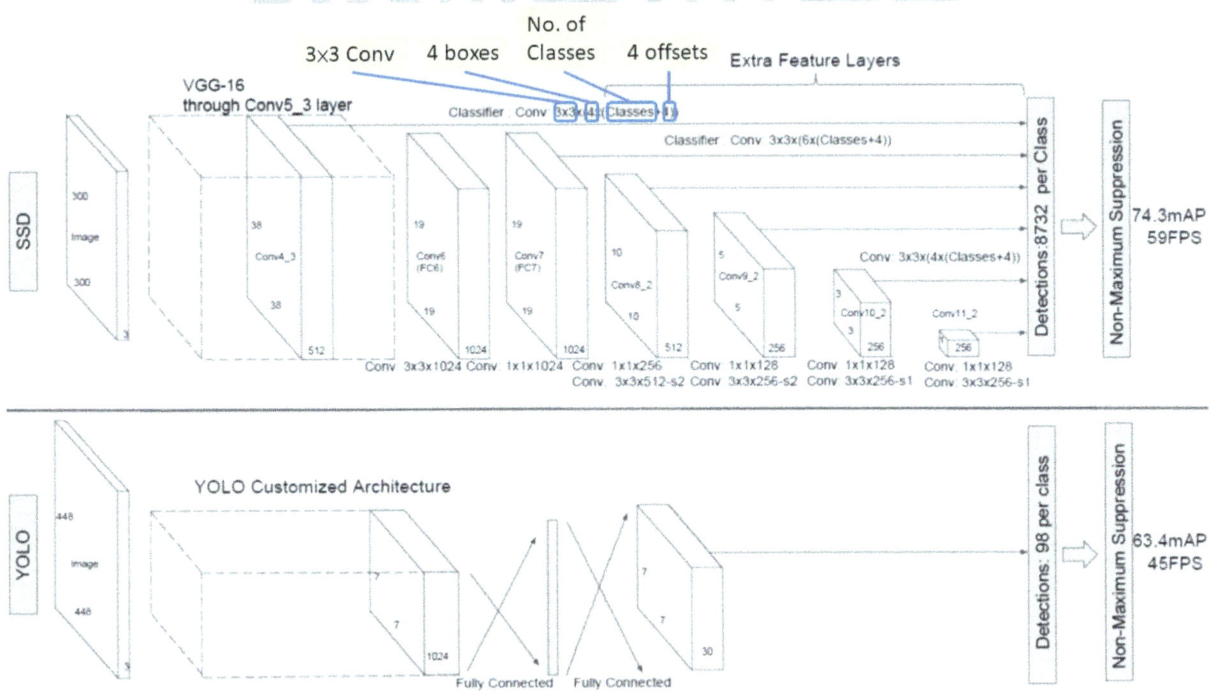

Faster R-CNN

Faster R-CNN (2015) is a two-stage detector improving on R-CNN/Fast R-CNN by integrating region proposals.

Key Features

- **Stage 1**: Region Proposal Network (RPN) shares backbone features (e.g., ResNet) to propose ROIs via anchors.
- **Stage 2**: ROI pooling + classification/regression heads for final boxes/classes.
- End-to-end trainable.
- **Advantages**: Highest accuracy, especially for precise localization.
- **Disadvantages**: Slower (not real-time without optimizations).

Faster R-CNN architecture diagrams:

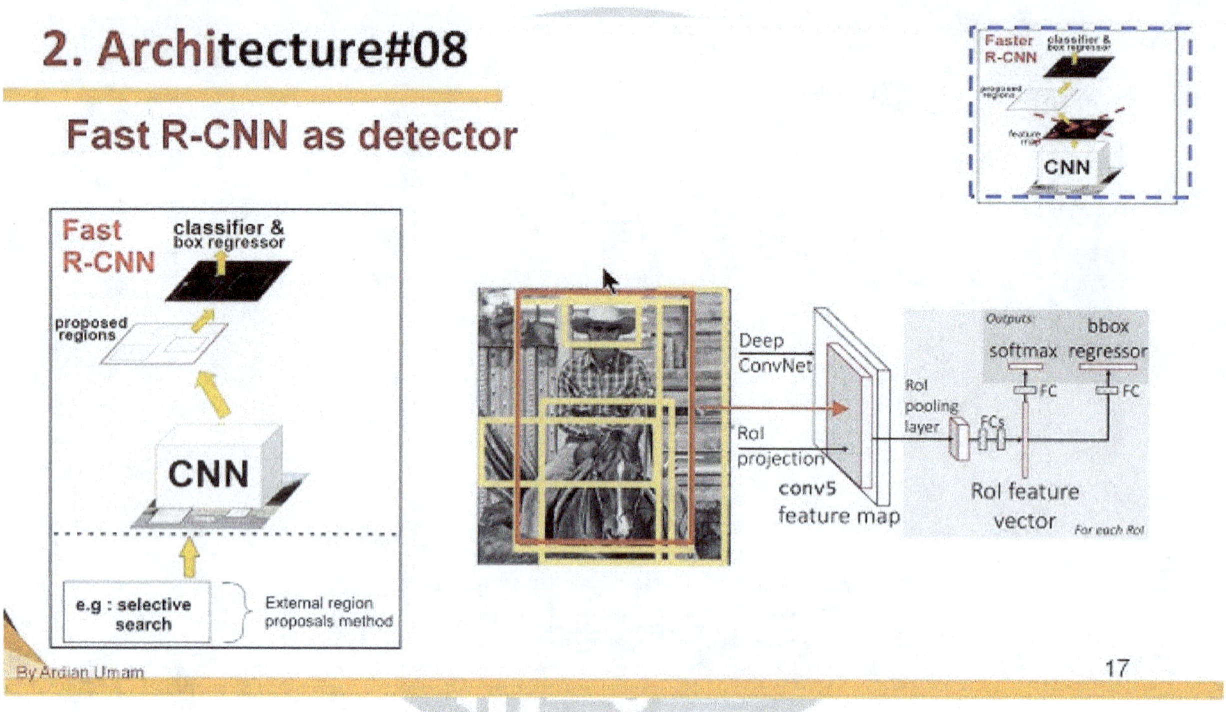

Comparison

Aspect	YOLO (Modern, e.g., v8/v11)	SSD	Faster R-CNN
Type	One-stage	One-stage	Two-stage
Speed	Fastest (real-time, 50-200+ FPS)	Fast (real-time capable)	Slowest (5-20 FPS)
Accuracy	High (competitive with two-stage in recent versions)	Medium (good balance)	Highest
Small Objects	Improved in later versions	Good (multi-scale)	Excellent
Use Cases	Real-time (video, robotics, edge)	General real-time	High-precision (medical, detailed analysis)
Parameters/Complexity	Low-medium	Medium	High

- Modern YOLO often outperforms SSD in both speed and accuracy.
- Faster R-CNN excels in accuracy but requires more compute.

Section-9

AI Applications

- Chatbots (Using NLP & Deep Learning)
- AI-powered Recommendation Systems
- AI-based Image Recognition

AI Applications

1.Chatbots (Using NLP & Deep Learning)

Chatbots are computer programs designed to simulate human conversation through text or voice interactions. Early chatbots were rule-based, relying on predefined scripts and keyword matching, but they struggled with natural, varied language. Modern chatbots leverage **Natural Language Processing (NLP)** and **Deep Learning** to understand context, intent, and nuances, enabling more fluid and human-like conversations.

NLP is the branch of AI that enables machines to interpret, process, and generate human language. Deep Learning, a subset of machine learning using neural networks with many layers, powers advanced NLP by learning patterns from vast datasets without explicit programming.

Role of NLP in Chatbots

NLP forms the core of intelligent chatbots, breaking down user input into understandable components. The typical NLP pipeline includes:

1. **Tokenization**: Splitting text into words or subwords (tokens).
2. **Part-of-Speech Tagging & Lemmatization/Stemming**: Identifying grammatical roles and reducing words to root forms.
3. **Named Entity Recognition (NER)**: Extracting key details like names, dates, or locations.
4. **Intent Classification**: Determining the user's goal (e.g., "book a flight" → booking intent).
5. **Slot Filling/Entity Extraction**: Capturing specifics (e.g., destination, date).
6. **Sentiment Analysis**: Detecting emotion or tone (optional for advanced bots).

These steps use a mix of rule-based methods and deep learning models for accuracy.

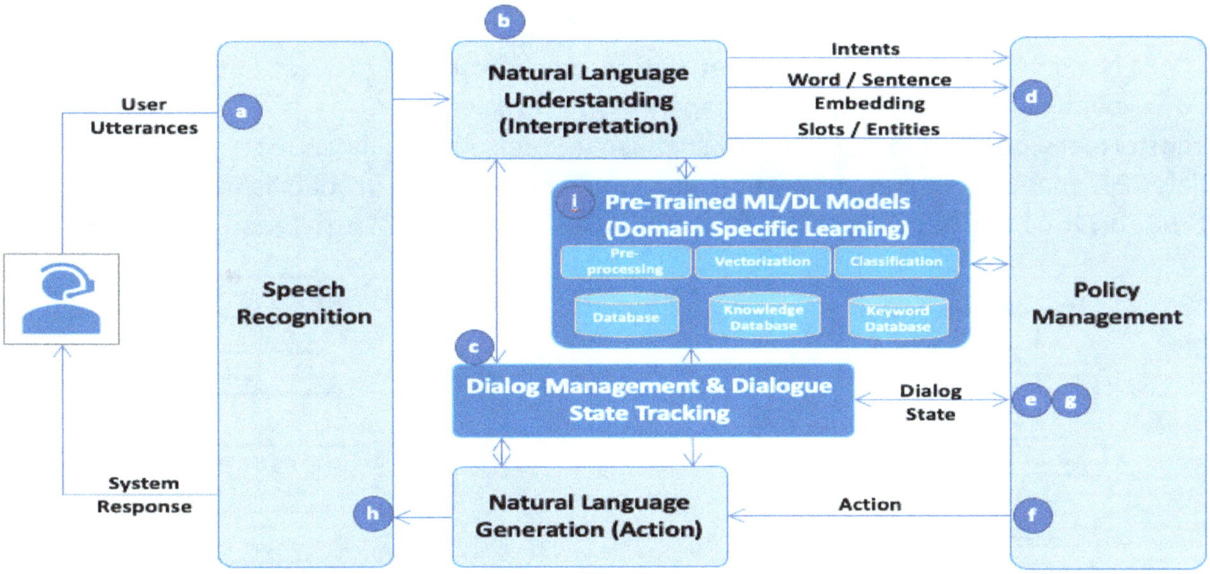

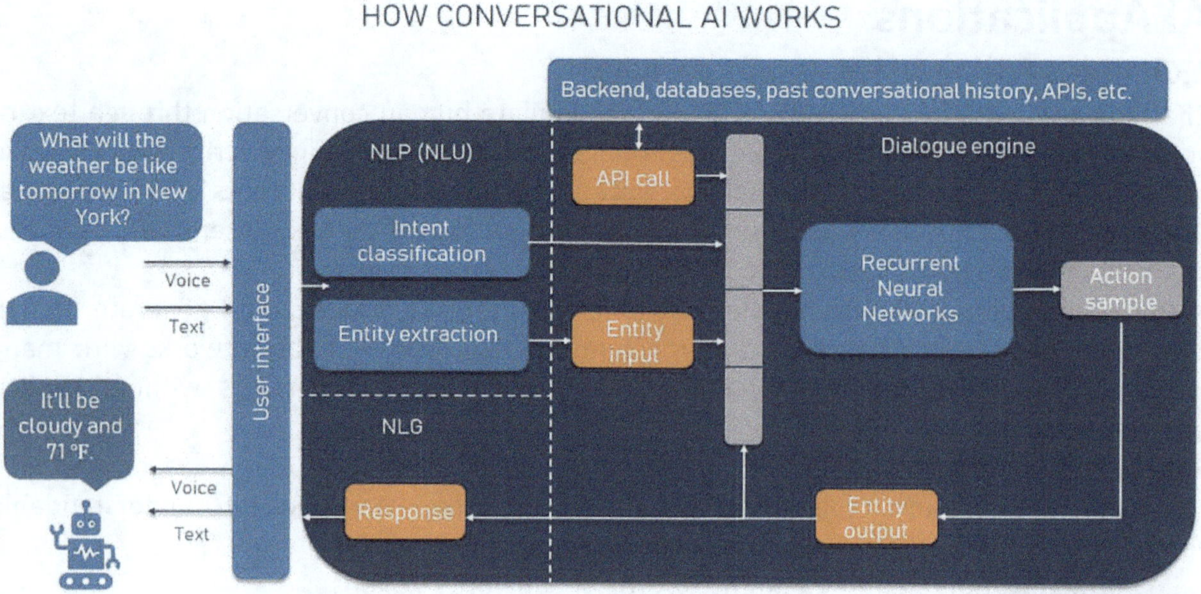

Role of Deep Learning in Chatbots

Deep Learning elevates chatbots beyond simple pattern matching. Key architectures include:

- **Recurrent Neural Networks (RNNs)**: Early models like LSTMs/GRUs handled sequences well, maintaining context over time.
- **Seq2Seq Models**: Encoder-decoder structures (often with RNNs) for translating input to output responses.
- **Transformer Models**: The breakthrough from the 2017 paper "Attention is All You Need." Transformers use **self-attention mechanisms** to process entire sequences in parallel, capturing long-range dependencies efficiently.

Transformers power modern Large Language Models (LLMs) like GPT series, BERT, and DialoGPT, enabling generative chatbots that predict next words probabilistically.

Scaled Dot-Product Attention

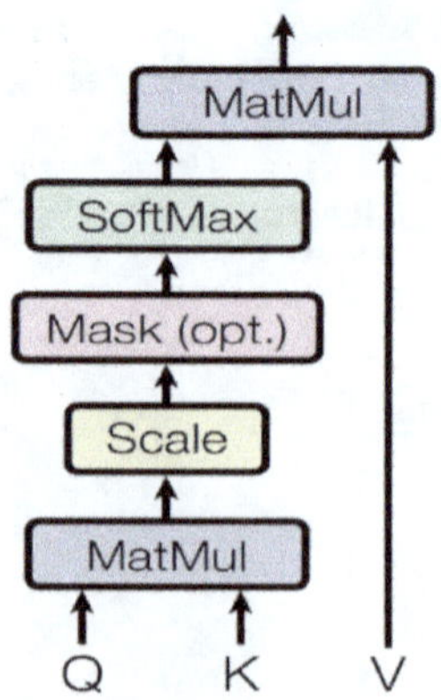

Multi-Head Attention

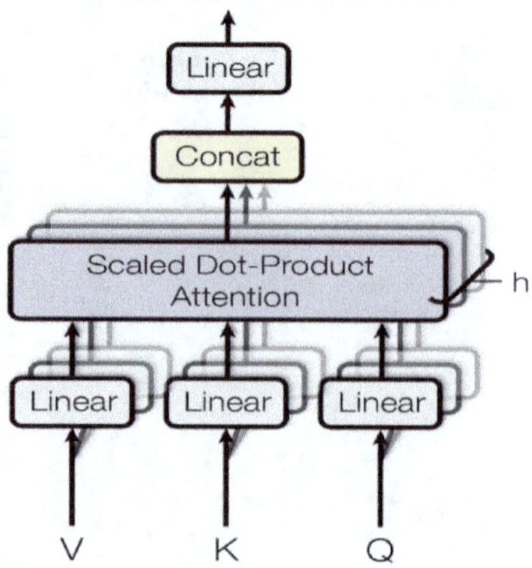

Types of Deep Learning-Based Chatbots

1. **Retrieval-Based**: Use NLP to understand intent, then retrieve pre-defined responses from a database. Reliable but less creative.
2. **Generative-Based**: Generate new responses on-the-fly using deep learning (e.g., Transformers). More natural and flexible, but risk irrelevant outputs.
3. **Hybrid**: Combine both for accuracy and creativity.

Most advanced chatbots (e.g., ChatGPT) are generative, fine-tuned with Reinforcement Learning from Human Feedback (RLHF) for better alignment.

Overall Architecture of Modern Chatbots

A typical deep learning chatbot architecture includes:

- **User Interface**: Text/voice input channel.
- **NLP/NLU Engine**: Processes input (intent + entities).
- **Dialog Management**: Tracks conversation state and context.
- **Deep Learning Core**: Transformer/LLM for understanding and generation.
- **Knowledge Base/Backend**: Retrieves data or integrates APIs.
- **Response Generation (NLG)**: Forms natural output.
- **Learning Loop**: Feedback improves the model over time.

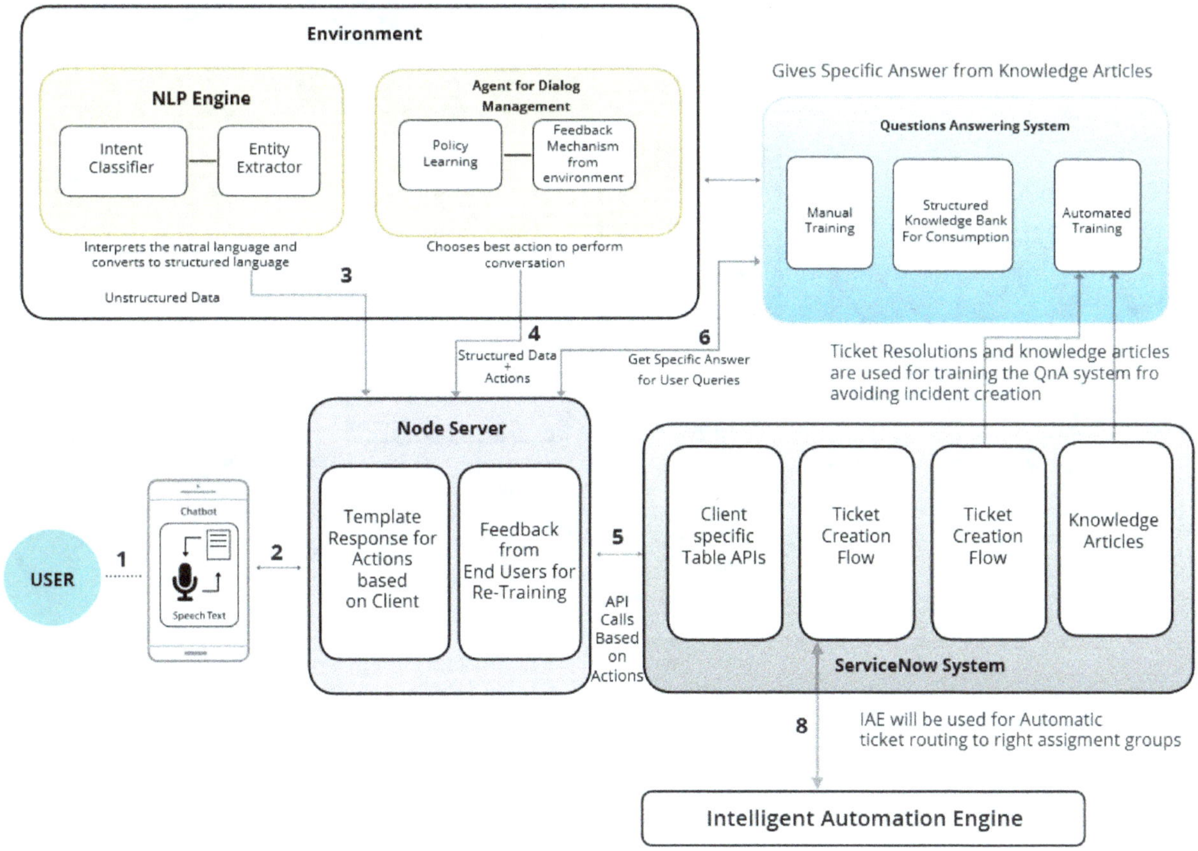

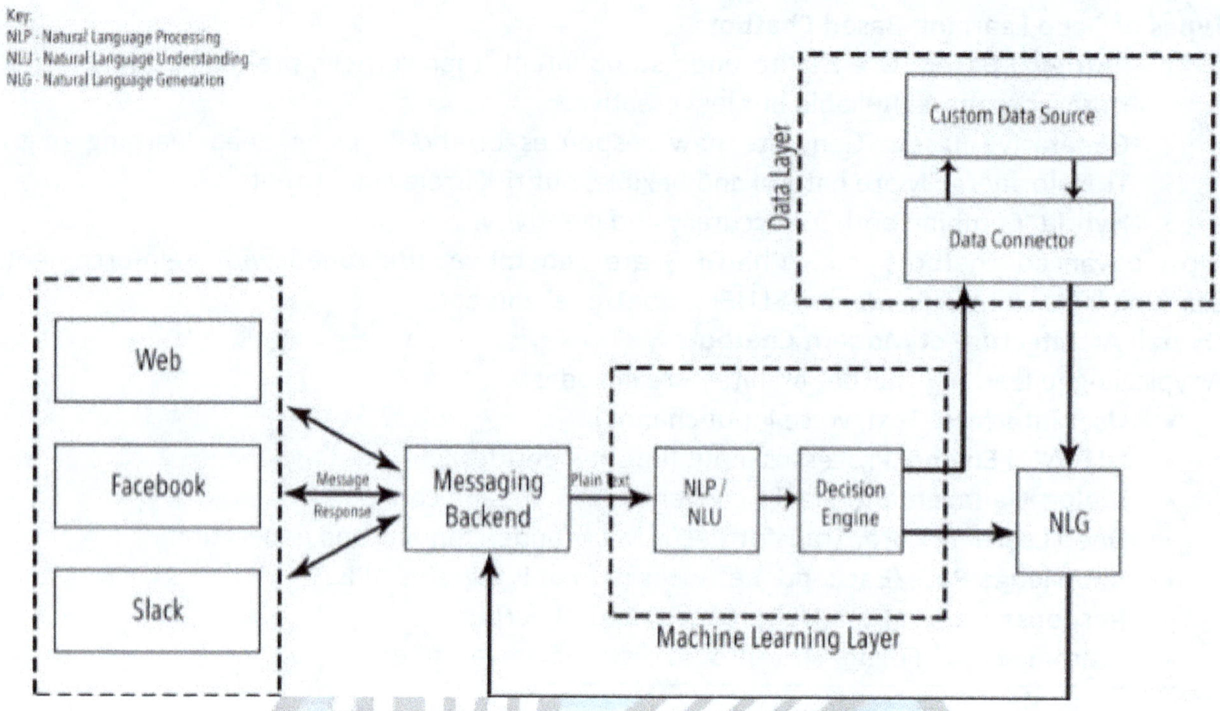
Key:
NLP - Natural Language Processing
NLU - Natural Language Understanding
NLG - Natural Language Generation
Data Layer
Custom Data Source
Data Connector
Web
Facebook
Slack
Message
Response
Messaging Backend
Plain Text
NLP / NLU
Decision Engine
NLG
Machine Learning Layer

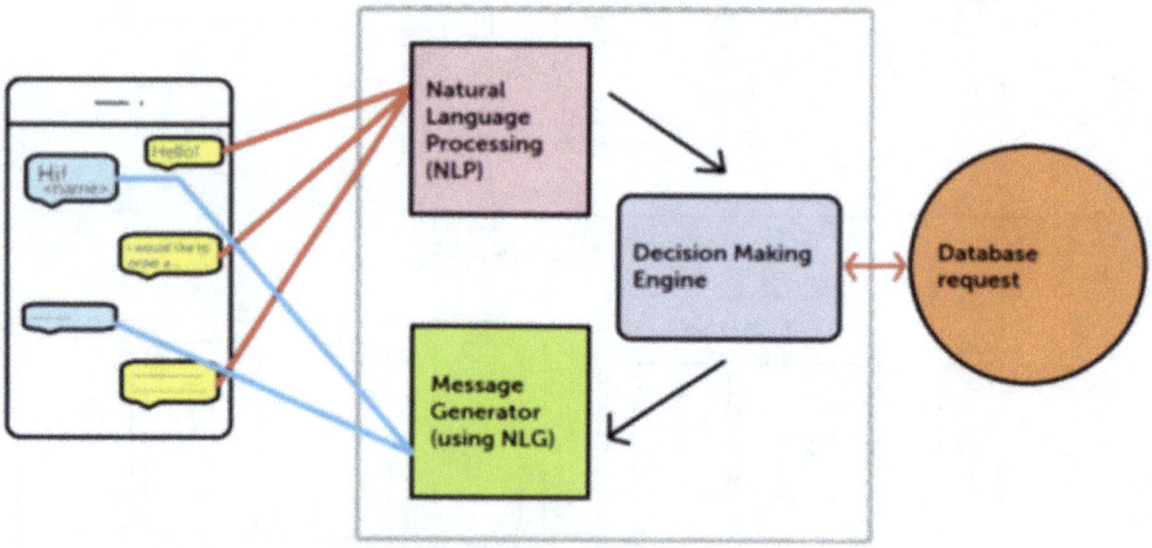
Hello!
Hi!
<name>
Natural Language Processing (NLP)
Decision Making Engine
Database request
Message Generator (using NLG)

How Modern Chatbots Work Step-by-Step

1. **Input Reception**: User types/speaks a message.
2. **Preprocessing & NLU**: NLP pipeline extracts intent and entities using deep models (e.g., BERT for classification).
3. **Context Management**: Maintains conversation history (Transformers excel here via attention).
4. **Response Decision**:
   - Retrieval: Match to best response.
   - Generative: LLM predicts tokens autoregressively (next-word prediction).
5. **Output Generation**: NLG refines response for fluency.
6. **Feedback & Improvement**: Logs interactions; models retrain/fine-tune.

Training involves massive datasets (e.g., Reddit conversations for DialoGPT), pre-training on language prediction, then fine-tuning for dialogue.

Advantages and Challenges

Advantages:

- Handle open-ended queries.
- Contextual awareness.
- Continuous improvement via learning.
- Scalable for 24/7 support.

Challenges:

- Hallucinations (generating false info).
- Bias from training data.
- High computational needs.
- Privacy concerns.

As of late 2025, advancements in Transformers and multimodal models continue pushing chatbots toward more empathetic, reasoning-capable agents.

This combination of NLP and Deep Learning has transformed chatbots from scripted tools into versatile AI companions used in customer service, healthcare, education, and more.

2.AI-powered Recommendation Systems

Recommendation systems (or recommender systems) are AI-driven algorithms that suggest relevant items to users based on their preferences, behavior, or similarities with others. They power personalized experiences on platforms like Netflix (movie suggestions), Amazon (product recommendations), Spotify (music playlists), and YouTube (video feeds). These systems analyze vast amounts of data to predict what users might like, increasing engagement, sales, and satisfaction.

Traditional systems used simple statistics, but modern AI-powered ones leverage machine learning (ML) and deep learning (DL) to handle complex patterns, implicit feedback (e.g., clicks, views), and massive datasets. As of late 2025, advancements in transformers and large language models have further enhanced sequential and multimodal recommendations.

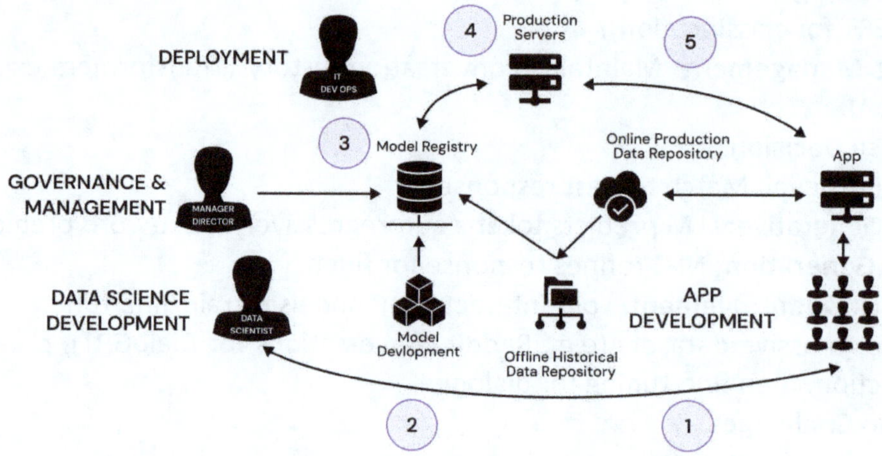
DEPLOYMENT
IT DEV OPS
4
Production Servers
5
3
Model Registry
Online Production Data Repository
App
GOVERNANCE & MANAGEMENT
MANAGER DIRECTOR
DATA SCIENCE DEVELOPMENT
DATA SCIENTIST
Model Devlopment
Offline Historical Data Repository
APP DEVELOPMENT
2
1

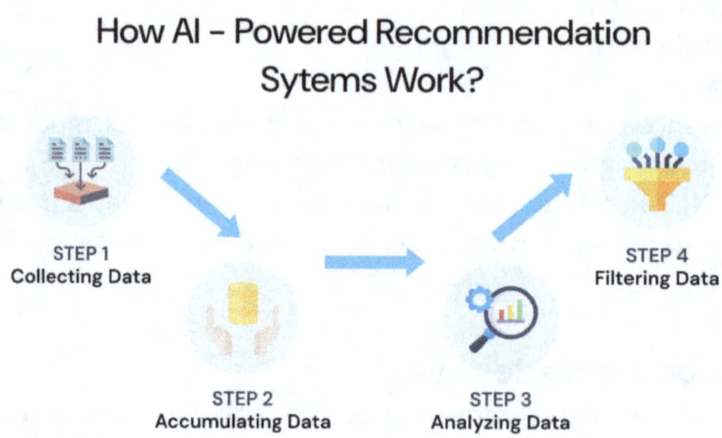
How AI - Powered Recommendation Sytems Work?
STEP 1
Collecting Data
STEP 2
Accumulating Data
STEP 3
Analyzing Data
STEP 4
Filtering Data

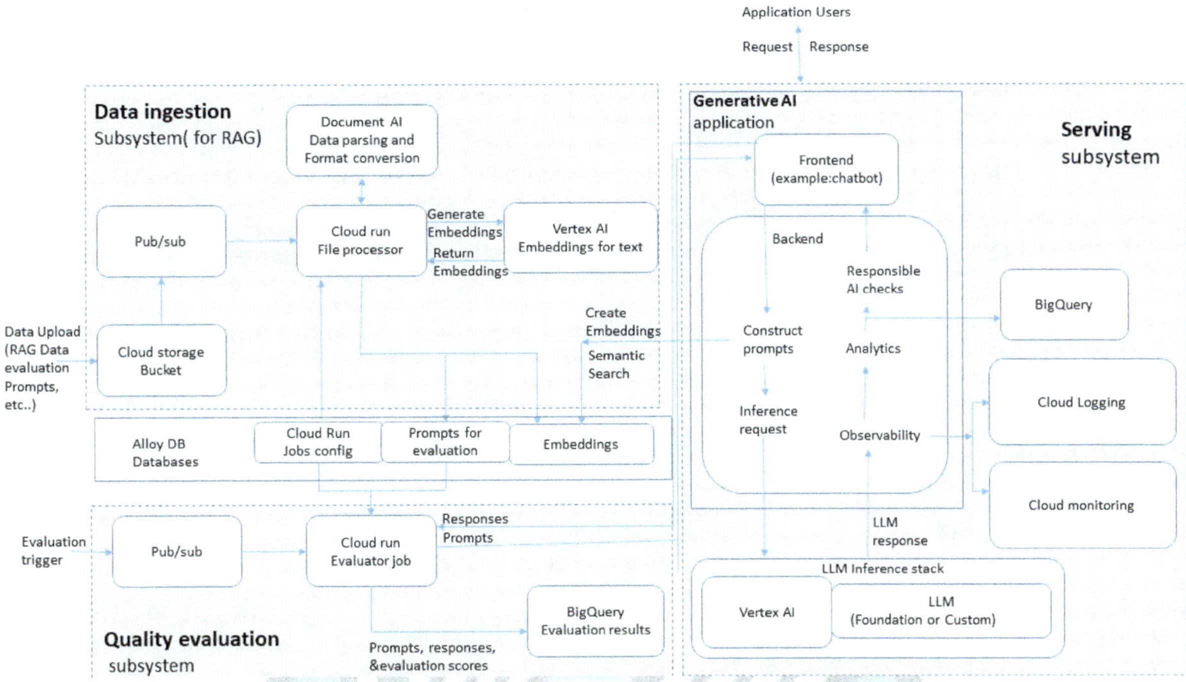
Application Users
Request
Response
Data ingestion
Subsystem(for RAG)
Document AI
Data parsing and
Format conversion
Pub/sub
Cloud run
File processor
Generate
Embeddings
Return
Embeddings
Vertex AI
Embeddings for text
Data Upload
(RAG Data
evaluation
Prompts,
etc..)
Cloud storage
Bucket
Create
Embeddings
Semantic
Search
Alloy DB
Databases
Cloud Run
Jobs config
Prompts for
evaluation
Embeddings
Evaluation
trigger
Pub/sub
Cloud run
Evaluator job
Responses
Prompts
BigQuery
Evaluation results
Quality evaluation
subsystem
Prompts, responses,
&evaluation scores
Generative AI
application
Serving
subsystem
Frontend
(example:chatbot)
Backend
Responsible
AI checks
Construct
prompts
Analytics
Inference
request
Observability
BigQuery
Cloud Logging
Cloud monitoring
LLM
response
LLM Inference stack
Vertex AI
LLM
(Foundation or Custom)

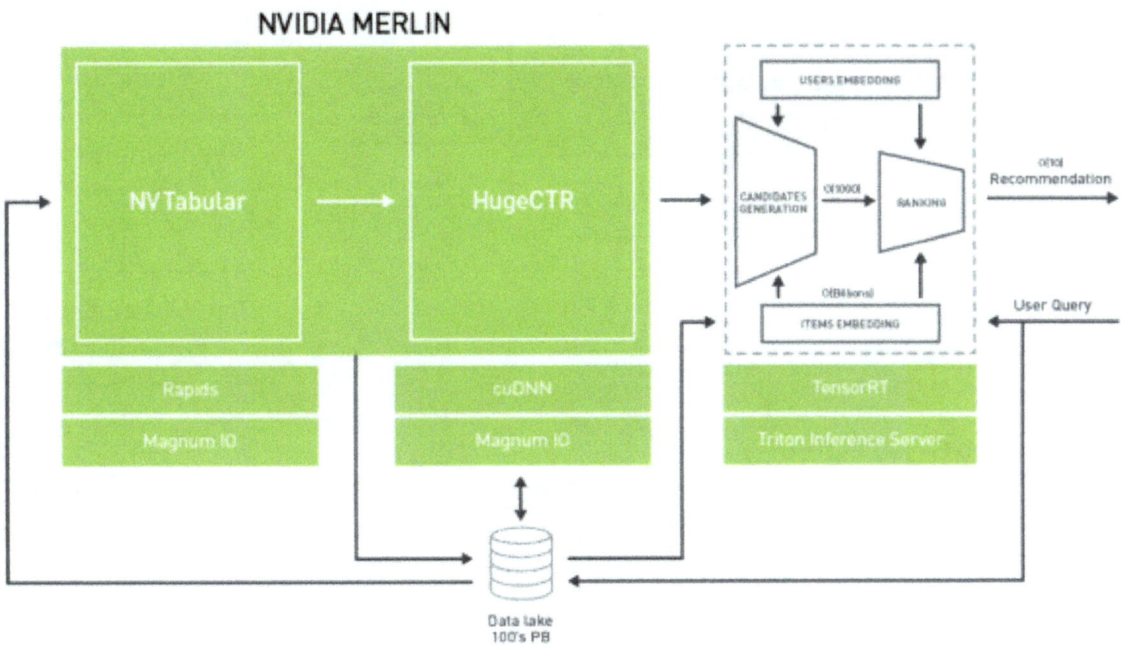
NVIDIA MERLIN
NVTabular
HugeCTR
Rapids
Magnum IO
cuDNN
Magnum IO
USERS EMBEDDING
CANDIDATES
GENERATION
RANKING
ITEMS EMBEDDING
TensorRT
Triton Inference Server
Recommendation
User Query
Data lake
100's PB

Core Types of Recommendation Systems

1. **Collaborative Filtering (CF):**
    - Relies on user-item interactions (e.g., ratings, purchases).
    - User-based: Finds similar users and recommends what they liked.
    - Item-based: Recommends items similar to those the user has liked (e.g., "customers who bought this also bought...").
    - Uses a user-item matrix where rows are users, columns are items, and cells are ratings (often sparse).
    - Traditional methods: Matrix factorization (e.g., SVD) decomposes the matrix into latent factors.

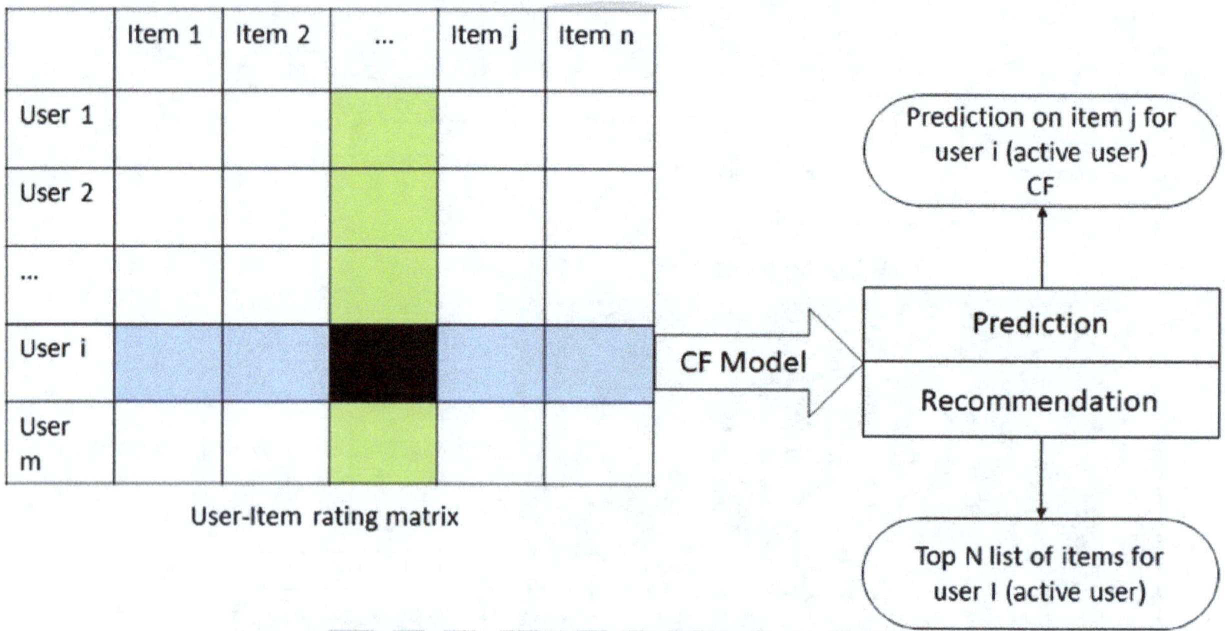

2. **Content-Based Filtering:**
    - Recommends items similar to those a user has liked based on item features (e.g., genre, description, tags).
    - Builds user profiles from past interactions and matches them to item profiles using similarity metrics (e.g., cosine similarity on TF-IDF vectors for text).
    - Strengths: No cold-start for items with features; avoids "filter bubbles" less than CF.

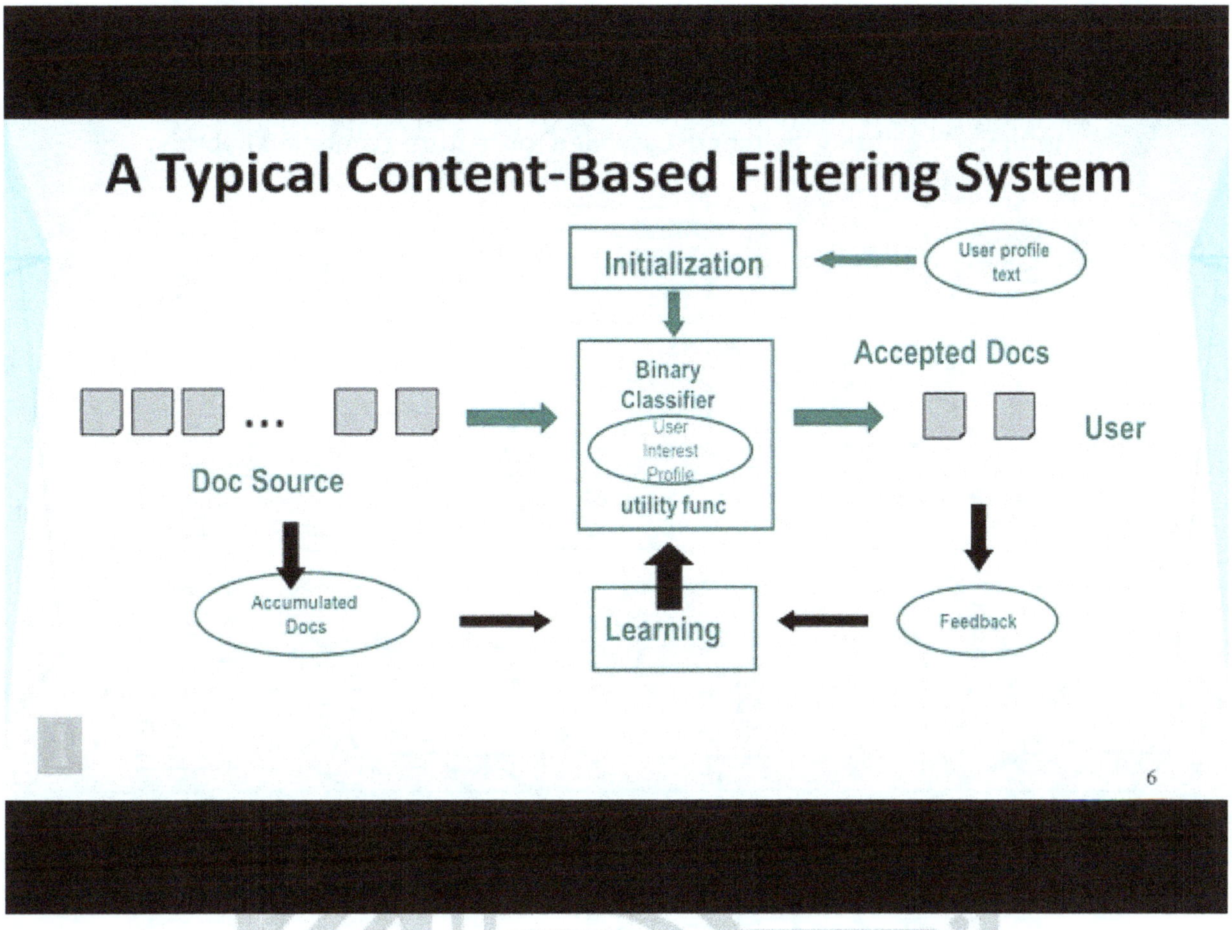
A Typical Content-Based Filtering System
Initialization
User profile text
Binary Classifier
User Interest Profile
utility func
Accepted Docs
User
Doc Source
Accumulated Docs
Learning
Feedback
6

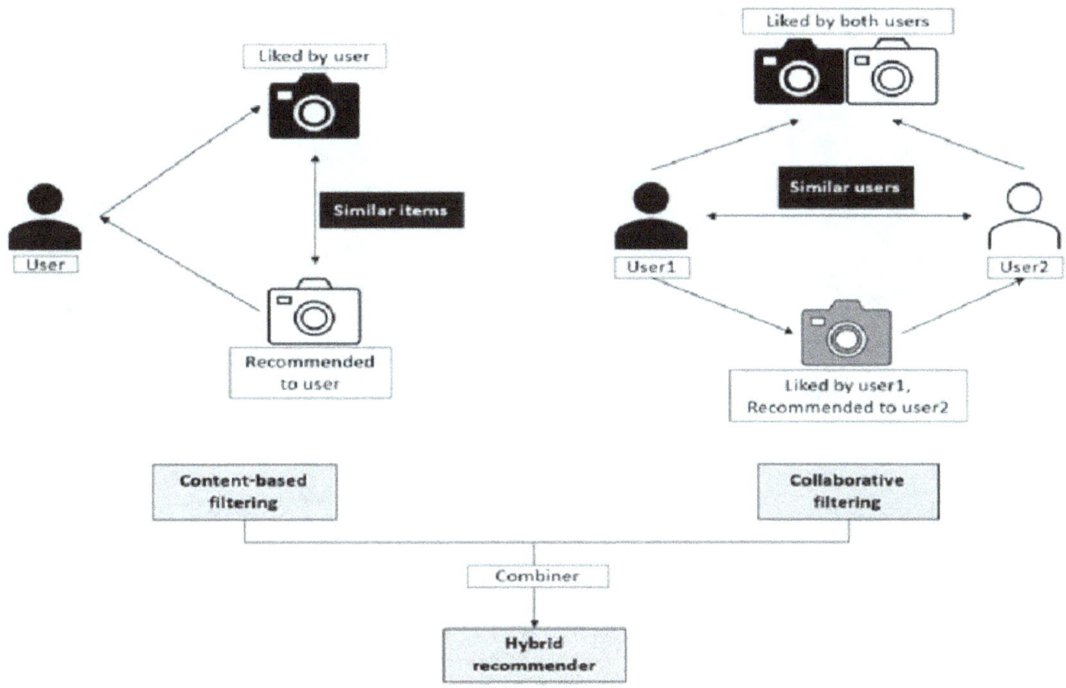
Liked by user
Similar items
User
Recommended to user
Liked by both users
Similar users
User1
User2
Liked by user1, Recommended to user2
Content-based filtering
Collaborative filtering
Combiner
Hybrid recommender

3. **Hybrid Systems:**
   - Combine CF and content-based (or others) to mitigate weaknesses like cold-start (new users/items) and sparsity.
   - Methods: Weighted, switched, cascaded, or feature-combined hybrids.
   - Most real-world systems (e.g., Netflix) are hybrid.

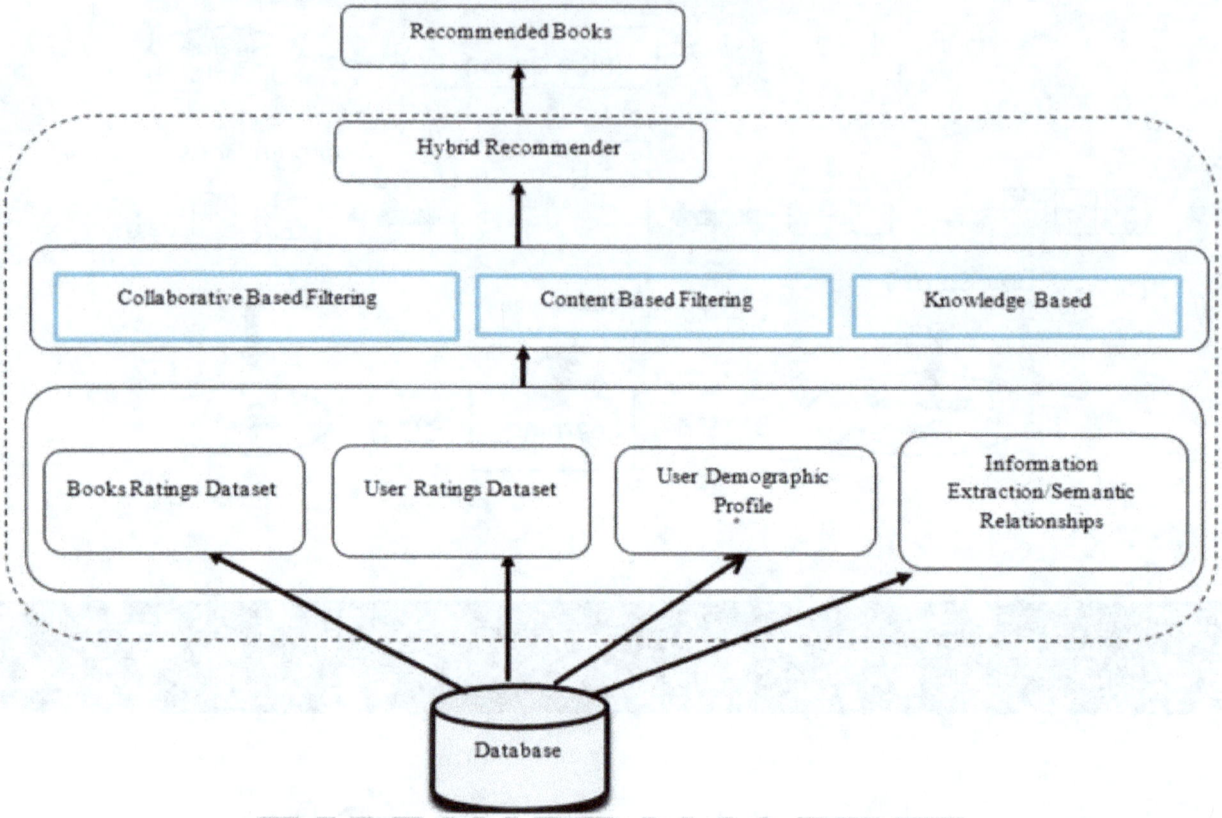

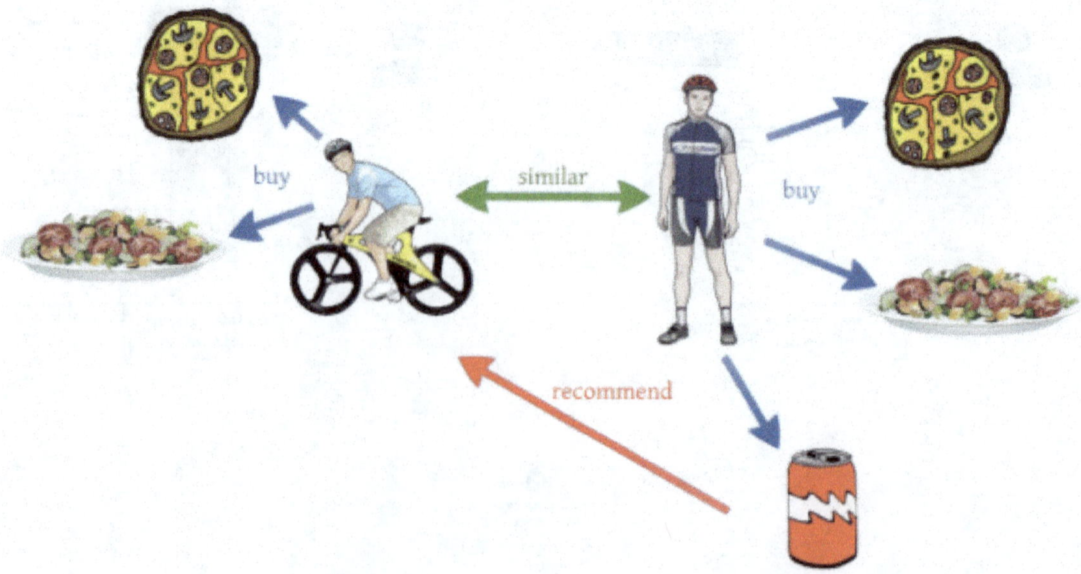

Role of AI and Deep Learning

Deep learning has revolutionized recommendation systems by handling non-linear patterns, sequential data, and multimodal inputs (text, images, audio).

- Neural Collaborative Filtering (NCF): Replaces inner products in matrix factorization with neural networks (e.g., MLPs) to learn complex interactions.

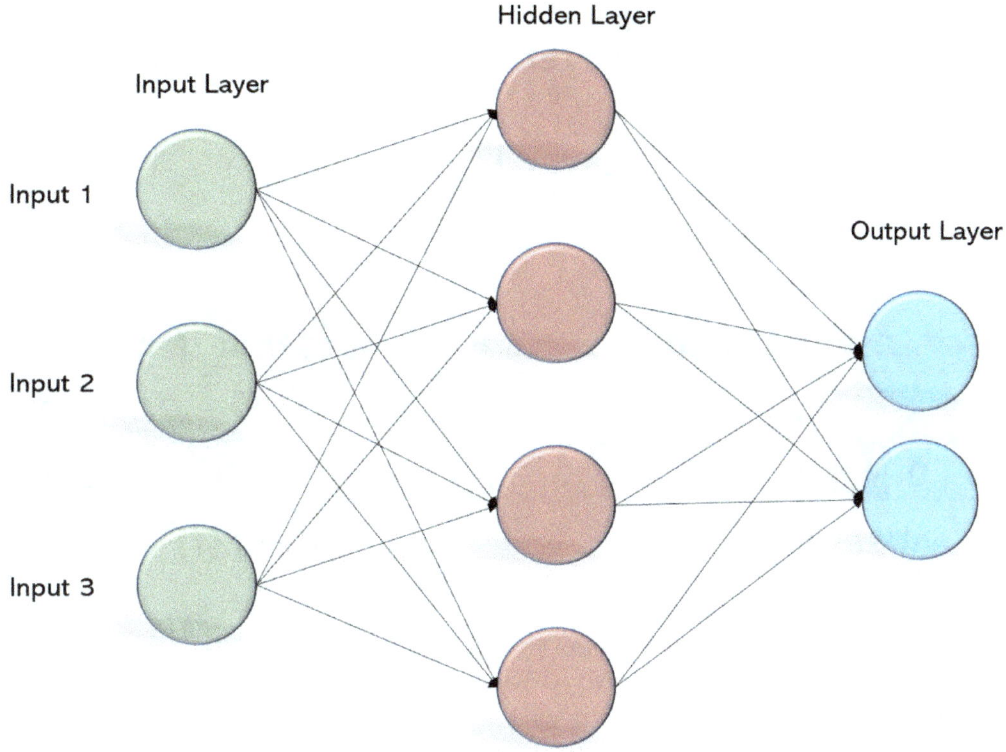

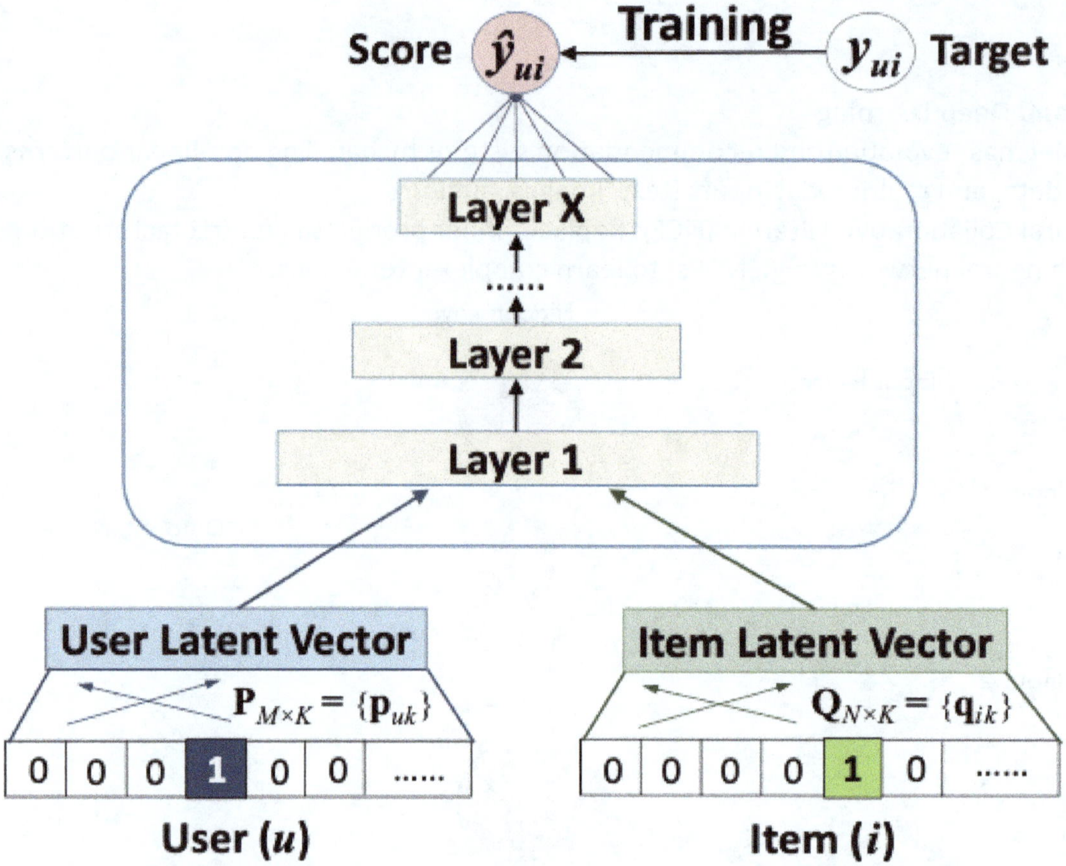

- **Autoencoders:** For denoising sparse data or learning embeddings.
- **Sequence Models:** RNNs/LSTMs/GRUs for session-based recommendations (e.g., next-item prediction in shopping carts).
- **Transformer-Based Models:** Self-attention captures long-range dependencies in user histories. Models like BERT4Rec or SASRec treat sequences of interactions as "sentences."

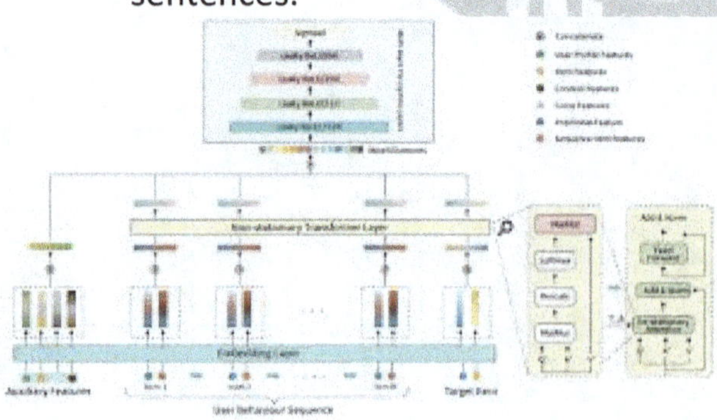

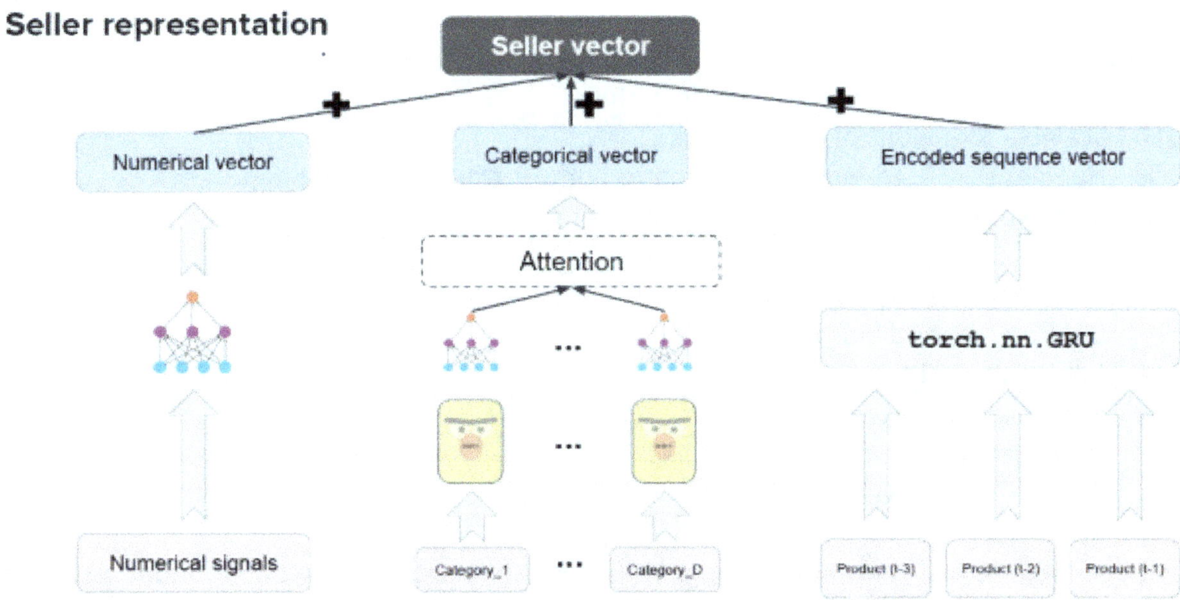

- **Graph Neural Networks (GNNs):** Model user-item interactions as graphs for better propagation of preferences.
- **Multimodal DL:** Incorporates images/videos (e.g., CNNs for product visuals) or text (LLMs for descriptions).

Overall Architecture

A typical AI-powered recommendation pipeline includes:

1. Data Collection: Explicit (ratings) and implicit (views, clicks) feedback; user/item features.
2. Preprocessing: Handling sparsity, normalization, embedding learning.
3. Model Training: Offline (batch) or online (real-time updates).
4. Candidate Generation: Narrow down millions of items (e.g., via approximate nearest neighbors).
5. Ranking: Score candidates with DL models.
6. Re-ranking: Apply business rules (diversity, freshness).
7. Serving: Real-time inference; A/B testing.
8. Feedback Loop: Reinforcement learning or bandit algorithms for exploration-exploitation.

Large-scale systems (e.g., YouTube's) use two-tower architectures: one tower for user embeddings, one for item, with dot product for scoring.

Advantages and Challenges

Advantages:

- Highly personalized and accurate with DL.
- Scalable to billions of users/items.
- Handles cold-start via side information or pre-trained embeddings.
- Improves over time with more data.

Challenges:

- Data privacy and bias amplification.
- Cold-start problem.
- Scalability and latency.
- Explainability (black-box DL models).
- Filter bubbles (over-personalization).

As of December 2025, generative AI (e.g., diffusion models for visuals) and foundation models are pushing recommendations toward more creative and contextual suggestions, like generating personalized playlists or outfits.

3.AI-based Image Recognition

AI-based image recognition, also known as computer vision, enables machines to interpret and understand visual information from images or videos. It involves identifying objects, scenes, patterns, faces, or actions. Early methods relied on hand-crafted features (e.g., SIFT, HOG), but modern systems use **deep learning**, particularly **Convolutional Neural Networks (CNNs)**, to automatically learn hierarchical features from raw pixels. As of late 2025, hybrid models combining CNNs with Transformers dominate, achieving near-human accuracy on complex tasks.

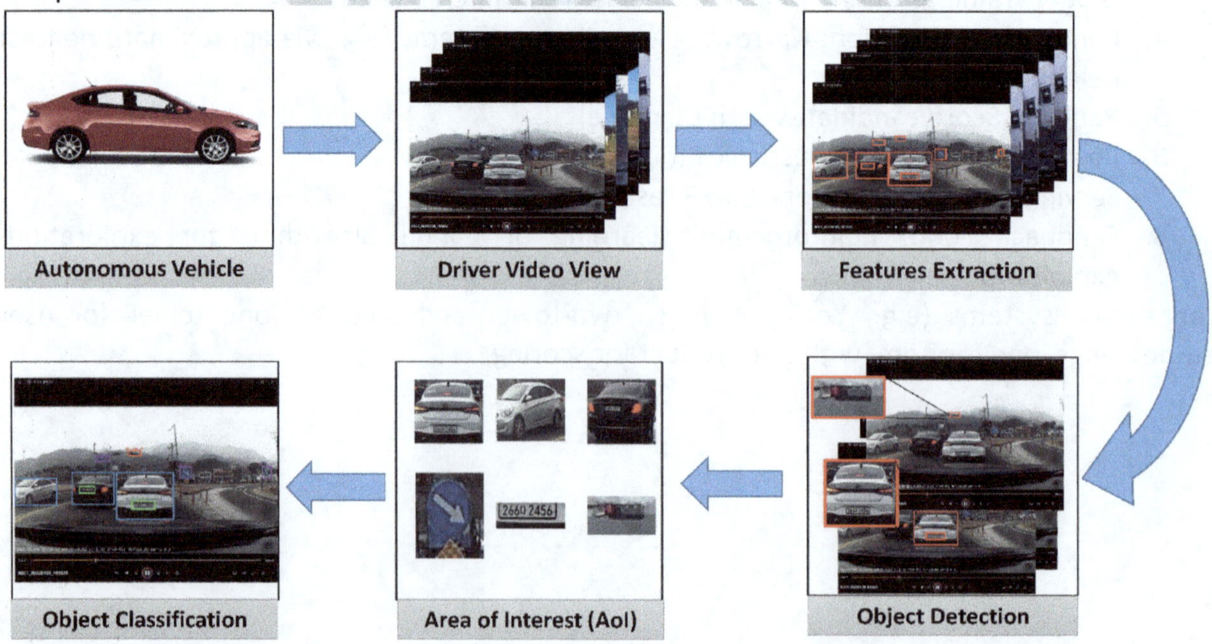

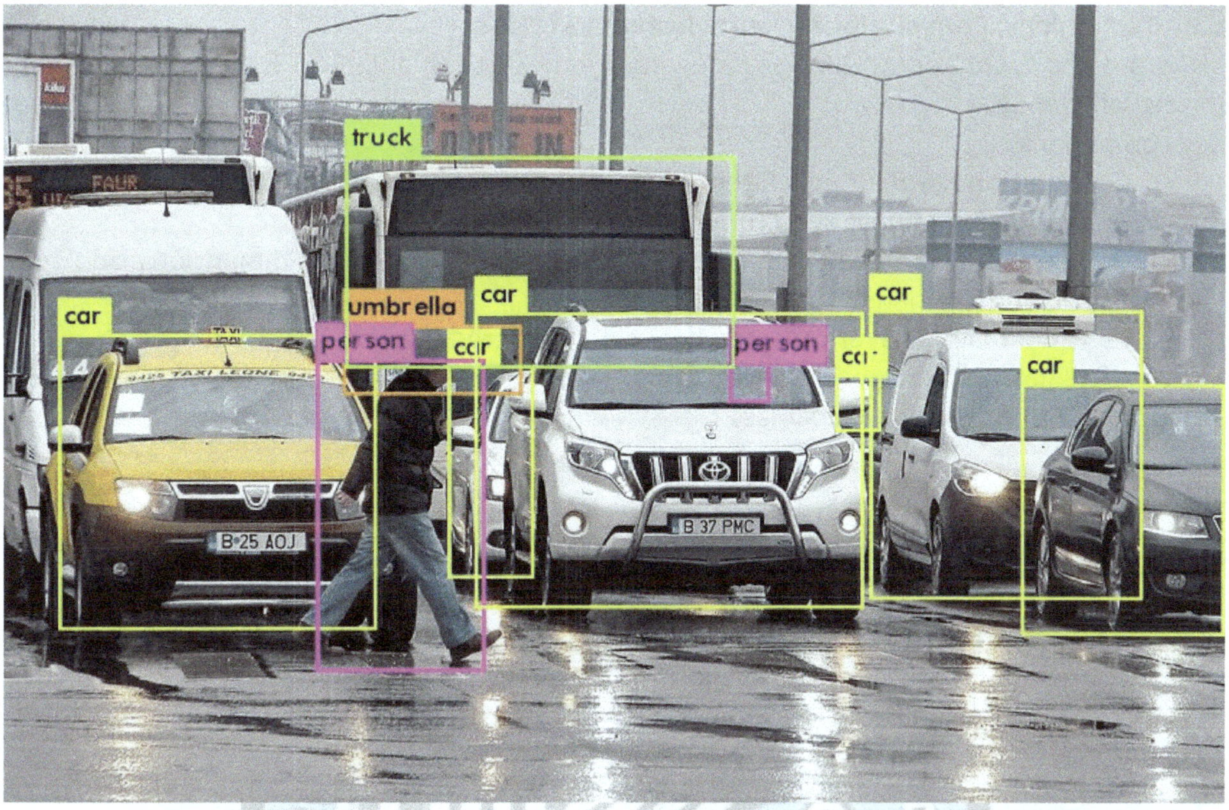
truck
umbrella
car
car
person
car
person
car
car
car
B 25 AOJ
B 37 PMC

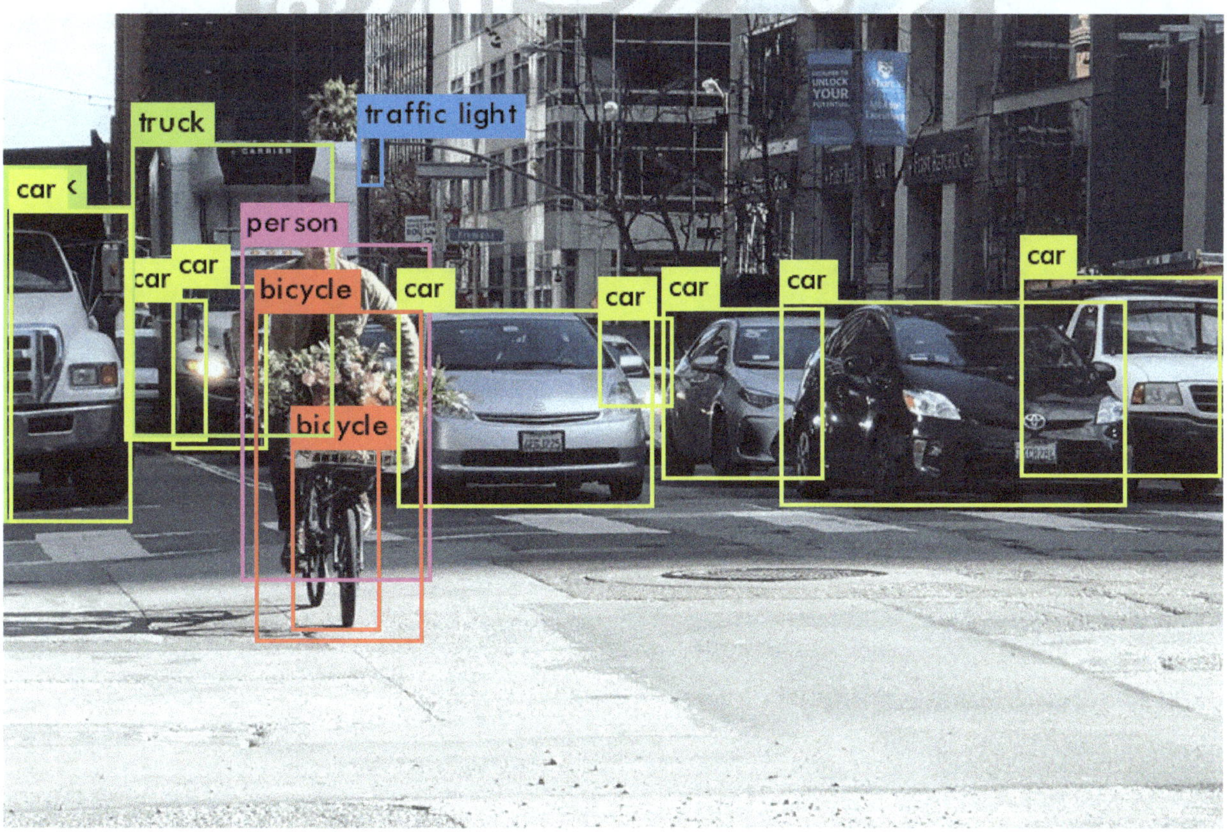
truck
traffic light
car
person
car
car
bicycle
car
car
car
car
car
bicycle

Core Technology: Convolutional Neural Networks (CNNs)

CNNs are the foundation of image recognition due to their ability to handle grid-like data (pixels) efficiently.

Key components:

- **Convolution Layers**: Apply filters/kernels to extract features like edges, textures.
- **Activation Functions**: ReLU for non-linearity.
- **Pooling Layers**: Downsample (e.g., Max Pooling) to reduce dimensions and gain translation invariance.
- **Fully Connected Layers**: Classify based on extracted features.

Typical pipeline: Input Image → Convolutions → Pooling → Repeat → Flatten → Dense Layers → Output (e.g., softmax probabilities).

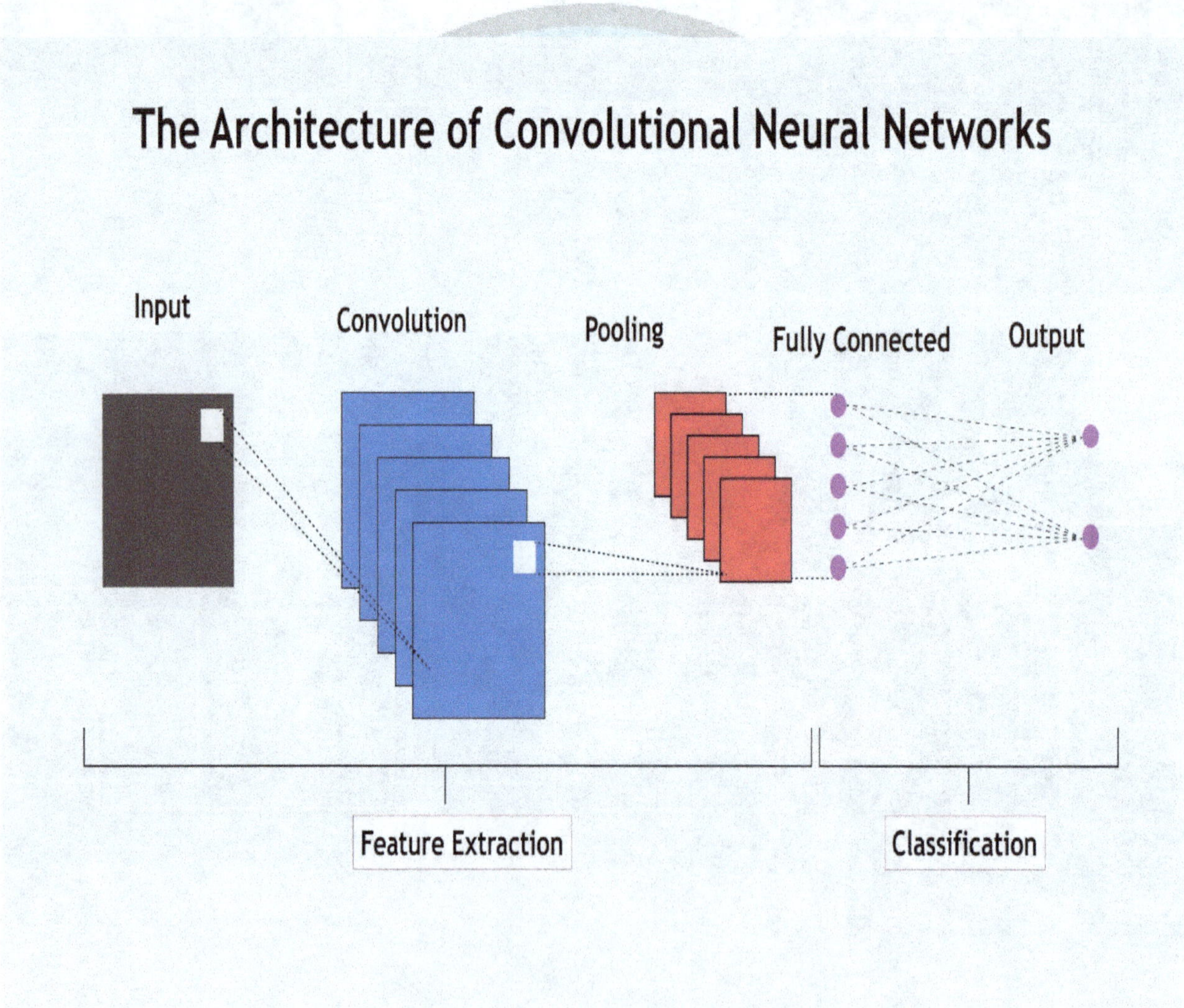

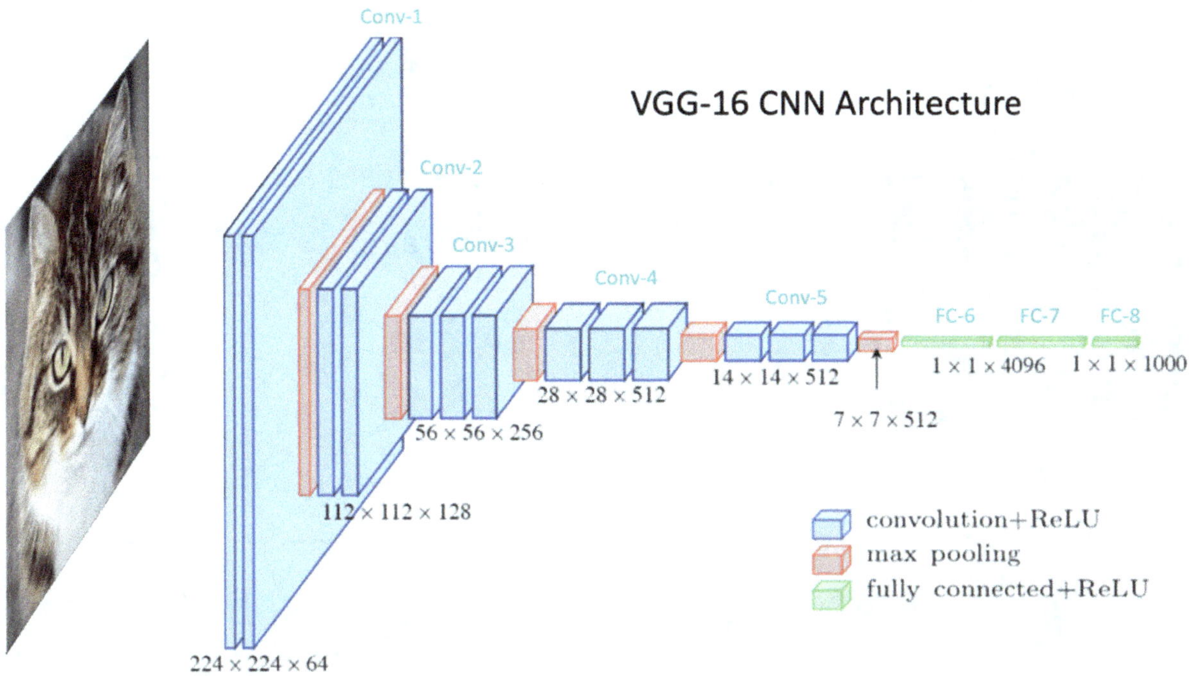
VGG-16 CNN Architecture
Conv-1
Conv-2
Conv-3
Conv-4
Conv-5
FC-6
FC-7
FC-8
224 × 224 × 64
112 × 112 × 128
56 × 56 × 256
28 × 28 × 512
14 × 14 × 512
7 × 7 × 512
1 × 1 × 4096
1 × 1 × 1000
convolution+ReLU
max pooling
fully connected+ReLU

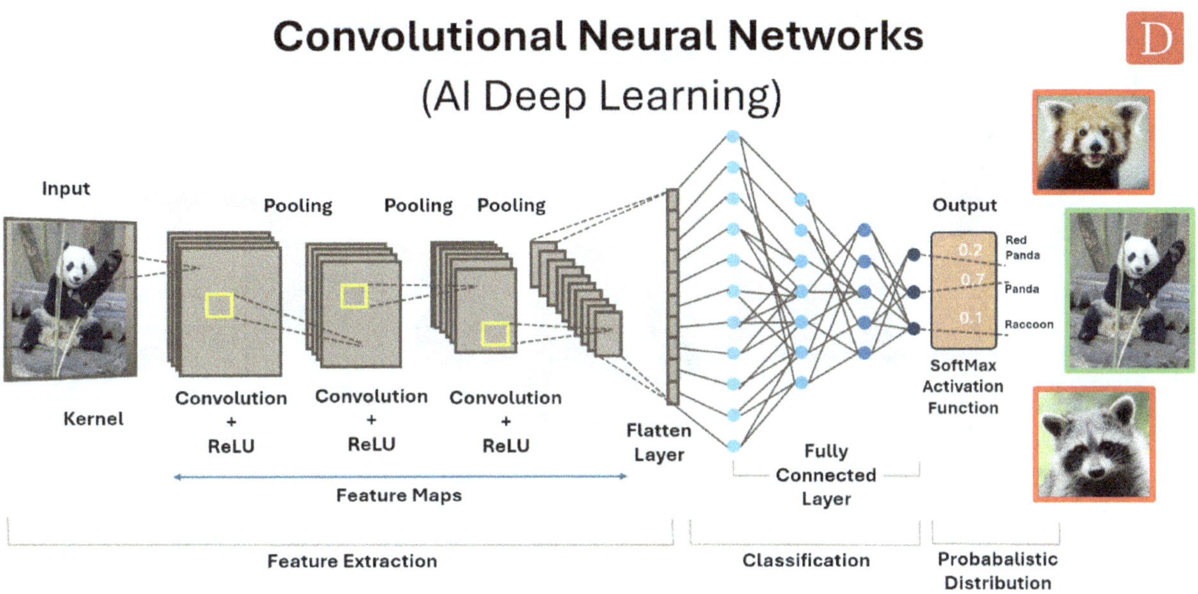
Convolutional Neural Networks
(AI Deep Learning)
D
Input
Kernel
Pooling
Pooling
Pooling
Convolution + ReLU
Convolution + ReLU
Convolution + ReLU
Feature Maps
Flatten Layer
Fully Connected Layer
Output
0.2
0.7
0.1
Red Panda
Panda
Raccoon
SoftMax Activation Function
Feature Extraction
Classification
Probabalistic Distribution

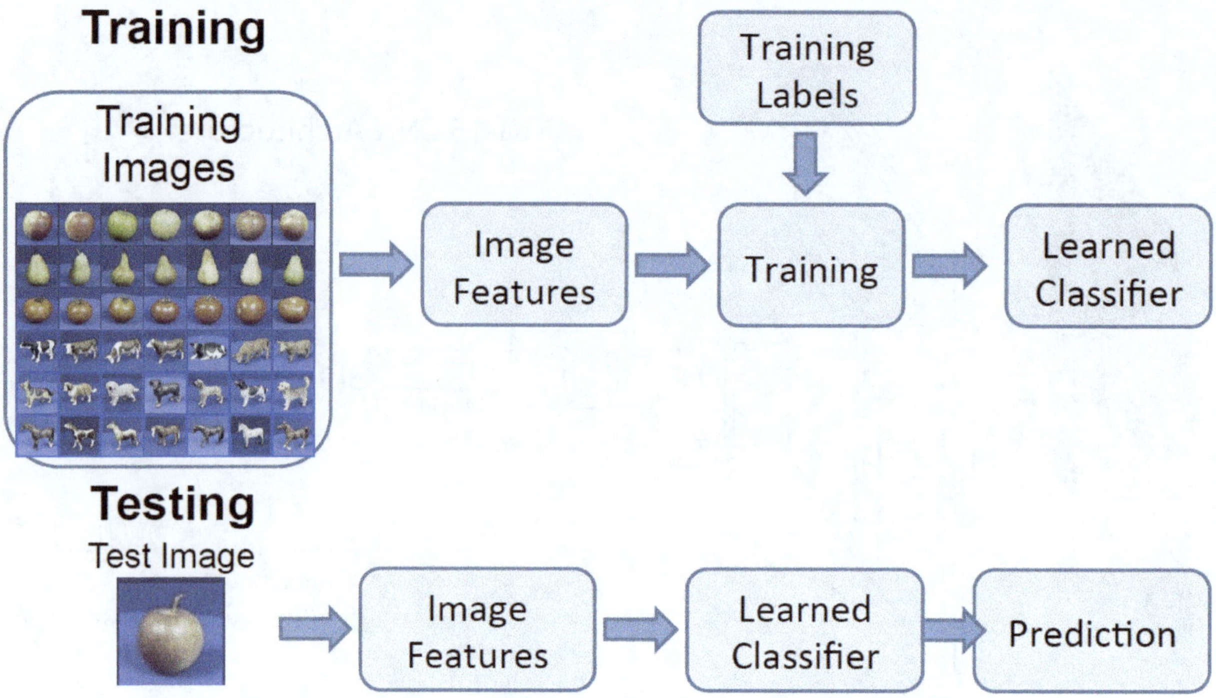
Training
Training Images
Image Features
Training Labels
Training
Learned Classifier
Testing
Test Image
Image Features
Learned Classifier
Prediction

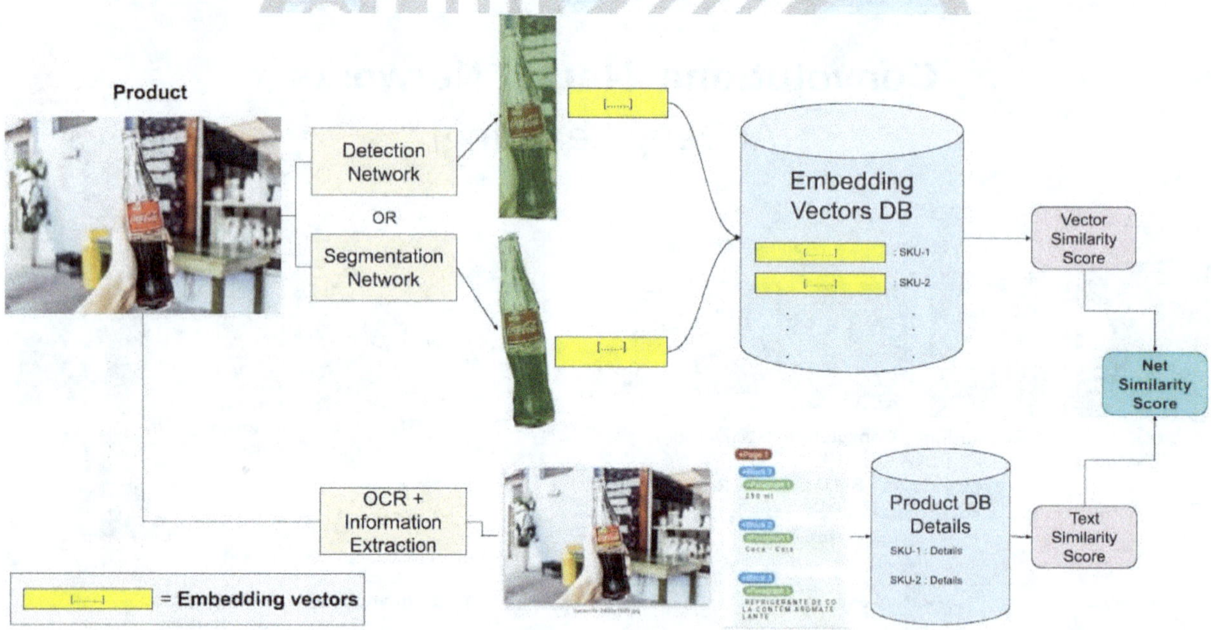
Product
Detection Network
OR
Segmentation Network
Embedding Vectors DB
: SKU-1
: SKU-2
Vector Similarity Score
Net Similarity Score
OCR + Information Extraction
Product DB Details
SKU-1 : Details
SKU-2 : Details
Text Similarity Score
= Embedding vectors

Evolution of Models

- **AlexNet (2012)**: Deepened CNNs, won ImageNet; used ReLU, dropout.
- **VGG (2014)**: Very deep with small 3x3 filters.
- **Inception/GoogleNet (2014)**: Multi-scale convolutions for efficiency.
- **ResNet (2015)**: Residual connections to train very deep networks (100+ layers).
- **EfficientNet (2019+)**: Compound scaling for better performance.
- **Vision Transformers (ViT, 2020)**: Patch images into tokens, apply self-attention; excel with large data.

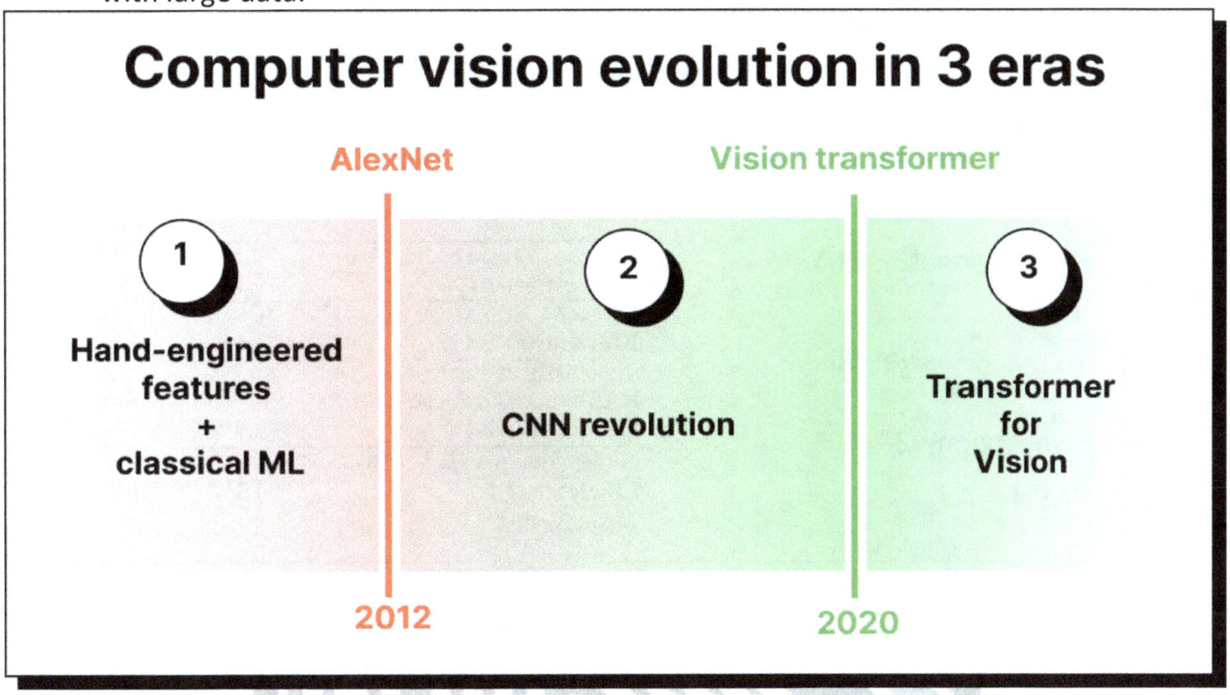

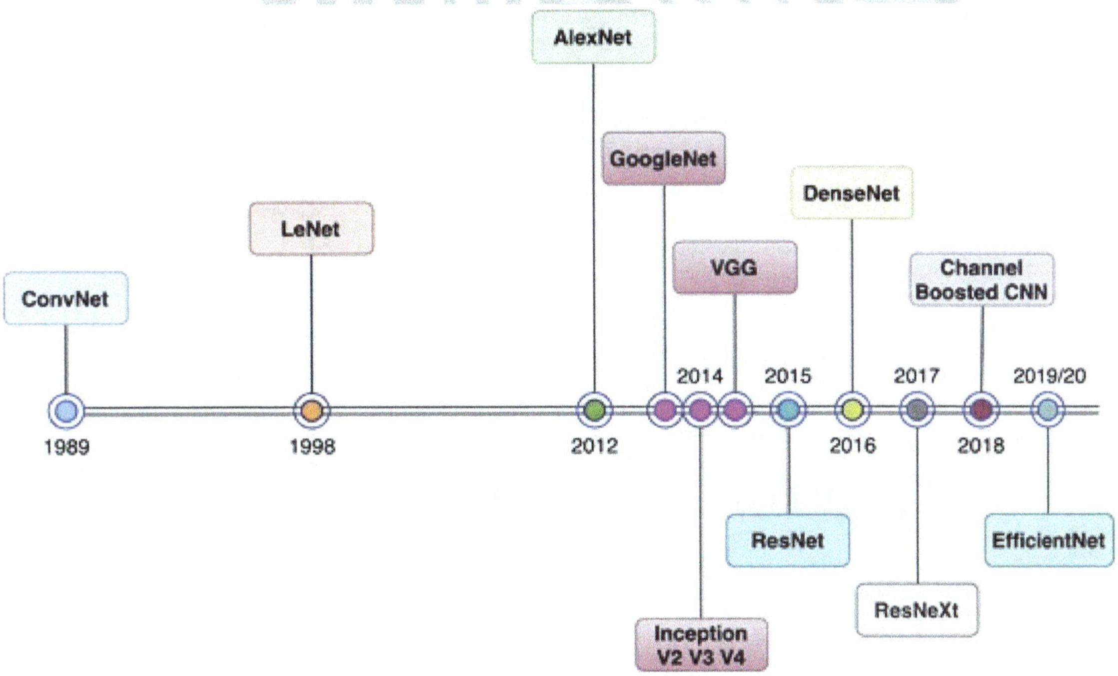

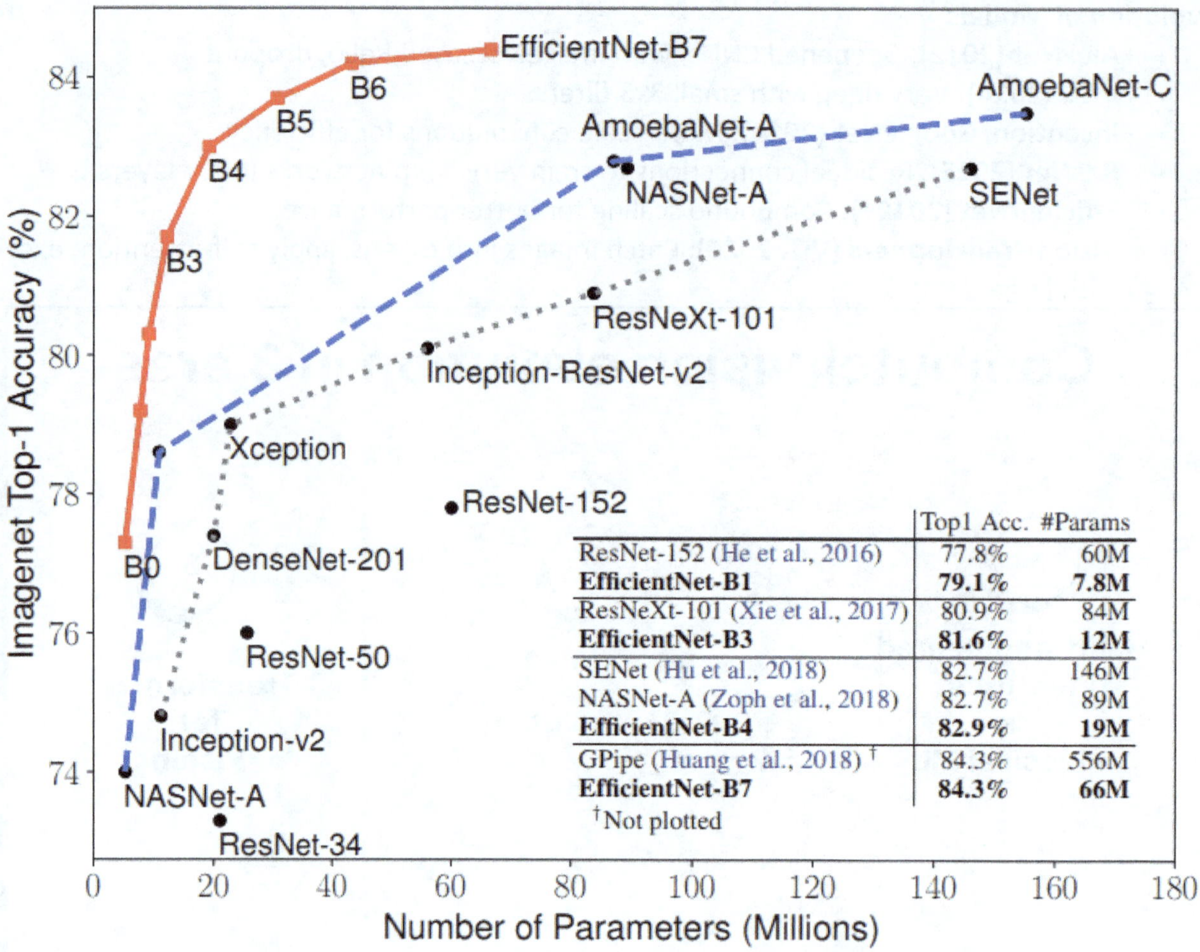

EfficientNet-B7
B6
B5
B4
B3
B0
AmoebaNet-C
AmoebaNet-A
NASNet-A
SENet
ResNeXt-101
Inception-ResNet-v2
Xception
ResNet-152
DenseNet-201
ResNet-50
Inception-v2
NASNet-A
ResNet-34
Imagenet Top-1 Accuracy (%)
Number of Parameters (Millions)
Top1 Acc. #Params
ResNet-152 (He et al., 2016) 77.8% 60M
EfficientNet-B1 79.1% 7.8M
ResNeXt-101 (Xie et al., 2017) 80.9% 84M
EfficientNet-B3 81.6% 12M
SENet (Hu et al., 2018) 82.7% 146M
NASNet-A (Zoph et al., 2018) 82.7% 89M
EfficientNet-B4 82.9% 19M
GPipe (Huang et al., 2018) † 84.3% 556M
EfficientNet-B7 84.3% 66M
†Not plotted

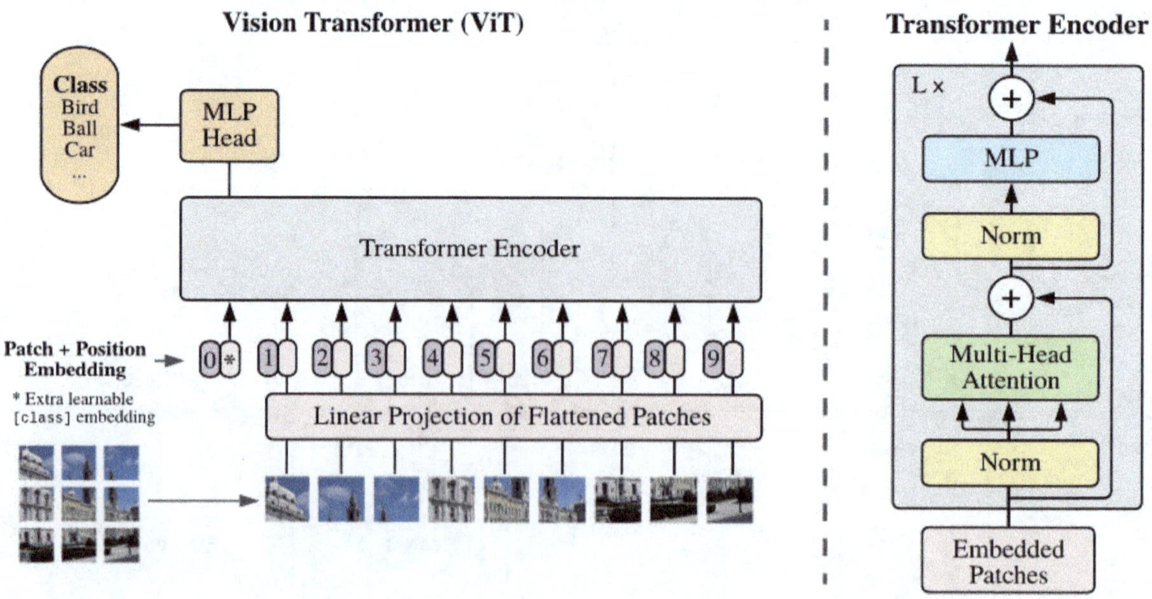

Vision Transformer (ViT)
Transformer Encoder
Class
Bird
Ball
Car
...
MLP Head
Transformer Encoder
Patch + Position Embedding
* Extra learnable [class] embedding
Linear Projection of Flattened Patches
L ×
MLP
Norm
Multi-Head Attention
Norm
Embedded Patches

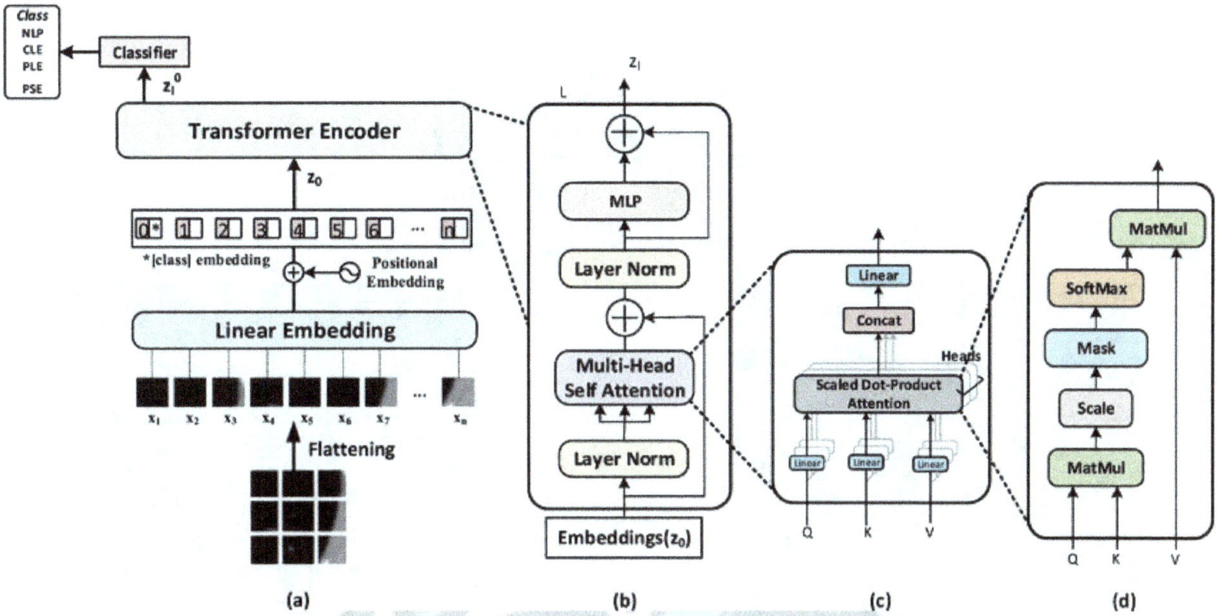

Key Tasks in Image Recognition

1. **Image Classification**: Assign labels to entire image (e.g., "cat" vs. "dog").
2. **Object Detection**: Locate and classify multiple objects with bounding boxes (e.g., YOLO, Faster R-CNN, SSD).
3. **Semantic Segmentation**: Pixel-level classification (e.g., U-Net).
4. **Instance Segmentation**: Detect and segment individual objects (e.g., Mask R-CNN).
5. **Facial Recognition**: Identify or verify faces.
6. **Image Captioning**: Generate descriptions using CNN + RNN/Transformer.

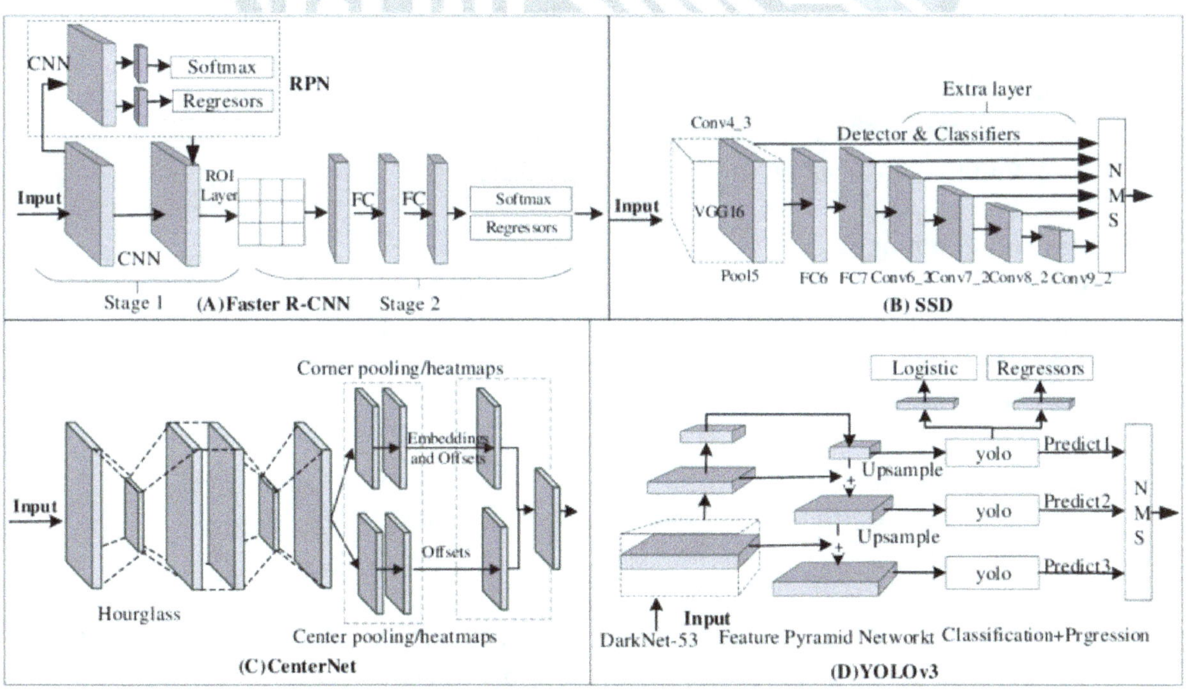

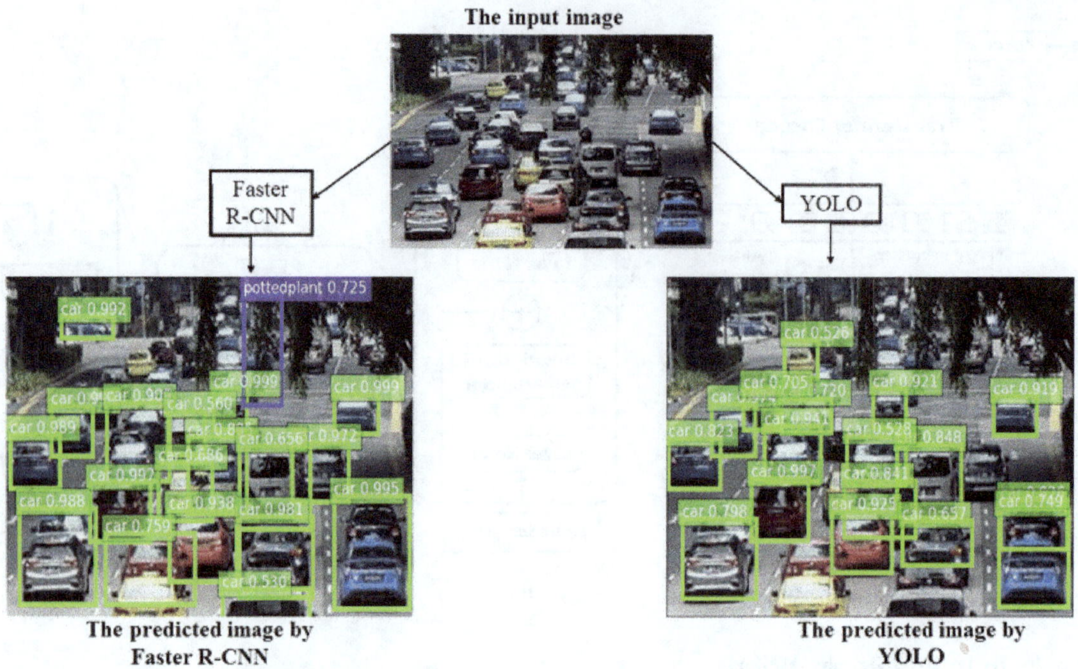

Training and Data

Models train on large datasets like ImageNet (14M images), COCO (for detection).
Techniques: Transfer learning (pre-trained models like ResNet50), data augmentation (flips, crops), fine-tuning.

Applications

- Autonomous vehicles (object/pedestrian detection).
- Medical imaging (tumor detection).
- Security (surveillance, biometrics).
- Retail (visual search).
- Social media (content moderation).

Advantages and Challenges

Advantages:

- High accuracy on benchmarks (e.g., >95% on ImageNet).
- Real-time inference with optimized models.
- Multimodal integration (vision + language).

Challenges:

- Bias in training data.
- Adversarial attacks (fooling models with perturbations).
- High compute requirements.
- Privacy concerns.

In 2025, foundation models like CLIP and multimodal LLMs (e.g., GPT-4V) enable zero-shot recognition, pushing boundaries toward general visual intelligence.
AI-based image recognition has revolutionized how machines perceive the world, powering countless real-world innovations.

Section-10

AI Deployment

- Flask / FastAPI (Deploy AI Models as APIs)
- Docker & Kubernetes (Containerization)
- Cloud AI (AWS, Google Cloud, Azure)

AI Deployment

1.Flask / FastAPI (Deploy AI Models as APIs)

Deploying AI models (e.g., machine learning or deep learning models from TensorFlow, PyTorch, scikit-learn) as **RESTful APIs** allows them to be accessed over the web by applications, mobile apps, or other services. This enables real-time predictions, scalability, and integration into production systems.

Python's lightweight web frameworks **Flask** and **FastAPI** are popular choices for this due to their simplicity and performance. Flask is a mature, flexible micro-framework, while FastAPI is modern, built for speed and developer productivity with automatic documentation.

As of late 2025, FastAPI has surged in popularity for AI deployments due to its asynchronous support and native integration with Pydantic for data validation—ideal for handling complex model inputs/outputs.

General Process for Deploying an AI Model as an API

1. **Train and Save the Model**: Use libraries like joblib/pickle (scikit-learn), torch.save (PyTorch), or SavedModel (TensorFlow).
2. **Load the Model in the API**: Load once at startup for efficiency.
3. **Define Endpoints**: Typically a POST endpoint for predictions (receiving JSON/data, returning results).
4. **Handle Input/Output**: Preprocess input (e.g., numpy arrays, images), run inference, postprocess output.
5. **Add Validation & Error Handling**: Ensure robust production use.
6. **Deploy**: Locally, via Docker, cloud (Heroku, AWS, Vercel), or serverless.

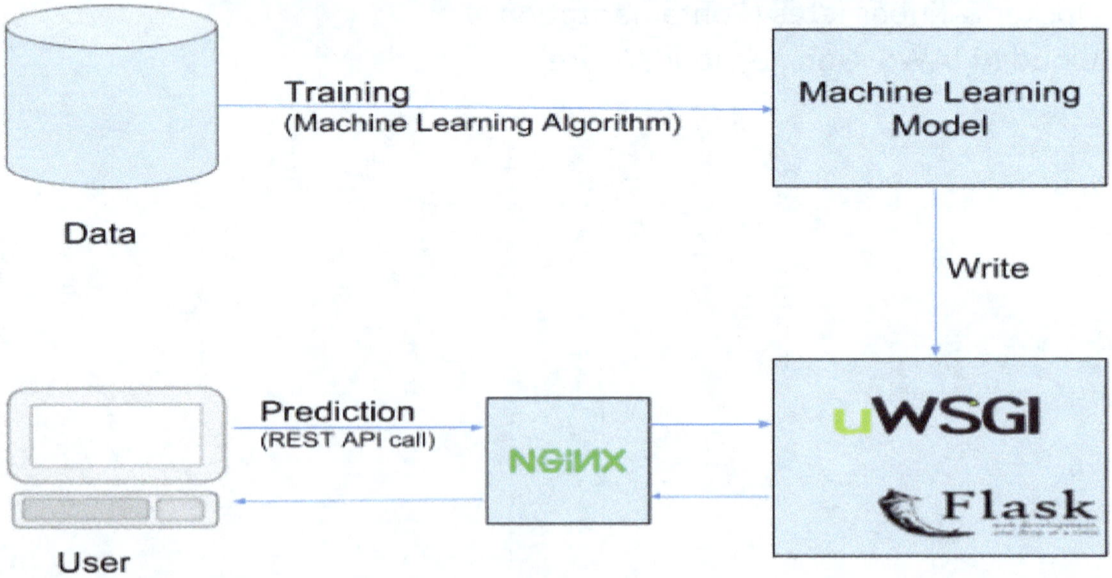

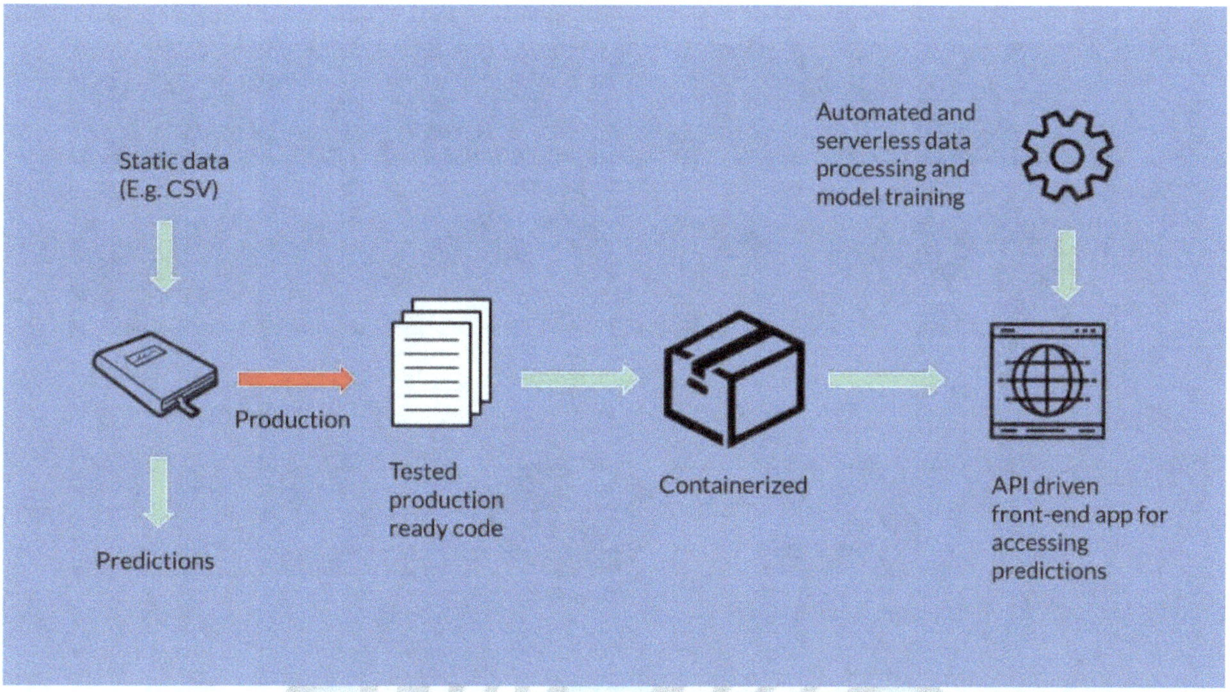
Static data
(E.g. CSV)
Automated and
serverless data
processing and
model training
Production
Tested
production
ready code
Containerized
API driven
front-end app for
accessing
predictions
Predictions

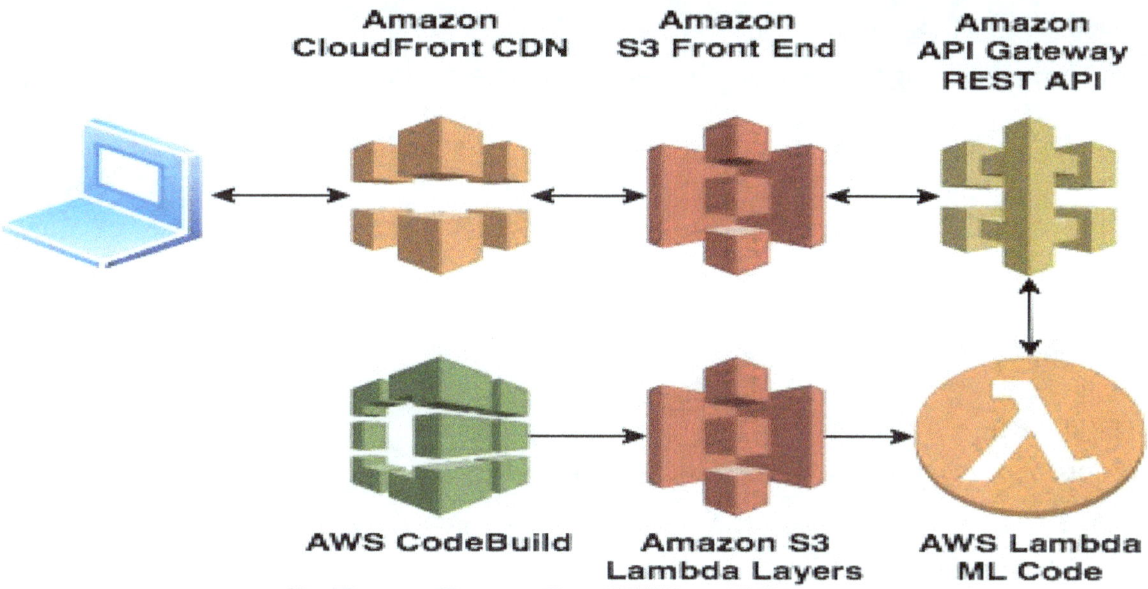
Amazon
CloudFront CDN
Amazon
S3 Front End
Amazon
API Gateway
REST API
AWS CodeBuild
Amazon S3
Lambda Layers
AWS Lambda
ML Code

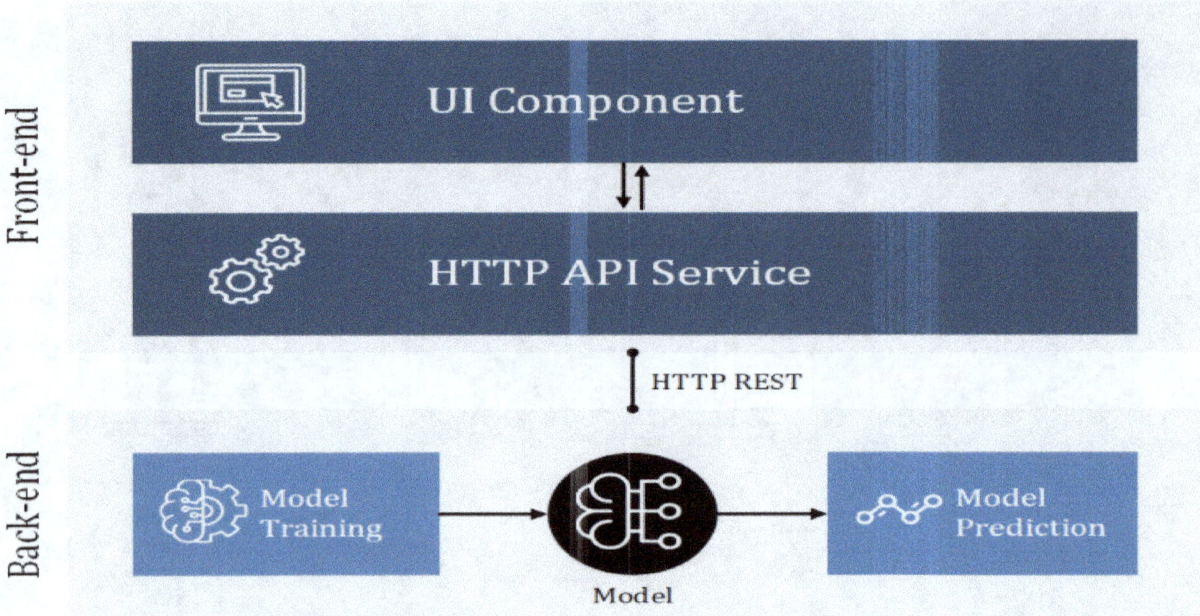

Using Flask for AI Model APIs

Flask is minimalist, giving full control. It's great for simple deployments or when integrating with existing Flask apps.

Example: Deploying a scikit-learn model

Python

```
from flask import Flask, request, jsonify
import joblib
import numpy as np

app = Flask(__name__)
model = joblib.load('model.pkl')  # Load at startup

@app.route('/predict', methods=['POST'])
def predict():
    data = request.json['data']  # Expect list or array
    input_data = np.array(data).reshape(1, -1)
    prediction = model.predict(input_data)
    return jsonify({'prediction': prediction.tolist()})

if __name__ == '__main__':
    app.run(debug=True)
```

For images (e.g., CNN model), use Pillow or OpenCV to process base64/file uploads.

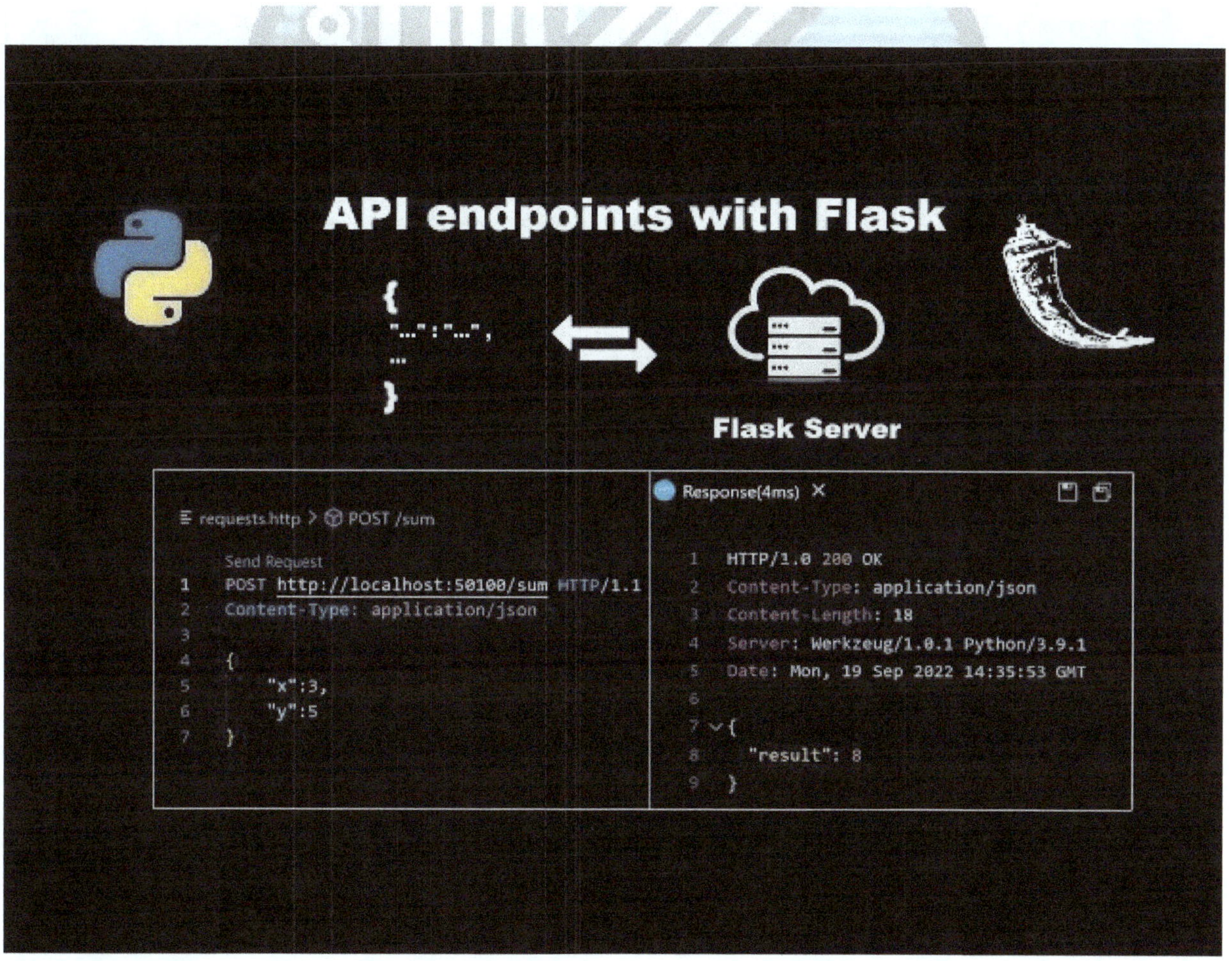

Pros: Lightweight, easy to learn, vast ecosystem (extensions like Flask-RESTful).
Cons: Manual validation, synchronous (slower for I/O-heavy tasks), no built-in async.

Using FastAPI for AI Model APIs

FastAPI uses Starlette for async and Pydantic for data models—faster, type-safe, and auto-generates OpenAPI docs (Swagger UI/ReDoc).

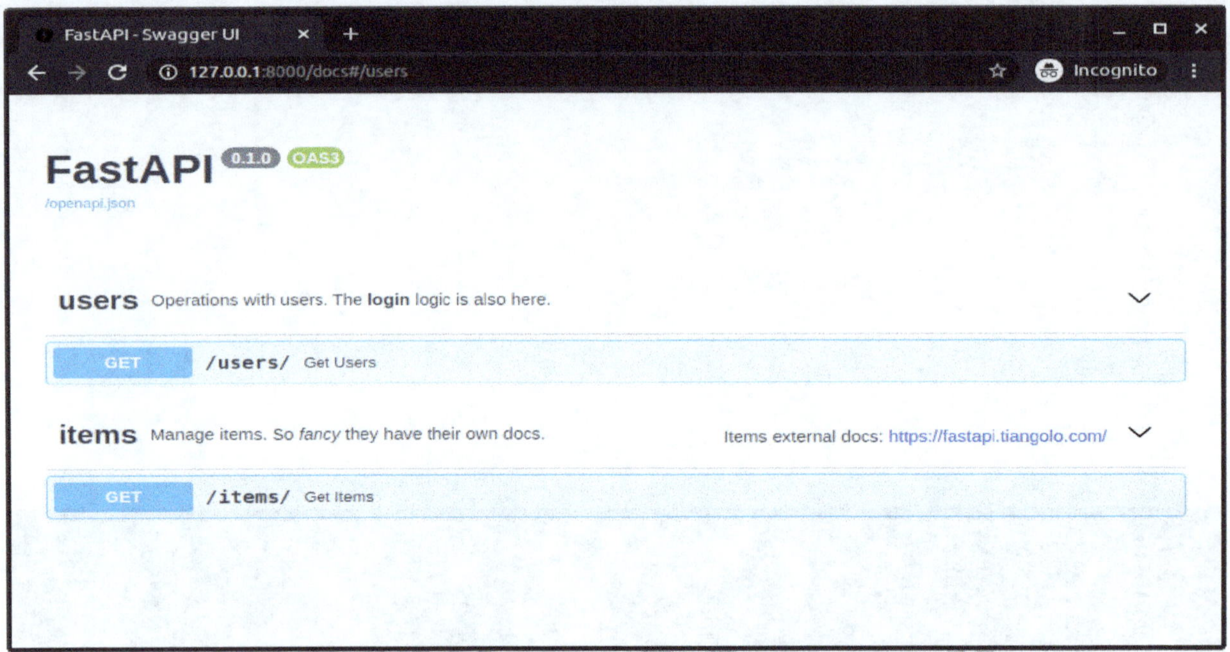

Example: Same scikit-learn model with validation

Python

```python
from fastapi import FastAPI
from pydantic import BaseModel
import joblib
import numpy as np

app = FastAPI()
model = joblib.load('model.pkl')

class InputData(BaseModel):
    data: list[list[float]]  # Validates structure

@app.post('/predict')
async def predict(input: InputData):
    input_array = np.array(input.data)
    prediction = model.predict(input_array)
    return {'prediction': prediction.tolist()}
```

Supports async for heavy inference or multiple requests.

```python
from fastapi import FastAPI
from pydantic import BaseModel

app = FastAPI()


class Item(BaseModel):
    name: str
    price: float
    is_offer: bool = None


@app.get("/")
def read_root():
    return {"Hello": "World"}


@app.get("/items/{item_id}")
def read_item(item_id: int, q: str = None):
    return {"item_id": item_id, "q": q}


@app.put("/items/{item_id}")
def save_item(item_id: int, item: Item):
    return {"item_name": item.pr, "item_id": item_id}
                             price           float
                             _process_values
                             parse_raw
                             parse_file
                             parse_obj
```

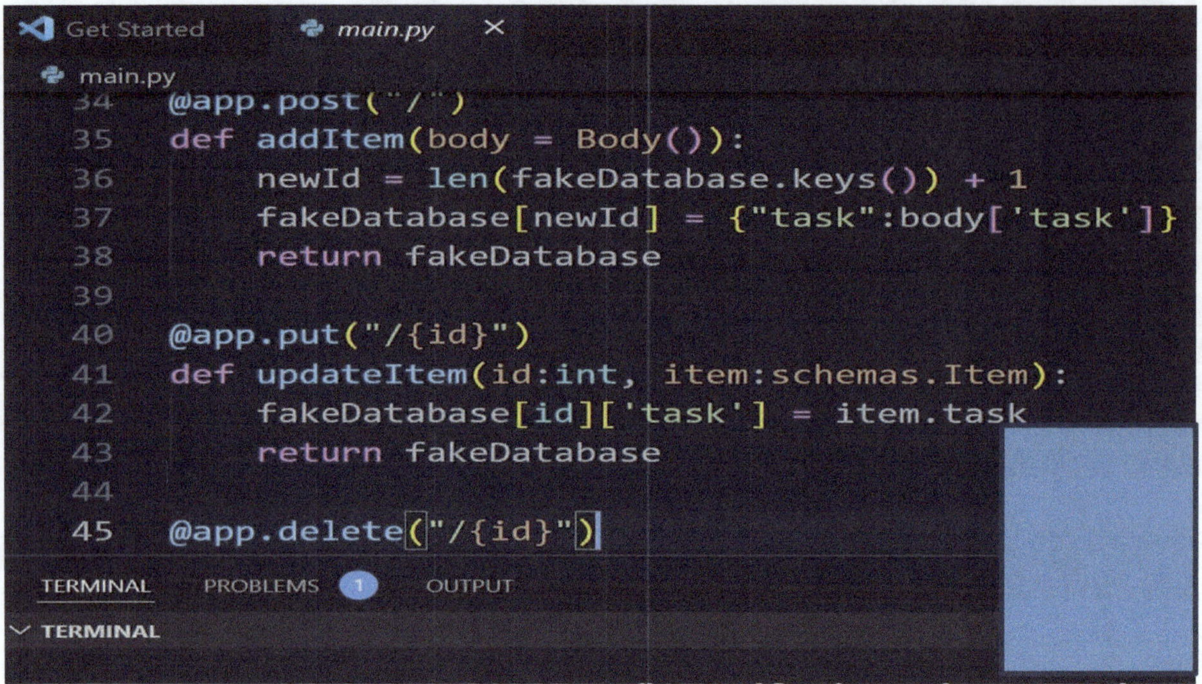

Pros: High performance (async), automatic docs, data validation, type hints for IDE support.
Cons: Slightly steeper learning curve if new to async/Pydantic.

Comparison: Flask vs FastAPI for AI Deployments

Aspect	Flask	FastAPI
Performance	Good (synchronous)	Excellent (async, often 2-3x faster)
Learning Curve	Very easy	Easy with Python type hints
Validation/Docs	Manual (e.g., Marshmallow)	Automatic (Pydantic + Swagger)
Async Support	Limited (via extensions)	Native
Ecosystem	Mature, many extensions	Growing rapidly, modern
Best For	Simple prototypes, legacy	Production AI APIs, high traffic

In 2025 benchmarks, FastAPI often outperforms Flask for concurrent requests, making it preferred for scalable AI services.

Production Deployment Tips

- **Containerization**: Use Docker for reproducibility.

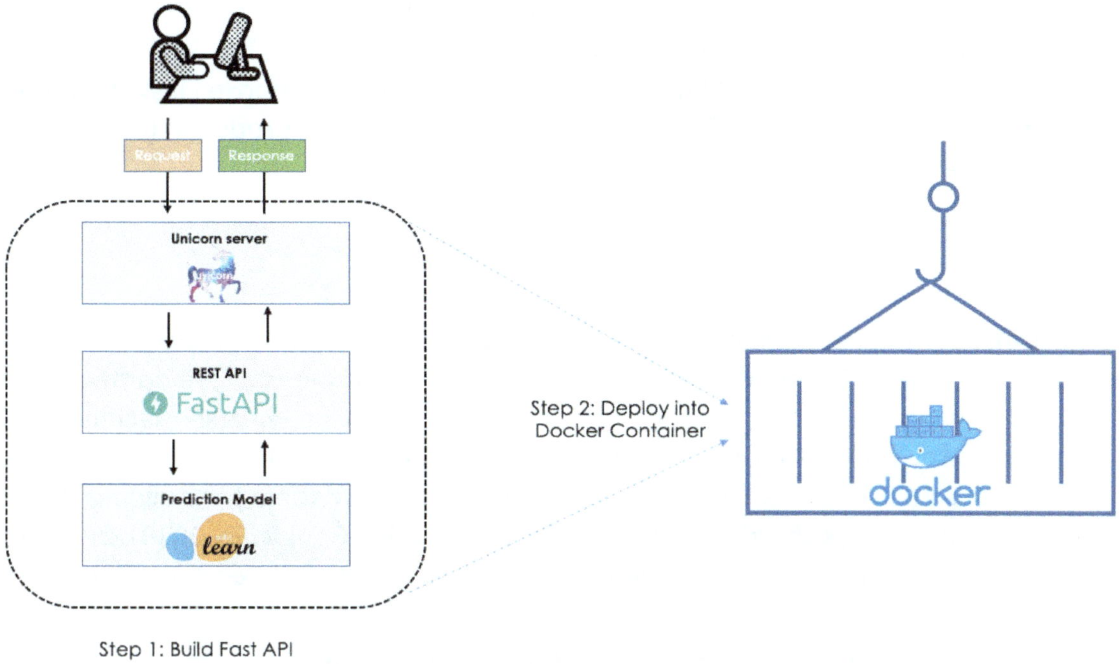

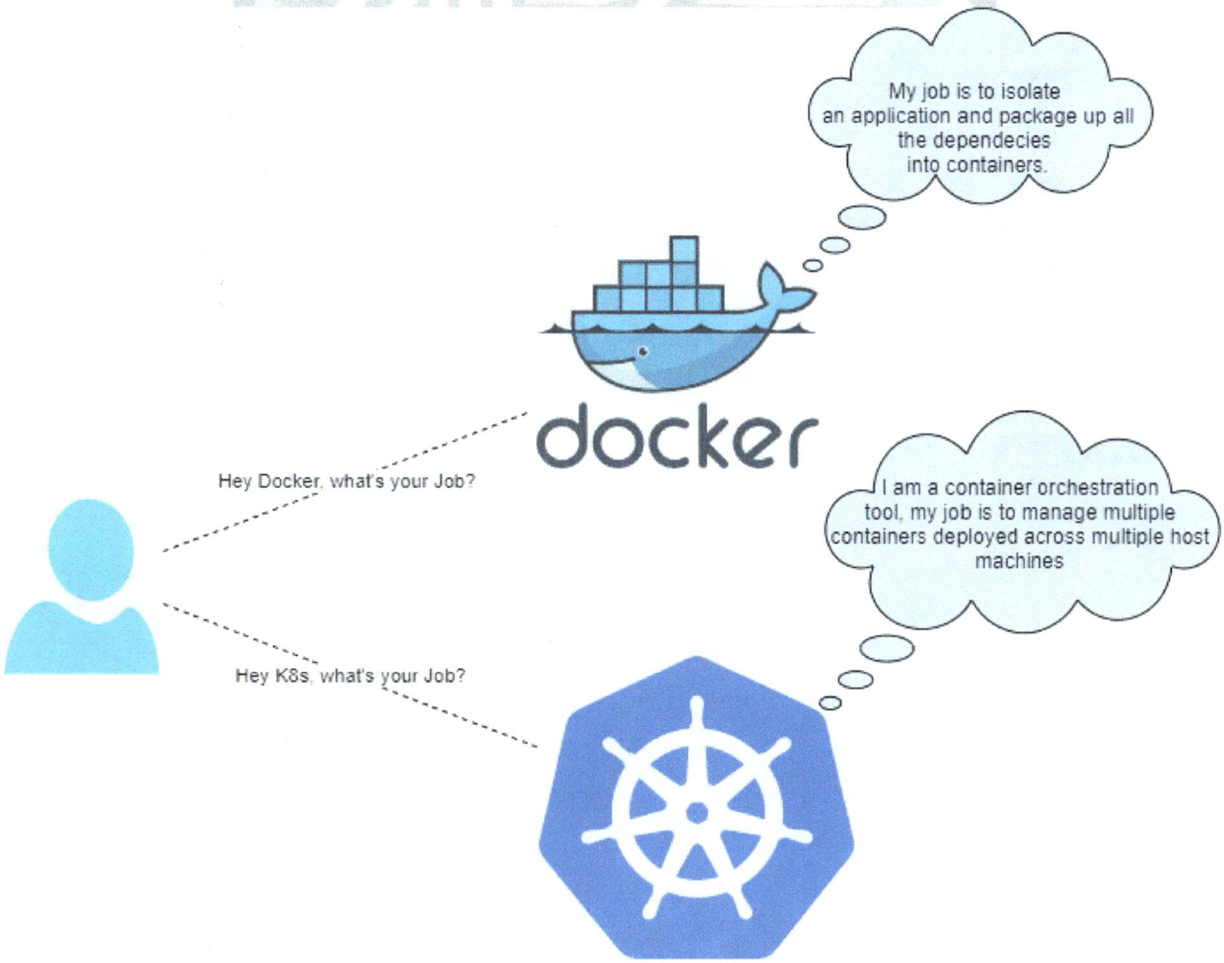

- **Serving**: Gunicorn + Uvicorn (for FastAPI async).
- **Scaling**: Kubernetes, AWS SageMaker, or serverless (Vercel for FastAPI).
- **Security**: Rate limiting, authentication (JWT), HTTPS.
- **Monitoring**: Logging, Prometheus for metrics.

Both frameworks excel at turning AI models into accessible APIs—choose Flask for simplicity, FastAPI for speed and modern features. Many real-world AI products (e.g., inference endpoints) use FastAPI today.

2.Docker & Kubernetes (Containerization)

Containerization packages applications and their dependencies into lightweight, portable units called **containers**. These run consistently across environments (development, testing, production), solving "it works on my machine" issues. Unlike virtual machines (VMs), containers share the host OS kernel, making them faster and more efficient.

Docker (released 2013) popularized containerization with easy tools for building, shipping, and running containers. **Kubernetes** (K8s, open-sourced by Google in 2014) orchestrates containers at scale—managing deployment, scaling, networking, and resilience across clusters.

eShopOnContainers reference application

(Development environment architecture)

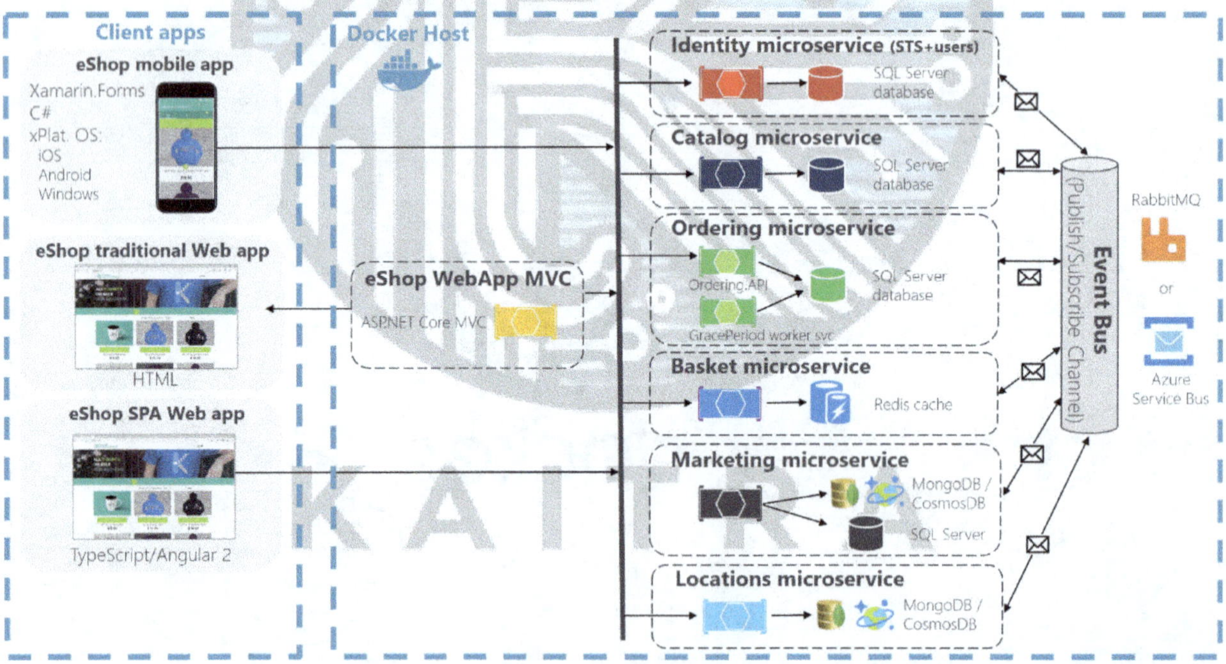

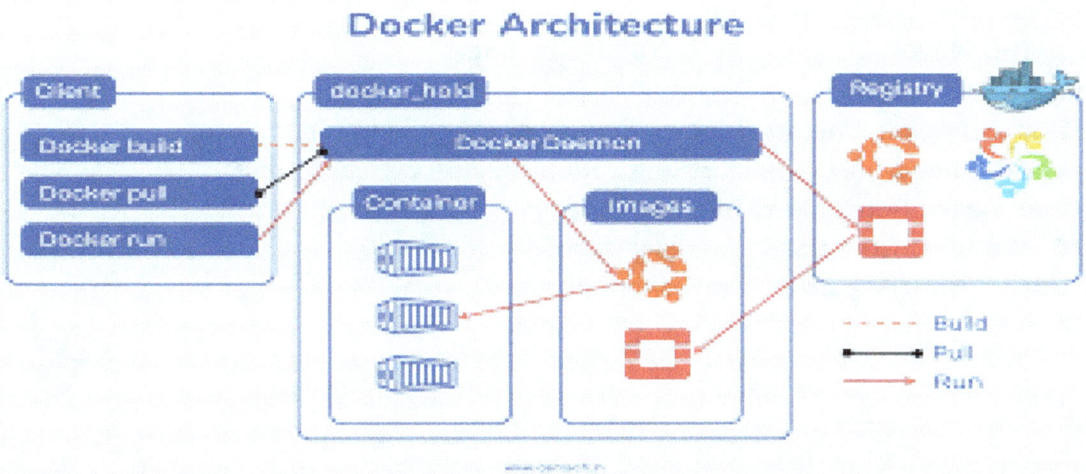

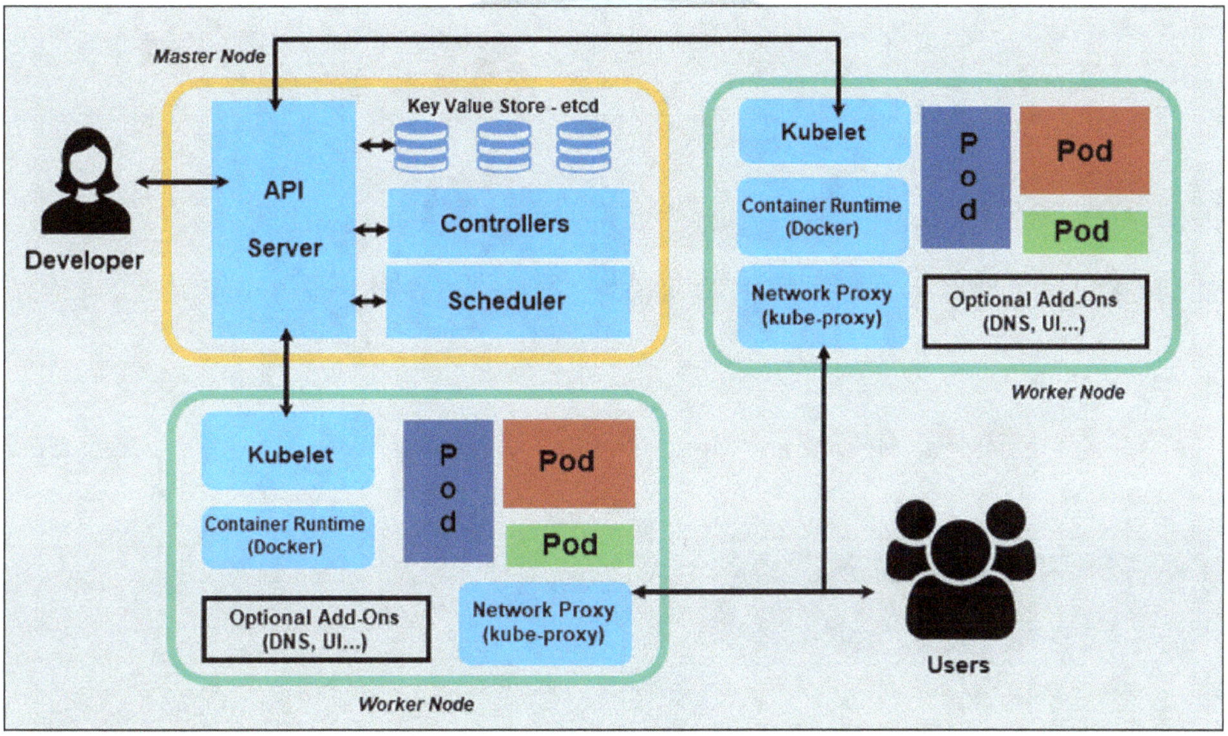

As of late 2025, Docker remains the standard for container runtime, while Kubernetes dominates orchestration (used by ~90% of organizations in cloud-native setups). They complement each other: Docker builds containers; Kubernetes manages them.

Docker: Containerization Platform

Docker uses OS-level virtualization to create containers.

Key Components

- **Docker Engine**: Daemon (dockerd) + CLI; client-server architecture.
- **Images**: Read-only templates (e.g., ubuntu:22.04 with app code).
- **Containers**: Runnable instances of images.
- **Dockerfile**: Instructions to build images.
- **Docker Hub/Registries**: Store/share images.

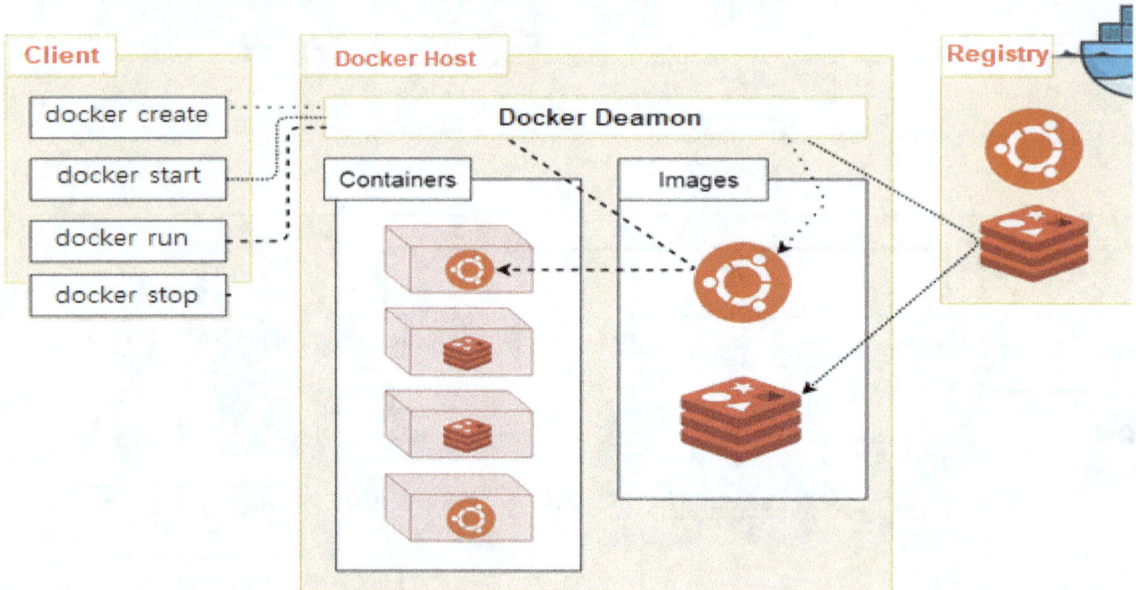

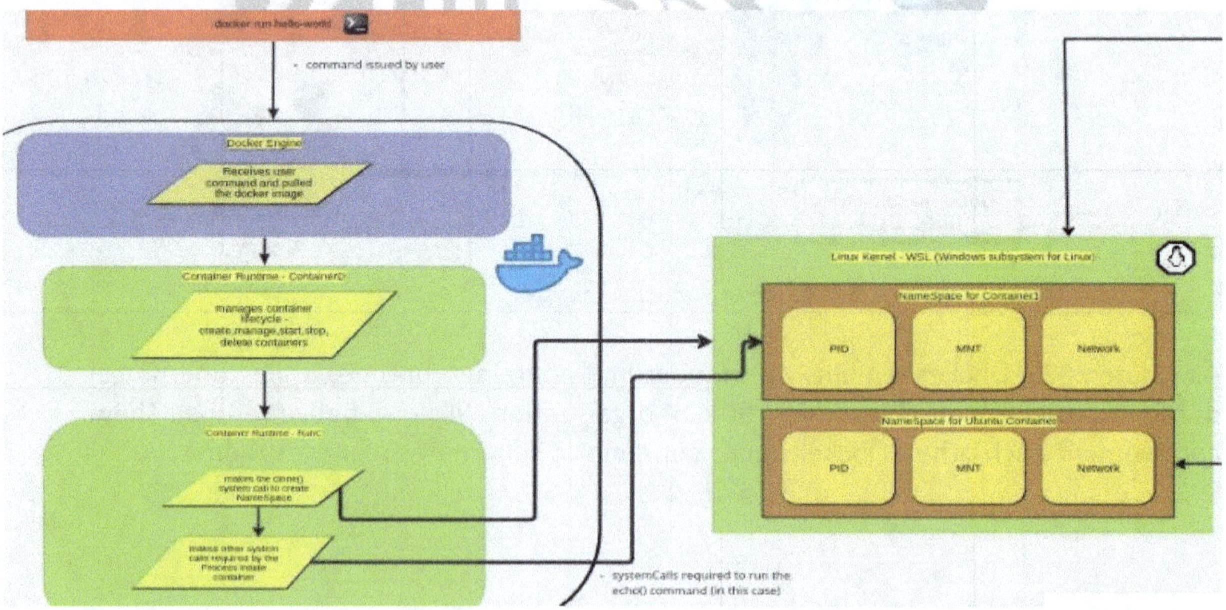

Basic Workflow & Commands

1. Write a **Dockerfile**:

dockerfile

```
FROM python:3.9
COPY . /app
WORKDIR /app
RUN pip install -r requirements.txt
CMD ["python", "app.py"]
```

2. Build: docker build -t myapp .
3. Run: docker run -p 5000:5000 myapp
4. Other commands: docker ps, docker logs, docker exec.

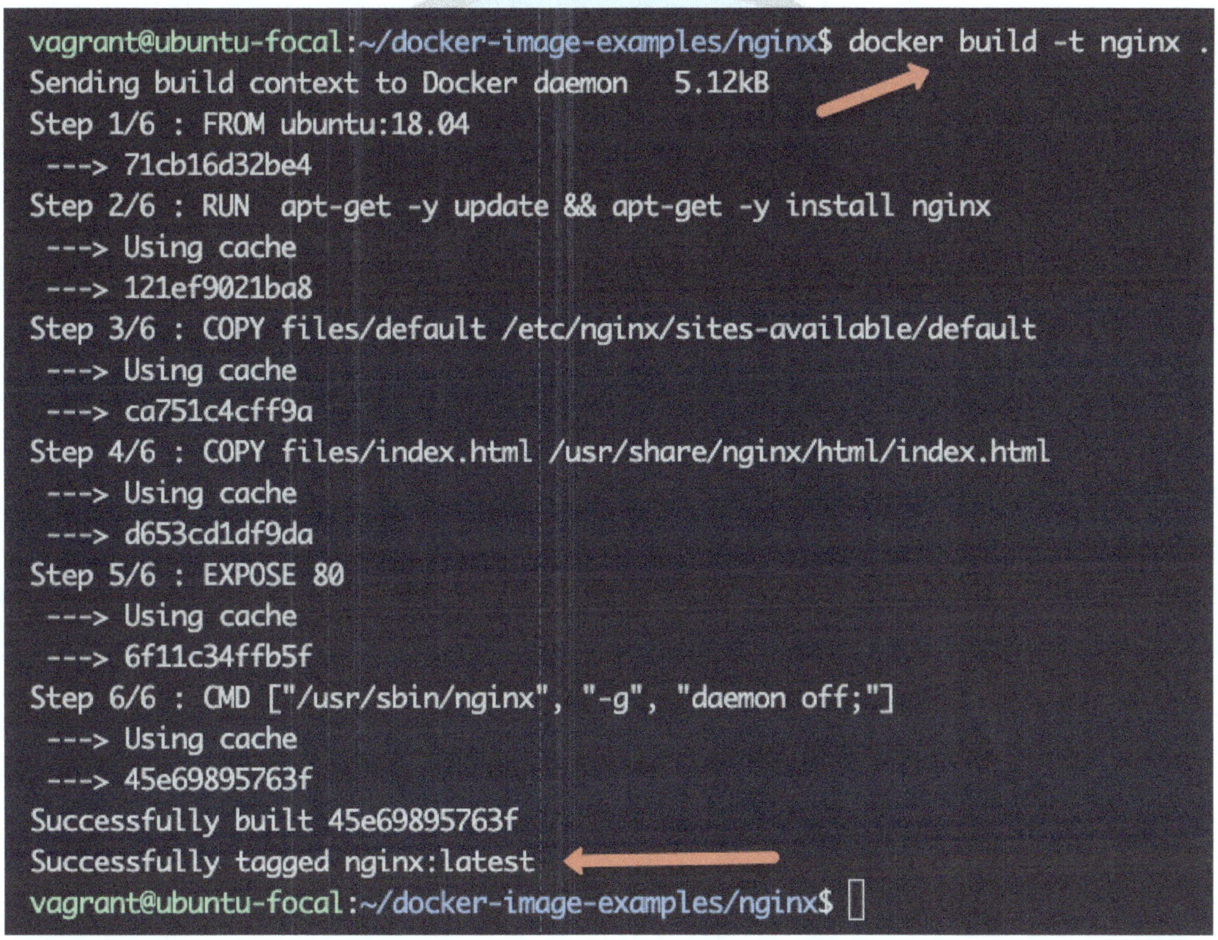

```
vagrant@ubuntu-focal:~/docker-image-examples/nginx$ docker build -t nginx .
Sending build context to Docker daemon   5.12kB
Step 1/6 : FROM ubuntu:18.04
 ---> 71cb16d32be4
Step 2/6 : RUN  apt-get -y update && apt-get -y install nginx
 ---> Using cache
 ---> 121ef9021ba8
Step 3/6 : COPY files/default /etc/nginx/sites-available/default
 ---> Using cache
 ---> ca751c4cff9a
Step 4/6 : COPY files/index.html /usr/share/nginx/html/index.html
 ---> Using cache
 ---> d653cd1df9da
Step 5/6 : EXPOSE 80
 ---> Using cache
 ---> 6f11c34ffb5f
Step 6/6 : CMD ["/usr/sbin/nginx", "-g", "daemon off;"]
 ---> Using cache
 ---> 45e69895763f
Successfully built 45e69895763f
Successfully tagged nginx:latest
vagrant@ubuntu-focal:~/docker-image-examples/nginx$
```

Image management commands

command	description
`docker images`	list all local images
`docker history` *image*	show the image history (list of ancestors)
`docker inspect` *image...*	show low-level infos (in json format)
`docker tag` *image tag*	tag an image
`docker commit` *container image*	create an image (from a container)
`docker import` *url*|- [*tag*]	create an image (from a tarball)
`docker rmi` *image...*	delete images

Docker Compose: For multi-container apps (e.g., app + database) via YAML.

Kubernetes: Container Orchestration

Kubernetes automates deployment, scaling, and operations of containerized apps across clusters.

Core Concepts

- **Pod**: Smallest unit; one or more containers sharing network/storage.
- **Node**: Worker machine (VM/physical) running pods.
- **Cluster**: Control plane + nodes.
- **Deployment**: Manages replicas, updates.
- **Service**: Exposes pods (LoadBalancer, ClusterIP).
- **Namespace**: Virtual clusters for isolation.

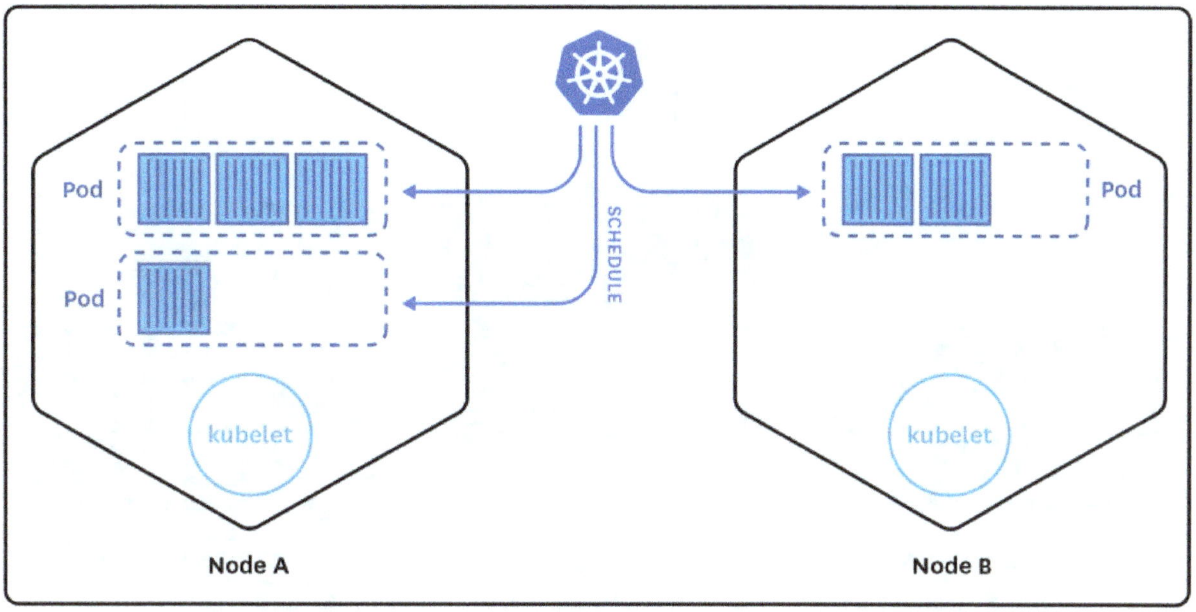
Pod
Pod
SCHEDULE
Pod
kubelet
kubelet
Node A
Node B
CLUSTER

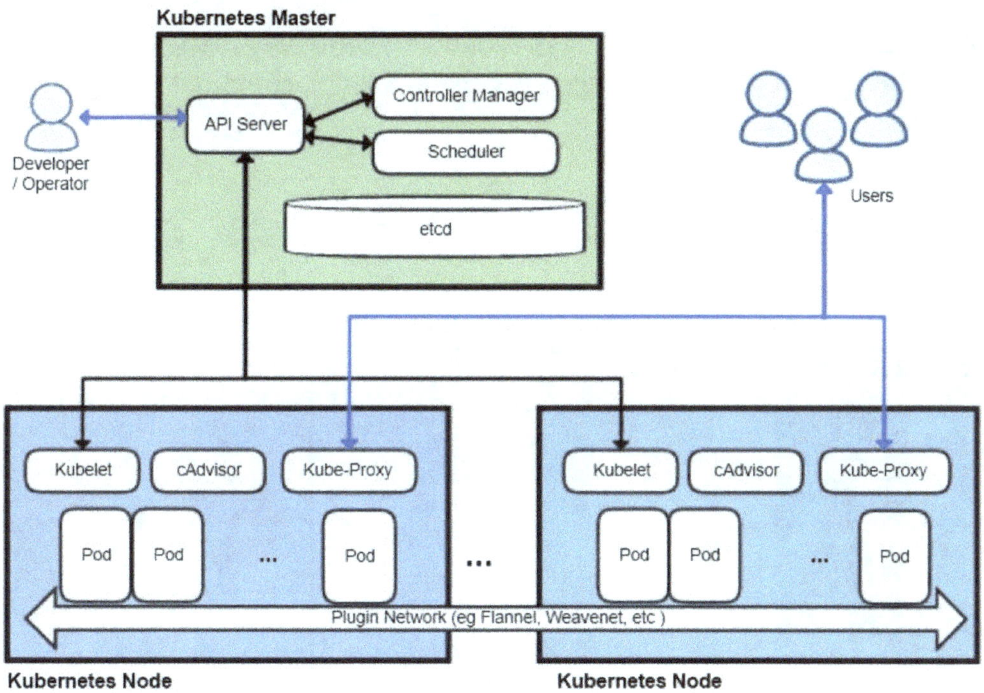
Kubernetes Master
Controller Manager
API Server
Scheduler
Developer
/ Operator
etcd
Users
Kubelet
cAdvisor
Kube-Proxy
Kubelet
cAdvisor
Kube-Proxy
Pod
Pod
...
Pod
...
Pod
Pod
...
Pod
Plugin Network (eg Flannel, Weavenet, etc)
Kubernetes Node
Kubernetes Node

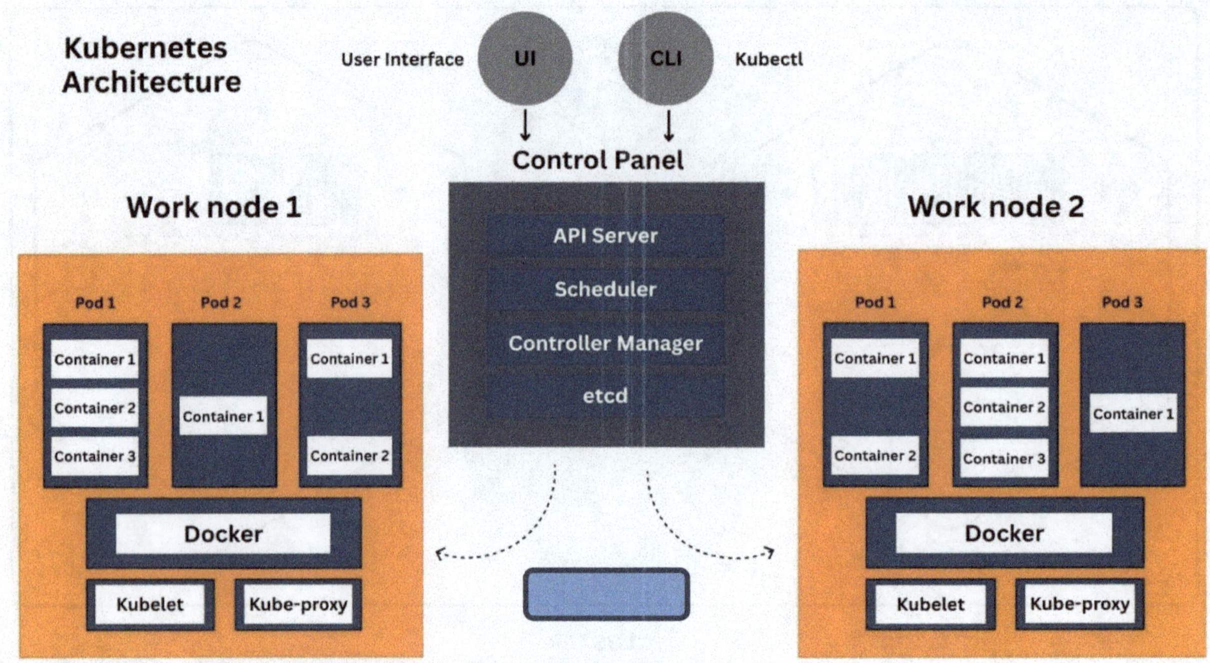

Architecture

- **Control Plane**: API server, etcd (storage), scheduler, controller manager.
- **Worker Nodes**: Kubelet (agent), kube-proxy (networking), container runtime (e.g., containerd).

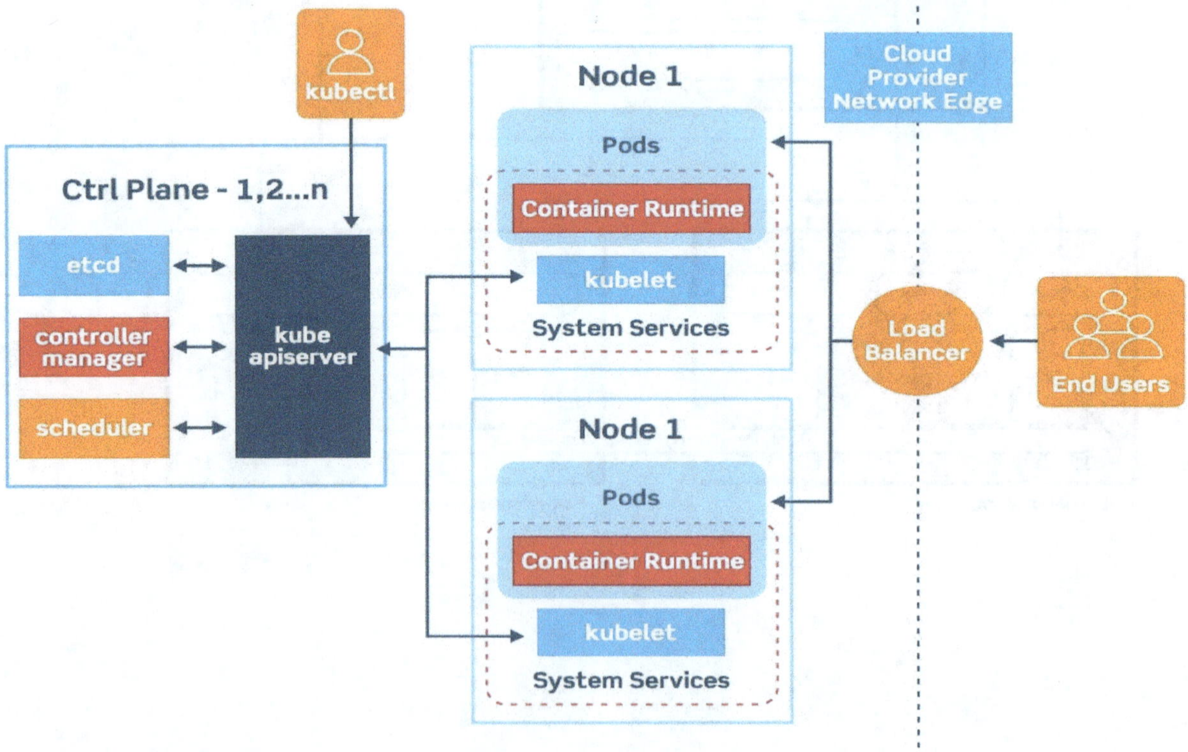

Example: Simple Deployment YAML

YAML

```yaml
apiVersion: apps/v1
kind: Deployment
metadata:
  name: myapp
spec:
  replicas: 3
  selector:
    matchLabels:
      app: myapp
  template:
    metadata:
      labels:
        app: myapp
    spec:
      containers:
      - name: myapp
        image: myapp:latest
        ports:
        - containerPort: 5000
---
apiVersion: v1
kind: Service
metadata:
  name: myapp-service
spec:
  selector:
    app: myapp
  ports:
    - protocol: TCP
      port: 80
      targetPort: 5000
  type: LoadBalancer
```

Apply with kubectl apply -f file.yaml.

Docker vs Kubernetes

Aspect	Docker	Kubernetes
Primary Focus	Building/running single containers	Orchestrating many containers
Scaling	Manual or Docker Swarm (limited)	Auto-scaling, rolling updates
Networking	Basic bridge networks	Advanced (CNI plugins, Services)
Management	Single host	Multi-node clusters
Use Case	Development, simple apps	Production, microservices

	Docker Swarm	Kubernetes
1	No Auto Scaling	Auto Scaling
2	Good community	Great active community
3	Easy to start a cluster	Difficult to start a cluster
4	Limited to the Docker API's capabilities	Can overcome constraints of Docker and Docker API
5	Does not have as much experience with production deployments at scale	Deployed at scale more often among organizations

Container vs Docker vs Kubernetes

Features	Container	Docker	Kubernetes
Definition	Application isolation and portability in a lightweight, portable unit	Platform for creating and managing containers, using a container runtime	Container orchestration for automating deployment, scaling, and management
Creation Tool	Various tools like Docker, Podman, etc.	Docker is a widely used tool	Manages containers created with Docker and other runtimes
Image Format	Uses container images (e.g., Docker format)	Docker uses its own image format	Supports various container runtimes and image formats
Orchestration	Add text here	Add text here	Add text here
Scaling	Add text here	Add text here	Add text here
Add text here	Add text here	Add text here	Add text here

Docker and Kubernetes integrate seamlessly—Kubernetes uses container runtimes like containerd (from Docker).

Advantages and Challenges

Advantages:

- Portability and consistency.
- Efficient resource use.
- Rapid deployment/scaling.
- Cloud-native foundation (microservices, CI/CD).

Challenges:

- Learning curve (especially K8s YAML/config).
- Security (image vulnerabilities, privileges).
- Complexity in large clusters.
- Debugging distributed systems.

In 2025, tools like Docker Desktop, Minikube (local K8s), and managed services (EKS, GKE, AKS) simplify adoption. Containerization with Docker + Kubernetes powers modern cloud computing, enabling resilient, scalable applications.

3.Cloud AI (AWS, Google Cloud, Azure)

Cloud AI platforms provide managed services for building, training, deploying, and scaling AI/ML models without managing underlying infrastructure. The big three—**Amazon Web Services (AWS)**, **Google Cloud Platform (GCP)**, and **Microsoft Azure**—dominate the market, offering a mix of pre-trained APIs, end-to-end ML platforms, and infrastructure for custom models. As of late 2025, these platforms have deeply integrated generative AI (e.g., LLMs), multimodal capabilities, and responsible AI tools. They enable enterprises to leverage AI at scale while optimizing costs and compliance.

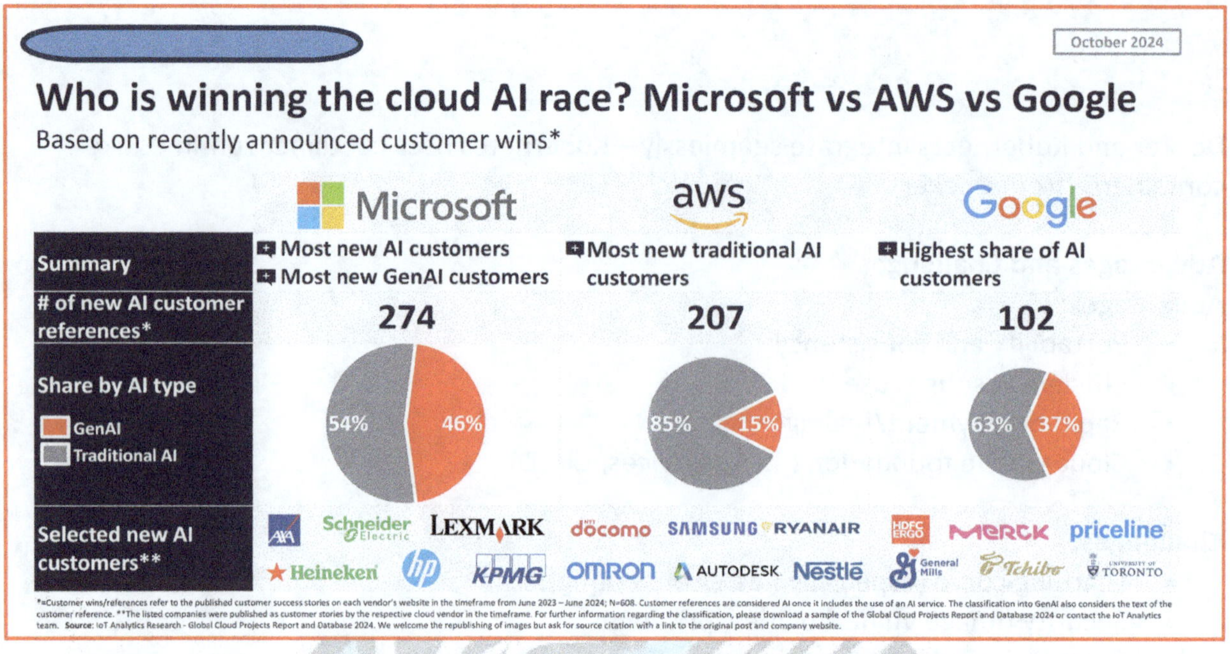
October 2024
Who is winning the cloud AI race? Microsoft vs AWS vs Google
Based on recently announced customer wins*
Microsoft
aws
Google
Summary
Most new AI customers
Most new GenAI customers
Most new traditional AI customers
Highest share of AI customers
# of new AI customer references*
274
207
102
Share by AI type
GenAI
Traditional AI
54%
46%
85%
15%
63%
37%
Selected new AI customers**
Schneider Electric
LEXMARK
docomo
SAMSUNG
RYANAIR
HDFC ERGO
MERCK
priceline
Heineken
hp
KPMG
OMRON
AUTODESK
Nestlé
General Mills
Tchibo
TORONTO

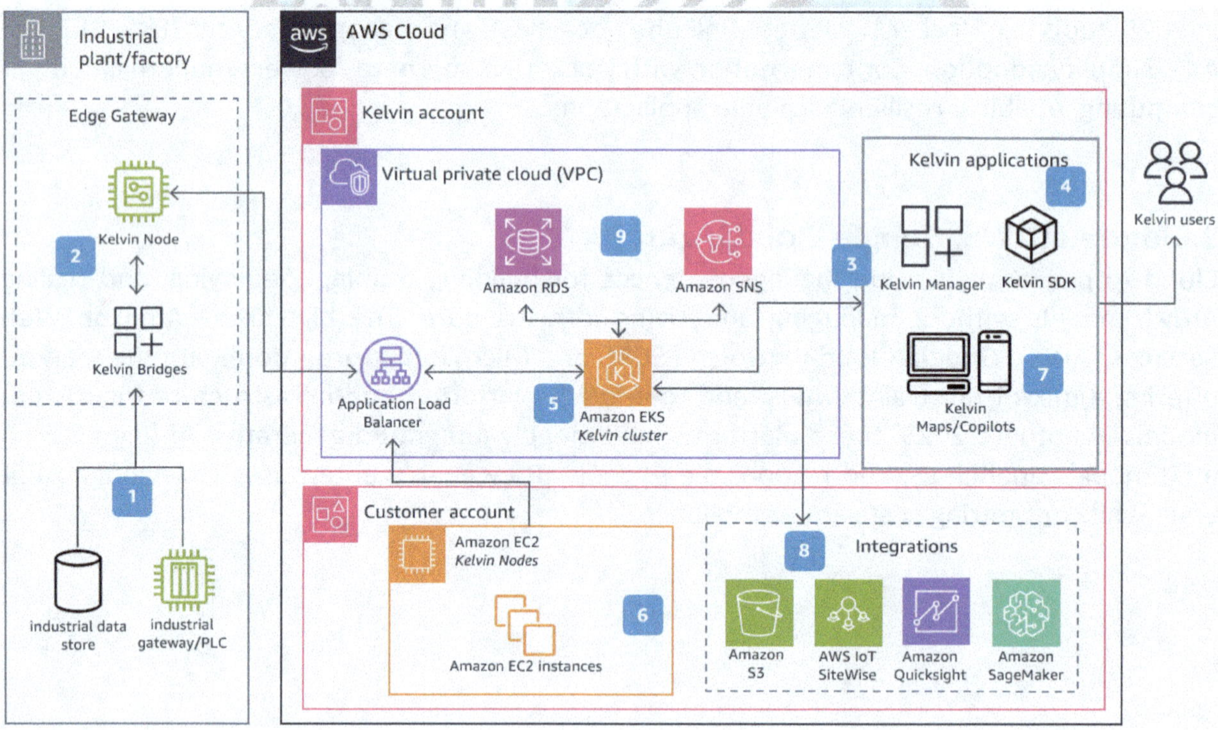
Industrial plant/factory
Edge Gateway
Kelvin Node
2
Kelvin Bridges
1
industrial data store
industrial gateway/PLC
aws
AWS Cloud
Kelvin account
Virtual private cloud (VPC)
Amazon RDS
9
Amazon SNS
Application Load Balancer
5
Amazon EKS
Kelvin cluster
3
Kelvin applications
4
Kelvin Manager
Kelvin SDK
7
Kelvin Maps/Copilots
Kelvin users
Customer account
Amazon EC2
Kelvin Nodes
6
Amazon EC2 instances
8
Integrations
Amazon S3
AWS IoT SiteWise
Amazon Quicksight
Amazon SageMaker

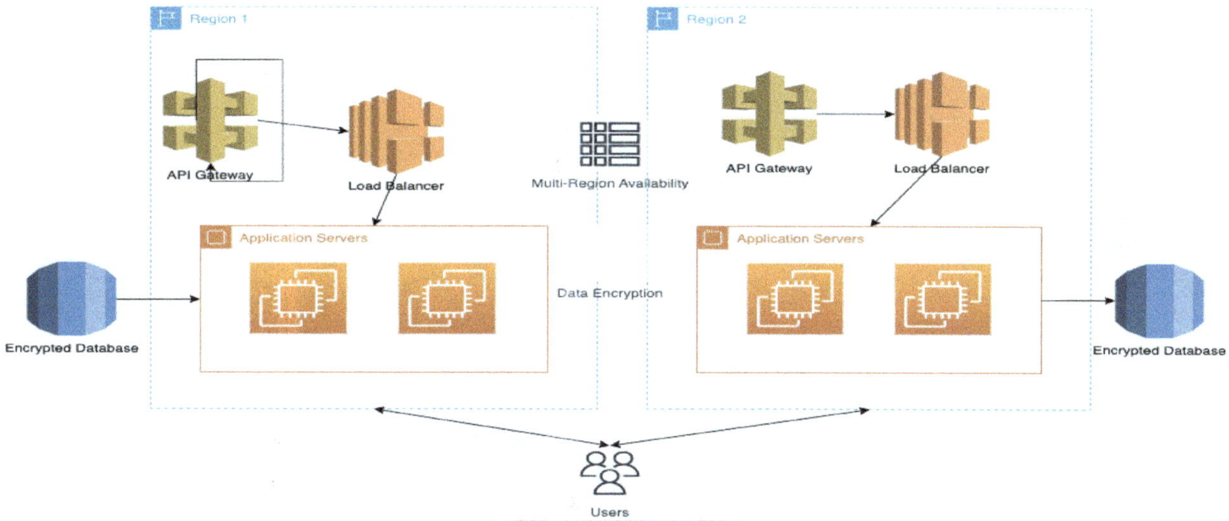

Key Components of Cloud AI Services

Most platforms offer:

- **Pre-trained AI APIs**: Ready-to-use for vision, speech, language (e.g., image recognition, translation).
- **ML Platforms**: Notebooks, autoML, training/inference engines.
- **Custom Model Tools**: Support for TensorFlow, PyTorch, etc.
- **MLOps**: Pipelines, monitoring, versioning.
- **Generative AI**: Access to foundation models (e.g., via Bedrock, Gemini).

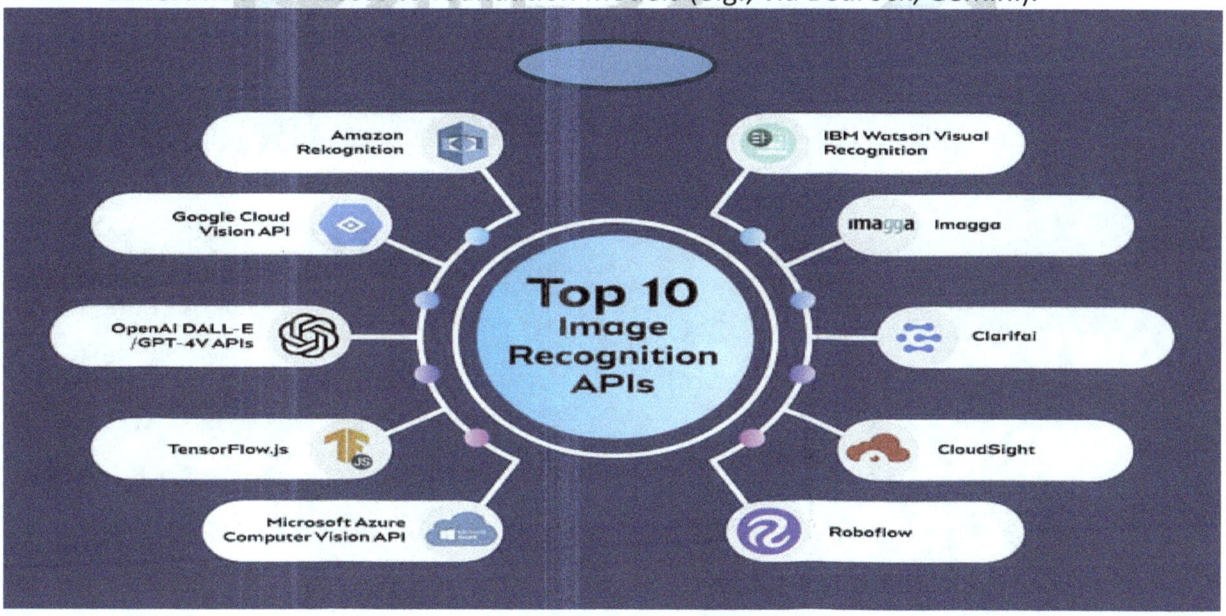

Best Image Recognition Software in 2025
Google Cloud Vision AI
Amazon Rekognition
Microsoft Azure Computer Vision
OpenCV + TensorFlow (or PyTorch)
viso.ai
clarifai
IBM Watson
Viso Suite
Clarifai
IBM Watson Visual Recognition

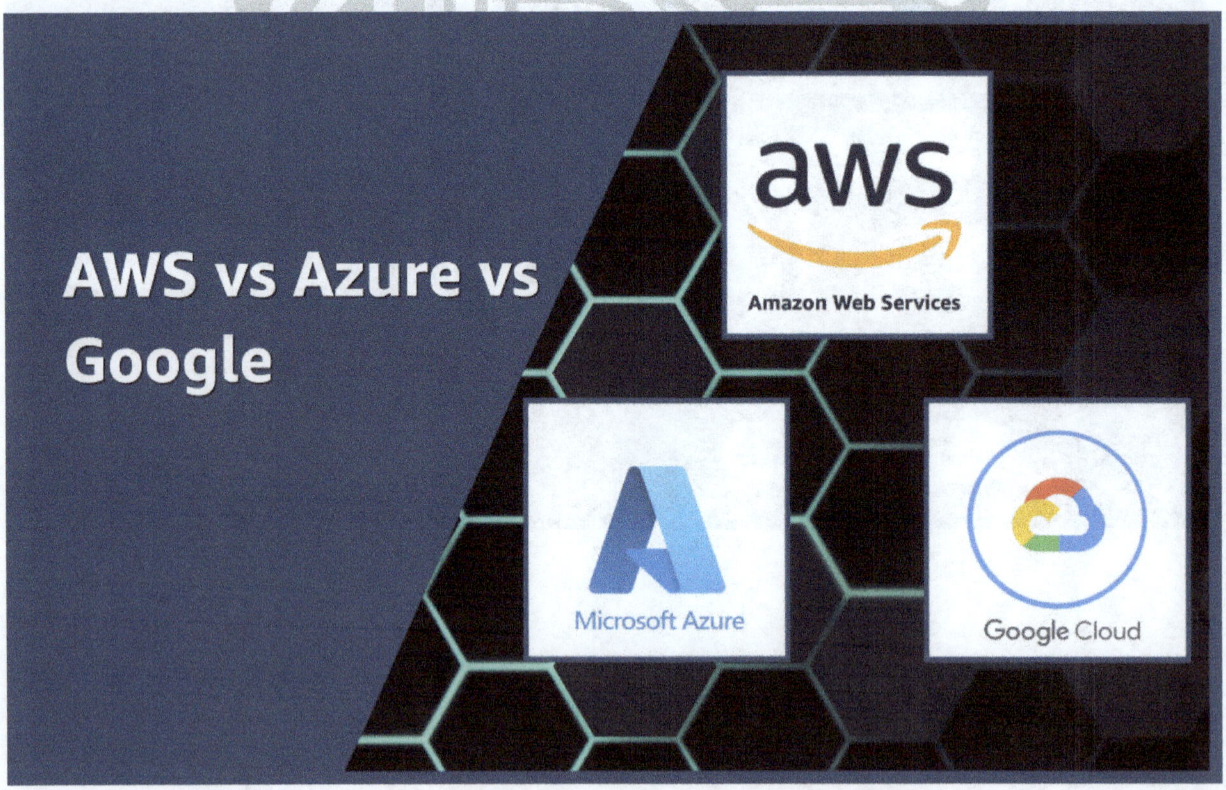
AWS vs Azure vs Google
aws
Amazon Web Services
Microsoft Azure
Google Cloud

AWS AI/ML Services
Core Platform: Amazon SageMaker – Fully managed for building, training, and deploying models.

Amazon SageMaker

Key Services:

- Pre-trained: Rekognition (vision), Transcribe (speech), Comprehend (NLP), Bedrock (generative AI with models like Claude, Llama).
- Infrastructure: EC2 with GPUs/TPUs, Inferentia/Trainium chips for cost-efficient inference/training.
- Strengths: Broadest ecosystem, strong in enterprise integration, serverless options (Lambda).

Google Cloud AI/ML Services
Core Platform: Vertex AI – Unified for AutoML, custom training, and generative AI.

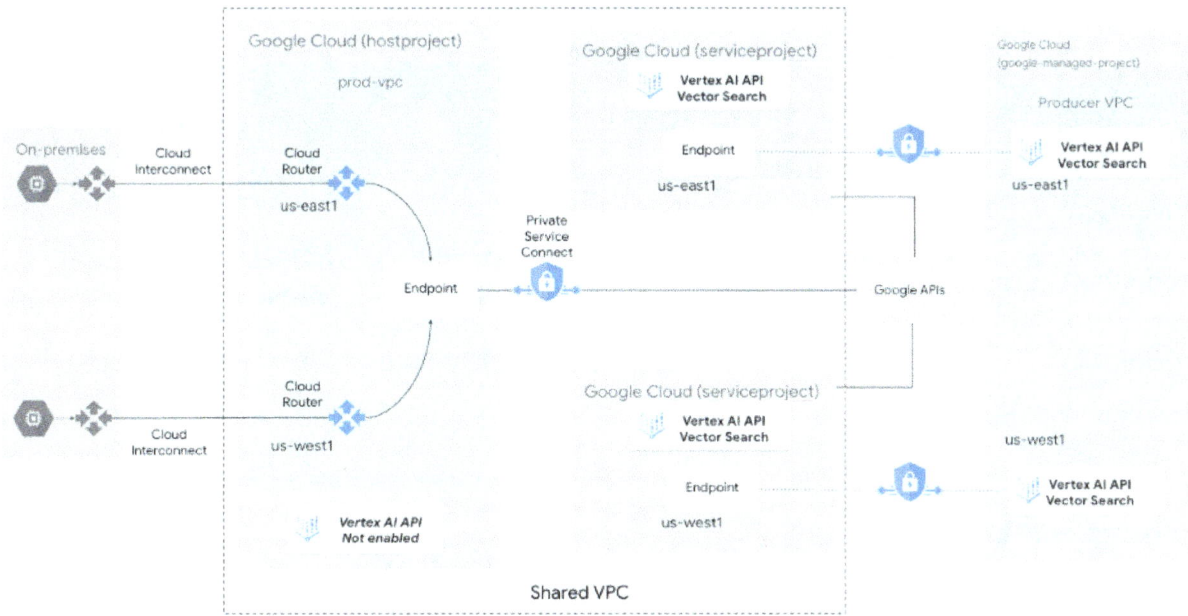

Key Services:

- Pre-trained: Vision AI, Speech-to-Text, Natural Language AI, Gemini (multimodal foundation model).
- Infrastructure: TPUs for fast training, AI Platform Pipelines.
- Strengths: Leading in research-backed models (from Google DeepMind), excellent data analytics integration (BigQuery), cost-effective for large-scale training.

Microsoft Azure AI/ML Services

Core Platform: Azure Machine Learning – Studio for no-code/low-code and pro workflows.

Key Services:

- Pre-trained: Computer Vision, Speech Service, Azure OpenAI (GPT models), Cognitive Services.
- Infrastructure: Azure ML endpoints, integration with ONNX, Phi models.
- Strengths: Seamless with Microsoft ecosystem (Office, Power BI), strong enterprise security/compliance, hybrid cloud support.

Comparison: AWS vs Google Cloud vs Azure

Aspect	**AWS**	**Google Cloud**	**Azure**
Market Share (2025)	Leader (~32%)	~11%	~23%
Core ML Platform	SageMaker	Vertex AI	Azure ML
Generative AI	Bedrock (multi-model)	Gemini	Azure OpenAI
Hardware Advantage	Trainium/Inferentia chips	TPUs	Close OpenAI partnership
Best For	Broad services, scalability	Research/advanced models, data	Enterprise/Microsoft integration
Pricing Model	Pay-as-you-go, savings plans	Sustained use discounts	Reserved instances

Advantages and Challenges

Advantages:

- Scalability and global reach.
- Reduced ops overhead.
- Rapid innovation via pre-built models.
- Responsible AI tools (bias detection, explainability).

Challenges:

- Vendor lock-in.
- Cost management (can escalate).
- Data privacy/regulations (GDPR, etc.).
- Learning curve for services.

In late 2025, the cloud AI landscape is highly competitive, with all three investing heavily in sovereign clouds and sustainable computing. Choose based on existing ecosystem, specific AI needs, and cost—many organizations use multi-cloud strategies.

These platforms democratize AI, enabling faster innovation across industries like healthcare, finance, and retail.

AWS SageMaker

Amazon SageMaker is a fully managed machine learning (ML) service from AWS that helps data scientists and developers prepare data, build, train, tune, deploy, and monitor ML models at scale. It covers the entire ML lifecycle, from no-code tools to advanced custom training. In 2025, SageMaker has evolved into **SageMaker Unified Studio** with enhanced AI agents, serverless options, and better generative AI support.

Key Components of SageMaker

- **SageMaker Unified Studio**: Web-based IDE for notebooks, experiments, and collaboration.

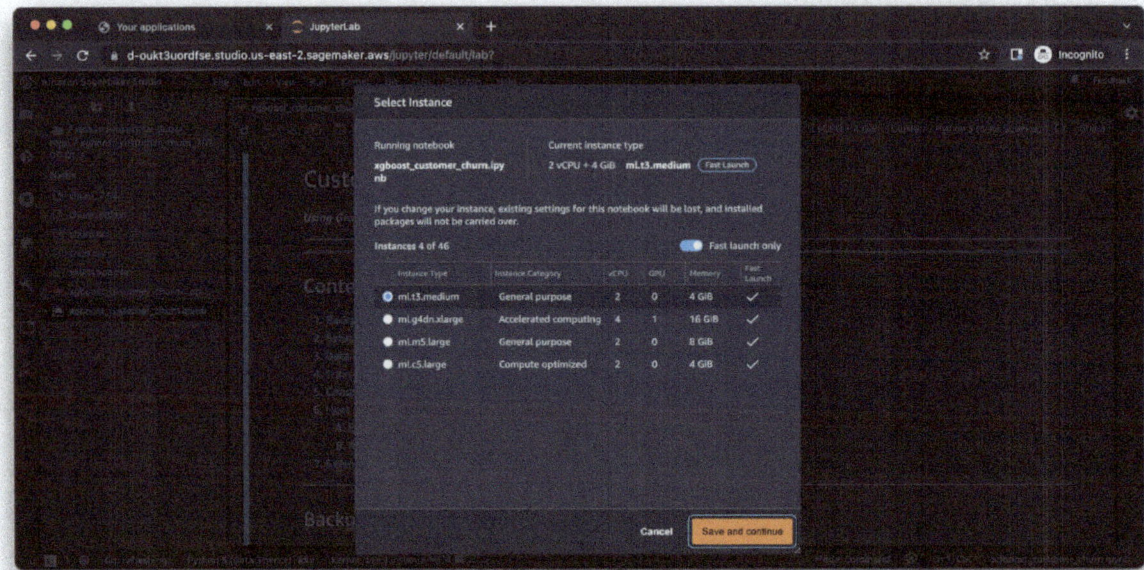

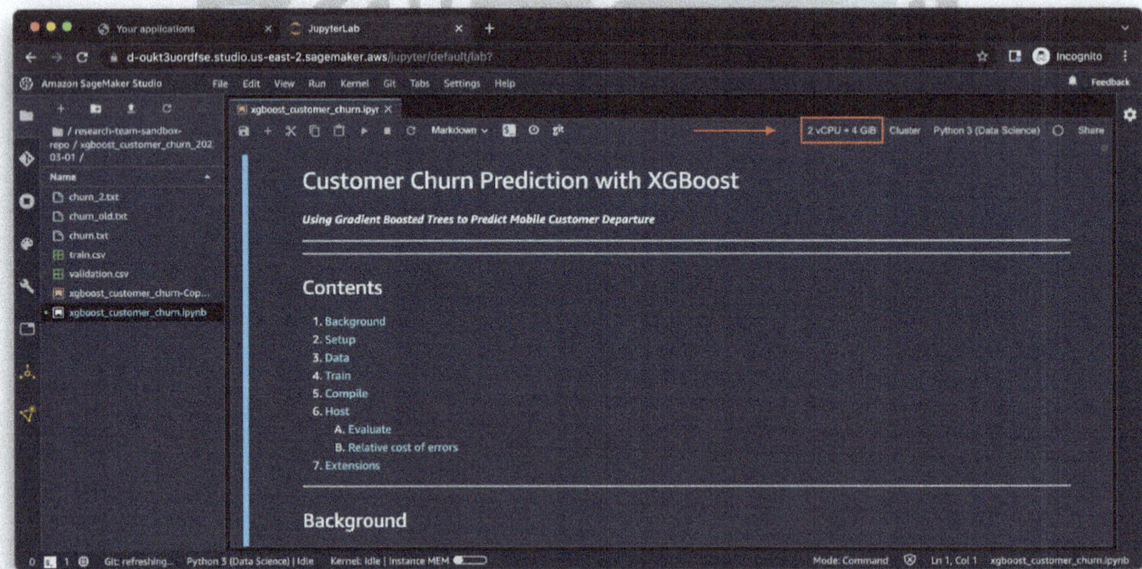

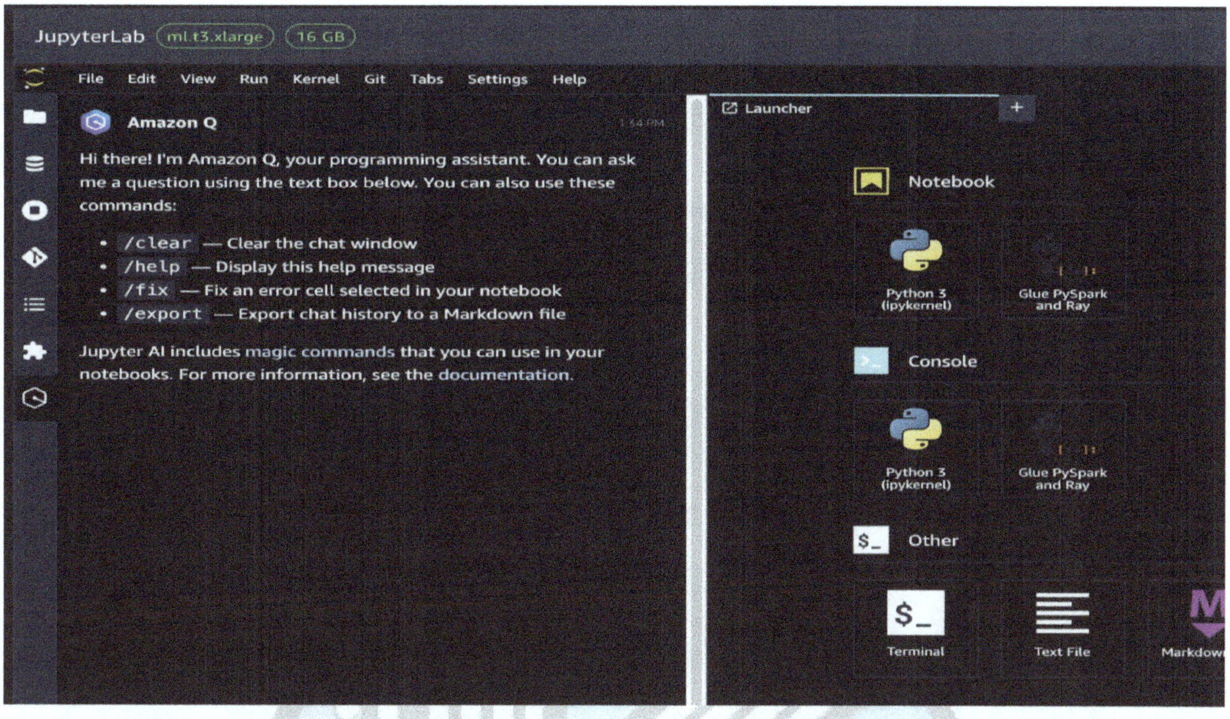

- **SageMaker Canvas**: No-code/low-code for business analysts (visual interface for building models).

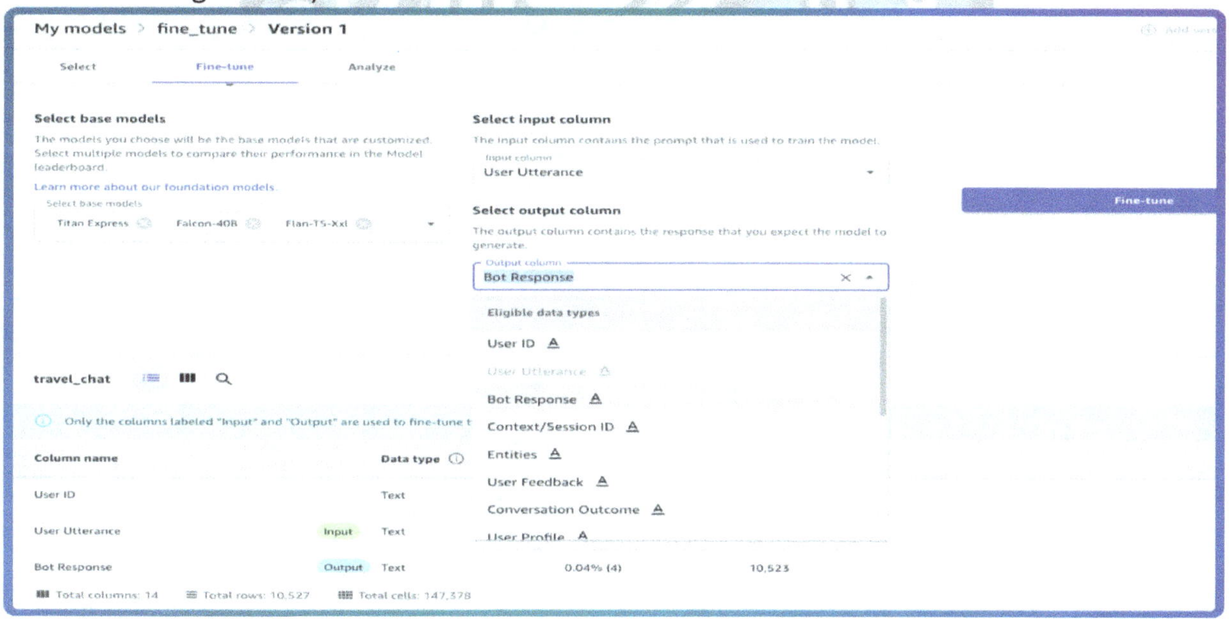

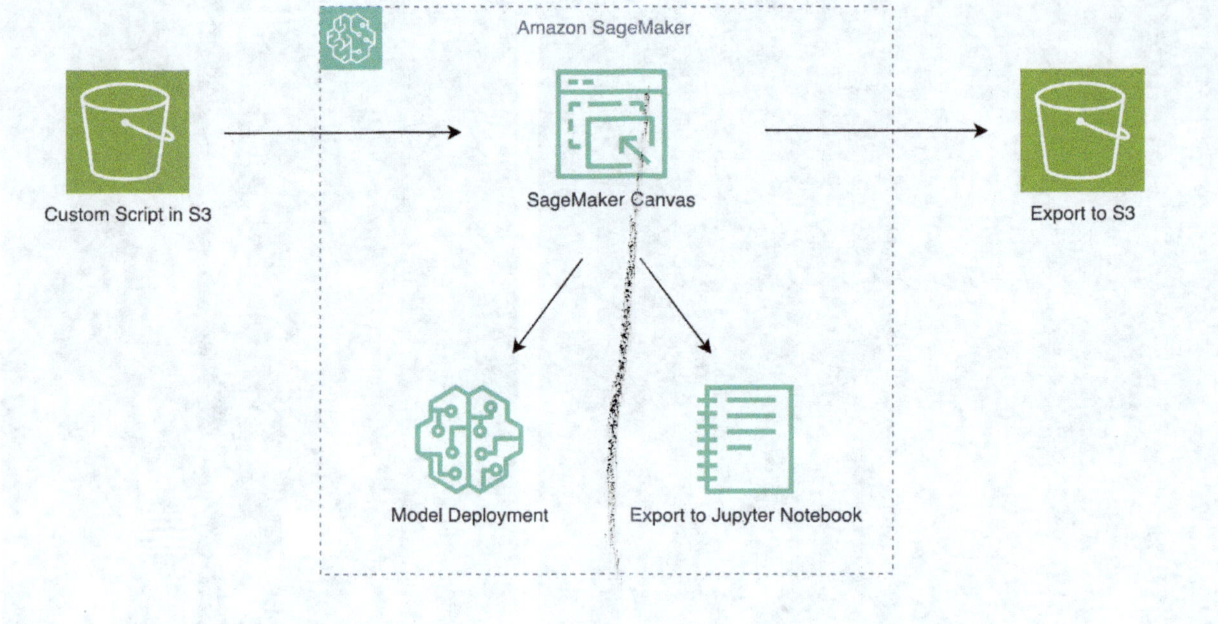

- **Built-in Algorithms & Autopilot**: AutoML for automatic model selection and tuning.

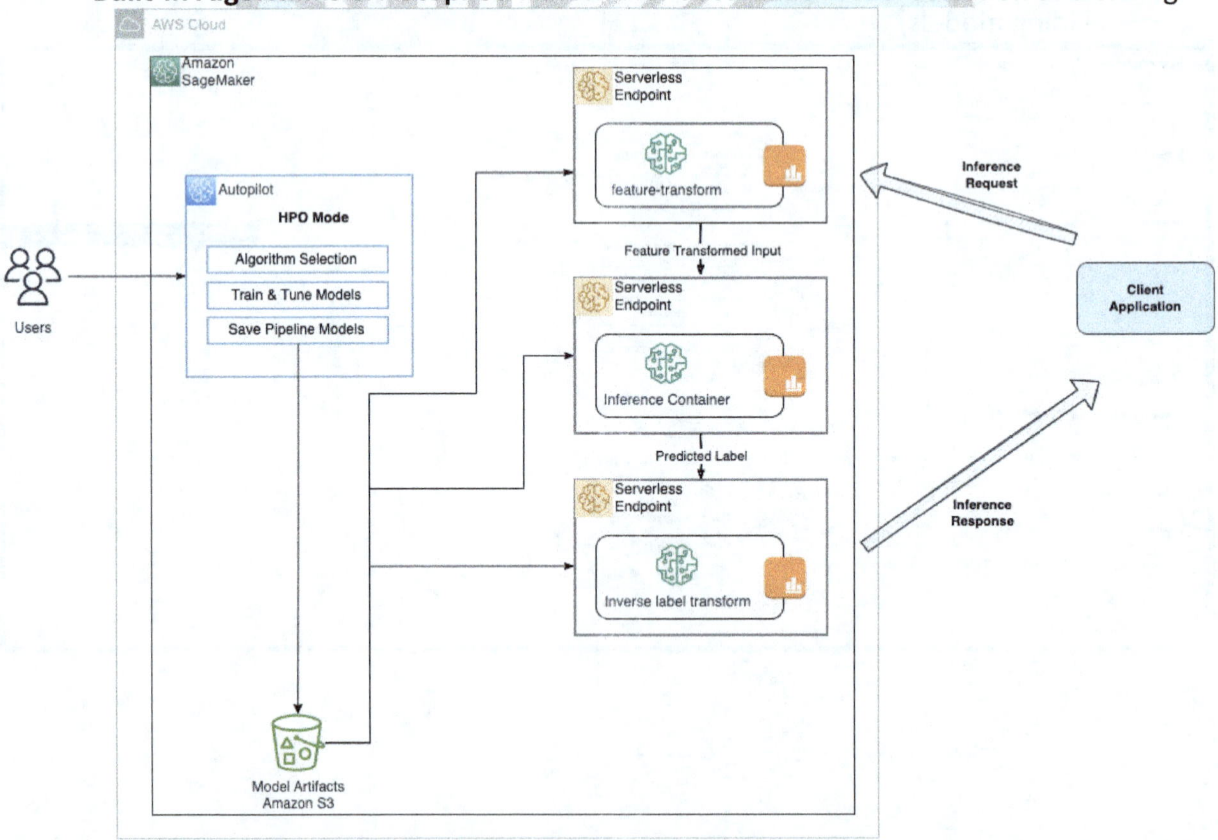

Deploy Amazon SageMaker Autopilot models to serverless inference ...

- **Training & Deployment**: Managed training jobs, endpoints (real-time/serverless), pipelines.

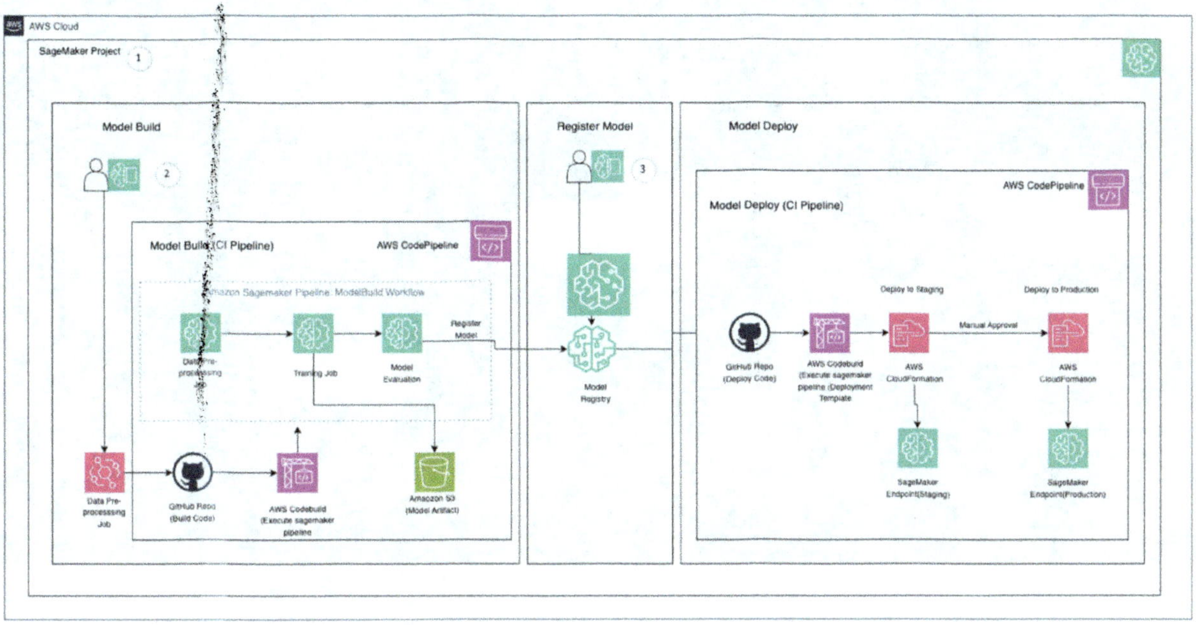

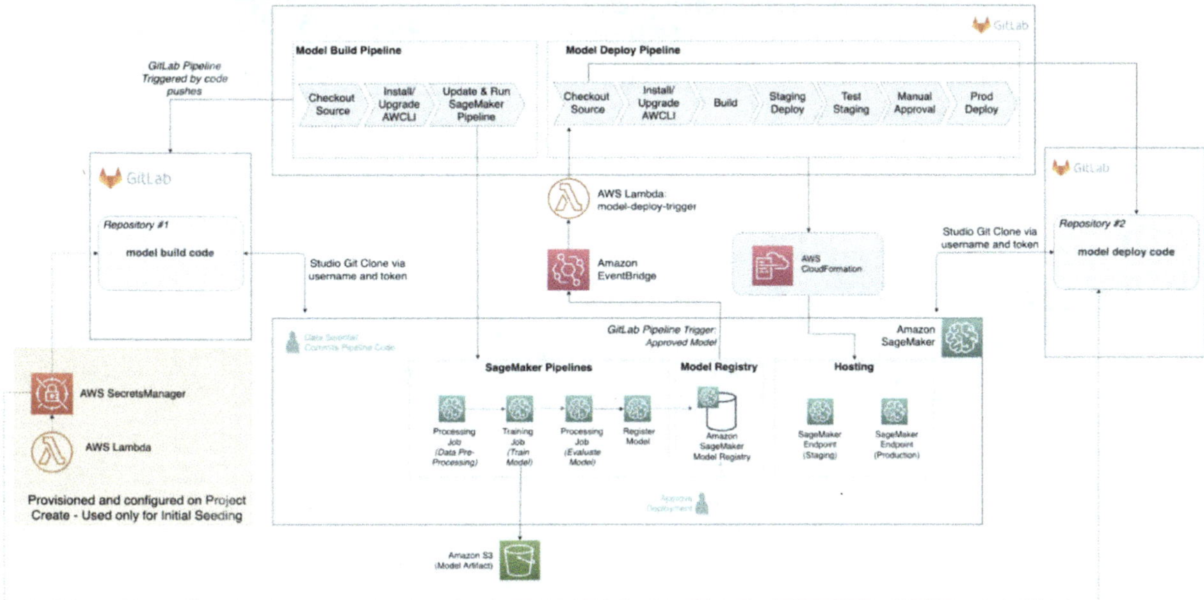

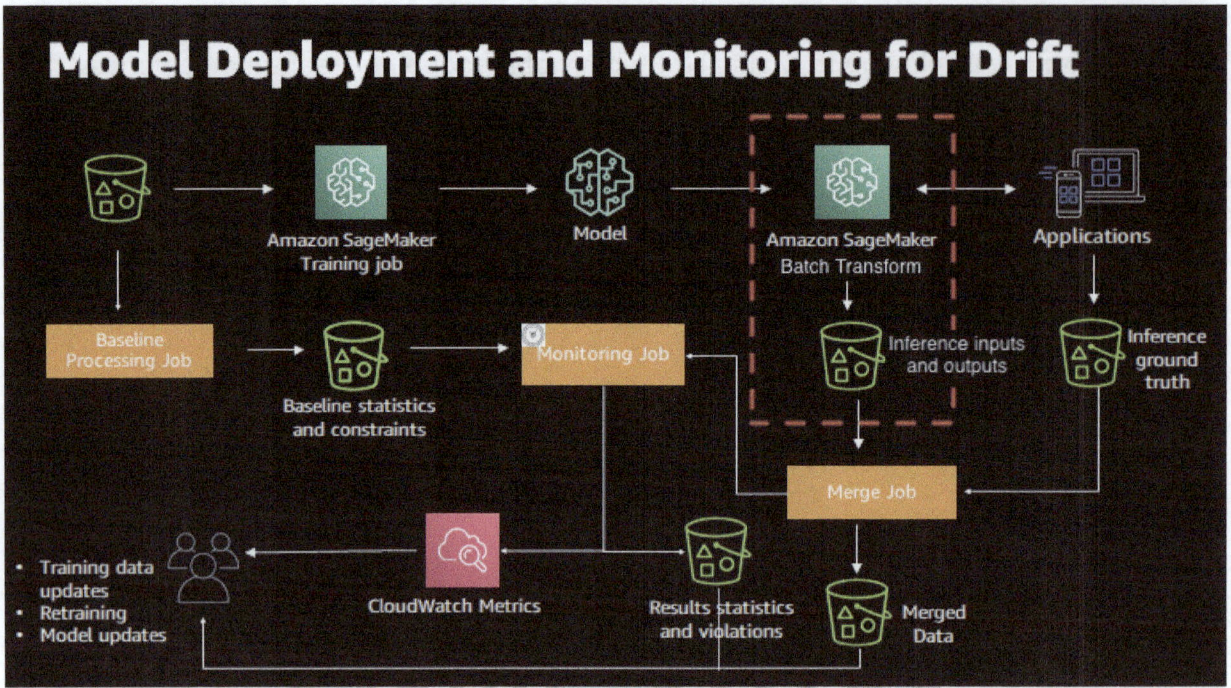

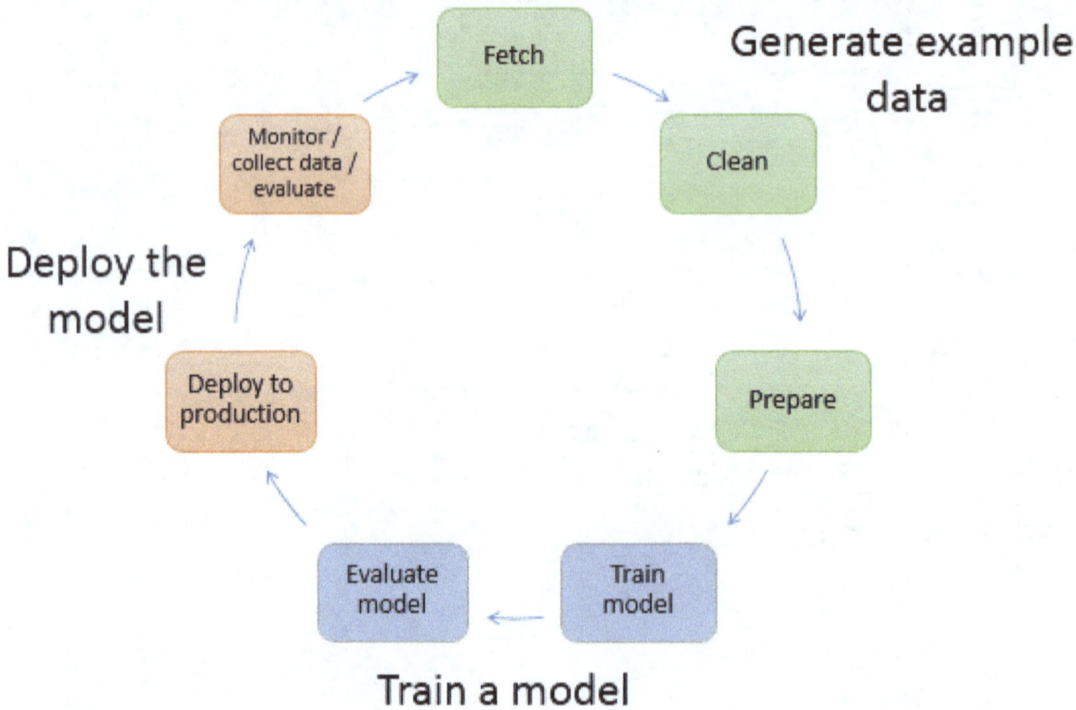

- **New in 2025**: Built-in AI agents for code generation, serverless model customization (fine-tuning with RLHF/DPO), notebooks with AI agents, and enhanced foundation model support.

Step-by-Step Tutorial: Build, Train, and Deploy a Simple Model
This beginner-friendly tutorial uses the classic XGBoost algorithm on tabular data (e.g., predicting customer churn). We'll use SageMaker Unified Studio and the Python SDK.
Prerequisites:

- An AWS account with SageMaker access.
- Basic Python knowledge.
- IAM role with SageMaker/S3 permissions.

1. **Set Up SageMaker Unified Studio**
    - Go to the AWS Console → Search for "SageMaker" → Open **SageMaker Unified Studio**.
    - If first time: Create a domain (quick setup recommended for individuals).
    - Launch a notebook environment (serverless or instance-based).

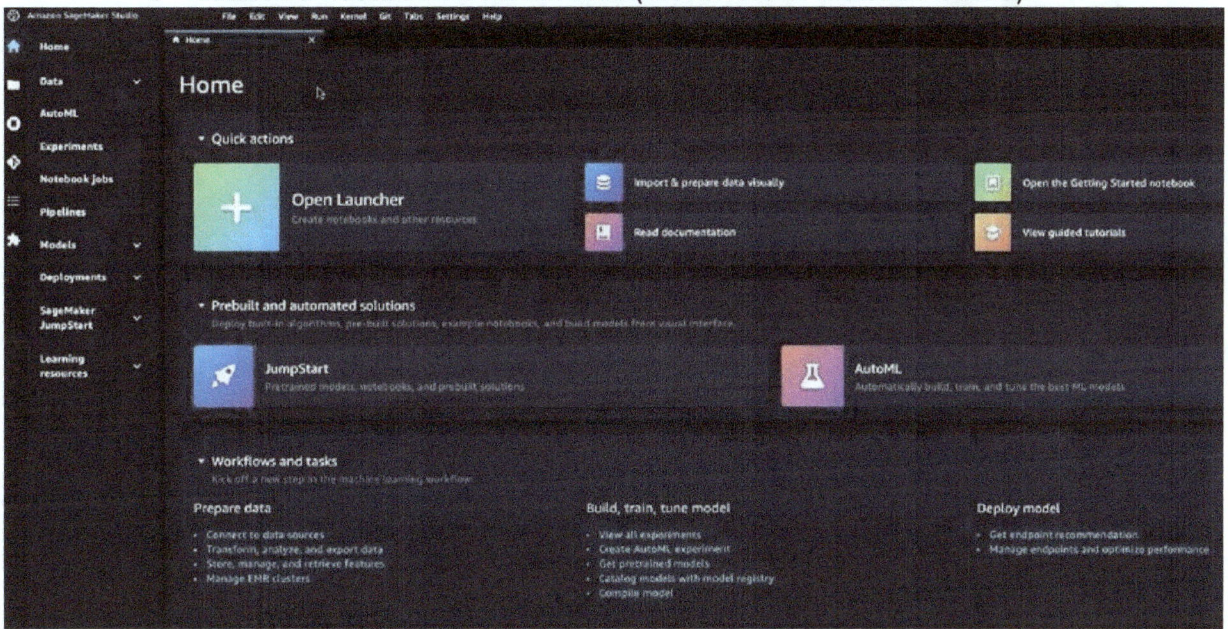

Amazon SageMaker Studio | Download Scientific Diagram

2. **Create a Notebook and Prepare Data**
    - In Studio, create a new Jupyter notebook.
    - Import libraries and set up session:

Python

```
import sagemaker
import boto3
from sagemaker import get_execution_role

sess = sagemaker.Session()
role = get_execution_role()
bucket = sess.default_bucket()  # Default S3 bucket
```

- Upload data to S3 (example: use a public dataset like Abalone or your CSV).

Python

```
import pandas as pd
data = pd.read_csv('your_data.csv')
train_data = data.sample(frac=0.8)
test_data = data.drop(train_data.index)
```

```
train_data.to_csv('train.csv', index=False, header=False)
test_data.to_csv('test.csv', index=False, header=True)  # For validation

prefix = 'sagemaker/xgboost-demo'
train_path = sess.upload_data('train.csv', key_prefix=prefix + '/train')
test_path = sess.upload_data('test.csv', key_prefix=prefix + '/test')
```

3. **Train the Model**
   - Use a built-in algorithm (XGBoost):

Python

```
from sagemaker.xgboost import XGBoost

estimator = XGBoost(
    entry_point='script.py',  # Optional: custom script; otherwise use defaults
    role=role,
    instance_count=1,
    instance_type='ml.m5.xlarge',
    framework_version='1.7-1',
    hyperparameters={'max_depth': 5, 'eta': 0.2, 'objective': 'binary:logistic'}
)

estimator.fit({'train': train_path, 'validation': test_path})
```

   - Monitor training in the console (Jobs tab).
4.
5. **Deploy the Model**
   - Create an endpoint:

Python

```
predictor = estimator.deploy(
    initial_instance_count=1,
    instance_type='ml.t2.medium',
    serializer=sagemaker.serializers.CSVSerializer()
)
```

   - Or use serverless inference for auto-scaling and no management.
6. **Make Predictions**

Python

```
import numpy as np
result = predictor.predict([[feature1, feature2, ...]])
print(np.argmax(result))  # For classification
```

7. **Clean Up**
    - Delete endpoint: predictor.delete_endpoint()
    - Stop notebook to avoid charges.

Advanced Features

- **Hyperparameter Tuning**: Use HyperparameterTuner for automatic optimization.
- **Pipelines**: Automate workflows with SageMaker Pipelines.
- **Generative AI**: Fine-tune models like Llama or Nova via serverless customization (new in 2025).
- **MLOps**: Use Model Registry, Experiments, and Feature Store.

www.ingramcontent.com/pod-product-compliance
Lightning Source LLC
Chambersburg PA
CBHW080242170726
48282CB00031B/1169
9789358128123